HARRY WHITE
AND THE AMERICAN CREED

HARRY WHITE

AND THE

AMERICAN CREED

How a Federal Bureaucrat
Created the Modern Global Economy
(and Failed to Get the Credit)

JAMES M. BOUGHTON

Yale

UNIVERSITY PRESS

New Haven and London

Published with assistance from the foundation established in memory of
Philip Hamilton McMillan of the Class of 1894, Yale College.

Yale University Press books may be purchased in quantity for
educational, business, or promotional use. For information, please e-mail
sales.press@yale.edu (U.S. office) or sales@yaleup.co.uk (U.K. office).

Set in Janson Text type by Newgen North America.
Printed in the United States of America.

Library of Congress Control Number: 2021935423

ISBN 978-0-300-25379-5 (hardcover : alk. paper)

A catalogue record for this book is available from the British Library.

This paper meets the requirements of ANSI/NISO z39.48-1992
(Permanence of Paper).

10 9 8 7 6 5 4 3 2 1

for Lesley Anne Simmons

It is quite possible that some day some scholar
will want to write on Harry as an economist.

—JACOB VINER, March 1951

Contents

Acknowledgments

THIS BOOK DRAWS ON a variety of sources, written and oral, including a substantial amount of archival material that was not public or was not easily accessible when the previous biographies were written. I am indebted to the proficient and helpful staffs of several institutions for much assistance.

One primary source for information about Harry White's own thoughts and actions is a collection at the U.S. National Archives in College Park, Maryland. The bulk of that archive is a chronological file of White's writing and outgoing correspondence throughout his career at the U.S. Treasury.

A second source is the Morgenthau Diaries, which are now available online through the Franklin D. Roosevelt Library and the National Archives and which include documents from White and transcripts of meetings in which he participated. That source is especially valuable for the period 1938–45, when White was a senior Treasury official.

A third, less comprehensive and more idiosyncratic collection of papers is in the Seeley G. Mudd Manuscript Library at Princeton University in New Jersey. That collection has two parts. The first comprises papers and other documents that White had in his possession at the time of his death and that were donated to the library by his widow, Anne Terry White. The second part, donated by the family much more recently, comprises additional material—both personal and professional—that was retained first by Anne and then by their daughter Joan White Pinkham until her death in 2012.

A fourth collection is in the archives of the International Monetary Fund (IMF) in Washington, D.C. That collection includes many documents relating to the Bretton Woods conference and to White's tenure as the IMF executive director for the United States.

For some specific episodes, I have drawn on archival material from the U.S. Treasury, the U.S. State Department, the Federal Bureau of Investigation, the Federal Reserve Board, the Harry S. Truman Library, the Universities of Delaware and Oregon, the Woodrow Wilson International Center for Scholars, and the State of Israel.

Research of this nature would also not be possible without help from librarians. I would like especially to thank the skillful and accommodating staffs of the Library of Congress, the Joint Library of the International Monetary Fund and World Bank, the libraries of the American University and Georgetown University, and the public libraries of Washington, D.C., and Sanibel, Florida.

In addition to archives, library resources, White's publications, and other documentary material, I have had the benefit of conversations, interviews, and correspondence with many people who had firsthand knowledge of his life and work or of the times and issues with which he lived and worked. When I began this research in the mid-1990s, several people who had known him were still alive. (A few still are, but none—so far as I know—who worked with him.) Their recollections have greatly informed my sense of the man and his times and of what he tried to accomplish. More recently, the White family and close family friends graciously made available to me a great many personal letters, photographs, scrapbooks, and mementos that have been invaluable in fleshing out the personal biography.

My debt to Harry White's granddaughter Claire Pinkham, for her very generous and capable help and encouragement, offered without any thought or effort to limit my free use of the family archive or to influence this narrative, is incalculable. To my wife, Lesley Anne Simmons, my debt is even greater. She encouraged me, pushed me along, helped me in ways small and large, read and gave feedback on the manuscript, and made the project both possible and fun. My heartfelt thanks also go to Seth Ditchik, whose careful and thorough editing greatly improved this manuscript. Ann Twombly's skillful editing of the final manuscript made it much clearer.

For sharing recollections, information, documents, and thoughts of many kinds, and without wishing in any way to implicate them in the account that follows, I am grateful to the following: Paul Blanc, John Morton Blum, Michael Bordo, Helen G. Burrows, Anand Chandavarkar, Svetlana

Chervonnaya, Piet Clement, Alexis Coe, Robert Coe, Bruce Craig, Margaret Garritsen de Vries, David Eddy, Pepe Epstein, Stanley Fischer, Bridgit Fitzgerald, Robert Flood, Richard Freeman, Randy Furst, John Kenneth Galbraith, Richard Gardner, Joseph Gold, Craufurd Goodwin, John Gunter, Thorvaldur Gylfason, David Hamilton, Howard Handy, Max Harris, David Hawley, Randy Henning, Peggy Bernstein Heyman, Barbara Hughes, Doug Irwin, Harold James, Andrew Kamarck, Joe Keyes, Craig Klemmer, Burke Knapp, Amy Knight, Julius Kobyakov, Claire Lipsman, John Lowenthal, Aarno Luiksilla, Allan Meltzer, Raymond Mikesell, Sandy Mountford, Claire Pinkham, Joan White Pinkham, Jacques Polak, Jay Reid, Sidney Rittenberg, Brian Rose, Andrew Roth, Paul Samuelson, Roger Sandilands, Philip Schlegel, Stephen Schuker, Kurt Schuler, Anna Schwartz, Robert Skidelsky, Mark Sobel, James Srodes, Landon Storrs, Victor Urquidi, Leo Van Houtven, David Vines, Howard Wachtel, Steve Wangh, Isabella Weber, Arnold Weiss, Thomas Weisskopf, Gordon Williams, and Juan Yepez.

Prologue

The Missing Legacy

My creed is the American creed.

—Harry Dexter White, testifying before the House
Un-American Activities Committee, August 13, 1948

THREE DAYS LATER, AGED fifty-five, he was dead.

The strain of testifying under severe pressure from congressional antagonists proved to be too much for a man who had already endured two heart attacks. White's death from a third heart attack, on August 16, 1948, caused a brief uproar. The pushback against the proceedings was led by the editorial board of the *New York Times*, which accused HUAC of "ignoring the Bill of Rights and outraging our American sense of justice."[1] His name then fell back into near anonymity until it was dragged back out in 1953, in the midst of the McCarthy era, as part of an effort to discredit former President Harry S. Truman for appointing White to his post at the IMF. More recently, the declassification of Soviet cables reporting on conversations between White and Soviet officials in 1944 and 1945 has resuscitated the attacks and has again overshadowed his accomplishments.

I first became interested in Harry White because of the sensational possibility that one of the main founders of the International Monetary Fund had led a double life. Was it possible that the principal designer of a major financial institution that was clearly intended to serve—and in fact has served—U.S. economic, political, and economic interests was secretly disloyal to his country? I was halfway through a thirty-year career as an IMF official and had been appointed the historian of the institution. For more than forty years, the IMF's senior management had been conflicted about White's story. Having once commissioned sculptors to produce busts of White and John Maynard Keynes (White's British counterpart in the design of the Fund), the IMF had long since squirreled away both statues in the basement to avoid seeming to take a position on the merits of the case. When Stanley Fischer—formerly chair of the Economics Department at MIT—arrived at the IMF as first deputy managing director in 1994, he asked me to investigate and report back.

It was soon evident that the conventional view was tainted. The presence of Communists and Soviet sympathizers within the U.S. government in the 1930s and early 1940s was well established, and it had become a common game to try to ferret out as many as possible. White had several friends and associates who were at least on the outer rings of the concentric circles of suspicion, some of whom he had hired for important Treasury jobs. Moreover, his own responsibilities brought him into frequent contact with Soviet officials, especially during World War II, when the two countries were allied in the war effort. From these professional and social interactions, it was easy to construct a narrative drawing White into the tighter circles. In contrast, if one started by looking at White's work and contacts from, in effect, inside his office, it was just as easy to construct a narrative in which the alleged wrongdoings and indiscretions were in fact benign and appropriate.[2] I reported back to Fischer that White was probably the victim of misunderstanding and excessive zeal. In due course, the IMF restored the founders' busts to a prominent place in the Executive Board room.

In response to an exchange of emails while I was conducting my initial research, Robert Skidelsky (a biographer of John Maynard Keynes) lumped me together with two other historians, John Morton Blum and Arthur Schlesinger Jr., as "American liberals" who "were reluctant to accept the view that White was a Soviet agent."[3] I accept the charge, and subsequent research has only reinforced my rejection of White's culpability.

Throughout World War II, Harry White was the chief U.S. negotiator on all aspects of international economic policy. As a representative of the U.S. government, he held a strong hand. Throughout the war, the U.S. economy was the strongest in the world and was becoming more so with every passing month. The United Kingdom, which had dominated world commerce throughout the previous half century, was declining, as was the prevalence of its currency, the pound sterling. The Soviet Union was on the ascendant but was being battered severely by the demands of the war. All other national economies were far lower in importance.

It was also an unusual moment in U.S. history, when isolationist tendencies were in relative abeyance. White himself was a committed internationalist, and the key role being played by U.S. military forces (albeit belatedly) in the fight against the Axis powers gave credence to the idea that the United States could be relied on to provide economic leadership as well. Whereas negotiators for Britain and the Soviet Union had to focus on the requirements for rebuilding their economies after the war, White and his colleagues could put more stress on broad global issues.

Beginning in 1942, White frequently emphasized that the U.S. economy could prosper only if other countries were able to buy its output. The idea that "prosperity, like peace, is indivisible" became something of a mantra for him throughout the war. (He first used the phrase in his April 1942 plan for postwar financial institutions, and he subsequently incorporated it into several speeches delivered by his boss, Treasury Secretary Henry Morgenthau Jr.) With Roosevelt in the White House, the Democratic Party in control of both houses of Congress, and the country united in a massive war effort, that global perspective had a greater chance of prevailing than at any other time in the twentieth century.

This combination of American power and a broadening domestic worldview enabled White to impose a universal vision on the process of creating institutions for postwar economic and financial cooperation. Across the Atlantic, Keynes—who was "fighting for Britain," as Skidelsky phrased it—had to fight a rearguard action to get as much help for his country and its commonwealth system as he could. Whatever Keynes's personal predilections might have been in this regard, he lacked White's freedom of action. Circumstances elevated Harry White to the primus inter pares in the pantheon of founders of the postwar economic system.

The Bretton Woods agreements that were the centerpiece of Harry White's life's work have been thoroughly analyzed in thousands of articles and books throughout the seven-plus decades since the end of World War II. White's central role in bringing them to fruition has, however, been obscured and downplayed, for three reasons. First, Keynes's luminosity has dominated the discussion and overshadowed all other strands of the narrative. Second, White's career as a government bureaucrat rather than an academic researcher or political star has muddled the effort to assess his contributions. Third, the espionage charges against him have further obfuscated the story and have led most analysts to downplay the positives in his career. The purpose of this book is to restore balance to the historical narrative. To borrow a phrase from the culinary arts, the goal is to "correct the seasoning." Throughout White's career, as this book tries to show, he put forth visionary positions on how to modernize the international monetary system, and he had the practical ability to bring them to fruition.

PART I

Becoming Harry Dexter White

CHAPTER ONE

Who—Really—Was Harry White?

Who Was Harry Dexter White?

—Cover story, *Life* magazine, November 1953

HARRY DEXTER WHITE HAS always seemed a bit mysterious. One of John Maynard Keynes's biographers regarded White as "a remarkable figure, who should be accorded an honourable place in British annals" but who instead was often regarded as "some dim scribe, some kind of robot, who wrote . . . an inferior version of the Keynes plan." Another summed up the problem by complaining that "almost everything about [White's] career . . . [was] mystifying."[1] In the United States, the FBI agents who investigated him extensively could not even figure out whence his parents had emigrated, or what the family name had been. White did little to dispel the mysteries. As one mundane example, he never publicly explained the roots of his middle name, which he took on himself as a teenager.

Origins

Like those of many nineteenth-century immigrants to the United States, the origins of the White family were never properly recorded. A century later, family members did their best to reconstruct the names and events, but some details remained unrecoverable. What emerges from the mist is the following account. In 1888 the thirty-eight-year-old Jacob

Fig. 1. *Harry's parents and their first five children, Boston, circa 1891. Family scrapbook, courtesy of Claire A. Pinkham*

Weissnovitz (a name that translates as "son of White") arrived in Boston, Massachusetts, from his native Lithuania (then part of czarist Russia) and promptly anglicized his name to White. His brother, Aaron, had immigrated some three years earlier. Both were married, but their wives and children remained in Lithuania until 1890, when the men were settled. Jacob's wife, Sarah (née Magilewsky, also from Lithuania), arrived then with their four children (three girls and a boy). The family reunification (fig. 1) soon produced three more boys. In October 1892, probably on the 29th, the seventh and final child, Harry, was born at home in Boston.

Many of the details are subject to dispute. Earlier accounts, derived mostly without access to the family's own research and memories or census records that have recently been declassified, related the origins a little differently, though still confidently. The FBI thought Harry's parents were from Russia or Poland. His first biographer, David Rees, relying heavily on a 1953 newspaper account[2] but also using official public records, gave the original family name as Weit. Harry White's birth certificate, as re-issued in 1928, listed the date of birth as October 9, as did passports issued in 1928 and 1935. His 1940 and 1942 passports, however, gave his birth-date as October 29. Harry himself always gave his birthdate as the 29th, the family celebrated his birthday on that date, and his death certificate gave his birth date as October 29.

While testifying before a grand jury in 1948, Harry was asked for his birthplace and date. He replied, "Born in Boston, October 29—at least, that's the date I always thought it was and the date on which I had my birthday celebrated. But I noticed some time ago, in looking over my mar-riage certificate—we were about to celebrate our 30th anniversary—that the date was the 9th. Now, whether the '2' was obliterated on my certifi-cate . . ." This soliloquy, understandably, was too much information for the prosecutor, who cut him off and just asked for the year, which Harry gave as 1892.[3]

Was he a Libra (if October 9), and therefore destined to concern himself with balance and justice; or a Scorpio (if October 29), and there-fore destined to be bold, confident, and controlling? The reader will have to decide.

According to Harry's reissued birth certificate, his father's name was Isaac. Other public records, including the 1900 census, support family rec-ollections of the father's name as Jacob, and the letterhead for his hardware store in Boston listed his name as "J. White" (fig. 2). In a 1947 passport application, Harry gave his father's name as Joseph (which Jacob appears to have used sometimes as a middle name). Harry's death certificate lists his father's name as Jacob White. Bruce Craig's biography of Harry cites a letter written by one of Harry's sisters in 1955, in which she gives her father's name as Isaac. In 1953, however, Harry's daughter Joan told a re-porter that her grandfather's name was Jacob, and that name is supported by other family records.[4]

As for the date of arrival in Boston, Rees states that immigration rec-ords list a Jacob Weit as arriving in April 1885; Craig cites that date as definitive, and it is consistent with information in Harry's 1947 passport application. When family members, including Harry's children, con-structed a handwritten family tree in the 1980s (now in the Princeton University archives), they wrote the immigration date as "1887 or 1888" and noted that the brother, Aaron, arrived in 1885. Craig asserts that "Isaac" had no relatives in America when he arrived, which could be true

Fig. 2. *One of the family stores where Harry worked before he enlisted in the U.S. Army. Family scrapbook, courtesy of Claire A. Pinkham*

if he arrived in 1885 but not if he arrived in 1887 or 1888. The 1900 census form, however, indicates clearly that Aaron immigrated in 1885 and Jacob in 1888.

As is evident from their given names, the Whites were Jewish. What this means, if anything, is less clear. Lithuanian Jews in the 1880s were subject to economic and cultural isolation and discrimination, both from ethnic Lithuanians and from the Russian government. Emigration to the West increased steadily, primarily in search of better economic opportunities.[5] Jacob Weissnovitz most probably had worked in Lithuania as a trader of some sort. The 1900 census and Harry's birth certificate gave the father's occupation as "Peddler." In Boston Jacob established himself as the proprietor of a hardware store at 99 Salem Street, where the North End Fish Market now stands.

Assimilation to the American way of life was swift and complete. Harry never did learn any of the languages that his parents might have spoken in Lithuania: Russian (which he did briefly study), Lithuanian, or Yiddish. Moreover, the role of religion in the White household was limited to the basic rites and was really just a matter of adhering to certain traditions. Along with many other family letters, a 1935 letter from Harry suggested that Christmas was the relevant winter holiday for the family.[6] When he got married in 1918, he insisted on having a proper Jewish ceremony, but only to please other family members, particularly an uncle who was religiously observant. Harry, his wife, and their children, however, were not religious, did not attend regular services, and did not observe dietary or other Jewish strictures.

Youth: From Child to Soldier

As was common among Jewish immigrants from Russia and Eastern Europe, Jacob and Sarah gave their children first but not middle names. That practice had the unfortunate side effect of making the children seem odd and thus increasing the difficulty of assimilating. Harry already had the challenge of being the youngest of seven children: his nickname in the family was "kid pants." Like many others in the Ashkenazic diaspora, Harry decided as a teenager that he should have a middle name, and he settled on Dexter. Family lore suggests that it was the name of a childhood friend, and it may have seemed quintessentially American. In any event, it stuck. From at least 1909, he became Harry Dexter White.[7]

As the hardware business got established, Jacob White moved his family into somewhat better accommodations. During Harry's preschool years, the family moved from 57 Lowell Street (where Harry was born) in the grimy immigrant section of the West End of Boston to 75 Prince Street, farther east, near the fabled Old North Church, though only briefly, and then a short distance to 109 Salem Street, a few steps down the street from the hardware store.

Salem Street was the address that Harry would remember later in life as the one that formed him as a person. In 1935, during his first European trip for the U.S. Treasury, he had occasion to meet the prime minister of the Netherlands, Hendrikus Colijn. After the meeting, he wrote home to his wife in amazement at how far he had come from his humble beginnings. "I could have laughed at kid pants from Salem Strasse chatting most informally with a prime minister. In another five minutes I'd have been telling him my stock of jokes."[8]

Harry began his schooling at the historic Eliot School where Paul Revere and many other famous Bostonians had studied. In 1901, however, when he was still in elementary school, his mother died. Jacob now had to raise the seven children on his own. In 1904 the family moved again, to a modest house at 20 Dyer Avenue in the northern suburb of Everett.[9] As a result, Harry transferred to Lincoln Grammar School, where he completed eighth grade in 1906.

The overall impression from the sketchy evidence is that young Harry was far more interested in the practicalities of becoming a normal American kid than in the culture and religion into which he was born. Though slightly below average in size, he played both tennis and baseball. As is common among men of slight stature, he tended to exaggerate his height. At times he claimed to be 5'7" or even 5'7 1/2", but his military records indicate that he was closer to 5'6" and that he weighed 132 pounds at age twenty-four.[10] He was a good student. He graduated from Everett High School a year early, in 1909, when he was just sixteen years old. Circumstances intervened, however, to prevent him from continuing his education.

No sooner had Harry graduated from high school than he was orphaned. His mother was already dead, as was his oldest sister, Ida (the latter probably a suicide),[11] and now his father died as well. Alongside three of his brothers, Harry went to work in the hardware store, which the brothers were soon able to expand into a chain of four stores selling automobile and bicycle supplies, wedding gifts, and other goods, as well as traditional hardware items.

After two years working in the stores, in September 1911, Harry matriculated at Massachusetts Agricultural College ("Mass Aggie," the forerunner of the University of Massachusetts Amherst). Despite having a good academic record, he stayed for only one term and returned to Boston in February 1912, presumably for economic reasons.[12] It is also likely and not surprising that he was unimpressed by what the college had to offer. Several years later, he took the initiative to write to Barney Kaplan, a boyhood friend who had enrolled there, telling him that he should really try to get into a better university. Harry urged his friend to transfer to Harvard. (Kaplan did so and graduated from both Harvard College and Harvard Law School.)[13]

For the next five years, Harry worked again in the family hardware business. During this time, he also volunteered at the Home for Destitute Jewish Children, on Canterbury Street (now the American Legion Highway) in the Dorchester neighborhood of Boston. To help raise young boys who had been orphaned or abandoned, he spent his Sunday mornings at the home, teaching classes and taking some of the older boys to a local park to play baseball. When Harry left to join the U.S. Army in 1917, the boys in that class established an essay prize in his honor.[14] This in loco parentis role, no doubt nourished by his own family hardships, evolved into a lifetime interest.

The death of his father and the apparent suicide of his sister Ida were not the only family hardships that Harry encountered while he was working in the hardware stores in his early twenties. By 1913 his sister Fanny had developed emotional problems that appear to have been symptomatic of a mental illness, and his brother Sam then also became emotionally disturbed, even more than Fanny. Because of the lack of knowledge about such illnesses at that time and the stigmas attached to them, little is known about the exact nature of their problems. What we do know[15] is that the circumstances had a profound effect on the direction of Harry's life and eventually revealed a silver lining.

Sam White, who was two years older than Harry, preceded him as a student at Massachusetts Agricultural College in Amherst. While he was studying there, he became friends with a classmate named Leon Terry. During their senior year, Leon introduced Sam to his much younger sister, Anne. Although Anne was just seventeen and still in high school in Springfield, Massachusetts (about twenty-five miles south of Amherst), she and Sam began dating. Before long, they were in love and "considered [themselves] to be engaged." By then, however, Sam was forced to drop out of school and take Fanny to Chicago for extended treatments for her mental illness. He returned to Massachusetts some months later, but his relationship with Anne did not survive the interruption.

Two years later, in the summer of 1915, Sam suffered a mental breakdown so severe that he was no longer able to recognize his own siblings, and the family had him committed to an institution. His friend Leon Terry did not know how to break this devastating news to his sister Anne, and so he asked Harry, as Sam's brother, to tell her. Harry had met Anne only once, at a party at her sister Elsie's house while Sam and Anne were dating, but he agreed to undertake the assignment.

That summer, Anne—who had just finished her freshman year at Pembroke College of Brown University in Providence, Rhode Island—was working as a nanny for a couple who lived in Somerville, Massachusetts, just north of Boston. Harry called her on the telephone and made an appointment to see her the next evening. Not having heard from Sam for a long time, she was puzzled as to why his brother would be calling on her. But Harry dutifully made the journey, escorted her to a quiet bench in the back garden where they could talk privately, and told her why Sam would not be coming back.

The story might have ended there, but Harry seems to have had trouble escaping the memory of his brief evening meeting with Anne. In the fall, when she was back at Brown, he called her again and asked if he could come over to see her. They met at the train station in Providence and spent an idyllic afternoon canoeing on the Ten Mile River. More dates followed, though not at first with any great romantic progress. After more than a year of sporadic afternoon adventures (more canoeing!), as Anne lamented later, "He had never so much as kissed me."

Harry's diffidence contrasted markedly with Anne's outgoing self-assuredness. Otherwise, they had much in common. In addition to canoeing, they both played a lot of sports, and they loved to sing and dance to popular songs. They both enjoyed serious reading, and they both indulged their love of children by getting involved with orphanages. The also shared a Central European immigrant heritage. Like Harry, Anne's ethnicity was Ashkenazic Jewish.

Anne was born in the town of Aleksandrovsk (renamed Zaporozhye in 1921), by the Dnieper River in southeastern Ukraine. Her native language was Russian, but her father, Aaron, was a multilingual lawyer, and Anne picked up languages easily. Her parents emigrated with her and her five siblings in June 1904, when she was eight years old. They settled in Springfield, Massachusetts, where some other family members were already living. Aaron bought a four-bedroom house (which he liked to call a "cottage") at 242 Dickinson Street, near Forest Park.

As the family settled in, they anglicized their surname from Teraspolsky (or possibly Tiraspolski) to Terry, and each of the children assumed American-sounding names. Born Anna, she first became Annie and then simply Anne. For a time as a young woman, for reasons that she never explained, she adopted a different family name. While a student at Brown

University, she was known as Anne Cutler. That surname was an anglicization of Kotlerevski, which was either the name of another branch of the family in Ukraine, or her mother's maiden name. Soon after, however, she returned to being known as Anne Terry.

The catalyst for a deepening of this friendship was the U.S. entry into World War I. When the United States declared war on Germany and Austria-Hungary on April 6, 1917, Harry immediately enlisted in the U.S. Army and applied for enrollment in the Officers' Reserve Corps. The army sent him to Plattsburg Training Camp in upstate New York. Meanwhile, Anne finished her junior year at Pembroke College (majoring in English literature) and took a summer job working at an orphanage in Pleasantville, New York. From there, she wrote enthusiastic letters to Harry about how much she wanted to adopt some of the children herself and how she wanted the two of them to run an orphanage.[16]

Harry was smitten. He invited her to visit him at Plattsburg. When she arrived, he finally found the courage to kiss her. Almost as if it were a reward for this show of bravery, the army commissioned him a few days later as a first lieutenant in the Infantry Section of the Officers' Reserve Corps (fig. 3). Harry had allowed himself to hope only to be named a second lieutenant. He wrote excitedly to his brother Nathan, "Luck [is] my middle name." To Anne he wrote that he had succeeded "beyond [my] wildest dreams."[17] Moreover, he had been selected for further specialized training at Harvard from a team of French officers in the Iron Battalion. Anne visited him again while he was training at Cambridge, and this time he gave her a diamond ring and asked her to marry him.

When his training was completed, Harry was assigned to the newly formed 302nd Infantry Regiment of the 76th Infantry Division of the Allied Expeditionary Forces. From September 1917 to July 1918, the regiment was posted at Camp Devens (also newly established), outside Ayer, Massachusetts. There Harry's duties included instructing soldiers in bayonet fighting and in the use and care of one of the army's newest light weapons, the Browning automatic rifle. Meanwhile, he and Anne began planning to have their wedding before he would be sent overseas.

On February 22, 1918, Harry and Anne were wed by the rabbi Harry Levi in a ceremony at the Temple Israel, a Reform synagogue then located on Commonwealth Avenue in Boston.[18] They remained in Boston for a hurried honeymoon, staying at the Copley Plaza Hotel. Lieutenant White then returned to Camp Devens, and Anne Terry White returned to Brown University to finish her undergraduate degree. When

Fig. 3. *Lieutenant Harry Dexter White, U.S. Army, circa
1917. Family scrapbook, courtesy of Claire A. Pinkham*

she graduated in May, the couple moved into a house for married officers
at the army base.

Normal married life was soon interrupted. In July 1918 Harry's regiment sailed via Liverpool to France and was stationed in Périgueux, in
the Dordogne region northeast of Bordeaux. It was designated as a "replacement" regiment, meaning that it was intended to help fill in gaps
in active regiments that were losing soldiers to casualties. For the next
few months, positioned far from battle, Harry had enough spare time to
play basketball, write letters and listen to American music at the YMCA,
and practice his French on dangerously attractive women he would meet
in town. More sedately, he offered English lessons to at least one young
mademoiselle, who wrote a charming letter of thanks to the lieutenant's
bride back home.[19]

As evidenced by the letters that he frequently wrote to Anne from France, young Harry took readily to army life.[20] He enjoyed the camaraderie of the barracks and the sense that he was part of a critically important project. Also, the army was "about the only place where I have not come into contact with any anti-Semitism." Moreover, he wrote that he was feeling "hatred" for the first time in his life, directed at Germany. "If any Boche prisoners fall in my hands, I can promise them a rough journey," he wrote in October 1918. This visceral antipathy toward Germany would only intensify when the Nazis took power in 1933, and it would remain with him for the rest of his life.

In September Harry was ordered to transfer to a camp in Châtillon-sur-Seine, in northeastern France, where he was given additional training to prepare him to help lead his troops—Company H of the 302nd Infantry—into battle. Four weeks later, he was put on a train of "cold box-cars" headed toward the front lines against the German army. Soon, he wrote home, he would be "in the trenches. . . . It cannot be too soon for me, I'm tired of schooling." For better or worse, he never made it. He and the other troops on the train were diverted to a replacement camp, where they were told to wait until they were needed to fill in other detachments.[21] Less than two weeks later, on November 11, 1918, Germany surrendered. The Great War was over.

With nothing useful left to do, Harry took advantage of his accumulated leave and headed south to the French Riviera for a two-week holiday in December. He then returned to camp in Burgundy and waited for orders to return home to the States. Finally, on February 7, 1919, he was aboard ship to sail from Brest to New York. From there he was sent to Fort Dix, New Jersey, until he could be released back into civilian life and reunited with his anxious bride.

Honorably discharged from the army on February 21, 1919, Harry seemed destined to the quiet life of a man of business. Ever restless, however, he soon left the hardware stores to his brothers. He and Anne moved to East Orange, New Jersey, where Anne's sister Ruth was living with her husband, Abe Wolfson. It appears that Harry and Anne lived with the Wolfsons, at least for a while. In the summer of 1920, Harry listed his address as 78 Rutledge Avenue in East Orange, which was also the Wolfsons' home address.

While living in New Jersey, Harry made a living running a settlement home: Corner House, at 21 Charles Street in Greenwich Village, New York City. Maurice Bernstein, a resident of Corner House who—as we shall see in the next chapter—became a close family friend, later wrote a firsthand

Fig. 4. *Harry (far left) directing the Blue Ridge Camp in Pennsylvania, 1919.*
Family scrapbook, courtesy of Claire A. Pinkham

account of Harry's work as director of Corner House, a home "for orphan asylum graduates who had no homes to which they might return."[22]

Earlier accounts have muddled this episode a bit. David Rees stated that in 1919 White became "the head of an orphanage for dependents of American Expeditionary Force servicemen killed in the war."[23] In another example, a 1943 story in the *New York Herald Tribune* (April 11) reported that White "served overseas in the last war and directed an A.E.F. orphan asylum." In White's own clipping of the newspaper story, he (or someone in the family) drew a penciled line through that statement. It seems most likely that the story conflated White's wartime service in the AEF with his later orphanage work and that subsequent accounts simply repeated the error.

In the summer of 1920, Harry also directed a camp for Jewish boys in rural Pennsylvania, the Blue Ridge Camp on Coolbaugh Lake in the Poconos (fig. 4). As the brochure for Blue Ridge Camp noted, Harry was "making the education of boys his life work." In addition, for a time in 1921 he sold office equipment for the American Kardex Company in Tonawanda, New York. These formative years would soon be at an end.

CHAPTER TWO

The Education of Harry White

If you have no family or friends to aid you, . . . turn your face to
the great West, and there build up a home and fortune.

—Horace Greeley

Columbia

In the fall of 1921, Harry White was turning twenty-nine years of age. He
had learned to run a business, he had served in the army in France, he had
married, and he had embarked on a career—running an orphanage—that
was perhaps modest but was probably emotionally satisfying. What he
most clearly lacked was a proper education, beyond the one term that he
had spent at the Massachusetts Agricultural College. That fall, he enrolled
at Columbia University in New York City.[1]

In his first year at Columbia, Harry studied government, social science, English, and two courses each in French and contemporary civilization. He received an A or a B in all courses. In his second year, he turned
to economics but got off to a remarkably slow start, receiving his first C
in Econ 1. Fortunately for the history of the twentieth century, he re-
bounded with an A– in Econ 2. Harry was now primed to prepare himself
for his true calling.

Like most undergraduates, Harry continued to pursue a variety of
subjects. In his sophomore year at Columbia, he took a course dealing

with the "nurture and education of children" (Education 187), suggesting that he might still have been considering going back to his earlier career ambition. He also took three more courses in French, two in English, two in government, and one on the history of philosophy. Only in the philosophy course did he receive a grade as low as C.

Harry also was reading widely and developing an interest in political philosophy and economics. A handwritten list of books that he compiled (undated but probably around 1923 or shortly thereafter) contains numerous philosophical works, including books by prominent figures such as Bertrand Russell, Thorstein Veblen, and Beatrice and Sidney Webb. The list also included several books on economic science, including one by Irving Fisher.[2]

Stanford

After two years at Columbia, Harry decided to move west. He initially planned to transfer to the University of Wisconsin, but after he contracted a serious case of influenza, his doctor advised him against relocating to a place with long, cold winters.[3] That induced Harry to make a major life-changing trip, following the steps that ambitious young Americans had been taking in great numbers since the middle of the previous century. He and Anne would move to California, and he would transfer to Stanford University.

The Whites left for California in June 1923 and spent the next two years in Palo Alto (living first in the suburb of Los Altos and then in Palo Alto itself, closer to campus) while Harry earned both a B.A. and an M.A. from Stanford.[4] Anne also resumed her studies in English literature and received an M.A. degree from Stanford in 1925. They began taking on the trappings of a typical American family life, acquiring a "dilapidated" Model T Ford, two Airedale terriers, and a cat. Although they did not yet have children of their own (two daughters would come later), they invited three orphan boys whom they had known from Corner House in New York to move to California and live with them so they could help the boys continue their education.

The temporary family that Harry and Anne set up in Los Altos succeeded remarkably well. The three boys from the orphanage all loved the chance to live in California in a real home with surrogate parents. The house was small enough that the three boys had to share one room, but the setting was bucolic, with a palm and fig trees in the garden (fig. 5). In

Fig. 5. *Harry and Anne at home in Los Altos, California, circa 1923.*
Family scrapbook, courtesy of Claire A. Pinkham

their late teens or early twenties, the boys did well in school, and all three committed to continuing their education and developing a career.

One of the boys, Maurice ("Bernie") Bernstein, had been having a difficult and unhappy time studying at City College of New York. Once in California, he got into Stanford with encouragement and help from Harry and Anne. Another, Irving Furst, finished high school and then enrolled at Reed College in Portland, Oregon. Bernie later joined Irving at Reed College, from which they graduated. Bernie had a successful career in social work. Irving had a successful career with the Jewish Federation in New Britain, Connecticut, until the FBI became suspicious of him in the early 1950s because of his past association with Harry and his continuing friendship with Anne. Irving was forced out of his job and spent the next several years eking out a living as a chicken farmer. The third boy, Dave Everall, finished high school (he had dropped out while in New York) and then left for the University of California at Berkeley, where he eventually earned a Ph.D. in philosophy. He became a professor of philosophy at City University in San Francisco.[5]

Throughout their lives, Bernie and Irving remained close to—really, a part of—the White family, as eventually did their children. Dave also remained fond of and loyal to Harry and Anne throughout his life, although he was always apart from the other two. Harry's original plan had been to invite just the two boys to move to California with them, but Dave—in his own words—"cried up a veritable storm" and made much of his suffering from recent ear surgery until he solicited the requisite sympathy to be added to the clan.[6] He and Harry reunited briefly in 1945, when Harry was in San Francisco for the conference that established the United Nations.

When Harry enrolled at Stanford, he still intended to major in political science, not economics. He went right to work, taking four courses during the summer: political theory, public finance (in the economics curriculum), and two courses in public speaking. He earned As in all four. Over the next year, though, he concentrated his studies heavily in economics, taking ten courses in that field while taking just three in history, two each in political science and education, and one seminar in Russian. After sixteen months of full-time study, Stanford awarded him a B.A. with "great distinction" in economics and honored him as a "Stanford Scholar" in recognition of his "special scholastic attainments."[7] He also was elected to the national honor society Phi Beta Kappa.

Eight months and eight economics courses later (all As), Harry held an M.A. from Stanford as well. His professors included at least two monetary experts: Murray S. Wildman, the author of a 1905 book on the history of financial panics in the United States that emphasized the psychological underpinnings of the problem; and Albert C. Whitaker, the author of a 1919 treatise on foreign exchange.

Studying for the master's degree gave Harry the opportunity to begin doing original research. As his thesis topic, he chose "European Loans Floated in the United States from 1919 to 1925." The thesis included a detailed accounting of the financial flows in the postwar years and an analysis of the economic implications. The United States, he noted, had always been a net borrower in international credit markets until the outbreak of the Great War in 1914. This was mainly because the young and rapidly growing country had a large and continuing need for capital beyond what could be raised through domestic saving. In addition, U.S. investors showed a "lack of interest" in lending abroad.[8] What changed because of the war was that the demand for financial capital in European countries ballooned while their traditional sources dried up. Great Britain, in particular, imposed controls on the outflow of capital with the aim of conserving it for domestic enterprises. Meanwhile, U.S. companies were able to gear up production of war materiel for European combatants. Banks and other financial institutions in New York and other major U.S. centers eagerly fulfilled the resulting demands for loans.

While at Stanford, Harry also first showed an interest in political activity. In a talk to the Parent-Teacher Association in nearby Atherton, he criticized the excessive dedication of federal government spending on the military, to the neglect of persistent and extensive poverty and the widening gap in the distribution of income and wealth.[9] As a representative of a "group of men consisting for the most part of mature graduate students of Stanford University," he wrote a fawning letter to Wisconsin's Senator Robert M. La Follette Sr., offering the support of the group if La Follette would run for president of the United States. Calvin Coolidge had just succeeded to the presidency on the death of Warren G. Harding, and Harry was unimpressed. "At no time has our country been more in need of a leader," he wrote to La Follette, who was known primarily for his opposition to corporate dominance of government but who was also an isolationist who had opposed both World War I and the League of Nations.[10] Harry's letter did not specify which of these views his group supported, but he himself was never an isolationist. At any rate, he concluded that "at no time since Lincoln's has there been a man more fitted to lead than you."

La Follette did run, on the third-party Progressive ticket, carrying only his home state of Wisconsin. The extent to which Harry followed up on his promise of support is not known, except that on at least one occasion he gave a public speech at Stanford in favor of La Follette's candidacy.

Harvard

When Harry received his master's degree, he was thirty-three, but he was not yet finished with his belated education. On the strength of his Stanford degrees, he moved back east in the summer of 1925 and enrolled as a graduate student at Harvard. The next seven years in Cambridge, Massachusetts, would finally establish Harry as a solid prospect for a career in economic policy. It was also time for Harry and Anne to form their family. Their first daughter, Ruth, was born in May 1926. Their second, Joan, arrived some three years later, in March 1929.

With the impending birth of Ruth and Harry's need to focus on his studies, Anne decided to stay with family members in Springfield, Massachusetts, some ninety miles west of the Harvard campus. For nearly two years during Anne's first pregnancy and Ruth's toddlerhood, Harry was again living on his own, in an apartment at 1 Chauncy Street, just off

Massachusetts Avenue in Cambridge and close to Harvard Yard. He often accepted dinner invitations from friends, without which he probably would have suffered from his own dietary choices. He discovered a Jewish deli near Harvard Square that sold sandwiches on black bread with spiced beef or pimento and cream cheese. Otherwise, as he admitted in his letters to Anne, bananas seem to have been a mainstay of his daily intake.

By the fall of 1927, Anne and the baby Ruth were back with Harry in Cambridge. The family now was living in a small apartment at 7 Merrill Street, several blocks east of the university campus. Anne presumably was providing both Harry and Ruth a more regular diet. She also resumed her literary pursuits at that time, including giving at least one lecture in Boston on three of the great Russian novelists: Dostoyevsky, Tolstoy, and Turgenev.[11] As the family grew, they moved into larger quarters: first a little farther north to 25 Hammond Street in Cambridge and then west and somewhat farther from campus, to 21 Holden Road in Belmont (fig. 6).

Harry's development as an economist began in earnest once he transferred to Harvard. While he pursued his one year of coursework there (receiving all A or A– grades), the Economics Department employed him

Fig. 6. *Anne and Harry with their daughters, Joan and Ruth, at home in Belmont, Massachusetts, 1932. Family scrapbook, courtesy of Claire A. Pinkham*

as "Instructor in Economics and Tutor in the Division of History, Government, and Economics," at a salary of $1,250 (equivalent to $18,500 in 2021).[12] He also began working with Professor Frank W. Taussig, who became his chief mentor and inspiration for the next few years. Though some thirty-three years older than Harry and already famous as the author of two major books on the principles of economics and trade theory, Taussig was culturally akin to him as a first-generation American descended from Jewish immigrants from Eastern Europe. At this time, he was preparing the third edition of his treatise on tariffs and protectionism, and he found Harry to be a valuable and sympathetic protégé. Over the next few years, Harry would not only write a new section for his professor's book and co-author a paper with him,[13] but occasionally teach his classes as well.

Harry studied both trade theory and the history of economic thought under Taussig and wrote his Ph.D. dissertation under his direction. The rest of his examination committee had a heavy emphasis on history. Abbott P. Usher was an expert on economic history, especially of Europe and the evolution of technology. Arthur E. Monroe was an expert on the history of thought, including monetary theory. William Y. Elliott was an expert on the history of political thought who later became famous as an outspoken critic of Marxist economics. The fifth member of Harry's committee was Arthur S. Dewing, a specialist on corporations. While at Harvard, Harry also took a course on monetary theory from Allyn A. Young and one on international finance from John H. Williams.[14]

Among these influences on Harry, Taussig's was easily the most important. First, he gave Harry a solid grounding in classical theory, with a keen appreciation of the benefits of international trade. As the Austrian American economist Gottfried von Haberler wrote a few years later, the "classical theory" of international trade was "accepted by the more theoretically-minded economists in the United States . . . notably by those under the influence of Professor Taussig."[15] Second, Taussig taught Harry the value of taking a practical and pragmatic approach to studying empirical questions and eschewing simplistic and ideological arguments.

Taussig was a past president of the American Economic Association and the longtime editor of the *Quarterly Journal of Economics* (*QJE*). His writings on trade theory were destined to become classics of that literature. He had absorbed and embraced the mainstream theory that open trade between countries improved aggregate welfare in both places, but he had developed a flexible and pragmatic approach to the study of individual cases. He wrote his first study of the appropriateness of tariffs in the late

1880s. The U.S. economy was generally thought to have matured by then to a point where John Stuart Mill's "infant industry" argument for tariffs no longer applied.[16] Taussig was not so sure, and he put forward the thesis that each industry's case should be studied on its own merits. New industries would arise, and even in an advanced national economy, entrepreneurs would need time to develop the methods, the skills, and the machinery to compete with established competitors overseas.

The first and second editions of Taussig's *Some Aspects of the Tariff Question*, published in 1915 and 1918, developed the theory of tariff protection and examined the effect of tariffs on selected major U.S. industries (iron and steel, sugar, and textiles) roughly from the end of the Civil War, in 1865, to the end of the Great War, in 1918. Harry's task was to update the study to include the early postwar years (to 1930) and to write a new section on an industry that had emerged after the period of the earlier editions. The infant industry was initially known as "artificial silk," later as rayon.

Rayon was invented by a French scientist around 1890, and the manufacture of rayon developed first in France and then in England and other European countries. U.S. companies tried to emulate the process but found early on that it was too complicated and too dependent on European expertise. Moreover, the start-up costs, including equipment and plants for manufacturing the cloth, were very high. Nonetheless, through perseverance over two decades, an American industry was established successfully. Throughout this emergent period, the U.S. industry was protected by tariffs on European imports ranging from 30 to 55 percent.

For the third edition of Taussig's book (subtitled as written "with the Coöperation of H. D. White") and in their jointly authored 1931 article in the *QJE*, Taussig and White analyzed this history and concluded that the development of a domestic rayon industry was beneficial. With no natural comparative advantage, U.S. firms would never have been able to get started against the established competitors without protection from the government. Once established, U.S. production was efficient and fully competitive with that of the European industry. It was, however, unlikely to have happened without assistance, owing to the high start-up costs and the difficulty of developing the necessary skills and infrastructure. Protective tariffs on rayon had been an appropriate application of the infant-industry argument. They cautioned, though, that it was too early to judge whether the mature U.S. industry had a comparative advantage over those in Europe. Without such an advantage, the normative case for a protective tariff could not be sustained.

While working with Taussig and completing his coursework, Harry suffered a brief setback when he failed his first attempt at the oral exams known as "generals" at Harvard. He pressed on and succeeded on his next try. He then began work on his Ph.D. dissertation: a study of the French international accounts in the prewar period. This topic was a natural outgrowth of his master's thesis, in which he had examined the effects of European lending to the United States. Now he would zero in on French loans and related capital flows, not just to the United States but to all countries. A consolidated set of accounts did not yet exist for France, so he constructed a data set covering 1880–1913, the bulk of the classical gold standard era.

To assemble such a formidable set of data, Harry applied for and got a grant from Harvard's Bureau of International Research, which enabled him to spend a few months in France gathering statistics. The $500 grant (equivalent to about $7,600 in 2021) was enough to enable Anne and Ruth to accompany him to Paris for the summer of 1928. They arrived in Cherbourg on June 9 and departed from the same port on September 14. In the town of Sceaux, just south of Paris, they rented an apartment in a suburban house with a walled garden at 19 rue du Lycée.[17]

France must have been a grand adventure for the young family: Harry spending his days in the library and the archives while Anne experienced the capital and possibly honed the writing skills that would become her life's work. For any young American, it was a magical time to be in Paris: the era of the "lost generation" of expatriates such as Gertrude Stein, Ford Madox Ford, F. Scott Fitzgerald, and Ernest Hemingway. In late July, Harry and Anne apparently attended a Davis Cup tennis match at Roland Garros Stadium between two of the great legends of the era: the American Bill Tilden and the Frenchman René Lacoste (won by Tilden).[18] That summer, Anne became pregnant with their second child. Back in Cambridge, Joan Terry White was born on March 12, 1929.

Harry's new data revealed that over the thirty-four years that he studied (1880–1913), between one-third and one-half of French savings had been invested abroad. Conventional theory of the time suggested that this practice must have reflected a shortage of profitable investment opportunities at home, relative to those available in other countries. It also suggested that the welfare consequences of investing on one side of a national border or another depended only on relative net returns, as long as the investor was seeking the highest risk-adjusted returns. The receipt of higher returns, the diversification of risks, and the enhancement of liquidity associated with these loans should have raised incomes and spurred economic growth in France.

Harry was skeptical on both counts. Individual choices had national consequences, and those choices might not fully reflect actual market risks. The question that he posed in his dissertation was whether the high rate of international lending (most of the outflows were in the form of bank loans) had improved "the welfare of France."[19]

Harry's dissertation disputed the classical analysis of foreign investment and found that the expected benefits had not materialized. Information about risks and rewards of foreign investment was not easy to obtain, and lenders were easily misled. French institutions had systematically underestimated the risks of lending abroad and had thereby systematically overestimated potential returns. Foreign lending had also drained resources away from the domestic economy. Starved of savings, domestic companies had been limited in their ability to create employment opportunities. Overall, foreign investing had probably done little or nothing to enhance the returns on savings or national income.

Harry concluded that the French experience showed that one could not just assume, on the basis of classical theory, that unrestricted capital flows would be beneficial. One would have to examine the data and the circumstances carefully. "The ramifications of exporting a large portion of a country's savings are too complex and the consequences too important to permit the continuance of capital exports without making some attempt at evaluating their effects on the well-being of the country at large."[20]

As Harry stood on the brink of his career as an economist, he was already revealing the hallmarks of the thought processes that would characterize his working style. He would start with the prevailing mainstream economic theory; he would test it against the data; he would keep whatever he found to fit; and he would reject whatever elements he found wanting. By the time he left Harvard, he had found reasons to be highly skeptical of unalloyed free trade and open capital, but the emphasis was on "unalloyed." At no time throughout his adult life would Harry turn away from trade and capital flows as the engines of economic prosperity, as long as they could be accurately assessed and effectively managed by public policy.

On the basis of this dissertation, the economic historian June Flanders in 1990 classified Harry as an important "late classical" economist who was "more original" than his peers in that group and who would have been a "major contributor" to the economics profession had he not worked primarily in government service and died young. She noted that the methodology in his dissertation "comes closer to Keynesian macro analysis . . .

[and] to developing a truly full-fledged general equilibrium system . . . than any of the others in" the late classical school of which Taussig was the leading figure and progenitor.[21]

The dissertation was a remarkable advance on prevailing theory, with important implications for international economic policy. Harvard recognized its value by awarding it the David A. Wells Prize for the best economics dissertation of the year and publishing it under the imprint of Harvard University Press.

The award of the Wells Prize was a great honor and carried a $500 cash prize, but Harry was furious at the way it was presented on the book's title page. Without notifying him, Harvard University Press described the prize in a way that made it look as if, in Harry's words, his "many years' labor" was just "a school boy's essay": "This prize is offered annually, in a competition open to seniors of Harvard College and graduates of any department of Harvard University of not more than three years' standing, for the best essay in certain specified fields of economics."[22]

While this wording was a technically accurate description of the terms of Wells's bequest, Harry noted in a diatribe to the publisher that the competition was effectively open only to Ph.D. dissertations, which had to be of publishable quality. Had he known that the press was going to "introduce my book to the public in such a manner," he averred, he "would never have consented" to its publication. "Please advise me," he concluded, "what you will do to rectify your unwarranted action." The press could only apologize.[23] What this contretemps mainly illustrates is a certain bristle and extreme focus, for which Harry would later become famous.

When Taussig saw how furious Harry was, he went out of his way to reassure him of the book's success and importance. It was "a real contribution to the theory, and to the verification and testing of theory," he wrote.[24] It would "take its place" alongside other important books published in the *Harvard Economic Studies* series. That list, Taussig noted, included such outstanding and seminal works as *Interregional and International Trade*, by the Swedish economist (and eventually Nobel laureate) Bertil Ohlin; *Twenty Years of Federal Reserve Policy* by Seymour E. Harris; and *The Theory of Monopolistic Competition* by Edward Chamberlin. "You and I can extend congratulations to each other," he concluded proudly.

Although Harry was destined to write other lengthy studies and make other major contributions to economics as his career progressed, *The French International Accounts* was the only book that he ever published.

The value of a university education is not limited to what one learns in class or writes in response. Both at Stanford and at Harvard, but especially at the latter, Harry developed contacts and made friendships that would be important to him (sometimes to his detriment) for the rest of his life. We shall meet several of these friends in later chapters, but one in particular is worth singling out here. Lauchlin B. Currie ("Lauch" to his family and friends) was ten years younger than Harry but was contemporaneous with him at Harvard. Despite their different backgrounds—Lauch was a lapsed Catholic from Nova Scotia—the two became good friends and, in Currie's words, "friendly rivals" while studying for their Ph.Ds. They frequently played tennis and bridge, cheered on the Harvard Crimson football and hockey teams, studied economics, political theory, and German together, shared their favorite novels, and went out for long walks or drives or to movies. Lauch would drop by the Whites' house for tea in the afternoon or for bootleg whiskey in the evening, or to sit for the Whites' baby girl, Ruth.

Harry's influence on his young friend was profound. In May 1926 Lauch recorded in his diary that Harry "appears to be extremely fortunate in his wife." Moreover, "What I want most in the world: a wife, intellectual and passionate." A few days later, Lauch took a young lady out on a double date with another couple, and he eventually married her. That same month, he took a big step out from his provincial upbringing when "White told me he was a Jew, to my surprise." The following week, after Harry invited him to tea and introduced him to another Jewish friend, Lauch proclaimed to his diary, "I'm becoming pro-Jew! Due to their history they are mostly very internationally minded." Soon, Lauch rented an apartment on the next street to the Whites'.[25]

Their friendship was not all sweetness. Lauch soon decided that he thoroughly disliked Anne, whom he found to be too intellectual and driven. "Being with her constantly [would] be too great a strain," he wrote in his diary.[26] And once the first glow of camaraderie faded, he began to have doubts about Harry's character as well. "He has his race's hardness," he wrote in his diary, "a certain aggressiveness, or intellectual pride. He is stimulating but not sympathetic. . . . A good friend when one feels strong & confident but not when one feels the contrary." Still, Harry was supportive of Lauch's prospects, and their friendship endured. And before long, Lauch reversed course on Anne once again, declaring, "I think I like her better than Harry."

Both men became Harvard instructors in economics. In 1932, together with their fellow instructor Paul T. Ellsworth, they wrote a memorandum urging a comprehensive policy of budget deficits and monetary expansion (through open-market operations) to combat the worsening economic depression in the United States.[27] It did not break ground that was not already being plowed by some other policy-oriented economists at the time, but it stands out as a clear and early statement of what we now call Keynesian macroeconomic policy. The government, they argued, should combat the fall in incomes with a program of deficit spending financed largely by injections of cash by the Federal Reserve System.

The memorandum is remarkable for the depth of its macroeconomic analysis and the clarity of its call for a comprehensive approach to demand management, four years before the publication of John Maynard Keynes's *General Theory of Employment, Interest, and Money*. But it is also an oddity in the curiosity shop that comprises the history of economic thought. Why did they write it, and for what audience? It was never published, and it is unlikely that it was ever submitted anywhere, but Harry kept the original draft for the rest of his life.

Harry's contribution to this paper probably focused on the international dimension, which was exposited in the last two sections. First, the United States should take the lead in reducing tariffs and other barriers to trade. Since 1925, rising tariffs had created a "mad dash toward declining trade, increasing costs, and economic maladjustment" and ultimately to the disasters of the Depression. Second, the United States should take additional action to reduce the burden of reparations and inter-Allied debts left over from the Great War in European countries. "Reparations . . . hang like a storm cloud over Europe," and the resulting "extreme distress in Europe must tend to retard our progress." The paper concluded with a call for "a *complete cancellation* of interallied debts and reparations," on the grounds that the direct financial costs to the United States would be more than offset by the benefits of economic recovery in Europe. In a pattern that was typical of Harry's writing, this proposal was documented with a lengthy accounting of the outstanding debts and their burden, followed by an emotional appeal for action. "Europe will have been relieved of the demoralizing burden of uncertainty and fear, and will have taken forward steps toward prosperity."[28]

None of this analysis of the international situation was completely new, but it was controversial. Keynes had railed against the burden of reparations and war debts since 1919 and had stirred up a lively debate on the associated "transfer problem" in 1929. His views were opposed by many prominent classical economists, led by Bertil Ohlin of the Stockholm

School of Economics. The debate was nominally about the technical issue of the effect of a reparations transfer on the country's terms of trade,
but the underlying normative issue was whether it was either wise or just
to try to force European countries—whether allies or enemies—to make
large payments after the war. As for the tariff issue, the Republican Party
platform of 1932 stated that the party "has always been the staunch supporter of the American system of a protective tariff. . . . The home market
. . . belongs first to American agriculture, industry and labor."[29] Harry and
his fellow graduate students were aligning themselves cleanly with the
other side, and with Keynes.

CHAPTER THREE

A Brief Academic Career

Teaching [is] of all things the work I like best.

—Harry White, 1935

HARRY COMPLETED HIS EDUCATION and finished his time at Harvard in 1932, just as the Great Depression was reaching its nadir. He was forty years old, was the head of a growing family, and had considerable real-world experience, but he had not yet embarked on an actual career. Despite his sterling academic achievements at Harvard, his prospects in that year of national misery did not look promising.

Harry began looking beyond Harvard as early as 1930, when he corresponded with the U.S. Tariff Commission in Washington about possible employment. He was probably encouraged to do so by Taussig, who had been the first chairman of the commission (1917–19). In January 1931, however, Harry decided not to pursue that prospect. He was still more interested in teaching than in a government career. With few jobs of any kind available in the depths of the Depression, in 1932 he accepted an offer from Lawrence College in Appleton, Wisconsin. It was quite a remote outpost after Harvard, but the job carried a good title (associate professor) and a decent salary: $3,300 (about $64,800 in 2021).[1] For Harry, the most important quality of the town of Appleton (population then 25,262) may have been its most quotidian: Appleton had a post office, through which

Harry could correspond with his former professors and colleagues and eventually find his way back east.

To be fair, Appleton was not without its entries in the history of the twentieth century, at least one of which brings us back to the story at hand. Appleton was the boyhood home of Harry Houdini, the great escape artist; and it is the burial site of Wisconsin's Senator Joseph McCarthy.

Why did Harry White, urban-bred and Harvard-educated, accept an offer from a little-known college in a small town in Wisconsin? No direct evidence is available. One factor, noted by Bruce Craig, may have been that Harry knew that simply because he was Jewish, "his chances for promotion at the Anglo-Saxon bastion [Harvard] were slender."[2] More generally, obtaining a permanent faculty position at Harvard or another elite university was a long shot for any student at any time, no matter how bright and regardless of ethnicity. The Depression made that challenge far greater when Harry was entering the market in 1932.

Wisconsin had a long-standing appeal for Harry because of its progressive politics. It was the home state of Robert M. La Follette Sr., whom Harry had supported as a presidential candidate in 1924. It also had an appeal for Anne, for that same reason and for its cool weather. They had considered moving to the state in 1923 so that Harry could study at the University of Wisconsin and had abandoned that plan only because Harry was having health issues that required him to live in a warmer climate. In any event, the most compelling explanation is just that Lawrence College, so far as is known, was the only academic institution to offer him a professorship.

As the U.S. economy continued to worsen and the electorate drifted left and elected Franklin Delano Roosevelt to replace Herbert C. Hoover in 1932, Harry concentrated on getting his nascent academic career up and running. He was teaching courses in economic theory, statistics, and "international economic problems." He was corresponding with Taussig on the final editing of their book manuscript. He was not yet writing original economics articles, but he was writing book reviews.

In Appleton, Harry was giving speeches debunking "technocracy," an increasingly popular movement that blamed much of the Depression on the interaction of technological advances and market economics. Its advocates, who most famously included the Norwegian economist Thorstein Veblen, called for turning control of the economy over to engineers and scientists. Despite the popularity of the movement in the early years of the Depression, it was an easy target for Harry.

In the fall of 1933, after just one year at Lawrence College, Harry was promoted to professor. He was awarded a nominal salary increase to $3,500 a year, but what the university gave with one hand, it pulled back with the other. Following the practice of the federal government in 1933, salaries were being reduced by 15 percent to reflect the general decline in consumer prices.[3] (From 1930 to 1933, the U.S. Consumer Price Index fell by a cumulative 23 percent.) The reduced salary was equivalent to about $58,400 a year in 2021.

At Taussig's invitation, Harry wrote a lengthy essay that fall for the *Quarterly Journal of Economics*. The essay reviewed two books on international trade: *Der Internationale Handel* by Gottfried Haberler (translated two years later from German to English and published as *The Theory of International Trade*) and *Interregional and International Trade*, by Bertil Ohlin.[4] Both books were destined to become the preeminent publications by those esteemed scholars. At the time, Haberler (teaching at the University of Vienna and writing in German) and Ohlin (a future Nobel laureate who was teaching at the Stockholm School of Economics and writing in English) were two of the most prominent economists writing about international trade, along with Taussig and Jacob Viner. All were connected as colleagues or by teacher-student relationships and friendships; the seventy-four-year-old Taussig served as the paterfamilias. Although Harry was the same age as Viner (forty-one) and several years older than either Haberler (thirty-three) or Ohlin (thirty-four), he was an academic novice.

Taussig was conveying quite an honor on Harry by asking him to write such a major review for one of the most prestigious journals in the field of economics. The master was initiating Harry into his inner circle.

On receiving the review in May 1934, Taussig declared it to be "first-rate" and accepted it for the journal without amendment. He could not offer much monetary compensation, he wrote, but the journal would send him a "modest check," which—Taussig noted with tongue in cheek—Harry should use "for something that your wife approves of."[5]

Harry was also searching for a fruitful research topic to carry him forward in his career. As the Depression continued to worsen, protectionism against import competition was becoming a major intellectual and political force in the United States. The most prominent example was the passage of the Smoot-Hawley Tariff Act in 1930, which sharply raised tariffs and thus suppressed demand for imported goods. The resulting contraction in international trade was also suppressing exports and adding to the

contraction of economic activity. Harry believed that protectionism had
to be stopped, and he began looking for alternatives.

One of Harry's first research tasks at Lawrence was to write a highly
critical review of the English translation of Mihail Manoilescu's book *Theory of Protection and International Trade*. Manoilescu—a Romanian fascist
politician and economist—promoted protectionist trade policy as a general and permanent condition. Harry's review argued that Manoilescu's
thesis was thoroughly flawed and that protection could be justified only
temporarily and in response to specific conditions such as the development of new industries. Unfortunately, Harry failed to get the review
published. After submitting it to the *Journal of Political Economy*, Harry
discovered that the journal had already published a similar critique by
another former student of Taussig, Jacob Viner. Moreover, the journal
Weltwirtschaftliches Archiv had published a critical review by Bertil Ohlin.[6]
The *American Economic Review* had a more favorable review by Leo Pasvolsky (whom we shall meet again in later chapters as an antagonist at the
State Department). Harry realized he was too late. He withdrew his effort
and did not attempt to find an alternative outlet.

International finance proved to be a more fruitful area for research
than did trade. Despite his confidence in the advantages of international
trade, Harry had a skeptical attitude toward unregulated flows of financial capital. The management of international exchange became the main
theme of Harry's brief academic career and the springboard into his Treasury career.

By 1933 the U.S. economy was in turmoil and in long-term decline.
Roosevelt had been elected president largely on the hope that he would be
more activist in responding to the Depression than his deeply conservative predecessor, Herbert Hoover. Roosevelt's first official act on assuming
office in March was to declare a bank "holiday" (briefly closing all commercial banks) as a temporary measure to halt the panic that was driving
thousands of banks into insolvency. Within days, Congress passed legislation declaring a national emergency and granting the president authority to
take necessary measures to stabilize the banking system and the currency. In
April, Roosevelt issued an executive order requiring citizens and businesses
to surrender almost all gold bullion, coins, and certificates to the Federal
Reserve System. In January 1934 he followed up by devaluing the dollar in
relation to gold, raising the official price from $20.67 an ounce to $35.

While these actions were happening in Washington, Harry was far
removed in his midwestern teaching post. Yet he was not so removed as

to ignore the threats to prosperity and the consequent seismic changes in the financial system. How should the system evolve, he wondered, so that the United States could have a stable dollar, the benefits of international trade, and a return to full employment? Roosevelt's New Deal program would help, but in addition some policy would have to replace the gold standard that was being abandoned.

As a research project, Harry decided to look at what other countries were doing in response to the same destabilizing force of internationally mobile capital. Shining examples were hard to find. Great Britain's 1925 restoration of the gold standard at the prewar parity had been a disaster. Germany was engaging in a stringent deflationary policy not unlike that of the Hoover administration. France was receiving large inflows of gold but was sterilizing them (hoarding the gold in the central bank) and thus deflating the economy. The value of the Canadian dollar was fluctuating wildly in a passive response to developments in the United States. Looking farther afield, Harry settled on the Soviet Union as a possible source of inspiration.

Initially, the focus of Harry's interest in the Soviet Union was its development of "planning" (that is, what became known later as central planning) as an alternative to reliance on price adjustments to balance supply and demand. In the economics literature, the study of central planning was still in its infancy. The practice of central planning dated back at least to the eighteenth century, but the economic theory was developed gradually in the twentieth century. In 1948 the economic historian Joseph Schumpeter wrote, "Economic theory is slowly developing the *mental instruments* that are necessary in order to 'rationalize' planning and to tell planners what they must do and avoid in order to attain given ends."[7]

Harry explicitly denied having any interest in "the success or failure of the Russian 'experiment.'" Instead, he was interested in solving the problems faced by the U.S. economy. Massive unemployment in the United States and other Western countries seemed to be associated with the absence of any government policy to control aggregate supply or demand. The publication of John Maynard Keynes's *General Theory* was still three years into the future, and Harry's thinking about this problem was essentially speculative. He wanted to study the theory and practice of planning to determine if it might do a better job of achieving high standards of living with full employment in the U.S. economy than a laissez-faire approach to economic activity. To study planning where it was being practiced most extensively, one had to go to Russia.

Harry's preparatory notes on the subject, written during his brief time teaching in Wisconsin, noted that both the United States and Great Britain had already adopted elements of planning in public institutions.[8] The British government was promoting industrial development through its Department of Scientific and Industrial Research and its oddly named Industrial Fatigue Research Board. Many of the U.S. federal agencies created in the New Deal were designed to create public-private partnerships or to add directly to government employment. The choice for a national economy was not between corner solutions: all private-sector capitalism versus fully planned government control. The choice, for Harry, was simply how much elements of planning might do to alleviate the dreadful shortcomings of Western economies in the 1930s.

After studying this issue for several months in 1933, Harry narrowed his interest to a more specific goal, which he explained in a letter that he wrote to Taussig in September:

> My interest has been aroused by the growing claims that our domestic economy must be insulated against outside disturbances, and that a greater reduction of imports should provide the insulation. This plea for virtual economic self-sufficiency needs, I believe, more critical treatment than has been forthcoming. I am wondering whether it may not be possible to develop feasible means of rendering our domestic affairs less sensitive to foreign disturbances without sacrificing either the stabilizing impact of international economic relations or the gains from foreign trade. The path, I suspect, may lie in the direction of centralized control over foreign exchanges and trade.
>
> I have been spending the spring and summer reading and thinking about the problem, but my opinion as yet is unsettled. I am also learning Russian in the hope that I may get a fellowship which will enable me to spend a year chiefly in Russia. There I should like to study intensively the technique of planning at the Institute of Economic Investigation of Gosplan. I expect to apply for a Social Science Research Fellowship, though my hopes of an award are not high.[9]

Harry was wise not to get his hopes up. He ultimately abandoned this ambitious project because he could not get financial support for it. The Social Sciences Research Council turned him down, as he half expected.

He then applied to the Guggenheim Foundation, which rejected his application because it arrived too late to be considered. Finally, he applied to the Commonwealth Fund in New York, which explained that it funded research only by British students.

These rejections ended Harry's quest. Spending a year in Moscow was not to be. He never went to Russia, he never learned much of the language, and he never again displayed any intention to study the techniques of central planning. The issue of "centralized control over foreign exchanges and trade," however, would continue to occupy him for many years.

In June 1934 Jacob Viner invited Harry to spend the summer at the U.S. Treasury in Washington working on "a comprehensive survey of our monetary and banking legislation and institutions, with a view to planning a long-term legislative program for the Administration."[10] Harry did not know it yet, but his brief academic career was at an end.

PART II

Becoming a Keynesian Internationalist

CHAPTER FOUR

What Next?

Dr. White Goes to Washington

Liberty's too precious a thing to be buried in books.

—Jefferson Smith, in *Mr. Smith Goes to Washington*

WHILE HARRY WAS STRUGGLING to find a way forward professionally, the administration of President Franklin Delano Roosevelt was struggling to find a way to restart economic activity and to end the Depression. Among the mass of legislation enacted during the first year of the New Deal, one would prove to be a decisive influence on Harry's career: the Gold Reserve Act of January 1934.

From 1879 to 1933, the U.S. dollar had been pegged to and freely exchangeable into gold at a fixed price of $20.67 an ounce. In the spring of 1933, Roosevelt—just weeks into his first term—abandoned efforts to restore the international gold standard through multilateral cooperation. The government devalued the dollar by 40 percent by letting the market price of gold rise for several months and then repegging it in January 1934 at $35 an ounce. Although the dollar was still pegged to gold and backed by the official stock of gold, it was no longer a true gold standard, because U.S. currency could no longer be exchanged for the metal except in official international settlements. Private entities—individuals, corporations, and other organizations—could no longer exchange currency for gold, and they were required to relinquish their holdings of gold coins. From that point, a license would be required for any large-scale acquisition or holding of gold in the United States.[1]

The 1934 legislation also transferred ownership of the stock of monetary gold (that is, the gold that served as backing for U.S. currency) from the Federal Reserve System to the U.S. Treasury. A portion of the profit from revaluing gold was used to create a $2 billion account at the Treasury called the Exchange Stabilization Fund (ESF). The ESF was to be used to stabilize the dollar in foreign exchange, and the Treasury was given wide latitude to decide on the methods for doing so.

The Gold Reserve Act marked a profound shift for U.S. monetary policy. The devaluation would arrest the destructive downward spiral in goods prices and help reverse the decline in export volumes that had resulted at least in part from earlier devaluations of other currencies. The elimination of gold coins and of the obligation for the Federal Reserve to sell monetary gold except in response to official claims would insulate monetary policy to some extent from market vagaries. It was the beginning of the end of U.S. reliance on the gold standard and the beginning of the beginning of what would become the modern discretionary control over the supply of money. When the act took effect in 1934, however, it was not at all clear what its consequences would be. The question for the U.S Treasury was simple: What next?

That first year of the FDR administration also marked a great shift in the intellectual basis for economic policy making. To guide the process, Roosevelt was seeking to attract a mass of academic firepower: what journalists soon began calling FDR's Brains Trust (soon shortened to Brain Trust).[2] For secretary of the Treasury, Roosevelt recruited an old friend and neighbor, Henry Morgenthau Jr. Morgenthau was not himself an intellectual, but he sensed that he needed a cadre of intellectuals to help him. He persuaded Jacob Viner to take a leave of absence from his professorship at the University of Chicago and come to Washington as special assistant to the secretary to help him assemble a team of highly capable economists. As that team assembled, it came to be known as "Viner's freshman brain trust."

On June 7, 1934, Viner wrote to Harry, inviting him to spend the summer at the Treasury, analyzing the recent changes in monetary policy and institutions, "with a view to planning a long-term legislative program for the Administration." The appointment was to start in less than two weeks, on June 20, and last for three months. Harry did not hesitate. Two days after Viner wrote his first letter, he wrote again to say he was "very happy" to hear of White's acceptance and offering to match his university salary "plus $200."[3]

Harry would soon learn that his old friend Lauchlin Currie was also going to the Treasury to work for Viner that summer.[4] When Currie informed Harvard University that he would not be able to teach two summer courses as he had planned, the university sent a telegraph off to White asking him if he could pick up the slack. As much as Harry must have loved the thought of returning to his alma mater, the siren call of public service, working with Viner on the design of the New Deal, was far more tempting. Within days, he was on his way.

On June 20, Harry began work as a temporary economic analyst in the office of the secretary of the Treasury (fig. 7), with a salary substantially higher than Viner's initial offer: $5,700 at an annual rate. He seems to have made a good initial impression in the capital city. When one of the Washington newspapers ran a story about Viner's Brain Trust, it noted approvingly that the "Lawrence professor, Dr. White, likes a dark blue coat with white flannels . . . [and] a bow tie." (Currie, in contrast, was characterized as one who "doesn't go in so much for clothes, but is a grand person.")[5]

Finding comfortable lodging at a reasonable price was a challenge in Washington in the depths of the Depression. Harry attributed the problem to there having been "no building for several years at least." To save money, he and Currie shared a suite with a bedroom and sitting room for

Fig. 7. *Members of the Viner "Brain Trust" in 1934. Jacob Viner is seated, front center. Harry is standing, far right. Others mentioned in this narrative include Frank Coe, standing, fifth from right, and Lauchlin Currie, seated, far right.*
From The Forward, *July 22, 1934.*

thirty dollars a month, at the elegant Powhatan Hotel, a 1911 building three blocks west of the Treasury. (Anne spent the summer in Massachusetts, staying with friends in Cambridge, raising their two daughters, and working to get her first two books published.) The Powhatan, like the Treasury and most other buildings in Washington, had no air conditioning, and the heat was oppressive for much of that summer. (The Powhatan Hotel was on the northeast corner of Pennsylvania Avenue and 18th Street, NW. It was demolished in 1975.) Harry and Lauch spent most evenings sitting around the apartment in their underwear, talking about work, women, and politics until the approach of midnight forced them to retire.[6]

Harry marveled at the amenities at work. He shared a large office with two windows that looked onto the East Wing of the White House next door. Never before had he had any real assistance for his research. Now what seemed like an army of assistants was available to type manuscripts, compute statistics, prepare tables and charts, or find whatever articles and books he might request. Every morning, as he reported to his daughter Joan, a "colored . . . messenger boy . . . comes in and sharpens my pencils, fills the ink bottle, and puts ice water in the pitcher. When I want something done I press a button and the messenger appears, like the fairies in the stories."[7] He also marveled that in the summer heat, most men in the office dressed without undershirts and shed their suit jackets. His previous life in Wisconsin must have seemed like a vanishing dream.

The background for Harry's work that summer—and later for almost all his work on international economic policy at the U.S. Treasury—was the future of the monetary role of gold. After all, the gold standard was the only monetary system with which he and other American economists of his generation had any experience. Most other major currencies were also pegged to gold from the late 1870s, and Britain's pound sterling was the dominant currency in international finance. The international settlement system broke down during World War I as most countries abandoned the peg to gold. After the war, a few countries restored the peg, most famously when Britain made the disastrous decision to return to the prewar parity in 1925 (discarded in 1931). By 1934, however, the prewar gold-based system was in a slow death spiral.

"What next?" was essentially the question that Viner wanted Harry to answer when he invited him to spend the summer in his coterie at the Treasury. What had been the effects of the devaluation of the dollar over the previous year? What had been the effects of the suspension of convertibility of the dollar into gold? What should government policy be regarding the monetary role of gold?

Harry had come of age as an economist when the continuation or restoration of the gold standard was being questioned by prominent economists as well as policy makers. During the era of the classical gold standard, criticisms of it had been largely confined to populist politicians, most notably William Jennings Bryan, who attacked it in 1896 as a "crown of thorns" and demanded that the government "shall not crucify mankind upon a cross of gold."[8] As the system's failures—repeated large and uncontrollable fluctuations in price levels—became evident, a serious search for alternatives commenced. The Yale economist Irving Fisher began developing an alternative policy scheme in 1911 and refined it repeatedly over the next two decades. The essence of Fisher's proposal was that the government should peg the dollar to a basket of commodities rather than to gold. Pegging to any single commodity rather than a basket was bound to lead to more instability of prices generally.[9]

Across the Atlantic, John Maynard Keynes had been attacking the gold standard as a "barbarous relic" since 1924. More recently, in his 1930 *Treatise on Money*, Keynes had argued that even if monetary authorities had flexibility to adjust parities in extreme situations, the gold standard would be unlikely to work. Would adherence to the gold standard be capable of preventing "violent disturbances and gross aberrations of policy?" he asked. No, because "experience . . . shows that, when severe stress comes, the gold standard is usually suspended. There is little evidence to support the view that authorities who cannot be trusted to run a nationally managed standard, can be trusted to run an international gold standard."[10]

Harry had a copy of the 1932 U.S. edition of Keynes's *Essays in Persuasion*, which included the *Auri Sacre Fames* ("Hunger for Gold") chapter from the *Treatise on Money*. In it he marked the paragraph in which Keynes mused on whether the world's fascination with monetary gold really existed because its advocates believed it was "the sole prophylactic against the plague of fiat moneys" or was just "a furtive Freudian cloak" arising from subconscious impulses. Keynes's conclusion was that gold had "become part of the apparatus of conservatism," which one "cannot expect to see handled without prejudice."[11]

Fisher's and Keynes's views notwithstanding, the prevailing but not universal view among economists in 1934 was still in favor of gold as the anchor for exchange rates and domestic price levels. Leading economists such as Gottfried Haberler, Joseph Schumpeter, and Parker Willis were arguing that the gold standard was the most reliable means of stabilizing foreign exchange markets and avoiding speculative and inflationary pressures in financial markets. Others, such as Allyn Young, who had taught both Harry and Lauchlin Currie at Harvard, argued that central banks should have as much discretion as necessary to stabilize the national economy. Still others, including Keynes (at times) and Harry's immediate boss, Jacob Viner, were trying to devise a halfway house in which money would be backed by gold but the government would have some flexibility to manage the supply of money. Within the Roosevelt administration, a fierce battle was taking place between gold's advocates and detractors.[12]

Harry's summer internship focused on finding a way forward. He obviously worked very hard (twelve-hour days, as he told Anne) and productively for those three months. On September 22, 1934, at the end of his assignment, he delivered a manuscript of more than four hundred pages to Viner, with the title "Selection of a Monetary Standard for the United States." Much of the report was a textbook analysis of the desirable qualities of a monetary standard and the evidence on the ability of different systems to deliver those qualities. Domestic price stability was obviously important, but so was stability of exchange rates. On both criteria, as well as the desirability of national sovereignty and policy independence, Harry found the gold standard to be seriously deficient.

The logic of Harry's argument was essentially what would become known in the postwar economic literature as the "trilemma" of monetary policy in an internationally open economy. If a country has a rigidly fixed exchange rate and is open to cross-border flows of financial capital, then it cannot independently control its domestic price level.[13] In 1934 Harry did not articulate that argument specifically, but the whole thrust of his report was on finding ways to limit the potential loss of control over the domestic economy by allowing for some flexibility in the exchange rate, controlling capital flows, or both.

Only two chapters were devoted to the domestic aspects of the issue: the effects on prices and economic activity. Although it had been widely argued that the gold standard was more likely to preserve price stability, Harry argued that the opposite was true, for two reasons. First, the supply of gold through mining or net imports matched changes in demand only by accident. Second, whenever the demand pressure on the stock of gold became too great, governments had no choice but to suspend convertibility. Expanding on Keynes's point, he noted that *every* country had suspended convertibility at least once in the preceding two decades.

Having dismissed the value of gold backing for domestic money transactions, Harry then expounded at length on the necessity of a metallic backing for international payments. Expecting a country or its residents to accept and hold another country's unbacked currency was—in 1934—completely impractical. The advantage of gold had nothing to do with any intrinsic value or characteristic of the metal. It arose entirely from its psychological effect on confidence, which existed simply because people believed in it. The logic, he knew, was perfectly circular, but logic it was. Without confidence, exchange rates would destabilize, the costs of international trade would escalate, and economies would stagnate or decline.

Although Harry was just a lowly and temporary employee that summer, he concluded his report boldly by proposing a "managed currency standard . . . for adoption by the United States." He acknowledged that his proposal "closely resembles the [standard] now in operation" in the wake of Roosevelt's actions of the preceding months. Essentially, he was making a case for those actions, proposing to embody them permanently in a comprehensive monetary policy, and tweaking the existing system a bit to make it more effective. These are the basic elements of his proposed system:[14]

- U.S. gold and silver reserves were to be used only for international settlements;
- the U.S. dollar was to be freely convertible for trade purposes, while capital transactions were to be subject to monitoring and potentially controlled;
- the price of gold was to be changed by the Federal Reserve Board when necessary to preserve the safety of the system, subject to the consent of the president;
- gold backing for domestic currency was to be eliminated; and
- the Exchange Stabilization Fund (ESF) was to be liquidated and the proceeds used for domestic expenditure. (As chapter 6 will show, Harry soon abandoned this idea and replaced it with a scheme to expand the use of the ESF.)

To ensure that the monetary system would be managed in a stabilizing and positive manner, Harry argued that the exchange value of the dollar should be kept fixed in relation to gold except in "periods of stress." Essentially, he was trying to define a standard for determining when it would become appropriate to alter the parity. War between countries would be an obvious example, but so would an economic depression or any situation in which alternative policy tools (tightening fiscal or monetary policies, reducing wages, or controlling goods' prices) would be inadequate or counterproductive. If the government could commit credibly to a policy of fixing the price of gold in normal times and to changing it without abandoning the system in periods of stress, then—he believed—the monetary system would surely function more smoothly and helpfully than under either of the corner solutions (pure fixing or pure floating, or, more generally, strict rules or completely discretionary management).

Harry's report thus went well beyond merely justifying Roosevelt's gold policy. Although the government did not adopt the specific recommendations for modifying the policy, the report offered a way to think about the longer-run consequences of an emergency action and converting it into a permanent policy regime. It contained the seeds of what would become the Bretton Woods system of "fixed but adjustable" exchange rates: the global system that prevailed from 1946 to 1973. It also prefigured the theoretical development that modern economists call "state-contingent policy rules."[15] And it clearly impressed Viner, who eventually would follow up by giving Harry a regular position as a Treasury economist and thus as a continuing member of his Brain Trust. In September, however, Viner did not have an open position to offer him.

As the summer job was coming to an end, Harry faced a different "what next?" question. What was he to do now to further his budding career? The obvious choice would have been to go back to Wisconsin to resume his teaching duties. Anne was eager for the cool Wisconsin air, and Ruth and Joan were eager to see their beloved German shepherd Ponto again (Ponto having been left in the care of their landlord for the summer), but Harry was less enthusiastic about the pedestrian intellectual environment. He applied for a job teaching at the University of Arizona, but negotiations broke down over salary.[16] A blank and potentially bleak future lay ahead.

CHAPTER FIVE

Settling into Morgenthau's Treasury, 1934–36

The charm of the work in Washington is so great that I feel that
I want to stay on for another year at least.

—Harry White, 1935

As the summer flew by without any clear prospect for escaping a return to Wisconsin in the fall, Harry White fretted about his highly uncertain future. "Don't feel too badly about it," he tried to reassure Anne
in mid-July. "The last bell has not yet rung down on us." And in his next
letter, "Maybe something else will turn up."[1] Increasingly, he wanted that
"something else" to be in Washington. Despite the oppressive heat and
his absence from Anne and their daughters, he seems to have been having
the time of his life. The New Deal was still taking form, and he was helping—as yet in a small way—develop the policy structure for recovering
from the Depression. Washington was the place to be.

Though the Treasury did not have a slot available for Harry in September, he managed, with help from a reference letter from Frank Taussig,
to get a one-year appointment with the Tariff Commission. Then his
prospects suddenly improved. After just one month at the commission,
he returned to Treasury as principal economic analyst in the Division of
Research and Statistics. Secretary Henry Morgenthau Jr. had created this
division just two years earlier as a vehicle for the agricultural economist
George C. Haas, who had previously worked for Morgenthau at the Farm

Credit Administration.[2] As an expert on international finance, Harry filled an important niche in the bureaucracy. For the next few years, Haas would rely heavily on Harry whenever the secretary needed advice on monetary issues or international finance.

Harry's salary was a bit less than in the summer but the same as at the Tariff Commission: $5,600 annually less a mandatory 5 percent reduction.[3] With prices still depressed in 1934, the salary was equivalent to about $102,000 in 2021. The job was fixed for only eight months, and the salary was being paid from an emergency fund established to cover the extra—presumably temporary—cost of devising responses to the Depression. Still, it established Harry in the government hierarchy, and it would ultimately get regularized. Treasury would be his professional home for the next eleven and a half years.

Harry was still on leave from Lawrence College as he began his first full year in Washington. In March 1935 the university president, Henry Merritt Wriston, wrote to express his hope that Harry would return to Appleton in the fall, while acknowledging "the great charm of the work in Washington." Harry wrote in response that although he loved teaching, he valued the work in Washington enough that he wanted to stay for at least another year. Reading between the lines of that response, however, reveals that Harry knew already that he would not be going back. His "pleasant" time in Appleton, he wrote, was "an association which I shall not lightly forget."[4]

Harry, Anne, and their two young daughters settled initially in a modest house that they rented for eighty-five dollars a month, at 1348 Madison Street, NW, just east of Rock Creek Park.[5] (Their dog, Ponto, sadly, had to stay in Wisconsin.) The two-story house had three bedrooms, a bathroom upstairs, a downstairs toilet, and a small but pleasant garden on a quiet residential street near a school. It was far from the Treasury but was well served by public transportation (an electric streetcar line on 14th Street, soon to be replaced by buses).

Gold and the Dollar

At work, Harry's first task in his new post was to pursue the policy implications of the work he had done during his summer internship. In that role, he carefully staked out a middle position between two virulently opposed camps on the monetary role of gold.

In January 1935, a few months after Harry took up his post, he managed to convey his ideas to Morgenthau. On this occasion, he drafted a memorandum with the title "Managed Currency and the Gold Standard." Again, he strove to define the intermediate ground between the two poles defined in the memo's title. The gold standard fell short because it could produce price stability only by accident and because it unduly constrained policy independence. An unconstrained managed currency ran the risk of being abused. Specifically, it was inappropriate to use currency devaluation "for the purpose of securing trade advantages." (This was more than two years before Joan Robinson popularized the phrase "beggar-my-neighbour" to describe such policies.) The best way to manage the currency while avoiding these dangers would be through international cooperation, possibly on the basis of rules or other formal agreements.[6]

By November 1935 Harry was able to develop his argument for a carefully managed currency in more detail. He drafted a thirty-nine-page paper, "Monetary Policy," covering six specific issues that "present major problems for the Treasury." The fourth topic—occupying nearly 40 percent of the document—dealt with international monetary policy, on which he argued that the problems were the "potential absence of national autonomy in the determination of monetary policy, the fact of international monetary instability, and the pressure to institute a universal international currency."[7]

In this note, Harry deconstructed and disputed the value of a gold standard for trying to stabilize domestic price levels. At the time, the United States held very large gold reserves, well in excess of what would have been legally required under the pre-1933 gold standard. Relying on the required gold backing to prevent excessive monetary expansion would have been destabilizing in the short run and procyclical in the longer run (once the excess had been eliminated). Better, then, to manage the currency sensibly than to rely on an unreliable rule.

The only real value to gold backing, Harry argued, was to help fix the exchange rate against other currencies. He was skeptical, however, that the gold standard could guarantee fixed exchange rates because "practically every country has abandoned the gold standard at least once"; or that fixed rates were even necessary for a well-functioning monetary system. He added hopefully, "Almost everyone knows better now." Unfortunately, "almost everyone" was a premature judgment. In stark contrast, a *Wall Street Journal* editorial a few months later (June 8, 1936) averred that "the desirability . . . of reestablishing an international gold standard . . . is questioned by very few."

Harry worried nonetheless that the debate over the gold standard was being distorted by a tendency to pose a choice between extremes:

"between fixed exchanges and broadly fluctuating exchanges . . . the evils of broadly fluctuating exchanges . . . are obvious and irrelevant." In practice, the choice should be "between an exchange rate fixed by law and a 'managed' currency."[8]

Even if the gold standard and its fixed exchange rates were no longer desirable, Harry did accept the need for policies that would produce stable exchange rates. Indeed, one issue on which all mainstream economists agreed in the 1930s was that stable exchange rates were a necessary lubricant for international trade. (Milton Friedman's seminal and influential article promoting floating exchange rates was not published until 1953.) If gold had become impractical as the means for stabilizing rates, then some other means would have to be devised. That task occupied Harry's mind greatly from 1934 for the rest of his life. In his November 1935 memorandum on monetary policy options, he envisaged a nightmare scenario in which disturbances from abroad would threaten the stability of the dollar, weaken international trade, and upend the recovery from the Depression. "Sooner or later," he wrote, "price movements may occur in other countries which are too drastic and too sustained to keep from increasingly disturbing our price structure."

The serious question raised by Harry's argument was *how* to manage the currency. The linchpin to his proposal was to retain a fixed gold price to underpin the market exchange rate of the dollar; gold would still be used to settle international payments balances. The memorandum alluded to the trauma of being forced to devalue "only after deflation has proceeded so far that abandonment of the gold standard is regarded as the lesser of two evils," as the Roosevelt administration had to do in 1933. It was better, in his view, to just change the price of gold "by administrative order when . . . it becomes necessary to do so . . . to achieve stability and sustained prosperity."

To limit the circumstances in which a devaluation (or upward revaluation) might be needed, Harry further proposed widening the spread between the buying and selling prices of gold (so as to allow for some flexibility without having to make a formal change) and having the ability (by means of "effective machinery") to impose capital controls "when there is a likelihood . . . that the price of gold is to be altered"—that is, the ability to suppress capital flight when it gets large enough to be an impending problem. This system, he argued, would enable the United States to have a fixed exchange rate for long periods *and* the ability to use its sovereign power to alter the rate infrequently but whenever it became helpful to do so.

These proposals resonated with Morgenthau, who quickly recognized brilliance in Harry's work and assigned him an ever-increasing portfolio of tasks. In April 1935, less than a year after Harry's arrival in Washington, Morgenthau named him a special agent for the Treasury and sent him to Paris, Brussels, and London, with instructions to go as well to "such other parts of Europe as you may deem advisable for the purpose of reporting upon the foreign exchange and other international monetary developments."[9] Belgium had just abandoned the gold standard, an action that the U.S. Treasury feared could set off a destructive cycle of instability in foreign exchange markets. Harry's task was to assess the situation firsthand and make recommendations for a response.

Harry left for Paris in early April, sailing first class on the German ocean liner the *Europa*. He was excited about encountering such luxury for the first time, notwithstanding his own and his family's disgust for the association with a country controlled by Adolf Hitler. He soon found himself uncomfortable, dining in his tuxedo on caviar and lobster and conversing with strangers whom he often found to be boring. In a letter home, he thanked Anne for making him pack the tuxedo, but he vowed to stop wearing it before the end of the voyage, "to maintain my self-respect." He spent much of his shipboard time preparing for the upcoming meetings and worrying about his ability to carry the trip off successfully.[10]

As he had feared, this first trip abroad for the Treasury did not go smoothly. No sooner had Harry arrived in Paris (where he found French people to be "as grasping as ever"[11]) than he received a cable from Morgenthau instructing him to skip Brussels and other possible stops on the Continent and proceed directly to London. There some of his British interlocutors found him unimpressive. By at least one account, staff at the U.S. embassy in London were so infuriated with his independent behavior, which they tried unsuccessfully to control, that they attempted to have him recalled to Washington. If true, that contretemps marked the beginning of a decadelong conflict between Harry and the State Department.

Nonetheless, the trip was ultimately successful. Harry met and had substantive discussions with many of the officials—most important, John Maynard Keynes—who would play key roles in the international financial negotiations of that crucial decade. In the end, after London, he did go to the Hague and Brussels before returning to London for a second time. By then, he was worn out. As he told Anne: "This is the end of a hectic week. I've been interviewing bankers, economists, public officials, big shots, little shots, hot shots and dead shots."[12]

By 1936 the last vestiges of the international gold standard were disappearing, as one country after another abandoned the commitment to sell their currencies for gold at a fixed price. Most of those countries were still trying to manage the exchange value of their currencies to prevent large movements against some standard, usually gold or dollars or pounds. Although Great Britain was no longer on the gold standard, the Bank of England was selling gold to France—which was still on the gold standard—when necessary to stabilize the value of the pound. As the ability of France to avoid devaluation weakened and a forced departure from gold became increasingly likely, the longevity of that tactic was being increasingly questioned. Officials in the Federal Reserve System, led by George L. Harrison, the president of the Federal Reserve Bank of New York, were pressing the U.S. Treasury to help Britain by selling gold to it. That would require a change in Treasury policy. Treasury practice at the time limited gold sales to countries with currencies freely convertible into gold, and the British pound had not been convertible since 1931. Morgenthau was reluctant to make such a change.[13]

On January 28, 1936, Morgenthau acquiesced and announced to his senior staff that he had decided it was time to allow "Central Banks of the world to buy and sell gold here. It looks as though it would make the exchanges flow more easily if the 52 Central Banks could operate here." He added that he "of course would not make this move until France straightens herself out again." Jacob Viner objected that this would mean placing the United States "back on an actual gold standard" and not just a "de facto gold standard." Viner also warned Morgenthau that the policy shift could give Britain a lever to "manage her currency against the other gold countries" and thus possibly destabilize the pound against the dollar. He suggested that the Treasury should wait until the British asked to buy gold and then ascertain what they intended to do with any gold they bought. Morgenthau agreed and thus put any shift on hold.[14]

Haas was present at that meeting but did not address the issue, even though it directly concerned his division. Afterward, he apparently went back to his office and asked Harry for an assessment. Harry drafted a five-page memorandum, which Haas submitted to Morgenthau the next morning. In it Harry proposed a scheme to turn Viner's objections into a strategy for moving forward. His memorandum began by explaining why, in general, buying gold from the United States instead of elsewhere should give rise to no advantage for countries not on the gold standard. Gold was a standard product traded in a global market. Britain, however, was an exception, because its primary source of gold was France. "For political reasons [Britain] would prefer at the moment not to appear to be making it more difficult for France to remain on the gold standard," Harry wrote. Letting Britain buy U.S. gold could therefore be politically valuable to Britain. It could also be valuable to the United States, because it would give the Treasury some additional leverage to try to keep exchange rates stable if France and other countries eventually abandoned their commitments to the gold standard.[15]

Morgenthau did not immediately act on the proposal to allow Britain to buy gold from the United States, but Harry kept pushing for it. Only after France departed from gold some six months later did the Treasury act to work with Britain and France to preserve a measure of exchange rate stability through what became known as the Tripartite Agreement.

The Tripartite Agreement of 1936

In 1936 deteriorating economic conditions in France contributed to an electoral victory on May 3 for a group of leftist parties known as the *Front Populaire*, led by the Socialist Party of Léon Blum. As Blum set out to implement a wave of reforms to strengthen the role of organized labor, he had to contend with a general strike and widespread unrest. Faced with a weakening economy, he sought vainly to preserve France's status as the de facto leader of the dwindling bloc of countries remaining on the gold standard (the others being Italy, the Netherlands, and Poland). The prospect of a French devaluation alarmed the British government because France was one of its major trading partners and because the British feared that a French devaluation would trigger retaliation by the United States. In fact, although France was not economically important to the United States, Britain was. The mutual fear of a series of cascading devaluations was suddenly a real threat to the still quite fragile recovery from the Depression.

For several days in early June, the U.S. Treasury was in panic mode, as capital flight out of France was putting upward pressure on both the pound and the dollar. Financial markets were increasingly skeptical of the incoming French government's promises not to devalue. Harry's nightmare scenario of a destabilizing shock from abroad was coming to pass.

Morgenthau organized an effort to contain the crisis, meeting and otherwise communicating frequently with officials from Britain and France, with bankers and other U.S. stakeholders, and with his own staff. Morgenthau began a meeting on June 4 with a British embassy official,

T. Kenneth Bewley, by telling him: "I want to talk to you straight from the shoulder and not diplomatically. The situation is so critical that if we use the usual diplomatic procedure we may have a smash-up in Europe." He continued by asking for assurances that if France were to devalue by up to 30 percent, Britain would not respond. Rather hyperbolically, he stressed how worried he was by concluding that "a similar situation started the march on Rome [which brought Mussolini to power]. The Hitler situation was just like this." Bewley promised to "put this [request] before my Government."[16]

In the event, the gold and exchange markets calmed down for the next two months, while the French government continued to try to muddle through and avoid a devaluation.[17] By September, though, pressures were building to a point that France had to act. Blum then developed a strategy to sugarcoat a devaluation by persuading the British and U.S. governments to enter into a joint agreement on exchange rates. His government even imagined for a time that France might persuade the other two countries to revalue their currencies upward, leaving the franc unchanged against gold but devalued relative to the other currencies. Blum also wanted the joint statement to include a commitment for all three countries to work toward an eventual restoration of the international gold standard. When his finance ministry presented these aspirations to the U.S. Treasury, Morgenthau rejected the idea out of hand. It then fell to the Treasury to devise an alternative plan.

Internal discussions at the Treasury (which also included State Department officials but pointedly excluded the Federal Reserve Board) intensified in the second week of September and culminated with the publication of a statement by the secretary on September 25, simultaneously with the issuance of similar statements by the governments of France and the United Kingdom. These statements jointly became known as the Tripartite Agreement.

In the run-up to the Tripartite Agreement, Harry participated in several meetings with Morgenthau, both in the office and at the secretary's Washington home. His role, however, was limited. Morgenthau himself uncharacteristically took charge of the discussions and also brought President Roosevelt into the process at key junctures. Assistant Secretary Wayne C. Taylor was the senior official under Morgenthau to be engaged in these deliberations, and Harry was also outranked by Haas, Viner, and a few others. Merle Cochran, the Treasury representative in the U.S. embassy in Paris, was the key interlocutor with the French finance ministry. Harry's role was confined largely to commenting on proposals and helping draft the final documents, but his contributions were important enough to warrant his inclusion in the official photograph of the Treasury team, gathered around Morgenthau behind the secretary's desk.[18]

Morgenthau's decision to exclude the Federal Reserve from the planning for the Tripartite Agreement was an early battle in a turf war that has continued through subsequent decades. In this instance, the Treasury's natural disdain for the central bank was augmented by personal animosity. At a meeting on September 18, Viner argued forcefully that Morgenthau should include Marriner Eccles, the chair of the Federal Reserve Board, in the deliberations or at least should inform Eccles right away on what was being decided. Morgenthau responded: "I don't trust Eccles. He is a liar." In the end, Morgenthau agreed to call Eccles to inform him, but only "five minutes before" going public with the agreement.[19] Across town at the Federal Reserve, Lauchlin Currie drew on his friendship with Harry to act "as go-between or peacemaker with Eccles and Morgenthau." When other Federal Reserve economists, including E. A. Goldenweiser and Walter Gardner, tried to persuade Eccles to press in the direction of a return to the gold standard, Currie tried to set up a lunch meeting between Eccles and White so that Harry could explain to him why it would be a bad idea. In the end, Eccles seems to have decided to stay out of the fray.[20]

Harry did have views on the proposed agreement, but in some ways his views were at odds with those of his boss. A year earlier, on his first overseas trip on behalf of the Treasury, he urged the British to stabilize the pound after devaluing by a modest amount. The British were unimpressed and continued to intervene to keep the rate in the vicinity of $4.86, the psychologically important rate that was equivalent to the prewar parity when both countries were on the gold standard. Harry continued to worry that the British would lose control of the rate and be forced into taking precipitous action, but by the summer of 1936 Morgenthau was worried more about the possibility that the French and British might get into competitive devaluing. His preference therefore was to persuade Britain to keep the rate unchanged and to persuade France to devalue but by no more than 25 percent. Morgenthau's diplomacy succeeded in achieving exactly that result, apparently to his own surprise. When it was over, he sent a triumphant handwritten note to his secretary: "My dear Mrs. Klotz: . . . after 3 months I have won against the career diplomats. Three cheers!"[21]

The issue on which Harry may have been most isolated within the Treasury was in his belief that retaining an international role for gold, although without a real gold standard, was important for financial stability. Morgenthau and Roosevelt were adamantly opposed to including any reference to the gold standard in the Tripartite Agreement. All that mattered was the set of exchange rates linking the three currencies. Harry realized, however, that the limited extent of formal central bank cooperation that existed in 1936 meant that exchange rates could not be kept within a narrow band without recourse to gold settlements. He also focused on the intellectual questions and the longer-run issues raised by the crisis.

In Harry's view, what mattered was not just getting France to devalue without triggering destabilizing responses elsewhere. What mattered was to devise a system of international exchange that would instill confidence, allow for policy flexibility and independence, and promote cooperation rather than competition. The Tripartite Agreement, for all its successes, did little to move the world in that direction. A full solution was still several years away and would be found only at the Bretton Woods conference in 1944, as we shall see in chapter 12. Harry's participation in the formulation of the Tripartite Agreement was an early step in his development of the ideas that led at Bretton Woods to the creation of the International Monetary Fund and an organized system of multilateral finance.

China and the Role of Silver

In the autumn of 1934, when Harry had just become a junior member of the professional staff at the Treasury, he grew concerned about the effect of U.S. silver purchases on the Chinese economy. This interest led him inexorably into an ever-deeper and ever more controversial involvement with economic support for China throughout his government career.

The Treasury had begun purchasing silver on the open market in December 1933, and the program had been extended by the passage of the Silver Purchase Act in June 1934. Purchases under that act began on October 26, 1934. Buying silver to raise its price was essentially a gift to U.S. silver miners and the associated industry, but it was also supported by many—including the farm lobby—who wanted to counteract the deflationary forces that were then so strong in the United States.

In addition to raising the domestic demand for silver, the purchase program stimulated silver imports into the United States. Because China's exchange rate was pegged to silver, the yuan appreciated vis-à-vis the dollar by about 40 percent in 1934 and 1935. That in turn aggravated deflationary tendencies in China. Silver hoarding in China made the problem worse. By November 1934, Harry reported, markets in China were in a state of "near-panic."[22]

That month, apparently just days after the silver purchase program began in earnest, Harry drafted a note in opposition to it, predicated primarily on the adverse consequences for China. Because U.S. silver purchases would aggravate the "business depression" in China through a deflation of the price level, the program should be either halted or restructured to avoid this consequence, he argued.[23] Indeed, from mid-1934 to the fall of 1935, the price of silver rose by more than 40 percent. Adhering to the silver standard was becoming a serious drag on the Chinese economy.

Morgenthau was trying to help by buying some silver directly from the Central Bank of China rather than buying it all on the open market. In November 1934 the Treasury entered into an agreement to buy up to 10 million ounces of Chinese silver. The Chinese had difficulty delivering that much, and a trickle of purchases was made throughout the next year.

The stress on China's economy, combined with the external pressure from Japanese aggression and the internal pressure from a Communist insurgency, forced the Chinese government to consider abandoning the silver standard altogether. Part of its plan was to seek financial assistance from one or both leading Western powers, Britain or the United States, by promising to link the currency to the pound sterling or the dollar. In Washington, Chinese officials first approached the State Department for help, to no avail. In February 1935 Secretary of State Cordell Hull, after consulting with President Roosevelt, informed the Chinese ambassador, Alfred Sao-ke Sze, that the U.S. government would consider only the possibility of participating in a *multilateral* lending program, if the Chinese were to request one.[24] Rather than accepting that the door was closed, the Chinese decided to take their plea to the U.S. Treasury instead.

On October 28, 1935, Sze called on Morgenthau at his home late in the evening to inform him that China was definitely planning to abandon the silver standard in favor of a managed fiat currency. To help rebuild the Central Bank's foreign exchange reserves for that purpose, Sze wanted the U.S. government to buy up to another two million ounces of China's silver reserves. Morgenthau immediately agreed, but only on one condition. The Treasury, he insisted, would pay for the silver by depositing the funds into a Chinese account at a U.S. bank and would have the account administered under U.S. supervision so that it could be used only to stabilize the value of the yuan and not to pay for military or other expenses.[25]

One reason for Morgenthau's enthusiasm (albeit restrained) was that he saw silver purchases as a way to strengthen U.S. influence and trading power in China over that of the United Kingdom. The British government had responded more positively to the Chinese overture than had the U.S. State Department and was actively courting China to replace the silver standard with a peg to sterling. In September, Britain sent Frederick Leith-Ross (chief economic adviser to the government) on an extended mission to China for that purpose. As Morgenthau told President Roosevelt in a phone call the day after his nocturnal meeting with Sze, "This is our chance, if they are down low enough, to hook them up to the dollar instead of the pound sterling. . . . It is very amusing to have the Chinese come to us with Leith-Ross sitting in China."[26] Whatever the secretary's motive, the effect was a U.S. commitment to provide further financial assistance to China.

Harry's influence on policy at this early stage of his Treasury career was limited. He had, however, argued against the Treasury's silver purchase program and paved the way for the use of the ESF to help countries that were not pegged to gold or to the dollar. Once Morgenthau decided to buy silver directly from China, Harry suggested a broader and more proactive program of support. On November 1, at the end of the week of Sze's appeal to Morgenthau, Harry drafted a memorandum for Haas to give to Morgenthau, warning that economic and political conditions in China were worsening, "owing to the increasing aggressiveness of Japan, and renewed Communist advance." The exchange rate against the dollar was depreciating because fear about the currency was leading to capital flight and smuggling of silver.[27] China had few good options other than seeking outside assistance.

China's abandonment of the silver standard on November 3, 1935, did little to reverse the deterioration in the Chinese economy. For the next five months, China kept the yuan fixed against sterling (though without an official peg) while continuing to seek financial aid from both Britain and the United States. Morgenthau wanted to help, but the long-standing reluctance of the State Department kept Roosevelt from agreeing to act. Finally, in April 1936, China sent a mission to Washington, headed by K. P. Chen, the influential Shanghai-based banker and adviser to the Chinese finance ministry, to negotiate financial support directly.

To help Morgenthau prepare for his meetings with Chen, Harry prepared a lengthy (fifty-eight-page) report on China that recommended stepping up U.S. purchases of silver from China in exchange for gold. The U.S. Treasury had more gold than it needed or wanted, and China had silver that it no longer needed as backing for its currency. Perhaps the deal would persuade China to link the yuan to the dollar and to increase its trade with the United States. In any event, it would help shore up the

Chinese economy and help the Nationalist government of Chiang Kai-shek resist the twin pressures from Japan and the Communist forces led by Mao Zedong. Three days later, Morgenthau approved a plan to purchase small amounts of silver from China gradually over a period of several months. On April 17 Harry followed up with a suggestion—this time sent directly to Morgenthau rather than in the form of a memorandum from Haas—to accelerate those purchases, restructure an existing loan to give it a longer maturity, and offer an additional loan.[28]

In May 1936 the Treasury approved a repurchase agreement for the ESF to acquire up to $20 million in Chinese yuan in exchange for U.S. dollars; the dollars were to be held in an account at the Federal Reserve Bank of New York *and* secured by an equivalent amount of silver held for China at U.S. depositories.[29] This arrangement—just the second of its kind, after one for Mexico five months earlier—was equivalent to a loan commitment from the Treasury to the Central Bank of China and was the prototype for the typical financial assistance now made by the International Monetary Fund (see chapter 6). This particular arrangement had a fourteen-month time span. Perhaps most important, by using the ESF, Morgenthau avoided having to seek approval from the State Department. In the event, China did not need to draw on it to defend its currency. Instead, the arrangement served to augment China's foreign exchange reserves with a right to borrow in case of need.

CHAPTER SIX

Rising into a Position of Influence, 1936–38

One of the ablest and brightest men in Washington.

—I. F. Stone, 1988

By 1936 HARRY WAS beginning to rise through the ranks. Having arrived at the Treasury in 1934 as a protégé of Jacob Viner, within two years Harry had shown his independence and had gained a more important patron: Secretary Morgenthau. He had become the Treasury's point man on all issues relating to international financial policy. At the same time, those issues were increasing in importance, as the U.S. economy gradually recovered from the Depression while Europe and Asia were languishing economically and drifting toward war. On October 1, 1936, Morgenthau promoted Harry to assistant director of the Division of Research and Statistics, at an annual salary of $6,500 (equivalent to about $120,300 in 2021). His long-term status was still uncertain. His Treasury post was not allocated within the regular budget, and his salary was still being paid from the emergency Depression-fighting fund. Even so, his prospects were improving.

Once Harry's position began to seem more secure, the family moved in 1936 from their rented house on Madison Street into a two-bedroom, fifth-floor apartment (#514) in a relatively new (built in 1929) Tudor and Gothic Revival building at 4707 Connecticut Avenue. It was in a more convenient and more upscale neighborhood (Forest Hills) that was well

64

served by streetcars and later by buses that went directly to the vicinity of the Treasury.

When Harry received his next pay increase, to $7,500 a year ($134,000 in 2021 prices), on July 1, 1937, the Treasury transferred the account from the temporary emergency fund to the Exchange Stabilization Fund (ESF).[1] Because Harry was working on international financial policy, the Treasury could justify his position as necessary for maintaining the stability of the U.S. dollar and therefore appropriate to be funded from the ESF. He still had an irregular position, but it no longer was under threat of abolishment for budgetary reasons.

In the fall of 1937, Harry found time to teach a course at the American University in northwest Washington: an introduction to money and banking for graduate students. This temporary reversion to academics did not, however, diminish his capacity to focus on his responsibilities downtown. As assistant director, he was reporting directly to Haas and was increasingly visible to Morgenthau.

In 1938 Harry and the family moved again to the near-northern suburbs, into a modest but elegant neo-Tudor house in the Edgemoor subdivision of Bethesda, Maryland, a neighborhood of single-family homes with mature trees and landscaped gardens (fig. 8). A photograph of the

Fig. 8. *Harry and Joan at the first home that the family owned (1938–46), in the Edgemoor neighborhood of Bethesda, Maryland. Family scrapbook, courtesy of Claire A. Pinkham*

house, which was built in 1932, illustrated a story about White in *Life* magazine in November 1953. As recorded by the county, Harry and Anne purchased the property for $10,000 in 1938 and sold it for $16,000 in 1946, a moderate gain after inflation. (It last sold for $1.9 million in 2015. The new owners then had the house torn down and replaced by one more than three times as large.)

After spending their first eighteen years together in a series of rented accommodations, Harry and Anne finally owned their own home. They soon acquired their fourth and probably final dog, which they named Kazan. The house was farther from public transportation than their apartment had been, and so it was probably at this time that Harry began commuting by automobile. They would live in this home at 7210 Fairfax Road until 1946. (At the time the Whites lived there, the address was 6810 Fairfax Road. The house numbers in Bethesda were reassigned and standardized by the U.S. Post Office after World War II.)

The move to the suburbs reflected a broader desire to escape the confines of the city. As early as 1936, Harry contemplated buying a farm near Washington to use as a retreat, but he abandoned that project after he had difficulty finding someone to manage it. In 1937 Harry and his family took a summer vacation at a fifty-five-acre farm near Hancock, New Hampshire, which was owned by their old friend Lauchlin Currie (fig. 9). Lauch had bought the property in 1934, using money that he had made buying stocks on margin in the late 1920s speculative market. He appropriately called the farm "Marginal Acres," and he regularly invited friends, including the Whites, to vacation there. Anne and their two daughters spent the whole summer at the farm in 1937, and Harry managed to escape the office for a week in early July and all of August.[2]

It was a happy time and an appealing place for Harry, Anne, and the girls. That fall Harry began looking for a house to buy in southern New Hampshire. In September he signed an agreement to buy a property in or near New Ipswich, New Hampshire, but the owner changed his mind and withdrew the offer to sell. At first, Harry threatened to sue the man, but he seems to have backed off.[3] Not until after the war would he finally succeed in finding the ideal spot for his summer home.

From Classical to Keynesian Economist

Harry's contributions to the theory and practice of economics have been largely neglected in writings on the history of economic thought. This

Fig. 9. *Harry and Anne at Lauchlin Currie's vacation home,*
"Marginal Acres," Hancock, New Hampshire, 1937.
Family scrapbook, courtesy of Claire A. Pinkham

neglect stems from the fact that after his brief academic career, he spent
most of his adult life working in government bureaucracies. He had little
opportunity to publish peer-reviewed articles. In addition, he had a dis-
concerting tendency to write at great length without ever quite finishing
his thoughts or polishing his prose. Teasing out the parts that were fresh
and quietly influential requires more digging than is the case with other,
more academically practiced economists of the twentieth century.

As we saw in chapter 2, the most extended discussion of Harry's work
by an economic historian was in June Flanders's book, *International Mon-*
etary Economics, 1870–1960. Because she considered only his Harvard dissertation, she classified him as a "late classical" economist. Even before he

left Harvard, however, he was already expressing the view that the federal government should shift to an active fiscal policy, supported by monetary policies at the Federal Reserve, to combat the Depression. Once he joined the Brain Trust at the Treasury, he evolved rapidly into an adherent of the activist policies that would soon become known as Keynesian economics.

Harry's responsibilities and interests at the Treasury were primarily and increasingly international. Only rarely did he weigh in professionally on a domestic policy issue, and then only because it related to an international issue. Perhaps the clearest example was a series of memoranda that he wrote in February and March 1935, just four months after assuming his regular duties at the Treasury.[4] The U.S. Supreme Court had just affirmed the legality of Roosevelt's suspension of the gold standard, which was a major element in the administration's program to restart economic growth. The question then was how to capitalize on the effective devaluation of the dollar so that the government could increase spending on domestic programs without inducing a panic flight out of U.S. dollars.

In a memorandum to Treasury Secretary Morgenthau on February 26, 1935, Harry made the case for an acceleration of spending programs. The slow pace of New Deal spending up to that point was, in his view, threatening the nascent recovery and contributing to populist discontent. In a second memorandum on March 14, he advocated taking advantage of a proposal circulating in the U.S. Senate to purchase silver on a large scale. Doing so, he argued, would help put more money in circulation and thus stimulate spending. The next day, he circulated a lengthy (fifty-eight-page) memorandum explaining why the administration's plans for public works and other spending increases should be accompanied by an active management of the exchange rate. Otherwise, uncertainty in the wake of the suspension of gold convertibility could undermine the country's ability to increase exports. Unilateral action to devalue U.S. currency would not work, he argued, because it would provoke competing devaluations by trading partners. The administration should, he concluded, seek cooperation with major allies, especially the United Kingdom and France.*

Another example came at the beginning of 1937, when the arduously slow recovery of the U.S. economy was faltering. Both the Federal Re-

---

* Eric Rauchway takes a more dismissive view of these 1935 memoranda, concluding that Harry merely "confirmed" Roosevelt's policies but "did not originate them" (*Money Makers*, 112). True, but the purpose was not to originate policies but to provide an intellectual basis and framework for them.

serve and the Treasury had been gradually tightening financial policies out of a misguided fear that liquidity growth was becoming excessive. In addition, the stimulative effect of one-off bonus payments to military veterans in 1936 was already wearing off. Banks were accumulating excess reserve balances because demand was weak and interest rates were low, but officials mistakenly inferred that the cause was an excess supply of bank reserves. In 1936 the Treasury began hoarding gold inflows rather than letting them drive up the money supply, and the Federal Reserve sharply increased reserve requirements. The combination of monetary and fiscal tightening resulted in a severe recession from the spring of 1937 through mid-1938.[5]

Even though Keynes's *General Theory* was in print and in the mix of discussion, and even though the New Deal emphasis on federally funded public works had been in effect for four years, the debate over how to respond to the recession extended deep within the administration. Morgenthau and Viner, along with James Farley (postmaster general and chairman of the Democratic National Committee), were in the camp of those who wanted to promote private investment indirectly by conveying confidence about government finances. Numerous other prominent economists in or close to the government—notably including Lauchlin Currie (then at the Federal Reserve Board), Louis Bean and Mordecai Ezekiel (Agriculture Department), Isador Lubin (Labor Department), and Leon Henderson (Works Progress Administration)—shared Harry's support for a stepping up of fiscal support for economic recovery.[6]

In April 1938 Viner abruptly resigned his position as adviser to Morgenthau with the intention of returning full-time to the University of Chicago, to protest what he viewed as the administration's policy of "heavy deficit spending . . . unaccompanied by genuine and courageous effort to eliminate the factors which . . . have forced us into a renewal of severe depression."[7] Although Morgenthau regretfully accepted Viner's resignation, Viner returned to the Treasury after a short interval and remained as a part-time consulting adviser to the secretary through 1942. Throughout that time, Harry continued to push for more aggressive action to stimulate the economy, even when that put him into direct conflict with his former patron. In a meeting on February 2, 1942, Harry told Morgenthau that he always consulted Viner and kept him in the loop except "on questions where I know we are opposed on domestic policy and in which I didn't think it would be a help but a hindrance."[8]

Harry's New Deal predilection sometimes clashed with his own cautious and conservative instincts. In 1937 prices were rising, but real

economic recovery was stagnant: a situation that four decades later would
be labeled "stagflation." At the end of March, Harry counseled strongly
against a proposal to fight incipient inflationary pressures by revaluing the
dollar against gold. He accepted that such a policy would certainly be effective if the change were large enough, but he argued that it was a "crude"
instrument and would be dangerous to use "when the recovery is still in
the sensitive stage it is now."[9] Two days later, in contrast, he cautioned
Morgenthau against trying to stimulate activity by supporting the bond
market. Even though interest rates were rising because of the Federal Reserve's policy of tightening, direct action by the Treasury to counter that
policy would be interpreted in financial markets as an effort to reduce the
Treasury's borrowing costs, not as a legitimate policy to ease monetary
conditions. He concluded by advocating a policy of "watchful waiting"
until the squeeze on the recovery became more acute.[10]

The clash of views between Keynesians and traditional fiscal conservatives in the Treasury came to a head in 1938. The economy was recovering from the recession, but much slack remained, and the unemployment
rate remained above 18 percent. Roosevelt was resisting any action that
would raise the federal deficit, and Morgenthau and some of his advisers
(notably Viner) supported that view. Harry pushed persistently to limit
the damage from this reluctance to act. For example, when Morgenthau
proposed to ask Congress to appropriate $2 billion for Roosevelt to use
at his discretion for public works, Harry argued that the amount was too
small. He suggested $4 billion and succeeded in getting Morgenthau to
ask for $3.5 billion.[11]

Beginning on Friday evening, December 9, 1938, and continuing on
Saturday afternoon and Monday morning, Morgenthau held a series of
lengthy meetings with advisers from the Treasury and other agencies, in
which Harry and Lauchlin Currie were the lead economists. (Alvin Hansen, the Harvard professor who was already the most prominent analyst
and interpreter of Keynes in America, attended part of the meetings but
did not take a major role.) Supported by instructions from Roosevelt,
Morgenthau wanted the group to devise tax increases that he could recommend to Congress and the president, to keep the deficit under control
without stifling economic activity. Throughout the weekend, Harry tried
to shift the discussion away from a national sales tax, which he argued
would be both highly regressive (falling heavily on lower-income groups)
and highly contractionary. As a less odious alternative, he proposed raising
estate and gift taxes, which were likely to have only an indirect effect on

consumer spending and would hit primarily those families that could most easily afford to pay them and that would have a relatively low marginal propensity to consume.[12]

The transcripts of those meetings convey a splendid snapshot of the state of the economics profession in the late 1930s, in the dawn of modern macroeconomics. In this discussion by policy makers, the theory was informed by the innovative work of Keynes, particularly the *General Theory*, with extended discussion of the fiscal multipliers for different types of taxation. The problem, though, was that no one had the data or the empirical tools to estimate numerical values for the concepts.* Modern computer-driven data analysis was still a quarter century in the future. The best they could do was to speculate whether a particular multiplier effect might be low, medium, or high.

For the final meeting on Monday, Currie and White prepared a draft report that included a clear statement of the Keynesian justification for not trying to balance the federal budget too soon: "Considering . . . on the one hand, the deficiency of consumer buying power during the next fiscal year in relation to our productive capacity, and, on the other hand, the inadequacy of existing outlets for the volume of accumulated savings, a continuing contribution by the Federal Government to the growth in buying power and the provision of an offset to savings, through deficit financing, is economically justifiable and desirable."[13] They continued, though, with an implicit acceptance that some form of tax increase was likely to be politically necessary in 1939. What mattered was that it should be the right sort of tax. The group had received Harry's proposal for higher estate and gift taxes with mixed enthusiasm, and the draft report alluded to it only indirectly: "If, therefore, it is felt that the proposed increased expenditures on armaments must be met by additional taxes, it is essential that the increased taxes must not reduce consumption." In the event, Roosevelt decided not to propose any new general taxes for the coming fiscal year.

By 1939 Morgenthau was coming around to the view that an aggressively expansionist fiscal policy could help stimulate recovery without

---

* The paucity of data and computational tools did not completely block attempts at estimation. Notably, in 1938 Currie employed a data set derived by Simon Kuznets to calculate investment multipliers for each year from 1919 through 1934. The results were highly variable from year to year, and Currie concluded that the data did "not appear to give much support" for the existence of a stable relationship ("Some Theoretical and Practical Implications," 18–22).

undermining the federal budget. At the beginning of June, he invited Harry to his home on a Sunday evening to discuss a plan that he (Morgenthau) was developing to generate an economic recovery in 1940. The centerpiece of the plan was some $4 billion in loans to finance infrastructure spending (equivalent to roughly 3.5 percent of total federal outlays). According to Morgenthau, "Harry was most enthusiastic and said his friends would not believe that I was going to suggest [such] a program." In addition, Harry offered several ideas for supplementing the secretary's plan, including setting up a corporation to buy land for farm tenants and making loans to China, Russia, and Latin American countries to help stimulate markets for U.S. exports. Enthusiasm, however, was not enough to win over the country. Although Roosevelt approved a modified version of the plan and submitted it to Congress, the legislature ultimately rejected it.[14]

Throughout the late 1930s, Harry's main focus was on ways to stabilize cross-border trade and finance in a world in which the international gold standard was no longer viable. As countries continued to abandon the gold standard and as political uncertainty increased in Europe in response to the worsening situation in Nazi Germany, gold flowed out of those countries and into the United States in vast amounts. Political pressure built up for the U.S. government to close off those inflows and take other measures to control the gold price and the money supply. Harry wrote numerous memoranda advocating resistance to those pressures. Even if the inflows were putting upward pressure on the value of the dollar and endangering the economic recovery, he argued that controlling capital inflows—possibly through taxes—was preferable to interfering directly with the gold market.[15]

The Case for Regulating Capital Flows

The 1936 devaluation of the French franc, France's departure from the gold standard, and the Tripartite Agreement all failed to help the French economy, which continued to decline and to suffer further downward pressure on the value of the franc. Most analysts have attributed the failure to what the economic historian Barry Eichengreen has called "a negative supply shock on a massive scale."[16] Fractious relations between labor and management intensified after the devaluation. Real wages rose, and profitability and real investment fell. For the next few years, the continuing weakness of the French franc was again a focus of concern for the U.S. Treasury.

In response to a request from Morgenthau, Harry wrote a memorandum at the end of April 1938 with advice on how to respond to the ongoing weakness of the franc. Some prominent politicians in France were urging the government to let the franc float downward until it reached a sustainable level. They argued that this policy would begin to bring financial capital back into the country, mainly from Britain and the United States, the markets to which capital had been fleeing for some time. In the U.S. Treasury, it was clear that a floating franc would raise the same issues that had precipitated the Tripartite Agreement two years earlier, and Harry and his boss were eager to dissuade the French from taking that course. An option under consideration in Washington was to encourage France to impose import controls to conserve scarce foreign exchange. Harry did not like that possibility any better. With no good options available, he settled on a singular alternative: "Of the three ways open to France to attempt to solve her acute exchange situation [further depreciation, import controls, or capital controls], the imposition of exchange controls over non-commercial transactions . . . seems to us now, as it has in the past, to be the best of the bad choices confronting her."[17]

More generally, the obvious first choice was always for a country to conduct its economic policy responsibly so that it could maintain a strong economy and a currency with a stable value. When policy or economic conditions went off track, however, the government would be faced with a range of suboptimal choices. Losing control of the exchange rate would not solve the problem. Restricting imports to conserve on gold and foreign exchange reserves would harm the economy and lead to unemployment. Restricting the outflow of financial capital by controlling access to foreign exchange was the only other practical option and was—so Harry argued—unambiguously preferable to the other options.

Harry pursued this idea of capital controls as a last resort ("the best of the bad choices") consistently throughout his years at the Treasury. He first articulated it in his 1934 report to Viner, where he argued that the United States could allow the open mobility of financial capital under normal conditions, but it was important to have legislation in place so that the Federal Reserve Board could impose controls quickly if capital flight became a problem. In January 1936, when gold inflows were threatening financial stability in the United States, he devised an elaborate scheme (which was not adopted) to impose a 100 percent reserve requirement on bank deposits owned by nonresidents, coupled with a tax on sales of securities to foreigners.[18] Then came the 1938 response to the French crisis described above.

In proposing a 100 percent reserve requirement on nonresidents' deposits, Harry doubtless was influenced by arguments in favor of imposing such a requirement on *all* demand deposits at commercial banks. That argument had a long intellectual history and was injected into the policy debates of the New Deal through memoranda written by economists at the University of Chicago. Irving Fisher popularized the idea in a 1935 book.[19] In Harry's circle, Currie was among the advocates.

When Harry drafted his plan for a postwar stabilization fund in 1942, he made the case that use of the fund should be contingent in some situations on the borrower's willingness to restrict the outflow of capital, because "there are situations in which many countries frequently find themselves, and which all countries occasionally meet, that make inevitable the adoption of controls." Also of note is that Currie argued in a 1936 paper that capital controls would generally be necessary for the maintenance of domestic macroeconomic equilibrium.[20] Currie's analysis was inspired in part by Harry's 1933 book and a 1935 article by Harry's Treasury colleague Frank Coe, both of which questioned whether international capital flows would produce the expected gains.

Across the Atlantic, John Maynard Keynes also argued in favor of capital controls, but he and Harry differed sharply on the rationale. In Keynes's view, capital flows were always potentially destabilizing and hence should always be controlled. His 1942 plan for postwar stabilization suggested that international cooperation on controlling capital flows was a key advantage of the scheme. Britain, he noted, had "gone a long way towards perfecting" the use of capital controls, and that experience should serve as an example to the rest of the world.[21] Rather than keep such controls in reserve for use in emergencies, Keynes wanted them to be encouraged for general use. As we shall see in chapter 10, what emerged from their negotiations was a compromise that was consistent with both views, but in practice it served Harry's purposes more directly than those of Keynes.

Tariffs and Other Trade Barriers

Although Harry was no fan of generalized tariffs or other trade restrictions, he recognized that openness required reciprocity and fairness on the part of all parties. The Tariff Act of 1930, commonly known as the Smoot-Hawley Tariff Act, after its two main sponsors, sharply (and disastrously) raised tariffs on imports to the United States. As we have seen,

Harry opposed the use of tariffs to protect American producers. Nonetheless, he saw that the Tariff Act could also be used to force other countries not to use trade barriers as a weapon against U.S. exports. Section 303 of the act obligated the U.S. government to retaliate with countervailing duties if another country imposed "any bounty or grant upon the manufacture or production or export of any article or merchandise manufactured or produced in such country." That issue generally lay outside Harry's purview (financial policy) in the Research Division of the Treasury, but he got involved in 1936 after Germany began using exchange rate policy as a form of trade barrier.

In the early 1930s, several Latin American countries began experimenting with various forms of exchange control, including multiple exchange rates that varied according to the type of goods being exported or imported.[22] As long as the practice was confined to relatively small countries with which the United States had friendly relations, these discriminatory practices were not viewed as a cause for concern in the Roosevelt administration. That changed in 1935, when Germany's minister of finance, Hjalmar Schacht, devised a set of multiple exchange rates so that exporters of certain goods could buy foreign exchange on favorable terms.

Economically, as became well understood much later, the use of multiple exchange rates was equivalent to providing direct subsidies to exporters. At the time, however, the practice was novel enough that it produced a muddled response within the U.S. government. The debate came to a head in the spring of 1936.[23]

At the end of March 1936, the interdepartmental Executive Committee on Commercial Policy, led by the State Department, issued a report recommending against invoking the Smoot-Hawley Act to apply countervailing duties in situations where the offending practice involved currency manipulation rather than a direct subsidy to exporters. The Treasury representative on the committee abstained. The report was otherwise approved unanimously. Part of the argument was that any U.S. action was likely to spur a spiraling course of action and reaction—in effect, a currency war. In addition, some argued that the 1933 devaluation of the U.S. dollar was at least partly responsible for the German policy and that the German reaction was to some extent justified.[24] Morgenthau was not satisfied, and he asked for further work within the Treasury.

Two of Morgenthau's senior advisers reached opposite conclusions. Assistant Secretary Wayne Taylor sided totally with the State Department (as he did on most issues), arguing that currency manipulation did not constitute a grant or subsidy to German exporters and therefore did not call for the imposition of countervailing duties. General Counsel Herman Oliphant took the opposite view, arguing that German currency manipulation was legally equivalent to a subsidy and therefore should be treated the same for purposes of the Tariff Act.

This disagreement distressed Morgenthau, who wanted nothing to do with the matter. The depth of his personal animosity to the Hitler regime in Germany and his limited understanding of technical economics made him uncomfortable. He refused even to read the various reports presented to him. On April 10 he told his senior staff, "All I know about countervailing duties in Germany is that I had a memorandum from Taylor, which I have not read; a report from the State Department, which I have not read; and a report from Haas, so my position up to date has been that I have taken no part in the consideration, for personal reasons, and . . . I know nothing about it."[25]

To resolve the matter, Morgenthau called in Jacob Viner, who had returned to his professorship at the University of Chicago but was continuing to serve as an occasional consultant to the Treasury. In two days in early April, Viner produced a fourteen-page report that concluded that for the most part, Germany's multiple exchange rates did not constitute subsidies. In a few limited cases, however, Viner found that Germany was guilty of subsidizing its exporters.[26] This attempt at reconciliation seems to have satisfied no one.

Roosevelt was inclined to approve the imposition of countervailing duties on selected imports from Germany, but he insisted on first getting the opinion of the attorney general. That delayed a final decision for several more weeks. Up to this point, Harry seems not to have been involved, except that he might have been the author or co-author of the "report from Haas" mentioned above. As the dispute dragged on, Haas sought Harry's advice.

On May 16, 1936, Harry responded with an unusually succinct four-page memorandum arguing that any time a country imposed discriminatory exchange rates on selected goods, it would have to be regarded as a subsidy (or "bounty," in the language of the Tariff Act). Trying to assess the validity of an exchange rate in terms of whether it was an appropriate response to another country's policies (as Taylor, Viner, and others seemed to be doing) was neither helpful nor necessary. "The Courts could not consistently take the position that multiple exchange rates do not constitute a bounty because in the case of Germany they serve merely to compensate for the depreciation of the dollar," he wrote. He cautioned, however, that imposing countervailing duties on all the imported goods affected by multiple exchange rates would be dangerous, because the amounts would be large enough to disrupt trade in the aggregate. He therefore urged a cautious application of the principle.[27]

The record does not show how far Harry's memorandum was circulated within the Treasury, or how much of a direct effect it had on the outcome. Circumstantial evidence, however, suggests that Harry's memorandum was an important influence. More than two years later, when the question arose anew, Harry circulated a package to Morgenthau of what he called "the significant material relating to the imposition of countervailing duties against German exports to the United States." That material began with his May 16 memorandum.

Morgenthau finally took charge of the matter and insisted, over the continuing objections of the State Department and others, on applying the Tariff Act in the way Harry was counseling. On May 22, Morgenthau obtained Roosevelt's authorization to proceed, with the caveat that it would be best to limit the action to Germany and not to the several other countries (including smaller European countries as well as in Latin America) that had similarly begun using multiple exchange rates.

On June 4 Morgenthau announced the imposition of duties on six categories of German goods ranging from 39 percent on gloves to 56 percent on surgical instruments. The policy quickly had the desired effect. Within weeks, Germany abandoned the multiple exchange rates, and the United States canceled the duties in early August.[28]

Two years later, in October 1938, Harry seized an opportunity to make a more general case for open multilateral trade. The occasion was the drafting of a letter for Morgenthau to send to Roosevelt (see chapter 7), appealing for the president to take bolder action in support of allies that were under threat from Germany and Japan. Harry's first draft included a reference to the restrictive trade policies that Schacht was still fostering in Germany, which Harry suggested were having indirect as well as direct negative effects on U.S trade. "Germany's resort to clearing agreements and barter devices is cutting heavily into Britain's exports in Latin America and elsewhere," he wrote. "England sells less and is therefore able to buy less, and so we find our business with third countries less than it otherwise would be."[29]

When Morgenthau read Harry's criticism of barter trade and bilateral deals, he interjected to remark that Keynes had begun suggesting that Britain should follow a path similar to the one that Germany was taking. "Did you see that cable of Keynes' statement?" Morgenthau asked Harry with evident incredulity. "I did," Harry replied. "I made a note to send it around. A very interesting idea. First case of a very able economist who has come out in favor of bilateral trade agreements. Very interesting."[30]

What they were responding to was a letter from Keynes published in the *Times* (London) on October 5, 1936, in which Keynes concluded: "In the circumstances of the moment I suggest that the balance-of-trade position and the net disinvestment in [Britain's] foreign assets . . . needs particular attention . . . by a new, and now necessary machinery for linking up exports with imports, so as to make sure that those from whom we buy spend a reasonable proportion of the proceeds in corresponding purchases from us. We can no longer afford to leave the barter aspect of foreign trade to look after itself."[31]

Morgenthau then asked Harry to add a mention of Keynes's position in the letter to Roosevelt. Harry responded in the second draft by adding this passage: "Only in the last week J. M. Keynes recommended that the British Government pursue a policy directed toward closer approach to bilateral balancing of trade. If Great Britain establishes such a precedent, it is difficult to see how any country can refrain from following, and the end result for us would be a complete rout of our commercial policy."[32]

In the end, Morgenthau decided that the draft letter was far too long, and the reference to Keynes was dropped along with much else. The argument nonetheless hung in the air, and it returned years later in the debates leading up to Bretton Woods, when Harry would prove to be a stronger advocate for open multilateral trade than his British counterpart.

The Exchange Stabilization Fund

The Gold Reserve Act of 1934 created a windfall profit of $2.8 billion for the United States by revaluing the U.S. official gold price at $35 per fine troy ounce, up from $20.67, where it had been valued since 1879. The act also transferred ownership of gold reserves from the Federal Reserve Banks to the Treasury, so that the windfall accrued to the Treasury. A large portion of the gain, $2 billion, was applied to create the Exchange Stabilization Fund, for the Treasury to use as it saw fit to help stabilize the value of the U.S. dollar in foreign exchange markets. Specifically, the ESF was to "be available for expenditure, under the direction of the Secretary of the Treasury *and in his discretion*, for *any purpose* in connection with carrying out the provisions of this section" of the Act; that is, "for the purpose of stabilizing the exchange value of the dollar."[33]

What Congress and the administration had in mind for the ESF was that the Treasury would use the funds to buy and sell gold and foreign currencies in reaction to market pressures against the established exchange rates and gold price. To execute that task, Morgenthau put Archie Lochhead, a former New York banker and an expert on exchange markets, in charge of the ESF. For the next five years, Lochhead steered the ESF carefully through the minefield of changing markets for gold and foreign exchange, including the Tripartite Agreement and the gradual dissolution of the gold bloc. Initially, the main activity of the ESF was to support the 1934 Silver Purchase Act by using the fund's $200 million working cash balance to buy silver in an effort to support the price of silver in an otherwise weak market.[34]

Watching from a nearby seat in the Treasury, Harry soon developed a broader interpretation of the role that the ESF could play. In June 1935 he sent a memorandum to Haas detailing just how broadly the Treasury could interpret Congress's intent in creating the fund. The memorandum noted that the Treasury's initial self-imposed limitation on the use of the gold holdings of the ESF—buying and selling gold as needed to stabilize the value of the dollar in relation to currencies that were officially pegged to gold—was unduly circumscribed. "Congress intended to give the Secretary broad powers in the use of" the ESF, he wrote. Most tellingly, Congress had voted down an amendment that would have made such stabilization the "sole purpose" of the act. Nothing in the wording of the act, or in its legislative history, need prevent the Treasury from using the ESF's gold holdings to stabilize the value of the dollar against, say, the pound sterling, even though the United Kingdom was no longer on the gold standard.[35]

Five months later, in November 1935, Harry's memorandum "Monetary Policy" (described in chapter 5) included a section detailing various options for expanding the use of the ESF. Much of the section was an overly complicated scheme that involved (1) converting the fund's holdings of gold into government securities; (2) selling the securities in order to buy silver; (3) converting the silver into coins with a higher face value; and (4) selling the coins to buy back the securities as well as the gold, the gold having been acquired through the revenue ("seigniorage") from step 3.

What mattered was not the scheme—which was not implemented in that era—but its justification. The case for an expansive use of the ESF caught hold. And many years later, a variation of Harry's scheme was enacted. In 1999 the IMF employed a similar series of maneuvers to convert a portion of its gold holdings into resources that it could use to reduce the external debts of low-income countries.[36]

The conception of the broad powers to use the ESF for stabilization purposes was put into practice just a few weeks after Harry sent the November memorandum to Haas. The weak international market for silver had been inducing price deflation in countries with currencies or economies linked to silver, notably China and Mexico. China had abandoned its silver standard (leaving Ethiopia as the only country still on silver) and had sold silver reserves to the United States. Mexico, the world's largest silver producer, needed to find a market for its output. The United States had the second largest output, from mines in western states. Political pressure from those states had led to the passage of the Silver Purchase Act and to ongoing efforts to prop up the price of silver or at least to put a floor under it. The ESF's working balance offered limited means for the Treasury to try to help these various players.

Harry's memorandum helped fuel a debate over how much more the Treasury could do. On December 8 Morgenthau wrote an aide-mémoire, starting with the observation that "our silver purchasing policy" was becoming "more and more stupid" because every country with any silver holdings was trying to dump them on the U.S. Treasury before the market collapsed completely. He then abandoned the practice of fixing the price of silver by setting a daily bid. The market price fell sharply amid confusion over U.S. intentions. Mexico was suddenly in a financial crisis.[37] If the Treasury was unwilling to buy newly mined Mexican silver, then the Mexican government would have to stop buying the silver from the mines, and the downward pressure on the Mexican economy would be severe.

At Morgenthau's request, Mexico sent its Treasury secretary, Eduardo Suárez, to Washington to try to arrange some financial support. Suárez was a formidable figure who would later be named to chair one of the three principal commissions at the 1944 Bretton Woods conference. When he arrived at the U.S. Treasury on December 31, 1935, for an urgent and well-publicized meeting, he suggested to Morgenthau that Mexico would like to have the ability to sell some of its silver reserves (and not just newly mined silver) to the U.S. Treasury in exchange for dollars. Morgenthau disliked the idea but promised to think it over until the two sides could meet again on January 2.[38]

Morgenthau also alluded elliptically to a question about "dollar exchange." The minutes of the meeting give no explanation, but Morgenthau raised it in response to an impasse over mobilizing silver reserves that Mexico held at the Federal Reserve Bank of New York. Suárez had asked the New York Fed if the Bank of Mexico could borrow against that silver as collateral, but the Fed had turned him down. The Treasury was about to offer a Plan B.

Who was responsible for the "dollar exchange" initiative cannot be determined. The Treasury participants in the meetings with Suárez, in addition to Morgenthau, were T. J. Coolidge (under secretary), Herman Oliphant (general counsel), Lochhead, and Haas. The first two can be ruled out because Coolidge was a conservative banker who resigned in mid-January over policy differences with the secretary, and Oliphant was engaged with legal, not financial, issues. All that can be said beyond that is that the outcome reflected the vision that Harry articulated in his memorandum to Haas: the ESF can and should be used in an expansive manner, not ring-fenced by a narrow interpretation of the mandate.

At the second meeting, on January 2, 1936, Morgenthau laid out the terms that the Treasury was offering. "The United States will purchase peso exchange with dollar credits up to $5,000,000 from time to time as requested, Mexico agreeing to repurchase such peso exchange at any time upon request. Such peso exchange is to be purchased at a fixed rate and repurchased at the same rate. . . . This . . . is on a month-to-month basis. . . . When you are using the exchange we will charge you 3% interest on the average balance." Suárez immediately agreed, and the arrangement was formally established later that month.[39]

The "dollar exchange" agreement was economically equivalent to a $5 million loan from the U.S. government to the government of Mexico, denominated in U.S. dollars, with a one-month renewable maturity and an interest rate of 3 percent per annum. Legally, however, it was not a loan, but an exchange of two sovereign currencies. Because the dollars provided temporarily to Mexico came from the ESF rather than from the Treasury's general accounts, the whole transaction could be—and was—kept secret. Mexico could use the dollars to bolster its foreign exchange reserves until the downward pressure was over. This procedure also enabled the Treasury to overcome resistance from State Department officials who viewed the Mexican government as "completely irresponsible."[40]

The use of the ESF to aid Mexico in January 1936 became the prototype for many similar arrangements with Mexico and other developing countries. During the first decade of ESF lending, through to the end of World War II, when Harry left the Treasury, the department entered into a total of twelve arrangements with seven different countries. Eight of the twelve were with four Latin American countries (Cuba, Brazil, Ecuador, and Mexico). The others were with China, Iceland, and Liberia.[41]

In 1939, when Lochhead left the Treasury, Morgenthau formally put Merle Cochran in charge of ESF operations. By then, however, Harry had charge of his own division and was the dominant force in deciding how the ESF was to be employed in pursuit of Treasury goals. Two years later, in December 1941, Morgenthau promoted Harry again and put him formally in charge of the ESF. (That prompted Cochran to resign and move to the State Department.) The payment of Harry's salary out of the ESF continued until his position was finally regularized through his appointment as assistant secretary in January 1945. The Treasury continued to draw on the ESF to pay administrative expenses (mainly salaries and travel) related to international financial policy for several decades afterward.

Harry's influence on the ESF was deep and lasting. As he recommended in 1935, the Treasury has continued to use it for a broad range of purposes through many and varied presidencies and secretaries. The ESF's biggest moment on the international stage came in January 1995, when an impasse between the Clinton administration and a Republican-controlled Congress blocked the approval of a loan to Mexico to help resolve a major financial crisis. In a "ghost of Harry White" moment, the Treasury activated the ESF to advance $20 billion to Mexico while the IMF offered an extended multilateral stand-by arrangement of unprecedented size ($17.5 billion). Some congressional leaders were furious, and they succeeded in temporarily demanding congressional approval of future such use of the ESF. Eventually, however, Treasury control over the account was restored.[42]

The Dollar Area

As the last remnants of the gold standard unraveled in the 1930s, each country that had formerly tied the value of its currency to gold had to find a new exchange regime. Measured by the number of participating currencies, the most common regime was pegging to the British pound sterling. The pound had long been the world's dominant reserve currency, and the practice was anchored by the existence of economic, political, and historical linkages across the vast British Empire. France also had colonial ties that facilitated the creation of a French franc zone in parts of Africa, the Pacific, and the Americas. Germany and Japan formulated similar but smaller arrangements. The U.S. dollar was a latecomer to this competition. In the 1930s the dollar area (including countries without formal pegs but with a policy of closely following movements in the dollar) consisted primarily of Argentina, Canada, Cuba, the Philippines, and smaller countries in Central America.[43] Morgenthau and White were determined, however, not to yield the floor to the more established players.

A recurring theme in Harry's work on international financial policy was the importance of the U.S. dollar as a reserve currency and as an anchor for exchange rates. Most famously, by insisting that the financial structure of the IMF be built on national currencies rather than a new international asset (see chapters 9–12), he ensured that the dollar would continue to play a dominant international role in the postwar era, as it already was doing during World War II. More generally, throughout his tenure at the Treasury, he took the view that if countries were to peg their currencies to the dollar, they would be more likely to buy goods from U.S. exporters, and the U.S trade balance and overall economy would tend to be more stable.

Harry's reasoning in favor of creating a dollar area was intuitive rather than theoretical or empirical. In basic theoretical models, the choice of currency peg does not have a predictable effect on the magnitude or direction of international trade. To derive such an effect requires additional assumptions. Modern economic analysis indicates that Harry's intuition was most probably correct because of factors such as the prevalence of "dollar invoicing" (setting international prices in terms of dollars) and "low pass-through" (small effects) of exchange rate changes on domestic prices in the United States. The intensive use of the dollar as an international currency helps insulate the U.S. economy from external price fluctuations.[44]

Because the major competitor to the dollar in Harry's lifetime was the pound sterling, promoting the international role of the dollar was an indirect threat to the health of the British economy. That threat was acute because Britain relied very heavily on the "sterling area" as a means of promoting trade with countries throughout the Commonwealth. (French policy was similar, but the franc zone was much less important internationally.) The diplomatic challenge for the U.S. Treasury was to encourage countries to link their currencies to the dollar and their trade to the United States without sticking too sharp a thorn in the side of its most important transatlantic ally.

Harry's advocacy for the international role of the dollar was consistent with the prevailing view in Morgenthau's Treasury. As we saw in the preceding chapter, the secretary eagerly sought to link the Chinese currency to the dollar in 1935 and was willing to do battle with the British to achieve a good outcome. In that campaign, Harry was a willing foot soldier. Later he took on a more active role in shaping policy. When he did, he tried to balance his desire for a strong U.S. position with a sensitivity to the interests of other countries.

Liberia offers a good example of the balancing act in Harry's approach to promoting the international use of the dollar. For seventy years after the country's founding, in 1847, Liberia had used the Liberian dollar as its currency and had pegged it to the U.S. dollar. In 1907, to facilitate trade with its neighbors, it switched to the British West African pound, which was pegged to the pound sterling. (In 1935 Liberia declared the U.S. dollar to be the official currency, but pounds continued to be the primary unit of account and medium of exchange.) When World War II began in Europe in September 1939, Britain imposed an embargo on the export of its currency. Firestone Tires, an American corporation that dominated Liberia's economy, decided to begin paying its employees in U.S. dollars. In response, the Liberian government informed the U.S. State Department that it wanted to switch the national currency from pounds back to dollars.[45]

On October 9, 1939, George Luthringer, an official at the State Department, telephoned Harry to get the Treasury view of Liberia's request. Harry replied that he wanted to defer a decision because he was not sure that it would be good for Liberia. "I can see where it might be desirable for the U.S to have Liberia adopt dollars, but whether it is for Liberia's interest, we wouldn't be able to tell unless we went into the matter more," he explained to Luthringer.[46]

In March 1942 Liberia renewed its request to switch to dollars. By then the wartime alliance between Britain and the United States was of far greater importance to Washington than any small economic advantage from expanding U.S. influence in West Africa. On March 16 Harry advised the Treasury to reject Liberia's request, which again had been conveyed through the State Department. It would create problems, he argued, "since it might very well be regarded by the British as an American effort to diminish British influence in Liberia." Some five weeks later, under unrelenting pressure from State, Harry renewed his objections, writing to Treasury Under Secretary Daniel W. Bell: "The argument that we should introduce American coins in order to orient Liberian policy toward the United States is unacceptable for two reasons," he explained. First, although the use of U.S. coins would generate seigniorage profits for the U.S. government, the amounts were not large enough for the United

States to worry about. Second, and more important, the move would offend the British.[47]

In the end, Harry was overruled. On May 8 he sent one of his staff, Frank Southard, to a meeting at the State Department that was also attended by the president of Firestone Tires, Harvey Firestone Jr. The diplomats and the industrialist ganged up on Southard and insisted that since the Liberians wanted to adopt U.S. coinage, the government should be prepared to do them "small favors." The Treasury gave up. Harry then devised a scheme to soften the blow on the British. The U.S. Treasury would grant an ESF arrangement for Liberia under which the ESF would purchase up to £250,000 ($1 million) in British coins from Liberians and then use them in military operations or sell them to the British.[48] He thus achieved several objectives at once, including a potential further expansion in the role of the ESF.

PART III

Wartime Finance

CHAPTER SEVEN

Preparing for War, 1937–41

The basis of the humiliation of the United States of America is being laid today.by a foreign policy that . . . shuts its eyes to German aggression in Europe and fails to offer moral and economic support to the victim of aggression in Asia.

—Harry White, October 1938

THE INTERNATIONAL ROLE OF the U.S. Treasury expanded greatly during Harry White's tenure there, owing partly to the country's needs and partly to the expansive vision of Secretary Henry Morgenthau Jr. As we saw in chapters 5 and 6, the chaos of international finance after the collapse of the international gold standard forced the Treasury to devise new policies and techniques to stabilize currency values and preserve international trade. Harry participated in and eventually dominated that process. At the same time, many U.S. trading partners and allies were threatened by the increasingly aggressive behavior of Germany, Japan, and other members of the Axis. The State Department, led by Secretary Cordell Hull, viewed dealing with that issue as its own turf, but Morgenthau was able to draw on his close friendship with President Roosevelt to ensure an important role for the Treasury.

Within the Treasury, Harry was already in a position of influence (fig. 10). Morgenthau recognized and acknowledged Harry's uncommon

Fig. 10. *U.S. Treasury portrait of Harry White, circa 1935.*
Family scrapbook, courtesy of Claire A. Pinkham

abilities and relied heavily on him to develop the strategies and tactics for aiding allied countries financially, both before and throughout World War II. Despite Harry's still-middling status in the bureaucracy, he was becoming Morgenthau's chief—really, his only—adviser on international financial policy. He accompanied the secretary on meetings with President Roosevelt and with foreign officials, and Morgenthau occasionally invited him to his New York farm on weekends to work on preparations for the coming week.

In March 1938 Morgenthau created a new division alongside the one headed by George Haas, where Harry had worked for nearly four years. The new Division of Monetary Research was to have a staff of some eighteen people. Morgenthau promoted Harry to be its director and raised his salary from $7,500 a year to $8,000 (equivalent to $147,000 in 2021). The promotion enabled Harry to communicate directly to Morgenthau by sending memoranda under his own name and participating in meetings in the secretary's office. In April Morgenthau made Harry a regular member of his "9:30 staff," the senior officials who met daily with the secretary at that time.[1] In July 1940 he named Harry to be a member of the Board of Trustees that oversaw the operations of the Export-Import (Exim) Bank. Other senior appointments followed steadily. By the time the United States entered World War II, in December 1941, Harry's division had expanded to more than fifty people.

Meanwhile, Harry's wife, Anne, was continuing to build her own career as a writer. After publishing books for children in the 1930s, she tackled the young-adult market in the early 1940s. Her two most successful books were *Lost Worlds*, on archeological discoveries such as the tomb of King Tutankhamen, and *Men before Adam*, a popularization of the story of human evolution and the work of Charles Darwin and other scientists to explain it. When *Men before Adam* was published by Random House in November 1942, Morgenthau sent a copy to President Roosevelt. Later, at the 1944 Bretton Woods conference, Harry gave a copy to John Maynard Keynes's wife, Lydia, who declared herself to be "enthralled" by it.

Anne wrote and published at least thirty more books over the next three decades and translated several major works of Russian literature. Not everyone, however, was enthralled by her often turgid writing style. Even Harry's opinion of *Lost Worlds* may have been more nuanced than his praise for *Men before Adam*. He sent a copy to the U.S. ambassador to Cuba, George Messersmith, as a gift for Messersmith's wife in thanks for her hospitality during Harry's 1941 visit to Havana. In a cover letter, Harry suggested that "it should be a good cure for any further attacks of insomnia that Mrs. Messersmith might experience. I venture the opinion that a chapter or two will do the work of ten grains of any soporific, with no after effects."[2]

By the late 1930s, in addition to the continuing economic depression, global political developments were forcing the U.S. Treasury into deeper engagement in international affairs. Roosevelt was trying to navigate a narrow path on which the United States would remain neutral as military conflicts flared around the world but would provide as much financial and material assistance to friendly countries as existing treaties and other constraints would allow. That drew Harry into the design and execution of aid policies, especially to China, Brazil, and other allies in Latin America, and to the efforts of the Soviet Union and Great Britain to resist German aggression. All these activities provoked controversies that raged throughout World War II and for decades afterward.

An Economic Response to Aggression

When the Axis countries intensified their aggressive militarization in 1939, Morgenthau responded by looking for ways to apply financial leverage against them. To that end, Harry wrote a detailed memorandum for Morgenthau to take to Roosevelt, setting out the rationale for seeking agreement with U.S. allies to pressure the aggressors by embargoing critical exports to them and by stockpiling strategic commodities.[3] He argued that stockpiling metals (copper, manganese, nickel, tin, and tungsten) and other commodities such as cotton, petroleum, and rubber would ensure an essential supply for the United States and would limit the aggressors' ability to wage war. Morgenthau conveyed the memorandum to the president on April 10 or 11 and recommended that he proceed to stockpile strategic commodities and embargo their export.[4]

Later that month, Morgenthau appointed Harry as the Treasury representative on the interagency Executive Committee on Commercial Policy, the group that oversaw U.S. trade relations with other countries. That gave Harry a perch from which he could monitor the trade and financial policies and activities of the Axis countries and help direct U.S. trade policy toward confronting the Axis. In the main, however, Harry's responsibilities focused on helping allies rather than confronting the Axis directly.

The dispute between the State and Treasury departments came to a head in October 1938. In Asia and Europe, early skirmishes were occurring in what would soon become a global war. The question in the U.S. government was whether the United States could and should remain neutral. Morgenthau concluded that neutrality had to be abandoned, and he decided that he had to make a strong case for action to Roosevelt. In an inspired move, he asked Harry to write a first draft of a letter to the president. Harry was a master at drafting clear explanations of financial policies, but on this occasion he would have to look well beyond his usual purview and make a compelling case for the United States to move off the sidelines of the struggle without—one had to hope—getting drawn into a military conflict.

Morgenthau gave Harry a weekend to prepare a draft. For this mostly noneconomic topic, Harry was out of his comfort zone. As he did occasionally throughout his career, he asked Anne to help him with the writing. She also must have been out of her comfort zone with the topic, but in that weekend, she helped Harry produce a powerful appeal for Roosevelt to ignore the timid and fearful responses to military aggression that he was seeing in Europe—Britain and France had just signed the Munich agreement that allowed Germany to annex part of Czechoslovakia—and that he was hearing from Hull and from many in the U.S. Congress.

Harry's draft letter had Morgenthau pleading with Roosevelt not to adopt the appeasement stance that had taken root in Europe: "With ever-increasing revulsion you and I have watched the long tradition of culture and civilization, so painfully acquired throughout thousands of years, being swept brutally and boastfully away, and in their place intolerance, cruelty, persecution, and spiritual degradation being enthroned. The bully's threat, oppressive power, becomes the arbiter of nations. Strong nations are made weak and weak nations crushed. The rules of gangsterdom become the laws of civilization. International anarchy looms."[5] To avoid that disaster, the letter urged Roosevelt not to let U.S. neutrality stand in the way of providing additional loans to China to help it resist Japanese aggression.

Harry finished his draft on Monday, October 10, and submitted it to Morgenthau. The next afternoon, Morgenthau convened a meeting with Harry, Herman Oliphant, and Herbert E. Gaston, a special assistant (later assistant secretary). As usual, Morgenthau's longtime private secretary, Henrietta Klotz, also attended the meeting and participated in the discussion. Morgenthau was simply blown away by the strength and clarity of Harry's draft. Several times he declared it to be "swell," and he concluded that it was "grand stuff" and "a magnificent job." Harry demurred, saying, "It's just something to begin with," but the secretary objected: "Well, it's more than that. It's a—it's a swell job." When Harry acknowledged that Anne (but no one else) had helped him, Morgenthau asked him to thank her on his behalf. Ten years later, in his public testimony to the House Un-American Activities Committee, Harry recalled that he was particularly proud of writing this memorandum. He cited it as an example of how hard he and his colleagues had worked to defeat the Axis.[6]

Despite the accolades, Harry's draft was overly long (more than 3,700 words) and emotional, and its conclusion—that the president should approve a loan to China—seemed too small a result to follow from such a sweeping moral appeal. In addition, it contained overtly negative references to Hull that were inappropriate for an official letter to the president. Morgenthau asked Harry to redraft it and resubmit it by the end of the week. The final letter (on which others in the Treasury also worked) was shortened by more than half, was a bit less passionate, and omitted personal references to Hull and his "adamant policy of doing nothing." It retained and emphasized the point that the foreign policy being pursued by the State Department was a large part of the problem. "The basis of either humiliation or war for the United States is being laid today by a foreign policy that shuts its eyes to aggression and withholds economic support from those who resist," read the final letter that Morgenthau sent to the president on October 17.[7]

The most important substantive change to Harry's first draft was the expansion of the recommended action to include loans to Latin America as well as China. "Germany, Italy and Japan will become bolder and more effective in their attempts to establish areas of economic and political support to the south of us," the letter warned. "We can stop that penetration by an intelligent use of our enormous gold and silver holdings."

Assistance to China

Before war broke out in Europe in 1939, a long-standing conflict between China and Japan erupted into open but undeclared warfare. Ever since the Japanese invasion of Manchuria in 1931, China had struggled to hold on to territory coveted by Japan. As the Roosevelt administration became increasingly concerned about Japanese territorial ambitions, it sought to support the Chinese government, led by Generalissimo Chiang Kai-shek, notwithstanding the reluctance of State Department officials who feared provoking Japan. The Japanese invasion of China in July 1937, followed by the indiscriminate slaughter of some 300,000 Chinese in the "rape of Nanjing" at the end of that year, brought the crisis to the forefront.

Because of these events, for four years before Japan's attack on Pearl Harbor, on December 7, 1941, forced the United States into World War II, the Japanese threat to China was a major foreign policy issue in Washington. It was also a major source of tension between State and Treasury. The sense of crisis was aggravated by the weakness of the Chiang government and by a second threat to stability from Communist forces led by Mao Zedong. The challenge was for the U.S. government to provide the financial support that Chiang needed to keep Japan at bay while ensuring that the Chiang regime could not waste or misuse that support.

Harry's role in monitoring developments in China and guiding Treasury policy toward helping China had begun even earlier, as recounted in chapter 5. The key issues in the mid-1930s had been stabilizing the exchange value of the Chinese currency in the face of volatility in the world market for silver and providing financial support in the form of an innovative currency swap through the U.S. Exchange Stabilization Fund (ESF). As hostilities between China and Japan intensified, these and other issues became more pressing.

The Treasury's support for China became more contentious after the de facto war broke out between Japan and China in July 1937. Cordell Hull's innate caution pulled the State Department further away from endorsing financial aid to China.[8] Morgenthau, in contrast, was steadfast in his desire to help Chiang, notwithstanding the apparent strictures of the 1907 Hague Convention. That agreement, to which the United States was a signatory, prohibited a neutral nation from making a loan to a country at war. Doing so would be tantamount to declaring war on the other country. In the late 1930s, China and Japan were engaged in hostilities but had not yet formally declared war on one another. Whether the convention applied in such circumstances had not been tested. Hull argued that a U.S. loan to China would provoke a legitimate response from Japan. Morgenthau argued that the risk was worth taking.

On July 8 he presciently told Harry and other staff that "fifty years from now the fact that China was not gobbled up by Japan and again becomes a strong nation may be the most important thing we did here." Hull approved a program of silver purchases from China that was announced on July 9, but he pulled back after the undeclared Sino-Japanese war broke out later that month. Still, over Hull's objections, Morgenthau won Roosevelt's approval to purchase another 50 million ounces of silver in December.[9]

In May 1938 Harry set out the case for increasing aid to China beyond the ESF currency swaps and small purchases of silver. With Hull still opposed on principle and Congress reluctant to act, Harry was continuing to look for actions that Roosevelt could take on his own. In addition to the ESF, he saw that the president could call on the Exim Bank without involving other departments or the legislature.

The problem was that if China borrowed from the Exim Bank to buy U.S. exports and then failed to repay the loan, the U.S. government would suffer a loss that would ultimately be borne by taxpayers. Even though the loss to the country as a whole would be minimal because exporters would still have gained a market for their output, the financial and political risks to the government could be substantial. Harry nonetheless proposed making a $50 million Exim loan to China to buy "surplus food crops from the United States and possibly some cotton." He acknowledged that it would be a "bad business risk for the Bank" and that the State Department would oppose it, but he made a case for proceeding on strategic grounds. In a follow-up memorandum a few weeks later, he concluded that "the risk is great—but so is the prize."[10]

After a further battle with the State Department, Morgenthau's appeal to Roosevelt resulted in a $25 million loan from the Exim Bank, secured by future Chinese exports of the strategic commodity tung oil, approved on December 13, 1938.[11] That was about as much as the administration could do without requesting additional authorization from a reluctant Congress. It was, however, too little to have much effect on China's ability to resist Japan. In the months that followed, Harry continued to push for bolder action.

At the end of March 1939, Harry proposed new loans from the Treasury to China, along with "real aid" to Latin America and Russia. Germany had just violated the terms of the Munich agreement by annexing all of Czechoslovakia, and Japan had occupied China's Hainan Island. In response, Harry argued that supporting China was the most urgent task because "China is the only country that is now resisting the aggressor nations and . . . there is a very good chance that China can seriously weaken, if not neutralize" Japan. He therefore suggested that Morgenthau should persuade the president to ask Congress to approve a ten-year loan of $100 million "to be used for China to buy whatever American products she wishes." Knowing that Congress was likely to resist, he further suggested that the loans could be financed by issuing special government-guaranteed notes off the federal budget or by drawing on the seigniorage revenues from issuing silver coins.[12]

While this proposal was languishing, China began borrowing reluctantly but heavily from the Soviet Union: $250 million in loans during 1939, with a requirement that the proceeds be used to buy goods from Russia.[13] China also began inquiring about the possibility of borrowing from the United States using future deliveries of tin as collateral, through an arrangement similar to the earlier one using tung oil. Harry still thought that it would be cleaner and quicker to draw on the Treasury's gold stock and make loans to China (and to allies in Latin America) through the ESF. On November 22, however, he came around to supporting the proposed "tin loan" as well.[14] All this discussion within the administration yielded some hope but very little financing for China. In March 1940

Congress approved a seven-year loan, secured by future tin exports, for just $20 million.

In May 1940 Chiang made an urgent request to Roosevelt, delivered first to the Treasury by Ambassador Hu Shih, for help in supporting the exchange value of the yuan. As part of the plea, Chiang wanted to be allowed to get part of the proceeds of the "tin loan" in cash instead of having to use it to buy U.S. goods. Harry was not keen. He told Morgenthau that a major reason for the weakness of the yuan was capital flight, and he suggested that the best way for the U.S. government to help Chiang would be to identify bank deposits and other investments by Chinese nationals in the United States. If the Treasury could block those balances and report them to the Chinese authorities, that would probably do more to prop up the yuan than lending cash, especially considering the likelihood that some of a cash loan would end up in Japanese hands and that it would further stimulate capital flight.[15] Harry's opposition effectively killed the proposal to lend cash.

Harry reiterated these doubts several weeks later, in July 1940. T. V. Soong—the Harvard-educated brother-in-law of Chiang Kai-shek—had just arrived in Washington as Chiang's emissary, replacing the banker K. P. Chen. Soong had arranged to meet with both Morgenthau and Roosevelt on July 1 to plea for more financial assistance. Harry warned his superiors that "a stabilization loan to China is beyond the legitimate scope of our [ESF] operations." In light of the chaotic conditions in Chinese currency markets, the United States could not hope to stabilize the exchange rate without undertaking unacceptably high risks, he argued.[16]

Soong continued to press for a stabilization loan, but he also embraced a suggestion from Morgenthau to involve the Soviet Union in a complicated scheme for the United States to aid China indirectly. Harry then worked out the details and submitted a plan to Roosevelt (through Morgenthau) on July 15.[17] The idea was for the United States to purchase manganese and other strategically important commodities from Russia, possibly with advance payment. Russia would agree to lend an equivalent amount of money to China. Russia would gain a market for its output of minerals and in exchange would accept the risk of lending to Chiang's unstable government.

That scheme never materialized, possibly because the Soviets were unenthusiastic. A few months later, however, Roosevelt finally was able to announce that more substantial aid to China was on its way. On

November 30, 1940, the White House issued a press release stating that the Exim Bank was prepared to lend $50 million to the Chiang government, to be used to purchase nonmilitary items from U.S. exporters. The press release also announced that the Treasury was preparing to enter into a $50 million arrangement with the Central Bank of China to help stabilize the exchange rate between the yuan and the U.S. dollar, for a total assistance package of $100 million.[18] Tellingly, neither component of the aid package involved providing cash to the Chinese authorities. The Exim Bank loan would provide cash to U.S. exporters, and the proceeds of the stabilization agreement would be under the control of the U.S. Treasury for intervention in foreign exchange markets. China would benefit from the facilities but would be constrained from abusing them.

The policy of limiting U.S. aid to direct provision of goods and services rather than cash was firmed up by Lauchlin Currie (then chief economic adviser in the White House), who visited China from late January to early March 1941 in response to an invitation from Chiang Kai-shek.[19] In Chungking (Chiang's wartime capital, now known as Chongqing), Currie met with numerous senior officials, including Chiang and his powerful wife, Soong Mei-ling, and Zhou Enlai, Mao's liaison with Chiang. He also met with senior State Department officials stationed in China. Those meetings reinforced the impression, which Currie had already gleaned from briefings in Washington, that the regime was rife with corruption and inefficiency. Nonetheless, he also came away convinced that U.S. support was essential if China was to avoid being consumed by civil war or overrun by Japan. On returning to Washington, Currie recommended that Roosevelt add China to the list of countries eligible for receipt of essential goods through the Lend-Lease program (see chapter 8).

Currie was not the only prominent American to see Chiang in Chungking in 1941 and then report back to the U.S. Treasury. While Currie was in China, the American journalist Anna Louise Strong visited the Treasury, met with Harry and others, and made a case for further aid to Chiang. Strong had just returned from a visit to China during which she had met with Chiang and other senior officials. She reported that what she called "fascist elements" within the Chiang government wanted to capitulate to Japan, but U.S. support was crucially important for those who were trying to resist. (Strong was personally sympathetic to Mao, not Chiang, and she may have been playing a long game to boost Mao's forces by keeping Chiang focused on the external threat.) Harry reported the conversation to Morgenthau, but it does not seem to have influenced either man's thinking in any significant way.[20]

The American writer Edgar Snow (the author of *Red Star over China*) was in China through much of the 1930s and in 1941, especially to cover the Communist movement. He and Harry met once, when Morgenthau asked Harry to take a courtesy call from Snow and his wife in March 1942.

More prominently, Ernest Hemingway—journalist, novelist, and adventurer—spent several weeks in China in March and April 1941. Newly married, he and Martha were on their honeymoon, and both were on assignment to write magazine articles. Shortly before leaving on this trip at the end of January, Hemingway spoke by telephone with Harry. (It is not clear how these two men of such different backgrounds and interests knew each other, but they might well have met when they both were in Havana, Cuba, the previous July. Hemingway was finishing the writing of *For Whom the Bell Tolls*. Harry was leading a Treasury mission to discuss plans for setting up an inter-American bank.) When Hemingway telephoned, Harry asked him to "look into the Kuomintang-Communist difficulties" (this was Hemingway's phrasing, some months later; *Kuomintang* was another term for Chiang's Nationalists) and to investigate transportation and disease issues along the river and railroad links between Burma and China.[21]

Not long after arriving in Hong Kong, Hemingway attended a dinner in honor of Currie, who cautioned him against writing anything in his magazine articles that could aggravate tensions between Chiang and Mao. (Hemingway complied.) After reaching mainland China in late March, Hemingway made an initial report to Harry by sending a letter through W. Langhorne Bond, an American airline executive based in China whom Hemingway befriended on this trip.[22] In April the Hemingways had a three-hour meeting with Generalissimo and Madame Chiang, and they returned to the United States in the second half of May.

On May 29, Harry reported to Morgenthau what he had gleaned so far from Hemingway and Bond.[23] That report dealt only with the transportation issues. Given the difficulties of moving people and goods through Burma, Hemingway suggested that the "best solution of the Chinese transportation problems would be the opening up of Canton" via Hong Kong. (Japan did not capture Hong Kong from the Allies until December of that year.) At the end of July, more than two months after returning home, Hemingway fulfilled his broader promise to Harry by writing a detailed and depressingly negative report to Morgenthau in a seven-page letter. He found that Chiang's government was divided; many officials wanted to capitulate to Japan, while Mao's Communists were reported to be ineffective fighters against the Japanese.

It is doubtful that Morgenthau took the time to read Hemingway's letter, because he asked Harry to summarize it for him. Harry sent him a two-page report on August 14. The next day, in a memorandum that Morgenthau promptly forwarded to Roosevelt, Harry further digested the report to its essence: "Mr. Hemingway reports of extreme bitterness between Kuomintang leaders, including the Generalissimo, and Communists. Some in Chungking favor peace with Japan and U.S. support for war against Communists. Hemingway agrees with U.S. policy of opposing civil war in China."[24]

Whatever the influence of these various reports might have been, substantial U.S. aid to China finally became a reality in the spring of 1941. In addition to the Exim Bank lending and the ESF arrangement to support the currency, Roosevelt accepted Currie's recommendation to add China to the Lend-Lease program. To limit capital flight and exchange speculation, the United States and Great Britain imposed sanctions in July, including a freeze on Chinese and Japanese assets.

Financial Diplomacy with Japan

While assistance to China helped Chiang continue his resistance to Japan, it did nothing to convince the Japanese to relent from their aggression and territorial quest. In November 1941, as the prospect of a widening conflict in Asia was becoming more dire, Morgenthau wanted to develop a strategy for applying economic leverage on Japan as an alternative to war. Harry responded with a proposal for an all-out diplomatic approach to Japan that relied heavily on U.S. economic leverage.

Harry began this effort by arguing that just as military preparedness demanded attention to a country's strengths, diplomatic strategy had to do the same. It "must make intelligent use of our geographical position, our rich resources, our vast labor power, technical equipment and democratic traditions . . . if it is to have any chance of success," he wrote on November 17. Anticipating that Hull's State Department would push back against his proposal, he warned that State's more cautious approach would be akin to the disastrous appeasement at Munich: his proposal "may be laughed at by the professional diplomats, but their ridicule will not alleviate the danger that confronts us, nor will their traditional method of handling the situation lead to any better results than have the efforts of their colleagues in Britain and France."[25]

While drafting this memorandum, Harry seems to have become overly enamored of his scheme. Perhaps feeling the need to make an over-the-top case to overcome the expected opposition, he launched into an unaccustomed eloquence: "If the President were to propose something like the appended agreement and the Japanese accept, the whole world would be electrified by the successful transformation of a threatening and belligerent powerful enemy into a peaceful and prosperous neighbor. The prestige and the leadership of the President both at home and abroad would skyrocket by so brilliant and momentous a diplomatic victory— a victory that requires no vanquished, a victory that immediately would bring peace, happiness and prosperity to hundreds of millions of Eastern peoples, and assure the subsequent defeat of Germany!"

More soberly, he set out a twenty-one-point plan for a joint agreement between the United States and Japan, to be supported by U.S allies. For its part, the U.S. government would commit to the following actions:

1. Withdraw most of its naval forces from the Pacific
2. Sign a long-term nonaggression pact with Japan
3. Promote a settlement of the status of Manchuria
4. Establish a five-power governance (U.S., Japanese, British, Chinese, and French) over Indochina
5. With Great Britain, end all "extra-territorial rights" over China, including the return of Hong Kong to China
6. End the prohibition of immigration to the United States by Japanese and Chinese peoples
7. Grant most-favored-nation (MFN) status and other trade advantages to Japan
8. Extend a long-term line of credit of $2 billion to Japan at 2 percent interest
9. With Japan, jointly endow a $500 million fund to stabilize the exchange rate between the yen and the dollar
10. Abolish controls on capital flows from Japan to the United States
11. Use its good offices to reduce tensions between Japan and its neighboring countries.

In return, Japan would be expected to commit to these actions:

1. Withdraw all its forces from China, Indochina, and Thailand
2. Withdraw support from "any government in China" other than that of Chiang's Nationalists
3. Withdraw all substitute currencies issued by Japan for circulation in China and replace them with yen
4. "Give up all extra-territorial rights in China"
5. Extend a line of credit of one billion yen (worth about $234 million at then-prevailing exchange rates) to China at 2 percent interest
6. Withdraw most forces from Manchuria, conditional on a similar withdrawal of Soviet troops from the region
7. Sell up to 75 percent of its output of war material to the United States
8. "Expel all German technical men, military officials and propagandists"[26]
9. Grant MFN status to the United States and China
10. Negotiate a nonaggression pact with the United States, China, the British Empire, the "Dutch Indies," and the Philippines.

Pointedly omitted from this detailed proposal was any direct mention of easing Japan's access to oil or other natural resources. From Japan's perspective, the need for secure access to those resources was a major justification for its territorial aggression. In the summer of 1940, Harry had prepared a plan at Morgenthau's request for limiting Japan's ability to acquire petroleum products from various sources.[27] Roosevelt had hesitated, and the United States had continued to sell oil to Japan until the summer of 1941.

In July 1941 Roosevelt defended his policy while addressing a group of civil defense volunteers, telling them that "if we cut the oil off, [Japan] would have gone down to the Dutch East Indies a year ago, and you would have had war. Therefore there was—you might call—a method in letting this oil go to Japan, with the hope—and it has worked for two years—of keeping war out of the South Pacific for our own good, for the good of the defense of Great Britain, and the freedom of the seas." He reportedly made a similar defense of his policy at a cabinet meeting that month, but he was then persuaded to shift course.[28] By late summer, even Hull finally became convinced that accommodating Japan was doing nothing to slow down Japanese military advances.

The omission of a proposal to restore access to natural resources is curious because it would have been a high priority for Japan. Perhaps Harry envisaged that the offer of MFN status would be an adequate substitute, but his memorandum also noted that Japan's ability to use the easing of tensions to increase its own military strength would be limited by "the scarcity of many raw materials."

It is difficult to argue with the observation by Morgenthau's biographer John Morton Blum that Harry's "hopes" in this proposal "were naïve, perhaps even fanciful . . . [but] reflected nevertheless a noble innocence." Even so, Morgenthau found the suggestions to be "very amazing," and he forwarded a slightly revised version of the memorandum to Roosevelt and Hull on November 18, 1941. The State Department then prepared a document to submit to Japan, based partly on Harry's draft.[29] Whether it would have had its intended effect of averting war will never be known. It was already too late, as Japan was preparing to attack Pearl Harbor.

While that process was evolving, Harry also drafted a letter for Morgenthau to send to Roosevelt, intended to strengthen the president's resolve in the resistance to Japan. There must be no "Far East Munich," he wrote. "The continuation and further intensification of our economic pressure against Japan seems . . . to be the touchstone of our pledge to China and the world that the United States will oppose Japanese aggression in the Pacific." Morgenthau produced a final draft, but he apparently decided that Roosevelt's resolve did not need a bolster. He filed it away and did not send it.[30]

Support for Latin America

As the U.S. government began preparing to combat Axis aggression in the late 1930s, it had to devise policies to cope with inroads that Germany and Spain were making in Latin America. From the outset of the Roosevelt administration in 1933, the overt policy of the United States had been to forgo intervention in Latin American affairs and to treat all countries in the Western Hemisphere as potential partners on an equal footing. This "Good Neighbor" policy, which Roosevelt announced in his first inaugural address, meant that the government had to shore up relations with its southern neighbors through diplomacy and economic support and not through the threat of military intervention. In 1938, as the director of the newly established Monetary Research Division in the Treasury, Harry became the point man for the Treasury's contributions to that effort.

Despite not speaking Spanish, Harry already had a keen interest in the financial development of Latin America. His succinct expression for this interest was "Prosperous neighbors are the best neighbors."[31] In his new position, he was a key player in the effort to establish an official inter-American bank and promote U.S. financial assistance to countries in the region. Later, both at the Treasury and as the U.S. executive director at the IMF, he provided advice to countries in the region on setting up central banks and stabilizing currencies. After retiring from the IMF, he served as a consultant to the government of Mexico. An early impetus for this work was the need to counter the economic influence of the European Axis countries, which were seeking to secure the region as a reliable source of strategic commodities.

Harry's early work on Latin America focused mainly on using the ESF to provide short-term financing for currency support, as discussed in chapter 6. He began to broaden that focus in 1938, in response to deepening economic problems in the region and the threat posed by German efforts to develop closer trade and financial relationships with several countries. The letter that Harry drafted and that Morgenthau sent to Roosevelt on October 17 (discussed earlier) lumped Latin America together with China as a top target for American aid aimed at thwarting Axis influence.

On November 5, 1938, Harry and a few colleagues drafted another letter for Morgenthau to send to Roosevelt. It laid out a detailed proposal for aiding Latin America, starting with Brazil. It had three goals: develop trade, stabilize currencies, and "encourage the growth of democratic institutions . . . and . . . check the incursion of political and commercial practices inimical to the . . . interests of the United States." The practices implied by that last point included bilateral trade arrangements with Axis countries and the use of multiple exchange rates and other restrictive trade policies. As an incentive to induce countries to abandon such policies, the letter proposed offering three types of loans, tailored to each country's circumstances: short-term ESF credits, revolving credit lines from the Exim Bank, and—subject to authorizing legislation from Congress—longer-term loans to help countries "develop their resources on a sound basis and . . . raise the standard of living."[32]

Loans for Brazil

Specifically for Brazil, the largest economy in Latin America, the November 5 letter proposed $200 million of assistance through three loan arrangements: $50 million through the ESF, $50 million through the Exim Bank, and $100 million through the Reconstruction Finance Corporation (RFC). The proposed RFC loan was especially controversial, because the Herbert Hoover administration had established the agency in 1932 to lend to *domestic* entities: businesses as well as state and local governments. Morgenthau was reluctant to approve the plan, and he asked Assistant Secretary Wayne Taylor to "go over it" before he acted on it. That initiated several months of negotiations before the Treasury finally came up with an agreed-on plan.

In February 1939 Morgenthau held a series of meetings on Brazil in which Harry participated actively. Perhaps unsurprisingly, proposals to help Brazil bogged down in a morass of diverging views between the Treasury and the State Department. Part of the problem was that Brazil was in arrears on obligations to U.S. banks and businesses. Morgenthau was prepared to set that problem aside and concentrate on financial relations between the two sovereign governments, but State was insisting that the government should not help a country that was in arrears on its debts to U.S. companies or citizens. The other part of the problem was that, while the Treasury had the legal right to support Brazil on its own with credits through the ESF, State was complaining that such action would violate the intent and the spirit of the legislation empowering the ESF. The fund was established to stabilize the exchange value of the dollar, not to help other countries service their debts. The legislation would soon be up for renewal, and Morgenthau did not want to take a chance on scuttling it.[33]

Harry suggested a way forward by having Roosevelt ask Congress to approve a "concurrent resolution" expressing approval for the proposed course of action. That seemed to be a winning formula. With the secretary's approval, the Treasury lawyers drafted such a resolution, and Morgenthau sent it to the president along with a detailed explanation of the plan. Roosevelt, however, nixed the idea, perhaps because it would have forced him to spend some political capital and might still have failed. Instead, he asked Morgenthau to use just the Exim Bank.[34] In the end, all that Brazil got from the United States was a small ($19.2 million) two-year loan, approved by the Exim Bank on March 2, 1939.

Aid for Allies through the Exchange Stabilization Fund

Harry continued to press for the use of the ESF to aid Latin American and other developing countries, usually with more success than in the 1939 Brazilian case. In July 1940, during a Pan-American conference of foreign ministers in Havana, Cuba, Secretary of State Cordell Hull asked Harry to devise a response to several requests for "monetary assistance" that he had received from Latin American countries. Harry responded by drafting a statement that Hull could give to delegates on behalf of the Treasury, conditionally offering support from the ESF, either to stabilize the country's exchange rate against the dollar or to strengthen the country's financial system, but only as part of a broader program of cooperation with U.S. objectives. Morgenthau agreed, and that established a policy of more actively encouraging countries to apply for such assistance.[35]

Overall, under Harry's direction, the ESF entered into credit arrangements with four Latin American countries: Brazil (1937 and 1942), Mexico (four arrangements through 1945), Ecuador (1942), and Cuba (1942); and three countries in other regions: China (1936 and 1941), Iceland (1942), and Liberia (1942). In most cases, the recipients did not draw on the arrangements. Instead, they used the ready availability of credit from the United States to gain credibility in financial markets and strengthen their external reserve position.

Technical Assistance for Cuba

In 1941 Harry also began providing technical assistance to Latin American countries, an activity he would continue intermittently through his tenure as executive director at the IMF and in retirement. His work in this field began with Cuba. In July 1940 Cuba adopted a new constitution, which called for the state to establish the National Bank of Cuba as a central bank. In August 1941 the Cuban government asked the U.S. government for advice, and the State Department arranged for Harry to lead a team of U.S. experts to Havana in October (fig. 11).[36]

Harry's team spent a month or so in Havana, and Harry joined them toward the end of the mission. He stayed at the home of the U.S. ambassador, George S. Messersmith, who had become well known and controversial in Washington while serving in the embassy in Berlin in the early 1930s for writing frequent warnings about the rise of Hitler and for enabling Albert Einstein to flee Germany and settle in the United States. Afterward, Messersmith wrote to Harry, "You made quite a conquest both so far as my wife and my mother-in-law are concerned. They both remarked to me again today that they hoped . . . that we would have the pleasure of having you at the house again. As I find it very difficult at times to please them, I think this is quite a feather in your cap." Messersmith also wrote to a State Department colleague that the Treasury team had done "a very

Fig. 11. *U.S. Treasury mission to Cuba, October 1941. Third from left is Frank Southard. Next to him is George Eddy, then Harry (in white shoes). On the far right in the white suit is George S. Messersmith, the U.S. ambassador to Cuba. (The two men on the left are unidentified.). Courtesy of David Eddy*

good job" and could not have been "a better group. Harry White came down for two days before they returned, and this was very helpful."[37]

The Cuban team was led by the economist Felipe Pazos, who was in the early stages of a highly successful and varied career. At the end of the mission, Harry recommended establishing a national bank that would function similarly to a currency board.[38] In that arrangement, Cuba would cease using the U.S. dollar as legal tender but would require the national bank (as the only bank of issue) to hold dollar assets equal to the dollar value of its liabilities.

Harry's proposal for Cuba was novel in that it combined the functions of a currency board with a more conventional central bank. In a pure currency board, the issuance of domestic money is determined automatically by the official stock of foreign exchange reserves, without action by a central bank. Before 1940, that system was in use primarily in British colonies. In the postwar era, currency boards and similar systems operated by central banks (as in Harry's 1941 proposal) were more widely used in countries where conventional means of stabilizing the value of the local currency were less likely to succeed.[39]

The world war delayed action on the report, but Cuba finally established the National Bank along similar lines in 1950. Its initial president was Pazos, whose colorful personal story adds background to this history. During the war, Pazos worked at the Cuban embassy in Washington, and he was a member of the Cuban delegation at the Bretton Woods conference in 1944. When Fulgencio Batista took power in a military coup in 1952, Pazos resigned from the National Bank. He later became a supporter of Fidel Castro, who reinstalled him as head of the bank in 1959. Pazos quickly became disillusioned as Castro shifted into Communism. He resigned again and moved to Venezuela, where he lived until his death in 2001. Two unrelated events add further color: his replacement as head of the National Bank in 1959 was the revolutionary hero Che Guevara; and his son, Felipe Jr., played the young apprentice to Spencer Tracy's fisherman in the 1958 film of Ernest Hemingway's *The Old Man and the Sea*.

The Proposed Inter-American Bank

Harry also took a leadership role in an effort to establish an inter-American bank to promote economic development in Latin America. That idea had been discussed since 1890 without resolution, but it appeared to be headed toward fruition after the U.S. State Department embraced it in 1939. That process began when Under Secretary Sumner Welles—the leading expert on Latin America in the State Department—was selected to chair the newly created Inter-American Financial and Economic Advisory Committee (IFEAC) in November 1939. One of the first goals of the IFEAC was to establish an inter-American bank.[40]

Harry was already focused on the task. In June 1939, as part of his effort to help Morgenthau develop an economic stimulus program, he set out a vision for a U.S. "government bank whose sole function should be to assist in promoting the long-run economic development of Latin America." That bank was to have a capital base of $300 million, financed from the ESF or the Treasury's holdings of unissued silver certificates. It would have made long-term loans at low interest rates, plus short-term stabilization loans and export credits. A large portion of the amount of the loans would have been tied to purchases from U.S. exporters. The proposal aimed to help stimulate the U.S. economy by increasing the U.S. share in world export markets.[41]

When Congress rejected the overall package in which Harry's proposed bank was embedded, he had to set the idea aside, but only for a while. As the Treasury's representative in the technical work of the IFEAC, he soon had the opportunity to revive it in a more general context. The committee moved quickly to get approval for the inter-American bank, and Harry took control of the negotiations and the drafting of a charter. When the committee approved the draft on February 27, 1940, Adolf A. Berle Jr.—the assistant secretary of state who ran the committee meetings—wrote to Morgenthau with praise for Harry, "who worked unceasingly, and who handled the final stages of the negotiations in the American Committee with entire success."[42]

At the time, this episode was a personal success for Harry. John Morton Blum later noted that the bank's "charter . . . owed its form primarily to Harry White." Even later, in a 1974 oral history interview, Emilio G. Collado—who worked on the IFEAC negotiations as an official in the State Department—recalled that Harry "was one of the principal authors . . . with Adolf Berle."[43]

All this work to establish a bank was—for the moment—in vain. Like Harry's 1939 proposal, the inter-American bank failed to win approval in the U.S. Congress. Without U.S. ratification, it could not come into being. Nonetheless, the idea of the bank was not destined to die. As we shall see in chapter 9, Harry revived it again less than two years later, in January 1942, at an inter-American conference in Rio de Janeiro. Although that revival also failed, it led fairly directly to the successful founding of the World Bank at Bretton Woods in 1944. That was as close as Harry ever got to realizing his dream of hemispheric solidarity in finance. Not until 1959 did the Organization of American States finally establish the Inter-American Development Bank.

The Special Case of Argentina

Argentina posed a particularly delicate problem for Roosevelt's Good Neighbor policy and for Morgenthau's Treasury because Argentina remained steadfastly neutral through the early years of the war. The Roosevelt administration was united in its desire to draw the hemisphere together in opposition to the Axis, but it was torn between the carrot and the stick. A case could be made either for pulling Argentina into the U.S. orbit through trade and financial incentives or for pulling it out of its traditional relationship with Germany through sanctions on trade and finance. Harry was firmly in the carrot camp.

In the spring of 1939, as the U.S. effort to provide aid to Latin America was gaining steam, driven by the tailwinds from the war in Europe, the Treasury could no longer ignore the Argentine dilemma. The October 1938 memorandum to the president did not include Argentina in the list of countries being considered for assistance. Harry's March 1939 memorandum calling for "real aid to Latin America" was silent on the selection of countries. In May, however, Harry boldly asserted that "Argentina is an excellent credit risk and by far the best in South America."[44] The U.S. government was justifying loans to most other countries in the region on political grounds, but Argentina stood out for its economic strength.

Harry's positive assessment was a response to a request from Argentina for a loan of the type that the Treasury was making through the ESF. Argentina was offering to pledge gold as collateral, but—in an exception to standard practice—it wanted to keep the gold in Argentina rather than in a U.S. repository (normally the Federal Reserve Bank of New York). In its view, having to ship gold to New York "would destroy public confidence in the currency," whereas strengthening that confidence was the intended purpose of the transaction.[45] Morgenthau was refusing the request, and Harry was trying to soften his resistance.

That effort failed, as the impasse over gold collateral continued, but it was not the last chapter of the story. In November 1940 Argentina's Finance Minister Federico Pinedo sent Raúl Prebisch to Washington to talk to Morgenthau about financial assistance and cooperation. Prebisch—the most influential Latin American economist of his generation, who was often referred to as the "Argentine Keynes"—was then serving as the head of the central bank. Morgenthau would have been happy to meet him, but he was away from Washington when Prebisch arrived. Instead, Prebisch met initially with Harry and Under Secretary Daniel W. Bell, and he called on Morgenthau only at the end of his trip. He made a case for financial assistance on the basis of the bilateral nature of international finance at that time. Because Argentina had been running a trade surplus with Britain and a deficit with the United States, it had accumulated sterling while using up its stock of dollars. Since sterling could not readily be converted into dollars, Argentina was obliged to purchase more goods from Britain and fewer from the United States. Dollar loans would help ameliorate that imbalance.

Harry was sympathetic to Prebisch's appeal, as he had been to Argentina's earlier request for support from the ESF. After meeting further with Prebisch and consulting with colleagues, he prepared a report advocating $100 million in assistance, half through the Exim Bank and half through the ESF. This time, Morgenthau agreed to support the request, and on December 27, 1940, the Treasury announced that it was entering into a stabilization agreement with Argentina. "As another practical proof that the Good Neighbor policy is a living force among American Republics, the United States and Argentina have completed a . . . cooperative arrangement between old and good friends," read the optimistic press release. In the following months, however, the government of Juan Perón was unable to pass the legislation that would enable it to meet its commitments under the agreement. The ESF arrangement never took effect.

In December 1940 Argentina did get a $60 million loan through the Exim Bank (where Harry had recently become a member of the Board of Trustees and the Executive Committee), but that was not enough to alter the course of relations between the two countries. Argentina remained neutral through much of the war, and it continued to show reluctance to enter into hemispheric agreements that might threaten its trade and other relations with Germany. Only in 1945 did it finally declare war on Germany, which by then was clearly headed toward defeat.*

Support for the Soviet Union

The Soviet Union (usually referred to as Russia by Treasury officials at that time)[46] was an essential temporary ally for the United States during World War II, codified in the formation of the Grand Alliance in January 1942. But the longer-term relationship was guided by mutual suspicion and systemic animosity dating from the Russian Revolution of 1917 and lasting through the Cold War until the demise of the Soviet Union in 1991. Even as the wartime alliance was being formed, fear of the spread of Soviet-style Communism was beginning to capture the national imagination, but it was largely overtaken by respect for the common good as long as the war was being jointly fought.

---

* When Harry was planning the Bretton Woods conference, he invited all countries in Latin America that were cooperating in the war effort. Nearly half—twenty of forty-four—of the countries with delegations at Bretton Woods were from the Americas. The Final Act of the conference included a special status for the American republics in the governance of the IMF and the World Bank. As a neutral state, Argentina was omitted from the list and was not invited to attend the conference or join the institutions. It joined only in 1956, and in 1959 the U.S. Treasury finally granted an ESF arrangement to help support the Argentine peso.

From 1939 to 1945, Harry worked diligently to use financial carrots—loans, Lend-Lease exchanges, and accommodations in the planning for the Bretton Woods conference—to secure and sustain a fragile wartime alliance between the two great emerging superpowers. His ultimate failure in this endeavor was a disappointment to him and a blow to world peace.

Harry's central role in organizing financial aid to Russia was a natural fit, in view of his cultural sympathy with the country. His parents emigrated from Lithuania when it was part of czarist Russia; he married a Ukrainian immigrant; and as an academic economist, he briefly studied the Russian language and hoped to (but never did) travel to Russia to study its system of economic planning. As the war progressed, he was impressed by the strength of the Soviet war effort in behalf of the Alliance and by the sacrifices being made by its citizens. Although that view might seem naive and short-sighted to Americans who grew up during the Cold War, Harry was far from alone among contemporary prominent Americans. The historian John Lewis Gaddis, for example, included General Douglas MacArthur, Vice President Henry Wallace, and the theologian Reinhold Niebuhr among those who expressed positive views of the Soviet Union during World War II.[47]

Although the Roosevelt administration did not begin serious discussion of financial aid until after Germany invaded Russia in June 1941, Harry made an initial suggestion two years earlier as part of a program for economic recovery in the United States. The essential idea was to lend $250 million to Russia, conditional on the proceeds being used solely to buy a specific list of goods from the United States. Topping the list was processed cotton, which was in excess supply in the United States and was being subsidized as a benefit to landowners in the politically powerful southeastern states. Harry's proposal noted that Russia had an ample supply of raw cotton but lacked the means to process it. Exporting American cotton to Russia rather than offering it for sale in market-based economies would be expected to limit the depressing effect on world market prices. U.S. leather and machine goods industries could be similarly promoted.[48]

Harry's memorandum gave an additional reason for the proposed loan. Diplomatic and commercial relations with Russia were complicated by the Soviet Union's refusal to honor debts incurred by Russia in the czarist era, including debts owed to U.S. investors. Harry was proposing to charge a high interest rate on the new loan and use the excess interest income above the U.S. government's cost of borrowing to settle the old debts. That would "clear the decks for future economic collaboration between the two most powerful countries in the world which, irrespective of their political differences, constitutes for the United States an important factor for economic improvement."[49]

This proposal for economic cooperation soon became temporarily moot. On August 23, 1939, Russia entered into a nonaggression pact with Germany through the Molotov-Ribbentrop pact. Russian forces then joined Germany in invading and occupying Poland in September, swiftly overwhelmed the Baltic countries in October, and invaded Finland on November 30. These actions naturally produced widespread outrage in the United States and made financial support for Josef Stalin both repugnant and impossible. Harry nonetheless maintained a pragmatic attitude. On June 15, 1940, the day after the German army conquered Paris, Harry drafted an aide-mémoire on what options might be available to the United States if Germany were to defeat both France and England. The possibility was very real. Three days later, Churchill would declare to the House of Commons: "The Battle of France is over. I expect the Battle of Britain is about to begin."

Harry speculated that in that scenario, the United States would be one of just four remaining great powers, along with Germany, Japan, and Russia. Economic relations with the first two would be attainable only by appeasing their military aggression and exposing the United States to the same fate as the great European powers. The combined manpower and productive capacity of the three remaining powers would be "far greater than our own." The only available options would be to try to stand alone against all the others or to reach some form of accommodation with Russia to form a united front against the other two. "To isolate ourselves from the support of an additional major power would be to create a political blunder that might well spell the doom of the United States," he wrote. The gravest danger of accommodating either Germany or Japan was that those two countries were aggressively pursuing policies of territorial conquest and expansion. Russia—in 1940—was "not interested in the near future in territorial expansion" and was "preoccupied with the industrial development of her own potentialities." Russia was practicing "ideological aggression" to establish Communism as the dominant global political system. No matter how threatening the ideology was, in Harry's view it was less dangerous than the territorial ambitions of Germany and Japan.[50]

This view that some form of cooperation with Russia was a necessity was shared by those above Harry in the government. Both Morgenthau and Roosevelt had demonstrated a willingness to cooperate with Russia when it would serve American interests. Morgenthau had been Roosevelt's emissary in 1933 when the newly installed president was preparing to extend diplomatic recognition to Russia for the first time since the 1917 revolution. Morgenthau's later (post–World War II) assessment of that move was that "recognition was one of Roosevelt's first attempts to create a community of good neighbors as the best security against the depredations of the neighborhood rednecks."[51] In July 1940, as discussed earlier, Morgenthau entertained the idea of drawing Russia into a coalition with the United States to provide loans to China. In October, however, he refused to make any commitment when the Russian ambassador sought his help in arranging for an exchange of Russian manganese and other raw materials for American airplanes and engines.[52] Russia's temporary entente with Germany made such an exchange impossible.

Discussions of possible exchanges continued to take place without any urgency through the first half of 1941, mostly through the State Department. Germany's invasion of Russia on June 22 totally changed the calculus. On July 2 Assistant Secretary of State Dean Acheson informed Morgenthau that Russia wanted to borrow $40 to $50 million to buy goods from the United States. Morgenthau did not object to the idea, but he wanted to keep the Treasury out of the deal and let the State Department make the necessary arrangements with the Commerce Department. In a meeting the next morning, Harry took a firmer line. Despite his support for good relations with Russia, he argued that Russia should be expected to pay cash. No one knew how much gold the Russians held, but since the country was a major producer, its stock had to be large enough to cover its immediate needs. "They should have plenty of money," he asserted. "They have plenty of gold." Morgenthau, however, was in no mood to listen. He was so angry at the State Department for the way he felt that it had treated him for the past eight years that he insisted on forcing it to arrange a loan itself without any help from the Treasury.[53]

The Commerce Department did lend the $50 million, which Russia quickly spent on U.S. goods, and Commerce then began advancing some $10 million a month. On September 26, Andrei Gromyko, then a counselor at the Soviet embassy in Washington, called on Morgenthau and Harry and asked for at least $100 million in sales on credit in October. Harry does not seem to have objected to that request, but he continued to insist on keeping Russia on a tight financial leash. On October 29, for example, he met separately with Gromyko and pressed him "to sell as much gold to the United States as it sells to England." Gromyko—already displaying the negotiating skills that would later become legendary when he served for almost three decades as foreign minister—demurred by claiming that his government's financial position was "difficult."[54] The next day, Roosevelt announced that he was adding Russia to the short list of countries eligible to receive large-scale assistance through the Lend-Lease program.

Support for Great Britain

In the second half of 1940, British forces successfully but at great cost defended England against a massive German air assault that became known as the Battle of Britain. France had capitulated in June, the United States was still unwilling to enroll in the war, and Great Britain had to find a way to continue its lonely defense despite its dwindling national treasury. (As is the case with the Soviet Union, a shorthand term is appropriate here. Although the formal name of the country since 1921 has been the United Kingdom of Great Britain and Northern Ireland, the terms Great Britain and just Britain were in common usage in almost all the source material for this account.)

The British government was ready to place large orders for both military equipment and consumer essentials from the United States, but it claimed to lack the cash to pay for them. With help from Harry and other Treasury economists, Morgenthau was determined to discover just how much Britain could afford. He was convinced that "the temper of the country is absolutely opposed" to granting a loan to Britain at that time.[55] If the British were short of dollar reserves, they would have to sell assets to raise the cash.

By siding with Morgenthau and taking the view that Britain's economic plight was less serious than the British negotiators were claiming, Harry opened himself to the charge that he was anti-British. The accusation has persisted and has been bolstered by the fact that Harry and his boss did seriously underestimate Britain's troubles, even if that error was miscalculation rather than malice.

At Morgenthau's request, in July 1940 the British Treasury sent its chief economist, Sir Frederick Phillips, to Washington to discuss the possibility of financial support. Phillips was an effective intermediary, and for the next few months U.S. industry was able to produce and ship a steadily increasing supply of goods across the Atlantic. Britain, however, was rapidly depleting its resources, and the Roosevelt administration had to start looking for other ways that the British might pay for the shipments. At one point, apparently at the request of Under Secretary Daniel W. Bell (and apparently reluctantly), Harry asked his staff to assess the possibility of taking sovereignty over certain British dependencies in the Americas in exchange for U.S. exports. Oscar Gass, an economist on Harry's staff, wrote a blistering response. The island dependencies, he wrote, "constitute a vast colonial slum. . . . To acquire sovereignty over the islands would plunge the United States Government into a very acute social and racial situation, which—it is quite possible—the British are handling better than we would." Harry passed the report on to Bell, and the idea quietly died. A bit later, during the war, the concept was revived in the form of long-term leases so that the United States could build military bases throughout the Caribbean. As the war wound down in the second half of 1944, Harry and Keynes informally discussed the possibility of a transfer of some Caribbean islands, but the idea again failed to get traction.[56]

In December 1940 Churchill wrote to Roosevelt with a plea for material support. After asserting that the war created "a solid identity of interest" between their countries, he confessed that the "moment approaches when we shall no longer be able to pay cash for shipping and other supplies." He then appealed to Roosevelt's good nature and sense of moral purpose not "to confine the help which they have so generously promised only to such munitions of war and commodities as could be immediately paid for."[57] Roosevelt responded by placing a challenge squarely in front of Morgenthau and the Treasury: how to give Britain the help that it desperately needed but could scarcely afford.

Roosevelt was already eager to help Great Britain. A week before Churchill sent his letter, Roosevelt took time to meet with Morgenthau, Harry, and Philip Young, another Treasury official, at the White House on a Sunday afternoon before leaving on a two-week holiday at sea. Morgenthau presented the case for complying with a British request for $2 billion in ships and other military hardware, which he explained would require U.S shipbuilders to incur an additional $700 million in capital outlays. Harry had prepared tables showing estimates of how much cash the British had in hand. Rather than forcing Britain to use too much of its dollar reserves, Roosevelt suggested financing the capital expenditures for shipbuilding through a U.S. government agency, the Reconstruction Finance Corporation, and then lending the ships to Britain.[58] In that context, though, the idea of a loan was impractical because the United States expected to have little use for the ships after the war. Nonetheless, it started a thought process that led quickly to a broader policy.

Roosevelt's idea was the germ that led a few months later to the passage of the Lend-Lease Act in March 1941. It authorized the president to provide military goods to nations wherever such assistance was deemed vital to U.S. national security, either by selling the goods or by lending or leasing them in return for future considerations to be negotiated case by case. Lend-Lease became the primary method by which the United States provided aid to its allies during World War II.[59]

Harry had little to do with the development of Lend-Lease, but once the act became an important vehicle for U.S. assistance to wartime allies, Morgenthau assigned him a major administrative role. The program started slowly with shipments to just a few countries, but it expanded greatly after the United States entered the war in December 1941. Eventually, thirty-eight countries received some $48 billion (equivalent to more than $700 billion in 2021) in Lend-Lease aid during the war. The bulk of it went to Great Britain and the Commonwealth countries (63 percent) and to the Soviet Union (22 percent).[60] Harry directed most of the Treasury's work on the aid program.

Although both Morgenthau and Harry were eager to help Britain through the Lend-Lease program, they were constrained by politics and law. Politically, Congress was unlikely to approve grants to a country at war when the United States was officially neutral and hoping to avoid being drawn into the war. Legally, the Neutrality Act of 1939 prohibited loans to belligerent countries and required that all military assistance be paid for upon receipt. In January 1941, to persuade Congress to enact Lend-Lease while the United States was still officially a neutral country, Morgenthau testified that he would require the British to sell whatever assets they held in the United States in exchange for the goods that the U.S. government would provide. Harry drafted text for that testimony, and he and his staff produced a set of tables detailing the assets that Britain had available to pay for U.S. goods and the liabilities that constrained the use of those assets.[61]

Those calculations and Morgenthau's public testimony led to a delicate balancing act. Because the Lend-Lease Act left completely open the determination of eventual compensation for American assistance, the Treasury continued to look hard for assets that would have value for the United States and that the British might be willing to give up.

A problem arose even as Congress was still debating whether to pass the Lend-Lease Act. In February 1941, during a meeting that Harry attended, Morgenthau expressed himself as "very much upset" because Phillips was telling him that his government was broke while an official from the U.S. Securities and Exchange Commission (SEC) was telling him that he had located "20 people . . . with their tongues hanging out" wanting to buy British companies operating in the United States.[62] Morgenthau told his staff to "bear down" on Phillips, and in March Britain agreed to sell its most valuable corporate asset in the United States, the American Viscose Corporation, to a group of American investment banks. The sale turned into a scandal when the exigency of selling it quickly resulted in a fire-sale price of $54 million, well below its expected market value.*

In July 1941 Harry sent one of his staff economists, V. Frank Coe, to London as a temporary attaché to Ambassador John G. Winant, with instructions to investigate reports that the British government was mishandling goods that the United States was providing under Lend-Lease. Coe confirmed that the British seemed to be charging consumers high prices for food and other goods, effectively shutting the poor out of the distribution and contributing to "grumbling about food." In addition, they were not adequately rationing scarce goods, were mishandling distribution in ways that were contributing to spoilage of fresh food, and were not doing much to ensure that the United States was getting proper credit as the source of the goods.[63]

Harry conveyed these concerns to Morgenthau on August 14. The next day, he and several of his staff met in his office with Phillips. Phillips, however, had a different concern: the U.S. War Department was reluctant to provide military equipment on the scale that Britain needed. Anticipating that the United States might soon be forced into the war, the army

---

* Although Harry had no substantive role in this episode other than providing Morgenthau with estimates of Britain's gold and dollar reserves, he was criticized posthumously for supporting it in internal discussions. The economist Charles Kindleberger, who observed some interagency meetings on Lend-Lease as a staff member at the Federal Reserve Board, recalled in a 1973 oral history interview that he "saw Harry White and saw some of his unpleasantness when he forced the British to sell American Viscose" (Kindleberger interview, July 16, 1973, HSTL, https://www.trumanlibrary.gov/library/oral-histories/kindbrgr). He elaborated on this false charge in his 1991 autobiography (*Life of an Economist*, 66), where he claimed that "White was determined to make the British turn their pockets inside out, and this led to their being compelled to sell a prize investment in the United States, the American Viscose Co., owned by Courtaulds." More recently, Benn Steil (*Battle of Bretton Woods*, 108) implied that White was somehow responsible because Morgenthau "was wholly dependent on White" for "gauging and monitoring" Britain's resources.

had concluded that it could not spare airplanes, tanks, or other materiel in large quantities. Harry agreed to ask Morgenthau to take the problem directly to the president and try to overcome the resistance. Neither Harry nor any of his colleagues mentioned any of the concerns that Coe had raised. In this setting, the goal was simply to get military equipment moving as quickly as possible.[64]

CHAPTER EIGHT

The Treasury Goes to War, 1941–43

I want it in one brain and I want it in Harry White's brain.

—Secretary Morgenthau, December 1941

WHEN THE UNITED STATES finally entered World War II, Henry Morgenthau elevated Harry to the post of assistant to the secretary and assigned him full responsibility for international economic policy. Morgenthau did not have a budgeted position for an additional assistant secretary, but he gave Harry the same level of independence and responsibility as the two men who had that title, neither of whom was an economist. The only higher staff position in the Treasury was the under secretary, Daniel W. Bell, a lawyer. Although Harry was technically in a lower position, he was effectively the department's chief economist.

It began on Monday morning, December 8, 1941, the day after the Japanese attack on Pearl Harbor, which pulled the United States into the war. Morgenthau told his staff that he was putting Harry in charge of all aspects of U.S. international economic policy. A week later, he issued a formal order expressing the elevation of Harry's role: "On and after this date, Mr. Harry D. White, Assistant to the Secretary, will assume full responsibility for all matters with which the Treasury Department has to deal having a bearing on foreign relations. Mr. White will act as liaison between the Treasury Department and the State Department, will serve in the capacity of adviser to the Secretary on all Treasury foreign affairs matters, and will assume responsibility for the management and operation of the [Exchange] Stabilization Fund without change in existing procedures. Mr. White will report directly to the Secretary."[1]

In February 1943 Morgenthau elevated Harry's wartime responsibilities further, directing him to "take full responsibility for Treasury's participation in all economic and financial matters . . . in connection with the operations of the Army and Navy and the civilian affairs in the foreign areas in which our armed forces are operating or are likely to operate." These matters had previously been handled by Bell, but Bell was feeling overwhelmed and asked to be relieved of some responsibilities.[2]

Although Harry had earlier shown substantial interest in domestic economic policies, dating back at least to his time at Harvard but continuing through his early years at the Treasury, by the time of World War II he was focusing entirely on international financial issues. A 1943 magazine profile described him as "considered by the Treasury as a practical, somewhat conservative economist, rather than a theorist. But he has gotten along well with the New Dealers, and leaves domestic matters to them."[3]

Throughout Harry's career, one characteristic on which everyone could agree was that he was extremely hardworking. After a full day at the office, he routinely took large batches of papers home to work on through the evening (fig. 12). Even when he was vacationing in New Hampshire, surrounded by his wife, children, and various visitors and with the radio on in the background, he was able to concentrate on whatever task was occupying him professionally. In November 1953 Anne responded to a request from Henry Suydam Jr., an editor at *Life* magazine, by providing brief written answers to questions. One question read, "We are told that Mr. White was an assiduous worker, often working at home late at night. Understand he often worked with a radio blaring." In response, Anne wrote that Harry "preferred to work with family around him so naturally radio was playing. [He] liked both classical and popular music."[4]

Eventually, Morgenthau became worried that Harry was overdoing it. In January 1941 he told Harry that he had to take some time off, and he told a Treasury official to find a location out of the country where something might need inspecting. He wanted "Harry to have a trip at government expense," perhaps to Cuba or the Virgin Islands. Three days later, Harry was off to Mexico for a week of big game fishing, reportedly interspersed with official meetings. Still, that sort of interlude remained exceptional, as Harry preferred work over play. In the summer of 1943, he and Anne traveled to Lake Ontario for a vacation, but he got bored

Fig. 12. *Harry working at home in Bethesda, Maryland, 1942.*
Family scrapbook, courtesy of Claire A. Pinkham

quickly, and they returned home. A few days later, Anne wrote to their daughter Ruth, "Dads [*sic*] is thoroughly enjoying his vacation at home. The ice box fascinates him."[5] (The "ice box" was probably an electric refrigerator, a device that was becoming more widely used in American homes at that time.)

For her part, Anne took several short-term jobs during the war, including one as an editor of a newsletter, the *Young Citizen*, for students in the fifth and sixth grades. In the summer of 1943, she worked at the Mil-Bur farm camp in Pasadena, Maryland, where high school girls picked beans and other crops under the aegis of the Victory Farm Volunteers. "I am an expert bean picker," she wrote to her daughter Joan that summer. "You should see me climbing on and off a truck!" Later in 1943 and in 1944, she worked at the Foreign Economic Administration and the Social Security Board, writing pamphlets and other promotional materials for government programs.[6]

The Morgenthau Diaries include a curious example of Anne's wartime writing. Submitted in November 1942, it is a rough handwritten draft of an embarrassingly obsequious tribute to Morgenthau. Its opening sentence reads, "Not many people, over and above those immediately around him, are aware that Henry Morgenthau, Jr., is quietly on the way to being the greatest Secretary of the Treasury the United States has had." There is no indication of why it was written or for what audience, but in the Treasury files it is marked as "received for filing" some six months later.[7]

Early Warnings of Trouble Ahead

Mr. White admitted, on his own initiative, that his wife had, for some time, been engaged in charitable enterprises.

—FBI report, 1942

Harry's role in providing financial assistance to wartime allies has been extensively scrutinized, but mostly through the prism of his supposed political biases. Some analysts have portrayed him as trying to help the Communist insurgency of Mao Zedong by limiting aid to the Nationalist Chinese government of Chiang Kai-shek during the war. Some have portrayed him as trying to promote the economic dominance of the United States by limiting aid to the British economy during the war. Some have portrayed him as promoting Russian interests by pressing for aid to the Soviet Union. All these assumptions appear to be dubious when seen from the perspective of Harry's role in the U.S. Treasury and the administration of Franklin D. Roosevelt. At least the main thrust of each of his activities was consistent with the overall strategy of the U.S. government and with the Treasury's mandate as pursued by Morgenthau.

The underlying issue was the unprecedented breadth and scale of U.S. financial support for other countries throughout the last ten years of the Roosevelt administration. To overcome political opposition, the Treasury Department had to devise innovative and complex financial arrangements. Harry was the main intellect behind those innovations, each of which has had important longer-term consequences. The way he used the Exchange Stabilization Fund (ESF) to help several countries stabilize their currencies against the U.S. dollar was the prototype for the financial practices of the International Monetary Fund (IMF) in the postwar period. The way he parceled out aid to a corrupt and inefficient Chinese government during the war was the prototype for IMF policy conditionality. His oversight of the Lend-Lease program, through which the large-scale international exchange of goods was restored after the interruption of the Depression despite the severe challenges imposed by the world war, helped inspire the development of a shared economic governance in the postwar era. The main avenues for these innovations were aid programs for China, Latin America, the Soviet Union, and Great Britain, each of which built on the prewar activities described in the preceding chapter.

Financial support for the Soviet Union, even in the context of the wartime alliance, was politically fraught because of the ongoing fear that the influence of Communism might be spreading in the United States. In June 1940 Congress passed (and Roosevelt signed) the Smith Act (formally, the Alien Registration Act), which made it illegal in the United States to advocate the overthrow of the U.S. government by force or violence or to be a member of an organization that so advocates. This development—aimed in large part to suppress the Communist Party of the United States—would not have affected Harry except for the fact that he had friends, family members, and colleagues who had been affiliated with the party in the 1930s or who were members of organizations that were sympathetic to Communism or to the Soviet Union. By 1941 the FBI—urged on by members of Congress—began investigating and arresting people for such associations. The U.S. Congress was also actively investigating people, through the House Un-American Activities Committee (HUAC), under the leadership of Martin Dies Jr., a Democratic congressman from Texas.[8] Eventually, investigations under the Smith Act would blow up into a countrywide witch hunt, usually summarized in the term *McCarthyism*: one of the most notorious and depressing eras of mass hysteria in U.S. history.

Martin Dies Makes a False Charge

The effects of the Smith Act first hit Harry indirectly through the activities of his wife. Anne was devoted to left-wing political causes and had joined at least two groups that government agents were investigating. One was the Washington Committee for Democratic Action, an affiliate of a national organization of the same name. The group worked in behalf of rights for minorities and other disadvantaged groups, and it opposed U.S. involvement in World War II. The other was the League of Women Shoppers, which pressured department stores and other retailers to serve "colored people" along with whites. As the historian Landon Storrs has noted, the founding members of the League of Women Shoppers included many women who were "prominent in their own right—as writers, artists, lawyers, and other professionals—and some of them married to prominent left and liberal men."⁹ Some members of those and other progressive groups may also have been members of the Communist Party. The organizations attracted the attention of HUAC and the Justice Department because of that overlap in membership.

The first allegation against Harry was made by Martin Dies, who included him on a list that his committee staff compiled of 1,100 federal government employees who were thought to be engaged in subversive activities. That charge was based on an FBI report that turned out to be comically misguided and inept. In January 1942 a bumbling FBI agent filed a report that Harry—not Anne—was a member of the Washington Committee for Democratic Action. The agent thought that his suspect was an "Underclerk" at the Treasury, because another Harry D. White had that title. That other Harry White was working for the Treasury in the Bureau of Customs in New York, but no one in the FBI seems to have noticed the anomaly until much later. The report also was replete with bizarre innuendo, such as the one quoted at the beginning of this section, implying that "charitable enterprises" were inherently incriminating. Despite the report's obvious incompetence, it was sufficient to induce the FBI to open a file on Harry and send agents out to interview him—and his neighbors—about his alleged activities.[10]

Harry of course vehemently denied the false charges, for which there was no evidence whatsoever. He also—accurately but perhaps unwisely—told the FBI agent that he considered Dies to be "a menace" and that his actions were "damnable, underhanded and cheap." The agent reported to FBI headquarters that Harry "became quite incensed . . . not only as [the accusations] concerned him, but [also] other responsible Government officials." Once the FBI realized that it had the wrong man, it dropped the inquiry and closed the file.[11]

Harry Defends a Friend

Harry next came to the attention of the crusaders in June 1942, when a friend, Nathan Gregory Silvermaster, was accused of being a Communist. Silvermaster was born in Odessa, Ukraine (then part of Russia), in 1898. He emigrated to the United States in 1915 and became a U.S. citizen in 1927. In the meantime, he studied at the University of Washington, where he earned a bachelor's degree; and then at Stanford as a graduate student. In 1932 he received a Ph.D. in economics at the University of California at Berkeley. From 1935 to 1946 he held various posts with the federal government, mostly in Washington and mostly in the Agriculture Department.[12] Although he and Harry both studied at Stanford, Harry left for Harvard before Silvermaster arrived. They met socially in Washington in the middle to late 1930s and became friends, primarily owing to the friendship struck up between their wives, both of whom were active in groups promoting social justice.

While in California, Silvermaster got involved in aiding striking agricultural workers, which in the early 1930s would have brought him into contact with Communists and others who would later be deemed subversives. In 1942, when he was working at the Board of Economic Warfare (an agency of the War Department), his earlier activities in support of unionization alerted investigators to the possible connection with Communism. On June 3 Colonel John T. Bissell, the head of counterintelligence at the War Department, submitted a report to the department asserting that Silvermaster was a Communist and should not have access to confidential material. That triggered an investigation, during which Harry was asked about his friend's character and activities. Harry responded that he knew of no reason to think that the charge was valid. He was certainly not alone in that view. On July 3 Under Secretary of War Robert P. Patterson, after personally reviewing the whole report, concluded that he was "fully satisfied that the facts do not show anything derogatory to Mr. Silvermaster's character or loyalty to the United States, and that the charges in the report of June 3rd are unfounded."[13]

The FBI tried for years to gather enough intelligence to seek an indictment against Silvermaster, without success. Silvermaster left government service in 1946 and moved to New Jersey with his wife, Helen, who by then was also being accused. Together with William Ludwig Ullmann (also accused), he formed a successful business constructing residences on Long Beach Island. He died in 1964. Much later, compelling evidence surfaced that the Silvermasters and Ullmann were involved in espionage for the Soviet Union, at least during World War II (see chapters 15 and 18). Whether Harry was ever aware of that activity has not been established, but his posthumous reputation continues to be haunted by this dubious friendship.

Wartime Aid to the Soviet Union

While Harry was being badgered by allegations of subversion and untoward friendships, he was called on to help design and implement the continuation of U.S. financial support for its Soviet ally.

The U.S declarations of war against Japan, Germany, and Italy in December 1941 brought the country into a military alliance with Russia. That relationship was formalized into the four-power Grand Alliance on January 1, 1942, when Roosevelt, British Prime Minister Winston Churchill, Ambassador Maxim Litvinov for Russia, and Foreign Minister T. V. Soong for China—joined by representatives of twenty-two other allied nations—signed the Declaration of the United Nations in Washington. This new diplomatic and military status opened the door to exploit the existing economic symbiosis. Of all the countries in the alliance, Russia had the most to offer the United States economically because of its rich lode of raw materials. Chief among them was manganese, which the United States needed to import as an input for its strategically vital steel industry.

As the war dragged on through 1943, the Russian need for manufactured goods and the U.S. need for raw materials increased dramatically. The discussions of tens of millions of dollars that had taken place before the U.S. entry into the war now ballooned into billions. Roosevelt sent Donald Nelson, the head of the War Production Board, to Russia to discuss mutual interests. Upon his return, Nelson reported that Russia wanted to acquire an additional $10 billion in goods from the United States to aid in reconstruction of the economy after the war. That prompted Roosevelt to ask Morgenthau to find out what U.S. industry needed from Russia that they might get in return.

Harry was out of the office at the time (in Cambridge, Massachusetts, at the invitation of the economics professor Seymour Harris, giving a lecture at Harvard University to explain the White Plan for postwar finance), but the secretary called in three economists from "Harry White's crowd" (Eddie Bernstein, Harold Glasser, and Thelma Kistler) and asked them to come up with a plan for "reverse Lend-Lease" (essentially, a barter arrangement) to get manganese, oil, lumber, and other strategic goods from Russia in exchange for manufactured goods.[14]

When Harry returned from his trip to Cambridge, he worried that making such an arrangement through the Lend-Lease program could be subjected to damaging criticism from opponents in Congress. Although the president had legal authority to do it, using Lend-Lease for postwar reconstruction could be viewed as violating the spirit of the act. Harry therefore urged Morgenthau, in a draft memorandum for the president dated January 5, 1944, to recommend a separate presidential request for legislation specifically authorizing the arrangement.[15]

That initiated a yearlong effort to negotiate a deal, which began with discussions that the U.S. ambassador, Averell Harriman, held in Moscow in January 1944. In March Harry presented a detailed proposal for a barter arrangement totaling $5 billion. The scaling down from $10 billion appears to have been necessitated by objections from other government agencies. In a Saturday afternoon meeting at Morgenthau's home on March 18, Harry and his boss agreed that $5 billion was too little: it would "not meet the needs of either the U.S. or U.S.S.R." Therefore "the larger program [Morgenthau] had had in mind would be more suitable."[16]

Harry's proposal was not for a monetary loan. The plan was that after the defeat of Germany, the United States would provide goods that Russia would need to rebuild its devastated economy. In exchange, Russia would provide essential raw materials to the United States, but it would do so over a period of several years. To ensure that the deal would be a "good business arrangement" that would "appeal to the American psychology" and thus be likely to clear Congress, the government would charge a rate of interest on the outstanding balance that would at least cover its borrowing costs.[17]

During this time, Harry was meeting regularly with the Soviet delegation that was in Washington to negotiate terms for Russia's participation in the Bretton Woods conference. On occasion, he took the opportunity to try to persuade the delegates that their government should consider asking for a larger arrangement, on the order of the $10 billion that Morgenthau thought was necessary for both countries. Separately, Morgenthau was negotiating with the State Department to win it over to the idea.

It was all for naught. The Russians resisted paying as much interest as the Treasury was demanding, and the State Department resisted making any accommodation while Russia was establishing puppet police states in the territories that the Red Army was liberating from German occupation in eastern Europe. In January 1945 Harry advanced one last proposal, designed to help Morgenthau persuade Roosevelt to take it directly to Stalin at the Yalta conference in February. The State Department blocked that avenue and ended the whole effort to reach a mutually advantageous deal.[18]

Wartime Aid to China

On December 7, 1941, the Japanese bombed Pearl Harbor. The United States immediately declared war on Japan, and all constraints on support for China were off. Within weeks, Chiang Kai-shek asked the U.S. government for a loan of $500 million for his government to use for a variety of purposes without restriction. Simultaneously, Chiang asked the British government for a similar loan of £100 million ($403 million). By this time, Morgenthau had given Harry full responsibility for international financial policy. Harry's main focus was on Latin America and on his initial work on what would lead to the Bretton Woods conference, but he made time to respond to China's needs. He met twice with Chinese officials in late December for initial discussions of the loan request, and on January 8, 1942, he convened a meeting with officials from Treasury and State, as well as Lauchlin Currie from the White House.

At the interagency meeting, Harry noted that the risk of such a large loan to China was "beyond the scope of anything undertaken by the Treasury previous to this." Participants agreed that economic considerations alone would dictate turning down the request, but "political and military considerations" might justify approving it.[19]

That agreement kicked off a series of almost daily meetings through the rest of January to determine exactly how to respond. During much of that time, Harry was in Brazil for a meeting of officials from across Latin America, but Treasury colleagues kept him informed. At first, Hull wanted to limit the loan to $300 million, but the Treasury team eventually won him over to approve the full requested amount. The British initially declined to make any loan to China, but they later agreed to lend £50 million, half of what Chiang had requested. At one point, Roosevelt suggested an alternative response in which the United States would pay up to a million Chinese soldiers each month, but Chiang quickly rejected that overture. At the beginning of February the administration requested, and Congress approved, the full amount of the $500 million loan.[20]

Harry was back in Washington in time to help with the negotiation of terms for the loan. As before, the key concern was ensuring that the loan would be put to productive use. State and Treasury agreed that the terms should be "in the spirit of Lend-Lease" (meaning that terms of repayment would be flexible and would be determined only after the war) and that the agreement should include a clause requiring that China consult regularly with the United States on the use of the proceeds. That latter provision alarmed Soong, who told Harry that he was afraid he would get caught in the crossfire if (as he expected) Chiang insisted on there being no conditions. The Treasury's first draft included a clause (Article II) that required consultations, but the Treasury team agreed to drop it after Soong objected.[21]

A snag arose when the State Department suggested that Article II should be retained. After further discussions, State Department officials proposed that the gist of Article II could be handled instead through a separate exchange of letters between the Chinese and U.S. governments. Harry and other Treasury staff found that idea to be insufficient, but Morgenthau overruled them.[22] That settled the matter, and Morgenthau and Soong held a public signing ceremony for the $500 million loan on March 24, 1942.

It did not take long for problems to arise. In early April, less than three weeks after the agreement was signed, Chiang announced publicly that his government was going to absorb excess liquidity in China by floating a bond issue, guaranteed by being backed by the first $200 million from the U.S. loan. He then asked the U.S. Treasury to transfer $200 million to China's account at the Federal Reserve Bank of New York for this purpose. Morgenthau was furious. Through his emissaries, Chiang had promised to consult with him on the uses of the loan, but on this first opportunity he had failed to do so. Morgenthau felt betrayed, and he told Harry and others in a meeting on April 11 that he doubted that he could trust Chiang to keep his word. How could the United States, he asked rhetorically, "send 100,000 American troops to China if we could not depend on the Chinese Government in a financial matter"? Harry pointed out that the Treasury had little choice because the agreement obligated them to transfer the money upon request. Once it was transferred, China could use it however Chiang wished.[23]

As Harry and his Treasury colleagues expected, China badly bobbled the bond issue. Instead of mopping up liquidity, it facilitated even more money creation. Inflation soared, and the fixed exchange rate became ever more unrealistic. When the minister of finance, H. H. Kung, sought to renew the 1941 ESF arrangement in 1943, Harry advised Morgenthau to refuse. It would be pointless, he observed, to try to defend a seriously overvalued currency. Morgenthau agreed. The arrangement lapsed and was never renewed.[24]

Of greater consequence, Kung also asked the Treasury to earmark $200 million in gold at the Federal Reserve Bank of New York for China to use as the second tranche of the $500 million loan agreement. Harry told Morgenthau that they should "get tough" with the Chinese and allocate the gold "only as rapidly as it could be shipped and sold in China." Morgenthau again agreed.[25] Through the rest of the war, the Treasury shipped small amounts of gold to China each month but never let the commitment get ahead of China's observed ability to use it.

In October 1943 Harry accompanied Morgenthau on a three-week trip to North Africa. The announced purpose of the secretary's trip was to meet with General Dwight D. Eisenhower in Algiers and with Allied troops in Italy and Tunisia to promote the sale of war bonds to finance the U.S. war effort. Harry's participation, which was kept secret, was in part to help prepare for a summit meeting of Roosevelt, Chiang, and Churchill, which was being planned to take place in Cairo the following month.[26] After Harry and the secretary met with Eisenhower in Algiers (where Harry dealt with the implementation of the occupation currency, as discussed below in chapter 14), Morgenthau traveled to Sardinia, Sicily, Naples, and Tunis. Meanwhile, Harry was meeting with U.S. officials in Cairo between October 17 and 23. Details are sketchy, owing to the extreme secrecy, but Harry had Solomon Adler—the Treasury's representative in China—travel from Chungking to Cairo to help with the planning.[27]

The secrecy was broken a few months later. A rather fanciful Associated Press story published in the *Boston Globe* (April 8, 1944) claimed that Harry had made "American and Allied diplomatic and military officials weary" with his lengthy explanations of "Lend-Lease and war financing. A celebrated British Minister actually fled from him in Cairo. He hung out there in the palace of Egypt's King Farouk . . . [and] an Arab chieftain personally gave him a seventeen-course birthday dinner . . . and Harry bawled him out because he had to sit on the floor, eat with his fingers and watch dancing girls, who, he said, 'didn't make sense.'"

At the November 1943 Cairo conference, Chiang asked Roosevelt for an additional loan of $1 billion. Roosevelt demurred. On returning to Washington, he told Morgenthau that he did not like the idea, but he asked him for an analysis. Morgenthau then met with a few of Harry's staff economists on December 17 while Harry was out of town delivering the lecture at Harvard University mentioned earlier. After some discussion of options, he asked them to "call up Harry on the phone" for help and then prepare a draft memorandum for him to send to the president by the next morning. Presumably they did consult with Harry before drafting the memorandum, which concluded that a new loan "could not be justified."[28] They recommended that the U.S. government should commit to help China in two other ways: by accelerating shipments of gold to China and by covering U.S. military expenditures in China by exchanging gold or dollars for yuan (at the black-market rate) to absorb some excess liquidity.

What happened next was highly unusual. Morgenthau sent the memorandum to the president, who approved it and asked Hull to forward it to Chiang for his approval. Hull, however, objected and held up delivery for several weeks. Only on January 11, 1944, did it reach Chiang (through the U.S. ambassador). Chiang asked for time to consider it, but a few days later he rejected the U.S suggestions and insisted on getting a $1 billion loan and having all currency transactions at the bloated official rate. Meanwhile, the U.S. Army was already beginning to buy yuan in the black market (one U.S. cent per yuan instead of five cents at the official rate) to finance its local expenditures. Harry set out to regularize this relationship through an equivalent above-board scheme under which the army would buy yuan at the official rate and the Chinese government would give it enough additional yuan to make up the difference. Otherwise, Harry worried, if the army relied on the black market, Chiang could simply shut it down. If necessary, Harry told Morgenthau, Chiang "can shoot as many Chinese as he likes" to get what he wants.[29]

Relations between China and the United States remained on edge throughout the remainder of the war. Although Chiang finally accepted a financial arrangement of the type that Harry was advocating (exchange by the U.S. Army at the official rate, compensated by transfers of additional yuan), he continued to press for the $1 billion loan, which neither Morgenthau nor Roosevelt was prepared to grant. Exasperated by Chiang's corrupt administration, the ineffectiveness of the Chinese military effort, and the arrogance of Chiang's (and Madame Chiang's) insistence on new loans, Morgenthau privately referred to Chiang's coterie as "bastards" and "crooks." In one meeting he told Harry that "we have always known that [Chiang] has financed himself through opium."[30]

While the Treasury continued to ship gold to China in accordance with the 1942 loan arrangement, Harry—with the concurrence of the State and War departments—kept the amounts to a bare minimum throughout 1944, out of concern that it would not be put to productive use in the war effort. This tactic was in keeping with the overall administration policy of doing as much as necessary to keep Chiang from caving in to Japanese demands, but no more than could be used productively. Morgenthau explained the U.S. hesitancy clearly in a letter to former Ambassador Hu Shih at the end of that year: "I . . . hope that the situation may improve in such way as to make possible increased military aid to China and that steps will be taken within China to make possible the maximum utilization of the aid which is given."[31]

The internal debate over how best to help China fight the war against Japan came to a crux in May 1945. Roosevelt had died in April, Truman had assumed the presidency, and Germany had surrendered on May 8.

That week Soong demanded to cash in on a promise that Morgenthau had made to deliver $200 million in gold as the final tranche of the $500 million loan. Harry tried to avert what he believed would be a total waste of money, suggesting as an alternative that the Treasury set up a $500 million fund to be used to stabilize the Chinese currency. Meeting with Harry and other senior members of his staff on May 15, Morgenthau agreed that sending the gold to China would be sending it "down a rat hole [and] was most distasteful to me," but he felt trapped because he had made a promise to the Chinese in writing almost two years earlier.[32]

Harry tried to find a way for his boss to meet his commitment to Soong without throwing away the gold. If his suggestion for a stabilization fund was a nonstarter, then perhaps they could just continue to send the gold in small amounts each month, as they had been doing throughout the war, but "accelerate" the pace a bit. Morgenthau was adamant that he should honor his own commitments. Still, in response to Harry's concerns about corruption and waste, he wanted to cover himself by getting something in writing from the departments of State and War telling Truman that "for political and military reasons they want to see this gold go out."

State Department officials were reluctant to bail the Treasury out of a bind of its own making. William L. Clayton—assistant secretary of state for economic affairs—asked Morgenthau (quite reasonably), "Why should we be asked to give political reasons for the Treasury to keep a commitment that it has made?" In the end, however, State agreed to provide a letter of support. On May 16, Morgenthau got Soong to admit privately that the Chinese government had misused earlier shipments of gold. Soong promised to do better. On that basis, Morgenthau agreed to have the gold shipped as soon as possible but told Soong that all future financial assistance from the U.S. government would depend on how well China used this gold.[33]

Despite the American skepticism toward Chiang and his circle, the Treasury respected the political judgment of Roosevelt and Hull that preserving the Grand Alliance was critically important to the war effort and would remain important for preserving the peace. Accordingly, Harry engaged China early and intensively in the planning for postwar financial cooperation that led to the Bretton Woods conference in 1944, and he ensured that China would be one of the top five members of the IMF and World Bank and would have the special privileges of that group. He consistently supported providing large-scale financial assistance to China throughout the war but insisted that it should be conditional on evidence that it was being neither stolen nor wasted.

Wartime Aid to Great Britain

Once the United States entered the war alongside Britain in December 1941, aiding the British war effort was no longer controversial. The entire Roosevelt administration was committed to carrying out the task on a grand scale. What remained controversial was the determination of appropriate compensation from Britain. The State Department negotiated an agreement with the British government under which compensation would be determined at a later stage and for the most part would be deferred until after the war. The Treasury, however, remained convinced that Britain should not take advantage of American largesse and rebuild its gold and dollar reserve position beyond a minimum sustainable level. Morgenthau's view was that the British should get as much as they needed and should pay as much as they could afford. Harry's job was to put numbers on the latter calculation.[34]

For this purpose, the British authorities had an incentive to make their financial balance appear as weak as possible, especially if they could manage to keep their projections secret from investors and speculators who might seek to profit from the weakness. In January 1942 the British emissary Sir Frederick Phillips told Treasury officials that his government would run out of dollars completely before the end of the year, and he asked them not to divulge the information publicly. Under Secretary Bell replied that secrecy was out of the question because Congress would demand to know the numbers. Harry's position was that Britain could work with the United States to generate additional cash. Britain owned companies in the United States that it could sell, as it already had done with American Viscose (see chapter 7). The U.S. military had forces stationed in the sterling area whom the Treasury could pay in dollars. South Africa, a Commonwealth member and major gold producer, could sell its current output for dollars. Harry's staff calculated that those three actions alone could generate a total of some $650 million in reserves, enough to give Britain a cushion at the end of the year.[35] How expensive and how comfortable that cushion would be were matters of perspective.

As the terms of the Lend-Lease agreement with Britain were being drafted in February 1942, the top British negotiators—Phillips and the ambassador, Lord Halifax—told Morgenthau that they needed to be assured of maintaining at least $600 million in reserves. This figure had first been mentioned by Phillips in December 1940 and had been confirmed in meetings in Washington between Harry and John Maynard Keyes in June and July 1941. Keynes and another British Treasury colleague, Lord Catto (Thomas S. Catto, later governor of the Bank of England), repeated the figure in a discussion with Edward R. Stettinius (director of the Lend-Lease Administration) in London the following year. Although $600 million would later be proved to be inadequate, it was what the British government then believed to be appropriate to its needs.[36]

With that figure in hand, Harry and the staff of the Lend-Lease Administration determined that the provision of Lend-Lease assistance should be scaled to keep British reserves at or above a floor of $600 million. Once the program was fully under way, however, reserves began rising above the floor. By December Britain's holdings of dollars exceeded $1 billion. That prompted Morgenthau to call Dean Acheson (Harry's counterpart in the State Department for monitoring the effects of Lend-Lease assistance) to set up an interagency discussion on the matter.

Morgenthau's initiative led to the establishment on December 23 of a cabinet-level committee chaired by Vice President Henry A. Wallace and a technical subcommittee chaired by Harry. The mandate for Harry's group was to examine the numbers, devise a criterion for judging recipients' compliance with the terms of Lend-Lease, and recommend remedial actions if necessary. The group met the next week and decided to recommend that Lend-Lease aid should be adjusted to keep British reserves in a range of $600 million to $1 billion. If reserves rose above that level, Britain would be expected to purchase nonmilitary goods for cash rather than acquiring them through Lend-Lease. Additional measures might include "reverse Lend-Lease" provision of goods by Britain and having Britain provide sterling to the U.S. government to pay U.S. military personnel stationed in the sterling currency area.

Wallace's committee accepted these recommendations at a meeting on New Year's Day, 1943. Wallace forwarded a report to that effect to the president, and Roosevelt approved the policy on January 4.[37] This policy, though necessary to keep Lend-Lease within the purpose for which it was enacted, created a conflict with Britain's growing need for reserves. The war was preventing Britain from producing goods for export in normal quantities. The country was running a persistent payments deficit with India and other countries in its Commonwealth, which it was settling by paying in sterling but holding the payments at the Bank of England and blocking the recipients from withdrawing them. This practice amounted to an ever-increasing postwar debt, which reached the equivalent of $7 billion by the fourth quarter of 1943. Britain would need much larger dollar reserves than it had initially counted on if it hoped to clear these obligations after the war.

On November 17, 1943, Morgenthau invited two officials from the British embassy—Lord Halifax and Sir David Whaley—to lunch with him and Harry for a discussion of what the secretary still saw as a growing problem. He began by offering to do whatever he could to help resolve Britain's payments deficit after the war, but he insisted that Lend-Lease was not the proper vehicle for dealing with postwar issues. For the British, Morgenthau's promise was too vague and conditional to be a comfort. The lunch ended inconclusively as both sides promised to try to find ways to alleviate the pressure on Britain's payments deficits.[38]

Later that day, Harry and his staff produced a draft memorandum for the president setting out the reasons for the limits on Britain's cash balance and recommending that the United States ask Britain to pay for "a larger proportion of civilian goods obtained in this country." Six days later, however, Oscar S. Cox, general counsel in the Foreign Economic Administration (FEA), proposed an alternative tactic of just cutting down shipments, one good at a time, and not adopting a new general policy. After Harry acknowledged that this plan might work, Morgenthau accepted Cox's proposal. The government applied it piecemeal over the next few months with some success. Nonetheless, without a clear understanding in place and endorsed by the president, the conflict with Britain did not diminish.[39]

The success of the D-Day landings in France in June 1944 gave impetus to optimism on both sides of the Atlantic that the war with Germany would soon be over. That was followed by the Bretton Woods conference in July, after which Harry accompanied Morgenthau on trips to France and England in August and to Quebec in September. On the trip to England, Morgenthau experienced an epiphany. He became firmly and finally convinced that Britain was "broke" and that the United States had a responsibility to "put England back on its feet economically" after the war. "I don't consider that the dollar balances are yardsticks any more," he opined at a meeting with State Department and FEA officials on October 6. "Our job is to . . . make it possible . . . for [Britain] to come back economically and really take her place in the family of nations on a successful financial basis."[40]

Harry was not convinced. If the United States were to make an open-ended commitment of that sort, Britain's need for dollars would rise dramatically. Perhaps for the first time, Harry went out on a limb and contradicted his boss in emotional terms in an interagency meeting. "What we are confronted with here is giving England many billions of dollars, giving it to her. . . . There is no limit to what she can absorb, and there may be no limit to what you can give her, except politically. . . . England could take without the slightest trouble, four billion, five billion, six billion, and ten billion dollars." He proposed settling on a dollar amount of assistance in advance, by asking the British authorities what they thought they needed and then determining how much the United States could reasonably provide.

After several weeks of discussions with the British, led by Morgenthau and White on one side and Halifax and Keynes on the other, the two sides agreed on a plan to carry Lend-Lease forward in 1945. Agreement did not come easily, and neither Keynes nor White demurred to make a heated case for his country's interests. By mid-November, Keynes had become so incensed by the atmosphere that his associates became apprehensive about his health and were trying to prevent any further meetings with Harry. They feared that Keynes had become "far too worked up . . . almost uncontrollable" and was being "appallingly rude" to Harry.[41] Nonetheless, negotiations continued.

Following the general tactic that Harry had recommended, the British team initially asked for $7 billion in aid for the year. The Americans countered with an offer of $5.5 billion, almost equally divided between military and civilian goods. Because everyone was assuming that the European war was about to end, this figure　a substantial reduction from the level of aid being provided in 1944—was thought to be high enough to enable Britain to make at least a start toward rebuilding its export capabilities, but not so high as to threaten the continuing success of U.S. industry.[42]

Although Harry clearly played the role of spoiler in tamping down Morgenthau's enthusiasm for helping Britain recover economically as the war wound down in 1945, he did not discourage and certainly did not prevent the government from meeting the bulk of British requests for assistance. Throughout the war, his primary role was to turn a policy devised by Morgenthau and endorsed unreservedly by Roosevelt into a concrete aid program. Overall, Britain and its colonies received about $29 billion (equivalent to about $432 billion in 2021) in wartime assistance through the Lend-Lease program, a substantial majority of which was not subject to compensation.

PART IV

Creating the Postwar Global Economy

CHAPTER NINE

Planning for a Stable Postwar Recovery, 1941–42

Without . . . planned cooperation, the economic dislocations of the war will result in widespread post-war depression.

—Harry White, August 1941

THE U.S. ENTRY INTO the war in December 1941 intensified Harry White's work in a direction that ultimately became the great purpose for his life. For the next four years, he devoted himself to two interrelated tasks: organizing the financing of the Allies' war effort and planning for economic and financial stability once the war was over. As we saw in the last chapter, the main elements of international wartime finance involved designing and producing financial support for the Grand Alliance members—China, the Soviet Union, and the United Kingdom—and shoring up relations with Latin America to insulate the region from Axis influence. The main elements of postwar planning involved designing and generating support for the institutions that would become the International Monetary Fund and the International Bank for Reconstruction and Development (commonly known as the World Bank). These were daunting challenges. They would exact an overwhelming toll on Harry's health, but he would ultimately succeed on all fronts.

The Birth of the White Plan

In the late 1930s, the starting point for anyone thinking about how to strengthen and stabilize economic and financial relations among countries was the failure of the Paris Peace Conference that had followed the Great War in 1919. U.S. President Woodrow Wilson went to that conference with the intention of getting an international agreement to set up an institutional structure for economic cooperation. The third point in his famous Fourteen Points speech to Congress called for the "removal, so far as possible, of all economic barriers and the establishment of an equality of trade conditions among all the nations consenting to the peace and associating themselves for its maintenance."[1]

Wilson's efforts in Paris succeeded in creating the League of Nations as a multilateral intergovernmental organization, but Congress refused to ratify U.S. participation. The League included an economics section, but it had little influence on member countries' policies. The consequent lack of effective institutions and the absence of rules or international agreements was widely seen as a major cause of the monetary chaos of the 1920s and 1930s, the Great Depression of the 1930s, and the economic pressures that were contributing to military tensions in Europe and Asia.

Harry White's thinking about how to develop a more cooperative financial system was also influenced by the shortcomings of other efforts in the 1930s. The most ambitious effort, the 1933 World Economic Conference in London, failed in part because it had the unrealistic aim of reestablishing a gold-based system of fixed exchange rates, but also because the Franklin Roosevelt administration lost interest in it and failed to take a leadership role. The 1936 Tripartite Agreement among France, the United Kingdom, and the United States was a helpful reaction to a specific potential crisis but did not lead to a more general structure for anticipating and resolving international financial tensions. As the Depression began to wind down in the late 1930s, Harry's work focused increasingly on the search for a broader, more sustainable, and more effective international monetary system.

Beginning in 1937, Harry used the U.S. Exchange Stabilization Fund (ESF) to provide financial assistance to economically struggling countries in the form of currency swaps. At Bretton Woods, that form of assistance became the core of the financial structure of the International Monetary Fund. Meanwhile, from 1940 through the early months of 1942, Harry was heavily involved in an effort to establish a regional bank for the post-Depression reconstruction of Latin American economies. Although that effort never came to fruition, it laid the table for the negotiations that would lead ultimately to Bretton Woods.

The focus began to shift toward Bretton Woods in August 1941, when Roosevelt and Churchill met—for the first time as leaders of their countries—on a U.S. warship, the U.S.S. *Augusta*, anchored in a quiet harbor off the southeast coast of Newfoundland. In the wake of Germany's invasion of Russia in June, the two leaders recognized the imperative of developing a joint plan to enable American support of the effort to resist the territorial ambitions of both Germany and Japan. Although neither the administration nor U.S. public opinion was yet prepared to go to war, Roosevelt wanted to issue a joint statement of principles expressing the solidarity of the United States with the United Kingdom and the alliance fighting the Axis. The result was the issuance of the Atlantic Charter.[2]

Watered down as it was with diplomatic obfuscation, the Atlantic Charter nonetheless boldly declared that Roosevelt and Churchill "desire to bring about the fullest collaboration between all Nations in the economic field with the object of securing, for all, improved labor standards, economic advancement, and social security." It was not quite a call for a new institutional structure to succeed the moribund League of Nations, but it was enough to justify the beginning of work in that direction on both sides of the Atlantic.

Back in Washington, on the same day that Roosevelt and Churchill were putting the finishing touches on the Atlantic Charter, Harry sent a memorandum to Treasury Secretary Morgenthau, urging immediate attention to planning for postwar reconstruction. The United States should begin working on the problem, along with the countries of the British Empire, he argued. "Without such planned cooperation," Harry warned, "the economic dislocations of the war will result in widespread post-war depression and economic and trade rivalries."[3] Whether by plan or by coincidence, Harry was to be the first one out of the blocks in the race to design a global economic system that would meet the challenges raised in the charter.

Many analysts have assumed incorrectly that because the Keynes plan for postwar monetary arrangements was published before White's, Keynes was the first to develop a plan. Notably, Armand Van Dormael's 1978 book on Bretton Woods included a chapter titled "Harry White Catches Up . . . ," followed by ". . . And Takes the Lead." In fact, as I discuss in the next chapter, Keynes began work a few weeks after Harry in the summer of 1941, and the two worked independently for the next several months.

In December 1941, in response to the U.S. entry into the war, Morgenthau telephoned Harry at home on a Sunday morning and asked him to do what Harry was already doing: develop a plan for international monetary cooperation both during and after the war. As Harry summarized the conversation the next day, Morgenthau "asked [me] to think about and prepare a memorandum and plan for setting up an Inter-Allied Stabilization Fund. The Secretary had in mind a Fund to be used (1) during the war to give monetary aid to actual and potential allies and to hamper the enemy; (2) to provide the basis for post-war international monetary stabilization arrangements; and (3) to provide a post-war 'international currency.'"[4]

A key part of Harry's elevated responsibilities as assistant to the secretary was to work directly with the State Department. Almost the first order of business was to prepare for a conference of foreign ministers, to be held in Rio de Janeiro in mid-January to solidify a hemispheric response to Axis aggressions. On Saturday, January 3, 1942, Harry participated in a meeting in the office of Under Secretary Sumner Welles of the State Department, who was to head the U.S delegation at Rio. When Harry mentioned his ideas for economic cooperation among the allied countries and an early start on planning for postwar economic cooperation and reconstruction, Welles responded enthusiastically. He asked Harry to prepare a proposal that he could introduce at the Rio conference.

Harry had been thinking, and discussing with Treasury colleagues, at least since August about possible plans for stabilizing the economies of all the allied countries: first during the hostilities, to help shore up their capacity to sustain the war effort, and then after the war to help secure the peace. Welles's request galvanized him into action. Three days later, on January 6, after reviewing his proposal with Jacob Viner and a few other Treasury colleagues, he sent a brief sketch to Welles.[5] (In a sign of how much independence Harry now had in his new role at the Treasury, he sent the draft to Morgenthau only on January 8, two days after he had sent it across town by messenger to Foggy Bottom.)

Key Elements

Though it was only nine pages, and so hastily written that it still contained several typographical errors, Harry's January 6 draft set out the key elements of what would transpire and then would be approved by all forty-four national delegations at Bretton Woods some three and a half years later. First, there should be two separate new institutions to promote economic recovery and cooperation after the war. One was to be a

"Stabilization Fund," which he hoped would establish monetary stability for the Allies during the war and for the world afterward. The other was to be an "international bank . . . to provide the capital necessary for postwar reconstruction and development." That phrasing is significant. The political scientist Eric Helleiner has stressed that development was included as a purpose of the World Bank from the beginning and was not an afterthought, as has sometimes been argued. Development economics was not yet a defined discipline, but the concept was already at the forefront of Harry's thinking.[6]

Second, the design of these institutions should be entrusted to a "special conference" of representatives of "the United Nations and the Associated American Republics." The reference to the United Nations was, as in all discussions during World War II, a reference to the alliance of countries at war with the Axis. The formal institution was not established until 1945.

Third, participation in the institutions "should be open to all countries that subscribe to the objectives of the Atlantic Charter—international security and economic progress." That is, membership should not be restricted to countries with certain economic or political systems.

Fourth, the stabilization fund would aim to establish stable exchange rates, enable international transactions to be free of "arbitrary and discriminatory restrictions" and bilateral clearing arrangements, and promote the adoption of "monetary policies that avoid serious inflation or deflation."

Harry continued to work on a design for the World Bank as a vehicle for reconstruction and economic development through the summer of 1943. He finished polishing it while he and Anne were vacationing on the south shore of Lake Ontario in August 1943. He then sent it to the British embassy, which forwarded it to Keynes in time for his September trip to Washington.[7] After that, Harry focused primarily on the design for the stabilization fund. (At Bretton Woods in 1944, he chaired the commission on the design of the IMF, while Keynes chaired the one on the World Bank.)

Rejection of an International Currency

One potentially important element that was *not* in Harry's plan for the fund was Morgenthau's request for a postwar international currency. From the outset, Harry argued that it was a bad and unnecessary idea. His first detailed draft included a lengthy explanation for the omission. A common accounting unit, he conceded, might be of some value, but that would just be a matter of defining such a unit—"a 'trade dollar' or 'Demos' or 'Victor' or 'what-have-you' unit"—as equivalent to a fixed amount of gold or other commodity. To go further by replacing national currencies with a common currency would require countries to give up sovereignty and independence with respect to monetary policies. The intermediate step of issuing a new currency for international transactions as a supplement to national currencies would just add a layer of hassle, expense, and bureaucracy to existing practices. Without naming anyone, Harry concluded that "the belief . . . held in some quarters that a common unit of currency will solve the world's foreign exchange problems" was misguided and unhelpful.

The names "Demos" and "Victor" were apparently being considered in the Treasury, probably because Morgenthau had suggested them. British officials in Washington told Keynes that they thought Roosevelt had suggested the names.[8] If so, Morgenthau would most likely have conveyed the president's suggestions to Harry. In any event, Harry's dismissal of them in his April 1942 draft was definitive. He also wrote a more detailed and equally vigorous denunciation of the idea in one of the drafts of his manuscript "The Future of Gold," discussed below.

Although Harry's rejection of an international currency was clearly aimed at dissuading his boss at the Treasury from pursuing the idea, it later put him at odds with Keynes, too. As we shall see, Keynes constructed his own scheme on an international currency unit that he called "bancor," a conflation of French terms for banking and gold. Keynes envisaged the creation of bancor as a way of reducing reliance on U.S. dollars as foreign exchange reserves.

For a while, Harry responded to that proposal by introducing what he called "unitas" as an accounting unit rather than an asset or a medium of exchange, but he eventually dropped the pretense and based his final plan simply on the gold content of the U.S. dollar.

The task at hand in January 1942 was merely to set in motion a process for creating a stabilization fund, as requested by Sumner Welles. The bank could wait, but the fund—if it could be set up quickly—could be an incentive for countries that were still neutral to join the battle against the Axis. The bulk of Harry's January 6 draft therefore focused solely on the possible design of the fund. Here again, many of the features prefigured the final outcome.

Harry envisaged that the fund should "have assets of $5 billion to $10 billion in gold, currencies and government securities." The final figure agreed on at Bretton Woods would be $8.8 billion if all the invited countries agreed to participate, and quotas of the countries that joined the fund as original members totaled $7.6 billion. Harry suggested that control should be spread across all members, and that votes be weighted according to financial contributions and the country's size. Small countries, he suggested, should be given "a share of voting power greatly in excess of their share of subscription to the assets of the Fund." At Bretton Woods, more than 10 percent of the voting power would be set aside for "basic votes" to amplify the voice of small countries.

The Role of Gold

The White Plan envisaged that the U.S. dollar would serve to underpin the postwar financial system, enabled by the dollar's convertibility into gold at a fixed rate that could be adjusted in extremis. The plan itself took that relationship as an implicit assumption, but Harry labored hard throughout the gestation of the plan to justify and explain it. In the event, his efforts remained unpublished.

In 1940 he began writing a manuscript that he titled "The Future of Gold." Nothing in the manuscript indicates who his intended audience was, but it reads as if he was trying to summarize his views for a general audience, and he circulated at least one draft within the Treasury. Three drafts, all incomplete, are in the Princeton archives. The first available draft, from 1940, is seventy-two pages long and concludes with a sentence promising more to come in "the next section."[9] Other, longer drafts appear to date from 1942 and 1944.

The initial impetus for this work was the onset of World War II in Europe and Asia, which had, as Harry noted in the opening sentence of the 1940 draft, "intensified the already chronic discussion concerning the future status of gold." As the largest neutral country, the United States was receiving large inflows of gold. In 1940 the United States already held some 63 percent of world monetary gold, and Harry predicted (correctly) that by the end of the war that percentage could rise to 75 percent or more. He also predicted that if the war lasted five years, "we would assuredly have most of the world's gold by the end of the war." That forecast assumed that the United States would remain neutral. In fact, U.S. official holdings topped out in the neighborhood of 75 percent of the total at the end of six years of war.

How could gold continue to serve as the foundation for international finance if one country held nearly the whole stock?

Harry concluded that as long as the United States accumulated no more than (roughly) 75 percent of the gold stock, the remainder would suffice to underpin international financial settlements between countries. He assumed, as did almost all economists at the time, that this link between gold and international settlements was—for the foreseeable future—essential and inviolable. Any careful exporter of goods "would demand payment in the form of his own currency, or of gold, or some currency that would give promise of being kept stable in terms of his own currency or gold. Since there is no currency that could give such promise unless backed by substantial sums of gold, gold in the last analysis is the only form of finally acceptable medium of international payment."[10]

The thrust of this manuscript was to argue that the future of gold as the basis for international settlements was secure, notwithstanding the end of the classical gold standard in the interwar period, a growing recognition that the role of gold as a backing for domestic money was no longer needed, and the concentration of gold in the U.S Treasury. He recognized that the international function of gold might be phased out eventually, but he thought that it would take "many decades at least . . . before many countries will elect to keep their reserves in the form of some foreign paper currency never redeemable in gold."[11] In practice, the evolution out of gold took only about two and a half decades, until the end of gold convertibility for the U.S. dollar and other major currencies by 1971 brought about exactly the result that Harry had projected. In the meantime, "those who are worried about the future of gold forget that gold is the best medium of international exchange yet devised."[12]

It seems extraordinary that Harry would have made time during World War II to draft such a detailed examination of the monetary role of gold. He had enough work on his desk to occupy him much more than full-time, without taking on this more abstract analysis as an extracurricular project. He started it a year or more before he was asked to prepare a design for postwar cooperation on international trade and finance: the task that would lead to the Bretton Woods conference and the creation of the IMF and the World Bank. He continued to work on it throughout the years leading up to Bretton Woods. A likely explanation is that by forcing himself to write a clear story about the future of monetary gold, he clarified his own thinking about the role that gold would have to play in his scheme for postwar cooperation. As we shall see in the next section, the White Plan that prevailed at Bretton Woods placed the U.S. dollar at the center of the future international financial system, but only because of the assurance that the dollar would remain convertible to gold. For the first quarter century after the war, the future of gold, the dollar, and the world economy would be tightly interdependent.

Building Support for the Plan

Harry recognized that much discussion would have to take place before the powers of the fund could be agreed on. The fund would have to be able to prevent countries from using its resources to pursue policies that would adversely affect other countries or that might destabilize the system, but how might it allocate its discipline between creditor and debtor countries? That issue would generate a bitter debate in the run-up to Bretton Woods, and it would never be satisfactorily resolved. Also, "to what extent," he mused, "and under what condition should the Fund be permitted to pass judgment on the monetary and credit policies of member nations?" That question would be left unsettled at Bretton Woods. Both issues would remain principal sources of controversy about the powers and policies of the IMF well into the twenty-first century.

Before members of the U.S. delegation left Washington for Rio, they agreed that Harry should begin the process by meeting informally and bilaterally with other countries' delegations to sound them out on the idea of holding a general meeting aimed at establishing a stabilization fund.[13] But once they were in Rio, Welles decided to act more decisively. He suggested to Harry that the U.S. delegation should introduce a formal resolution to the conference, calling for a conference of the whole United Nations alliance aimed at establishing the fund. That made Harry a little nervous because no one other than the Latin American countries represented in Rio had yet been consulted on the proposal.

On the morning of January 15, 1942, Welles sent a cable to the State Department, and Harry sent one to the Treasury. At the State Department, Assistant Secretary Adolf A. Berle Jr. checked around and obtained a general approval to go ahead. At the Treasury, Under Secretary Daniel W. Bell called a meeting of staff who had been involved (Jacob Viner, Frank Southard, Frank Coe, and Bernard Bernstein). They agreed that the resolution could be presented, but only after consultation with Secretary Morgenthau (who was out of the office that day), Federal Reserve Chairman Marriner Eccles, and "the British," and after informing President Roosevelt. Harry had informed them in his cable that all these steps had to be completed by the next morning, because the deadline for submitting resolutions to the Rio conference was noon on the next day.[14]

Bell then telephoned Morgenthau, who asked him to hold off. He liked the proposal, but he thought it was premature to raise it formally in Rio, where participation was limited to the American nations. Bell informed White by cable, and it appeared that the proposal was dead.

Welles was not happy. On Saturday, January 17, he telephoned Morgenthau and made a personal plea for him to reconsider his opposition. Morgenthau next called Harry, and they agreed to scale down the resolution by limiting it to the Western Hemisphere and deleting a few references that could have been interpreted as promoting "dollar diplomacy" by the U.S. government. With those changes, Welles introduced the resolution, which was adopted by the assembled foreign ministers.

The proposal to establish what would ultimately become the International Monetary Fund thus made its first public appearance in Rio de Janeiro in the form of a recommendation to hold a hemispheric conference of finance ministers to discuss creating a fund to "promote stability in foreign exchange rates, encourage the international movement of productive capital, facilitate the reduction of artificial and discriminatory barriers to the movement of goods, help correct the maldistribution of gold, strengthen monetary systems, and facilitate the maintenance of monetary policies that avoid serious inflation or deflation."[15]

The foreign ministers agreed that the hemispheric conference should be held within two months, in Washington, beginning on March 15. When the U.S. team returned home, however, cooler heads prevailed. After all, it was never anyone's preference to limit the discussion to the Americas. The scope had been confined only because time had not allowed for wider consultation.

Morgenthau finally had a chance to explain the situation to the British authorities on January 22, 1942, when Sir Frederick Phillips called on him to discuss Britain's perilous financial condition. Phillips asked the secretary what was going on in Rio, to which Morgenthau replied that he had vetoed the proposal for a full conference of the allied countries and had insisted that it be limited to the Americas until the other allies could be consulted. Morgenthau then agreed with Phillips that, in Phillips's words, "this is really nothing more than extending to the South American countries the privilege of joining the old Tripartite Agreement" of 1936.[16] Ultimately, it would turn out to be far more momentous than that, but the process was still in an early stage.

The hemispheric conference was quietly abandoned, but Harry and his staff went to work fleshing out the proposal for a stabilization fund. By

April 1942 Harry had a detailed (155-page) plan for how the fund and the bank might be conceived and organized.[17] He proposed to Morgenthau that the Treasury get approval from other government agencies and then move quickly to convene an international conference to get the project under way. On May 15 Morgenthau was satisfied enough to send it to Roosevelt for approval.

The spirit of American idealism with which the White Plan was conceived, and with which it was conveyed to the president, seems remarkable when viewed through the lens of cynicism that one picks up more naturally in the early decades of the twenty-first century. World War II was an era of internationalism in much of the United States and especially in the Roosevelt administration. That spirit made possible the Bretton Woods agreements in 1944, the creation of the United Nations in 1945, and the implementation of the Marshall Plan in 1948. And the spirit was evident already in 1942, when Morgenthau informed Roosevelt of the purposes of the proposed fund and bank: "The purpose of these two agencies is to meet the inevitable post-war international monetary and credit problems—to prevent disruption of foreign exchange and the collapse of monetary and credit problems, to assure the restoration of foreign trade and to supply the huge volume of capital that will be needed abroad for relief, for reconstruction, and economic development essential for the attainment of world prosperity and higher standards of living."[18] Partly because the enemy was so greatly reviled and the threat that it posed was so dire; partly because the dominant economic strength of the United States meant that its own national interest dovetailed with the restoration of global prosperity; partly because of a widely held faith that economic progress was essential for the preservation of peace; and partly because Roosevelt had led the country for an unprecedented ten years (and counting) as much by inspiration as by action: for all these reasons, the moral high ground on which the White Plan was founded was both genuine and credible in the dark early days of American engagement in the war.

The president approved the White Plan on May 16, 1942, and Morgenthau then invited the State Department, the Board of Economic Warfare (BEW), the Export-Import Bank, and the Federal Reserve Board to designate representatives to participate in a meeting at the Treasury on May 25.[19] Morgenthau opened the meeting by asking Harry to explain the purpose of his plan for postwar financial stabilization and to suggest how the group should proceed. Morgenthau then suggested that the group appoint a subcommittee, to be chaired by Harry, to develop the plan into a formal proposal of the U.S. government. Finally, he asked each agency representative whether he thought that Harry's proposal was a good basis for discussion by such a committee. In turn, Jesse Jones (secretary of commerce), Marriner Eccles (chair of the Federal Reserve Board), Frank Coe (representing Henry Wallace, who headed the BEW), and Herbert Feis (representing Secretary of State Cordell Hull) all gave their support and agreed to nominate members of their staff to serve on Harry's committee.

The Export-Import Bank did not send a representative to the May 25 meeting and did not participate in subsequent committee meetings, but the other groups did. With Morgenthau's approval, Harry invited a few economists from other agencies to join in the work of his subcommittee on a personal basis. That led notably to the participation of a distinguished Harvard professor and leading Keynesian scholar, Alvin Hansen, who was then a consultant to the National Resources Planning Board.

Although Under Secretary of State Sumner Welles had been an enthusiastic supporter of Harry's proposal, and although Feis approved the plan at this initial meeting, the State Department now became a thorn in Harry's side as he tried to put the plan into action. The conflict was institutional, not personal. A few months earlier, when Morgenthau had elevated Harry to the status of an assistant secretary and made him the principal liaison with the State Department, Hull had responded that Harry was "a mighty suitable man . . . a very high-class fellow . . . capable."[20] On this occasion, Feis designated Leo Pasvolsky to serve on Harry's committee. For more than a year, Pasvolsky would oppose many of Harry's proposals, principally because of Harry's intention to create two new institutions.

Pasvolsky—a Ukrainian-born journalist who was serving as a special assistant to Secretary Hull—had been working quietly for years to develop a new global institution to replace the ineffectual League of Nations, and in 1942 he set out his own scheme for postwar economic planning. That scheme went nowhere, but he would eventually be credited with being the principal author of the United Nations charter, as adopted in 1945.[21] In 1942 the idea that the U.S. Treasury was going to begin planning for two more specialized multilateral agencies seems to have struck him as a complicated diversion and a potential threat to his own project. In September Pasvolsky added Eleanor Lansing Dulles to his staff working on the bank and fund proposals. She had been working separately, at the BEW, on a proposal to establish an international central bank to replace the Bank for International Settlements. Already bitter because her work was not being given serious consideration, she shared her boss's disdain for Harry's complicated scheme and spent much of her two-year stay at State writing memoranda challenging it.[22]

More generally, the State Department view—expressed most clearly by Dean Acheson, assistant secretary of state (and later secretary of state under President Truman)—was that the other major powers wanted to be able to shape the proposals before they were presented to the alliance at large. The British had "a rather pathetic feeling" that the U.S. government was going to "write the ticket" and prevent them from being "in on the formulation at the start." Acheson proposed a series of bilateral meetings, starting with the British and then with the Russians, "the Dutch, the Belgians, and others, before we get into a large meeting."[23] Because State Department officials did not think any new institutions could be created until after the war, they did not see the point in rushing ahead.

The turf battle with State did not delay action for long. After a series of meetings of Harry's subcommittee and of the cabinet-level committee chaired by Morgenthau, Harry got a green—or at least an amber—light in early July.[24] He had the support of both Morgenthau and Roosevelt to present his plan to the other leading members of the alliance: Britain, China, and Russia. The caveat was that the White Plan was not to be presented yet as an official U.S. proposal. It was merely a set of preliminary ideas to stimulate discussions within the alliance. That was enough for the time being. Within a week (by July 8, 1942), the plan was in British hands, and a new battlefield was in play.

CHAPTER TEN

Negotiating with Keynes, 1942–43

In many respects [Harry] is the best man here.

—John Maynard Keynes, 1943

WHILE HARRY WHITE WAS developing the American plan for postwar financial cooperation and stability, John Maynard Keynes was developing a British plan to secure continuing American financial support and preserve as much as possible of Britain's prewar colonial system. Although the motivations were strikingly different, the purposes and structures were similar enough to lead ultimately to a successful compromise.

Harry's role in these preparations and their consequences has been underappreciated. Part of the problem has been his personal and professional obscurity and the overarching obsession with the scandalous accusations that later came to define him. The other part has been the respect and even devotion that has naturally been attached to Keynes, who was already the most celebrated economist of the twentieth century before he began working on plans for postwar finance. Keynes was the author of best-selling books and of masterworks that had transformed the theory and practice of economic policy. He was also a cultural icon who had famously been a conscientious objector in the Great War; a member of the literary and artistic Bloomsbury Group; the husband of a famous Russian ballerina, Lydia Lopokova; and a lecturer at and financier to the University of Cambridge. He would soon become a peer in the House of Lords.

The separate plans developed by White and Keynes were reconciled and amended in a lengthy process that culminated in the United Nations Monetary and Financial Conference in Bretton Woods, New Hampshire, in July 1944. As this process evolved, Keynes was occasionally appalled at White's crude and undiplomatic behavior, but he praised his contributions. After meeting with him in Washington to prepare for Bretton Woods, Keynes wrote to a colleague that Harry was "over-bearing, a bad colleague . . . but I have a very great respect and even liking for him. In many respects he is the best man here." Keynes's acolyte and first biographer, Roy Harrod, made a case for elevating White's reputation as a contributor to the postwar system. "In Britain," he wrote, White "is too often thought of as some dim scribe, some kind of robot, who wrote . . . an inferior version of the Keynes plan—mainly to vex the British! Far different was the real man. He was a remarkable figure, who should be accorded an honourable place in British annals."[1]

Without any doubt, Keynes was by far the more remarkable of the two collaborators, in every way. Still, in their efforts to create a secure system for the postwar world economy, White was by no means either the junior partner or an obstructionist. In the end, he won both the battle and the respect of his adversarial colleague.*

The Birth of the Keynes Plan

Robert Skidelsky's biography of John Maynard Keynes provides an intimate portrait of Keynes quickly drafting his initial plan for an international clearing union (ICU) in the course of a single weekend at his country home in Sussex in September 1941.[2] Perhaps to clear his own mind from the straitjacket of prewar international finance, Keynes began the weekend by writing a note on the shortcomings of the gold standard, which he had come to regard as a "doctrinaire delusion." Exchange rates

---

* Some more recent authors have taken a decidedly less positive view. Keynes's most recent biographer, Robert Skidelsky, relegated most of his discussion of White's role to a chapter in *John Maynard Keynes: Fighting for Britain* titled "The Strange Case of Harry Dexter White." The subtitle of Eric Rauchway's 2015 book on the period made an oddly lopsided pairing: "How Roosevelt and Keynes Ended the Depression, Defeated Fascism, and Secured a Prosperous Peace." Another recent book by Benn Steil (*Battle of Bretton Woods*, 5) characterized White's role as being "the chief barrier to Keynes's blueprint for the postwar monetary order."

and capital flows had to be controlled by government action, not left alone in a laissez-faire indifference to action in private markets.[3] Looking backward was not to be an option for a Britain that would be attempting to recover from a depression and then the devastation of war.

The motivating purpose of Keynes's proposal for postwar finance was to obtain as much external support as possible for Britain's economic recovery. Although his scheme was described as open to all central banks that were willing to adhere to its requirements, Keynes developed it with specific objectives designed to benefit his own country. One problem with the gold standard, he wrote, was that its rules were "*compulsory* for the debtor and *voluntary* for the creditor."[4] He would remedy that defect by imposing requirements on creditor countries, which at the time meant just the United States. If the United States was to continue to amass a large surplus after the war, he imagined that it could be required to revalue the dollar and to surrender part of its reserves to the ICU.[5] Not only would this requirement alleviate the adjustment burden on debtor countries such as the United Kingdom, it also would establish a fund that could be used to help war-torn countries recover. Keynes proposed setting up a Relief and Reconstruction Council for this purpose, which would be funded, at least in part, by transfers from the ICU.

A critical issue for Great Britain (and thus for Keynes) was that the colonial structure that Britain had been exploiting economically for centuries was in decline and was likely to come under increasing pressure after the war. That structure relied on a system of "imperial preferences" on trade, a currency system in which many countries either used the pound sterling or linked their own currencies to it, and a central role for the Bank of England as the repository for sterling balances that belonged to Commonwealth countries but that were blocked from being withdrawn except under agreement.

Keynes was acutely aware that all elements of the imperial system were under threat and were unlikely to survive unscathed, even assuming a full victory in the ongoing war. In a footnote to the opening paragraph of his ICU proposal, Keynes mused on how he might try to limit the damage: "Perhaps we could not expect the new sterling area to be as large as what we now call the sterling area, but we should try to make it as large as possible. Could we persuade Australia, New Zealand, and India, and even South Africa, to remain within it? I should have a good try."[6]

Keynes envisioned a governance structure that put the United Kingdom and the United States on a par, each country appointing one of the eight governors. But the British vote would be enhanced by the inclusion of one governor from the rest of the Commonwealth. The remaining five governors would represent the Soviet Union ("Russia," in Keynes's draft), the rest of Europe (with two seats), South America, and everyone else (whom he called "odds and ends countries"). The multi-country governors would be elected by their constituent countries using weighted voting.

Although halting Britain's decline was Keynes's primary purpose, he also had the global economy very much in mind. Prosperity depended on the restoration of international trade, which in turn depended on the ability of countries to finance the balance of trade. At the time he was writing, the only financial buffers enabling countries to run trade deficits were their holdings of gold and the two widely acceptable currencies, the U.S. dollar and the pound sterling. By holding such balances in reserve, a country could then draw on them to settle a deficit. Collectively, though, the withdrawal of gold and currencies from circulation into reserves exerted downward pressure on spending and thus on output and incomes. Replacing those reserves with a new international asset that Keynes called "bancor" would offset the downward pressure.

Keynes also understood that the scheme would have to be beneficial to the United States in some way, or it would never get approved. Part of his plan was to convince the Americans and any other potential creditors that the new reserve asset would enable them to hold on to their accumulations of gold without stifling the ability of debtor countries to buy their exported goods. In addition, he designed the scheme to limit potential abuses by debtor countries. He intended that it would buy time for debtor countries to adjust their policies but not avoid the need for adjustment altogether. Participating countries would have an automatic right to draw from the ICU up to a specified amount, but prolonged or large-scale drawings would be discouraged.

To limit abuse, Keynes first proposed to fix a ceiling on the size of any country's debit balance, determined in relation to the amount of its international trade. He called this ceiling an "index-quota" (later, just "quota"). For symmetry, he proposed that every country with a debit *or credit* position exceeding 25 percent of its quota would pay interest to the ICU. These interest charges, he believed, "would be valuable inducements towards keeping a level balance." In addition, if a country wanted to borrow larger amounts from the ICU, the Governing Board could require the debtor to devalue its currency, surrender gold, or "to take measures to improve its position." Similarly, as noted above, the Governing Board could require a country with a persistently large credit position to appreciate its currency, raise domestic wages, reduce tariffs or other import barriers, or make loans to "backward countries."[7]

Over the next two months, Keynes received comments from several British colleagues in the Treasury, the Bank of England, and universities. He then circulated a second draft in November 1941, taking account of those comments and including a lengthy justification of his reasoning. In the commentary, he acknowledged that the main point was to find a way to get financial help from the United States without making too blatantly obvious or direct an appeal. "If we are to attract the interest and enthusiasm of the Americans, we must come with an ambitious plan of an international complexion, suitable to serve the interests of others besides ourselves, which to a hopeful spirit may carry a chance of making the postwar economy of the world more reasonable and promising than it was before."[8] His commitment to that "international complexion," however, was only skin deep. The two dominant Anglophone countries would be "joint founders of the Club" and would invite in other countries only when they were "capable of sustaining the obligations of membership."

In a third draft, which Keynes circulated in December, he added the rather hopeful proposal that interest would be paid to the clearing bank by both debtor and creditor countries: 1 percent annually for relatively small balances and 2 percent for larger ones. Only by staying in balance on international payments could a participating country avoid paying interest charges.[9] This suggestion had a certain internal logic as a method for applying symmetric pressure on creditors and debtors, but Keynes must have sensed even at that early date that U.S. officials would never agree to it. Even if the scheme appealed to the "hopeful spirit" of the Roosevelt administration, it was inconceivable that the U.S. Congress would ratify an agreement requiring it to pay interest to an international agency on its accumulated surplus.

In March 1942, still unaware that Harry was preparing a rival scheme across the pond, Keynes produced a fourth draft, which became the first version to be discussed outside his circle of British colleagues and friends.[10] Within a few months, the principal task would become to try to reconcile his plan with White's and produce a joint proposal to take to the rest of the wartime alliance. As Keynes put it in May, "Now it is a question of capturing American sympathy."[11] Up to this point, Keynes was focused on sharpening and strengthening his arguments. From then on, he would have to focus on trying to salvage as much of his ambitions as possible.

Throughout these first six months of work on postwar financial planning, Keynes became increasingly delusional about the role that Britain
could expect to play. In each successive draft, that intended role became
stronger and more specific. In September 1941 Britain was to be one of
three countries (along with the United States and the Soviet Union) entitled to select one of the eight governors of the international clearing
bank. The November draft elevated Britain to the role of a "co-founder,"
alongside only the United States. By December, those two countries were
to be given an unspecified "special position" in the ICU. Finally, in March,
Keynes found a way to place his country a nose *ahead* of its transatlantic
rival: "I conceive of the Bank as substantially under Anglo-American management, especially in its early days. It would be easy to give it a constitution which would ensure this. In view of our experience and of our geographical and political position in relation to Europe, the United States
and the British Commonwealth, we could justifiably ask that the head
office should be situated in London with the Board of Managers meeting alternately here and in Washington." Moreover, he wrote hopefully,
"there should be a provision, at any rate for some years, by which the British and American members when acting in agreement could outvote the
rest of the Board."[12]

The Death of the Keynes Plan

By April 1942 Keynes and White had independently prepared two very
different plans for organizing postwar finance. Both plans envisaged creating a new institution with two main powers: to mobilize or supplement
gold and foreign exchange reserves to clear international payments balances, and to restrict the continuation of imbalances through some form
of disciplinary measures. They differed in almost every detail on how to
structure and organize those powers. They also differed on how widely
shared the powers should be: whether it would be primarily an Anglo-
American system into which other countries would be invited (as Keynes
wished), or a creation of the whole anti-Axis alliance from the outset (as
White preferred).

The most crucial difference in the American and British plans was
the choice between pooling or supplementing official reserves. In Harry's
conception, each country would deposit designated amounts of gold and
currencies in the stabilization fund. In return, the country would have
the right to borrow from the fund when it needed to cover a deficit in its

balance of payments. Borrowing rights would be limited to a multiple of the size of its subscription (that is, its deposit), but the limit could be overridden in exceptional cases. In Maynard Keynes's conception, the ICU would be empowered to issue a new international currency (bancor) and lend it to deficit countries to settle payments deficits with other participating countries. Borrowing rights would be linked to the country's economic size and trade volume but would not be constrained by its ability to deposit gold with the new agency.

These two conceptions were not mutually exclusive. Much later, in 1969, the United States and the United Kingdom led a drive to amend the IMF Articles of Agreement to enable the Fund to issue a new international asset, bizarrely named the Special Drawing Right or SDR, to supplement official foreign exchange reserves. Since then, these SDRs—a sort of bancor-lite—have functioned alongside the IMF's lending to member countries as a source of reserves and a means of settling payments imbalances. In 1943, however, that solution was not considered. The entire debate was over which option to choose, not how to combine them.

A second crucial difference concerned whether and how to discipline countries with persistent large surpluses in their balance of payments. As I noted earlier, that issue was central to Keynes's purpose in proposing his currency union. He planned to discourage surpluses by charging interest on them and by requiring surplus countries to transfer a portion of their accumulated balances to the union. Initially, the White Plan was silent on this issue, and Harry showed no interest in it. He did not expect the U.S. surplus to persist after the war was over, and he knew that any institutional plan to penalize it would be extremely difficult to sell to the U.S. Congress.

Before these differences could be bridged, each side had to share its plan with the other. As early as February 1942, British officials urged the U.S. ambassador, John Gilbert Winant, to use his influence to get a delegation of U.S. officials to go to London for preliminary discussions of the Keynes Plan. Winant delayed acting on that request, as discussions were taking place simultaneously in Washington about how and when to begin sharing the White Plan with the British, the other key members of the Grand Alliance (the Chinese and the Soviets), and the broader alliance. No one in Washington expected the Chinese or the Soviets to have a substantial say in the design of the postwar financial system, but White and his colleagues believed that those and other countries should be consulted at an early stage to avoid any misunderstandings or resentments later. The challenge in Washington was to get enough agreement among the several federal agencies involved on what exactly to propose, and to whom.

The May 25, 1942, interagency meeting at the Treasury evolved into a regular technical committee, with Harry as chairman. Formally, it was a subcommittee of the "Cabinet Committee on a Stabilization Fund and a Bank for Reconstruction and Development of the United and Associated Nations." Morgenthau chaired the Cabinet Committee, and White chaired the subcommittee. After two informal meetings, on May 28 and June 3, the subcommittee recommended to Morgenthau that the U.S. government invite representatives of "all friendly nations" to a technical conference in Washington. The State Department, however, was reluctant to go along, on the grounds that the British should play a special role and not be relegated to the same list of invitees as other countries.[13]

Not until July 10 did the whole interdepartmental group agree to proceed with multilateral discussions aimed at eventually holding a formal international conference. Even then, to placate the State Department, they agreed to start discussions with just six countries: the United Kingdom, Canada, Australia, Brazil, Russia, and China. The last two were included only "for political reasons."[14] By that time, however, Harry had already decided to move ahead on his own. He had leaked his plan to the British, giving one copy to Frederick Leith-Ross, an official at the Treasury in London who was in Washington for talks on postwar inter-Allied economic relief plans, and another to Frederick Phillips, who represented the British Treasury in Washington. Phillips sent the plan's summary to Richard Hopkins (permanent secretary of the U.K. Treasury) on July 8, and Leith-Ross circulated the full document to Treasury officials in London the next day.[15]

Harry was now waging a two-front battle. On one front, he was working within the U.S. bureaucracy to arrange informal technical meetings with several key allies. On the other, he was opening a bilateral dialogue with the British to unite the two parties who were bound to be most actively involved. He had not yet seen the Keynes Plan, but he had heard that such a plan was being prepared.

Despite Harry's fervent desire to involve all the allies at an early date, he also understood the State Department position that it was imperative that he first try to get the British on board. Presenting two competing plans to a large conference would risk disaster. In addition, as long as State was objecting to the process, he would have only the most reluctant support from his own government. Negotiating with the British would take matters out of the American bureaucracy into a forum where he might have more control. The new challenge, though, was that he would be up against one of the greatest economists, and one of the most formidable intellects, of the century. Keynes also possessed an intimidating level of fame and prestige. By coincidence, on the same day (June 5, 1942) that Harry sent the recommendation to Morgenthau to hold a multilateral conference, King George VI granted Keynes a hereditary peerage, with the title Baron Keynes of Tilton.

On July 24, 1942, Lord Keynes took his copy of the White Plan to his country home, Tilton, to read it at leisure. He was not impressed. In an oft-quoted response, he wrote to Hopkins on August 3: "It obviously won't work."[16] Just as obviously, Keynes was wrong. The basic structure of Harry's plan survived in the Articles of Agreement of the IMF as approved in 1944, albeit with many revisions. Whatever one might think about the subsequent effectiveness of the IMF, the plan did work. Where did Keynes go wrong?

Keynes had two primary objections to Harry's plan, both of which he described somewhat cryptically in his initial response. The American plan, he wrote, "makes no attempt to use the banking principle and one-way gold convertibility and is in fact not much more than a version of the gold standard which simply aims at multiplying the effective volume of the gold base."[17]

The reference to the avoidance of "the banking principle and one-way gold convertibility" meant that the White Plan relied on pooling official reserves rather than supplementing them. Moreover, White's fund could lend gold as well as accept it as subscriptions and repayments (that is, it had *two-way* gold convertibility). Keynes's ICU scheme would have created an institution with the power to create bancor as a reserve asset in response to demand from member countries with deficits in their balance of payments. It could choose to lend gold, but no country could demand gold. The stock of bancor outstanding at any time would be constrained by disincentives to borrowers (that is, interest charges) and by requirements that borrowers take policy actions to reduce their payments deficits. The outstanding stock of credit under the White Plan would take the form of gold and national currencies (in practice, at least initially, mostly U.S. dollars) and would be limited by ceilings on borrowings in relation to each country's contributions to the fund.

Keynes's second objection was that the White Plan appeared to be a throwback to the gold standard; each country's ability to draw on the fund would be limited by the amount of gold that it was able to pay in as part of its subscription. This objection had merit, but it ignored White's preemptive attempt to overcome it. In the April version of the plan, White's fund could lend as much as necessary without regard to the subscription-based ceiling as long as the loan was approved with 80 percent of the voting power in the fund. If the borrower lacked the gold holdings to cover the excess amount of the loan, the fund would have to be satisfied that "the 'excess' could be disposed of within a 'reasonable' time."[18] In other words, the borrowing country would have to present a plan for how it could reduce its external deficit by enough to generate the revenue needed to repay the fund.

The underlying problem was that the Keynes and White plans were formulated on the basis of the British and American financial systems, respectively. Keynes was trying to extend the British banking system, with its use of overdrafts as the normal method of extending credit, to the international sphere; and he was trying to generalize the abandonment of the gold standard. White was trying to extend the U.S. Treasury's practice of using the Exchange Stabilization Fund (ESF) to extend credits to other countries through currency swaps, and he envisaged a continuing role for gold as an anchor for currency values and as a medium for the settlement of international balances. Either scheme had the potential to work effectively, but neither seemed to be compatible with the other.

Harry's adaptation of the ESF as the prototype for IMF lending irritated Keynes because he saw it as unnecessarily complex and obscurantist. To Harry, those qualities were a great advantage, because they helped disguise the fact that the IMF would in effect be lending U.S. dollars to countries that were likely to be facing financial difficulties. Like the ESF, the IMF would not (in a legal sense) be making loans. Instead, it would be entering into agreements with its member countries to exchange dollars and possibly other internationally usable currencies for the borrowers' own domestic currency. By presenting the process as a simple exchange of currencies, Harry made the proposal much more appealing to Congress and the American public. Keynes, however, repeatedly referred disdainfully and condescendingly to the financial structure of the White Plan as a form of "Cherokee." (During World War II, the U.S. government employed members of the Cherokee tribe to convey coded messages because virtually no one outside the tribe understood their unique language.) The criticism did not faze or divert Harry at all.

Harry got his first look at the Keynes Plan at the end of August 1942, when the British embassy sent a copy to the State Department with a request to begin informal bilateral discussions.[19] Like Keynes, Harry was unimpressed by what was being proposed on the other side of the Atlantic, but he tried to formulate a constructive response to it. On September 10 he participated in a meeting at the State Department at which two British officials—Phillips from the Treasury and Redvers Opie from the embassy—presented the Keynes Plan. Adolf Berle and Leo Pasvolsky were there as well for the State Department, and the meeting turned into a three-way dialogue during which Pasvolsky and White occasionally argued against each other, forcing Berle to try to forge a common American view.

This meeting in Berle's office was the first opportunity for the two sides to compare the two plans. It ended with a proposal for Pasvolsky to submit a list of questions to the British on how their plan might work in practice. The next day, Harry reported to Morgenthau that the Keynes Plan was "similar in its essential principles" to their own, but it differed in "important respects." He was particularly scornful of Keynes's proposal that the United Kingdom would have both the largest borrowing quota and the largest voting power. "Keynes's plan seems to provide voting power in proportion to the right *to borrow*!" he wrote emphatically.[20]

In early October the interdepartmental technical group met to consider how to respond to the Keynes Plan. Whatever reservations these individuals or their agencies might have had about Harry's proposals, they all preferred them unambiguously over those from the British. Nonetheless, they decided to keep options open by responding to Keynes with a list of questions about his plan. Pasvolsky had assembled a list of eighteen questions. Separately, White's team from the Treasury (principally William H. Taylor) had produced thirteen questions. In a meeting on October 5, the group managed to combine the two lists more compactly into a set of just eleven questions to be put to the British. The next day, Berle gave the questions to Phillips, who promised to convey them to Keynes personally, as he would be in London around the middle of the month.[21]

Throughout the summer of 1942, Harry had been trying to shift the focus of work to the broader alliance. On July 21 he suggested to Morgenthau that they arrange a meeting of technical representatives of eight countries: the United States, the six countries agreed to by the interdepartmental committee earlier that month (Australia, Brazil, Canada, China, the Soviet Union, and the United Kingdom), and Mexico. At the State Department meeting on September 10, he noted that the other allies had an interest in the postwar planning, and he asserted that several were already circulating "projects . . . covering more or less the same ground" as the U.S. and British plans. That may have been little more than a bluff, but he succeeded in getting the State Department and the British to agree to continue discussions with other governments.[22]

With that agreement in hand, Morgenthau told Harry on September 12 that he could go ahead and organize a meeting with representatives from several allied countries. That plan was interrupted, however, when the secretary told Harry that he wanted him to accompany him to Europe. Much of the trip would focus on inspecting and learning about U.S. and Allied military activity and logistics, but it would include nearly two weeks in London. Harry would now be able to meet directly with Keynes to discuss their plans.

Although this trip would present the first opportunity for the two men to discuss their plans for postwar finance, it would be their third meeting overall. They had met for the first time during Harry's trip to London in 1935, and for the second time during Keynes's trip to Washington in June 1941. That second meeting dealt with Lend-Lease matters, not postwar planning.

Flying across the Atlantic in those days, even discounting the risks of war, was a slow and uncomfortable affair, not to be undertaken lightly. On this occasion, miserable weather hampered travel throughout the trip. Morgenthau, White, and a military aide left Washington on October 13; rested in Gander, Newfoundland, at a refueling stop; arrived in Glasgow, Scotland, on the 15th; transferred to a smaller plane; and flew on to the Royal Air Force station at Northolt, just west of London, arriving in the late afternoon. They were met by Ambassador Winant and a military escort and were taken to Claridge's Hotel in Mayfair, close by the U.S. embassy on Grosvenor Square.

Morgenthau was whisked around southern England in a whirlwind tour, sometimes on military planes but often in cars or trains when air traffic was grounded by the weather. Harry accompanied him on occasion, but on several days he stayed in London to meet with finance officials, including a lunch with Keynes and a few others on October 23. The two Americans did manage to see a couple of plays at West End theaters, but Harry seems to have been left behind when the secretary met with Prime Minister Churchill at 10 Downing Street and later dined with the king and queen at Buckingham Palace. Harry was struck by how stoically the British people dealt with the hardships of the war: the "surprisingly normal aspect of London, . . . people . . . hard at work . . . without any flag-waving or hurrahs. . . . Apparent acceptance of war's annoyances and inconveniences . . . without any semblance of grousing or ill-will."[23]

Winant organized for Harry to have a substantive meeting with Keynes toward the end of the visit, but it almost got scuttled. On the appointed day, Keynes was scheduled to address a meeting of technical experts from six Commonwealth countries, where he would be presenting his plan for an International Clearing Union in public for the first time. When the Treasury explained the schedule conflict to Harry and suggested he meet with other officials instead, Harry insisted that he would speak only to the great man himself. Keynes's schedule was hastily rearranged, and bilateral negotiations finally began in earnest.[24]

From England Harry and the secretary traveled to Lisbon, Portugal, made two quick stops in West Africa, and returned to Washington via Brazil, Puerto Rico, and New York.

When Harry chaired the next meeting of the interdepartmental group in Washington on December 1, he reported that Keynes had stressed three key points. First, countries' quotas, in his view, should be in proportion to trade volume, rather than being determined by contributions to the fund. Second, he had some sympathy for retaining a role for gold, although the only reason for doing so was "popular feeling" in favor of it. Third, the two countries should agree on a joint plan before approaching other countries. No one in the group seemed particularly impressed by these concerns, and no one suggested trying to amend the U.S. proposals in the direction of Keynes. Neither White nor Keynes reported on their discussion of the American questions on the Keynes Plan, but Keynes did produce a revised draft a few weeks later (dated November 9, 1942).[25] In the same spirit, Harry produced an amended draft of his plan in mid-December.

One of Harry's amendments would ultimately prove to be a breakthrough in the Anglo-American standoff, but the initial British reaction was mixed. This technically obscure proposal was the "scarce currency" clause—or, as it became known in the U.S. Treasury, the "$carce ¢urrency" clause. Harry evidently became convinced by Keynes's argument that his original plan lacked a means of disciplining countries with persistent trade surpluses (which were likely to include the United States). Moreover, if the United States did continue to run large surpluses, the stabilization fund would eventually run out of dollars to lend to deficit countries. To cover that eventuality, Harry added four paragraphs spelling out a two-step reaction from the fund. First, the fund should issue a report to the surplus country and specify how the scarcity should be eliminated. If that did not solve the problem, then the fund could start buying the currency from other countries. That would put upward pressure on the value of the currency and force the exchange market back toward equilibrium.

When Keynes read the amended White Plan, he was gobsmacked. Surely, he thought, the Americans had failed to understand their own proposal. It was "a half-baked suggestion, not fully thought through, which was certain to be dropped as soon as its full consequences were appreciated." He worried particularly that "Harry White has put a quick one across the State Department and that the real significance of this provision has escaped notice." Once officials in the State Department figured it out, he feared they would kill it.[26]

Keynes was brought around gradually to a greater acceptance by the enthusiastic arguments of his friend Roy Harrod. On March 2, 1943, Harrod took a midnight train from London's Paddington Station to Oxford. He had just obtained the latest redraft of the White Plan. His copy had been printed by the British Treasury on flimsy paper with single-space type on both sides of the sheet. The light on the train was dim, the train was crowded with soldiers on leave, and Harrod struggled to read the document and to make sense of Harry's difficult prose. When he got to the newly introduced scarce currency clause, he was "transfixed":

> This, then, was the big thing. For years we had complained of the United States' attitude as a creditor. . . . Now they had come forward and offered a solution of their own, gratuitously. . . . They had said in a document . . . that they would . . . accept their full share of responsibility when there was a fundamental disequilibrium of trade. As I sat huddled in my corner, I felt an exhilaration such as only comes once or twice in a lifetime. There were the disheveled soldiers sprawling over one another in sleep; and here was I, tightly pressed into my corner, holding these little flimsy sheets. One had the urge to wake them all up.[27]

Fortunately for his own safety, Harrod resisted the urge to wake the exhausted soldiers, but upon reaching Oxford around two o'clock in the morning, he wrote immediately to Keynes to convey his wonder and enthusiasm. After some reflection, Keynes had to admit that Harry had found a way to ensure that creditor countries would have to shoulder some of the burden of adjustment if trade imbalances became large and persistent. Indeed, the scarce currency clause seemed to make the White Plan much more palatable. "Without this provision the logic of the whole scheme breaks down," Keynes wrote in April.[28]

In the end, events proved to Keynes that the clause was a serious offer from the U.S. side. It survived intact in the IMF Articles of Agreement that were approved at Bretton Woods.[29] Although the clause was never invoked, it stood there in the Articles like a boarding-school teacher with a ruler ready to smack an unruly hand.

Although neither man liked the other's plan, Keynes and White both were determined to develop a common proposal. Even so, they had incompatible tactics in mind. Keynes was convinced that the only practical way forward was for the two countries' teams to work together and develop a document that they could present jointly to the rest of the alliance. Harry was convinced that cooking up and serving an Anglo-American plan would alienate everyone else and would create an unacceptable risk of ultimate failure. The American team therefore had to keep working with the British to develop a joint proposal while they simultaneously began to meet with officials from other countries to incorporate their views into the White Plan. Harry's hope must have been that he could drag out the bilateral negotiations with the British long enough to get everyone else on board. Keynes could only wail in frustration. "Is Harry White giving any sign of life?" he wrote to Phillips in December, without receiving any encouragement in return.[30]

Keynes was confused, and that led later chroniclers down a rabbit hole. Armand Van Dormael's generally authoritative account of the negotiations asserted incorrectly, "After the meeting with Keynes in London, Harry White disappeared from the scene for several months, and the conversations were carried on in the State Department."[31]

Harry, of course, was full of life but was moving the process toward multilateral discussions. On January 23, 1943, Harry got approval from Under Secretary Daniel W. Bell to begin sounding out other countries on the idea of holding a multilateral conference aimed at establishing an international stabilization fund. By the end of April, Harry had held meetings only with Canada and the Netherlands but had sent requests to thirty-two other countries. Of those, fifteen planned to send delegations soon, and in fact an Australian delegation arrived in mid-May. Eight other countries had expressed interest in the proposal. Nine had not yet replied. In addition, the Soviet Union had not responded to communications extended through the State Department. By the end of May, however, Harry received a positive reply from Andrei Gromyko (then chargé d'affaires at the Soviet embassy in Washington), stating that his country was "definitely interested" and had delayed responding owing to a misunderstanding.[32]

The two competing plans were now entering the public consciousness and being debated in the news media. In the United States, Morgenthau announced the existence of the White Plan in a news conference on April 1. On instructions from Roosevelt, he did not make the details of the plan public right away, but he presented the plan to three congressional committees a few days later.[33] The *New York Times* published the full text of the White Plan on April 7. *Time* magazine ran prominent stories about both the Keynes and White plans later that month. The *Time* article on the White Plan was accompanied by a photo of Harry (dubbed "Planner White"), pointer in hand, apparently explaining his proposals in front of a large display of statistical charts. A few weeks later, on May 18, Keynes made his maiden speech in the British House of Lords, which he used to make the case for his own plan while praising the competing efforts of Morgenthau and White. Critics, noted Lord Keynes, "have overstated the differences between the two plans, plans which are born of the same climate and which have identical purpose."[34]

Harry's outreach soon resulted in the first large-scale technical meeting in Washington, at which representatives of eighteen countries participated, along with a sizable U.S delegation. Many of the foreign delegates were already in the vicinity, having just participated in a forty-four-nation conference on food and agricultural security at the Homestead Resort in Hot Springs, Virginia. Thus, the Treasury was able to convene an informal but good-sized meeting in Washington on short notice.

The meeting, with Harry in the chair, lasted three days, June 15–17, 1943. It was held in a large room on the third floor of the Treasury, as more than fifty participants faced each other around a U-shaped table. According to one British delegate, Lionel Robbins, the arrangement was crowded and chaotic and plagued by "dreadful acoustics." At the head of the table, "Harry White, who has a very resonant and penetrating voice, shouted all day like a man directing the movements of a ship without a rudder in a hurricane. No doubt at the back of the room his voice sounded just right."[35]

The goal of the meeting was to begin the delicate process of trying to shape the proposal for an international financial agency into a form that would satisfy each country's interests—or at least would not work against whatever was most important to it—while retaining its essential structure and its appeal to the U.S. government, which would be its principal financier. Harry had prepared the agenda by circulating a preliminary draft of the White Plan for an international stabilization fund, and a list of ten questions to all the potential participants. Almost everything about the proposed fund, it seemed, was up for discussion. How big should quotas be? Should silver play a role? How should initial exchange rates be determined? Should countries be allowed to change exchange rates without approval from the fund? How should "excessive credit balances" be constrained? How should voting rights be apportioned? The question-naire focused on the White Plan, but it was accompanied by a copy of the Keynes Plan for an international clearing union that had been published in April. Separately, the Canadian delegation circulated its own plan.[36]

Correspondence and bilateral conferences before the June 15 meeting had generated more than eighty questions and suggestions for amending the White Plan. Ten countries made suggestions: Australia, Belgium, Bra-zil, Canada, Czechoslovakia, Mexico, the Netherlands, Norway, the Phil-ippines, and the United Kingdom. Several other countries seem to have come more to listen than to argue for amendments: no suggestions were submitted by China, Ecuador, Egypt, Luxembourg, Paraguay, Poland, the Soviet Union, or Venezuela.

The Soviets were particularly reticent. They apparently decided to attend the meetings only at the last minute, as their lone delegate's sur-name—a Mr. Tepliakov—was just penciled in on the provisional list. The minutes contain no record of his speaking at all during the group meeting, though he and Gromyko met separately with Harry on June 16.[37] The delegate was most likely Valentin F. Tepliakov, who later served as a Soviet official at the United Nations, including a position on the commission that drafted the Universal Declaration of Human Rights in 1947. He had no further involvement in the discussions leading to the creation of the IMF and World Bank.

Some of the suggestions at the June meeting aimed to fill in gaps that the plan had neglected. The Czech delegation, for example, suggested that the base period for determining quotas should be updated every five years. Some aimed to redirect the proposal toward specific national interests. The Norwegians, for example, wanted the quota formula to take account of shipping services as a component of foreign trade, since that would in-crease their borrowing rights. Similarly, Mexico (a major silver producer) was keen to introduce a role for silver alongside gold. A few suggestions conveyed a surface appeal but would eventually prove to be impractical. Mexico, for example, proposed that disputes about exchange rates be-tween a country and the technical staff of the fund should be resolved by an external committee of experts, "selected from a list of economists of world-wide reputation."

The most important suggestions for modifying the White Plan came from Canada. That might seem surprising, given Canada's small economic size. In this instance, its significance in the proceedings was partly due to the intervention of one man: Louis Rasminsky, a senior official in the Bank of Canada (later its governor). Rasminsky had worked in the economics section at the League of Nations in Geneva throughout the 1930s and was thoroughly steeped in the issues that the White and Keynes plans were addressing. When he saw the White Plan in March 1943, he judged correctly that it had the better chance of the two to be adopted, but also that its chances would rise if it was tweaked to be more palatable to the British and other potential borrowers. He quickly drafted an alternative proposal for what he called an international exchange union and circulated it to other Canadian officials on March 24, 1943.[38]

Some four weeks later, Rasminsky and a few colleagues went to Washington for five days of meetings with Harry and his staff at the Treasury.[39] They argued principally for four amendments to the White Plan, and they were successful on two of the four arguments. First, they wanted a larger fund than the figure in the latest U.S. proposal. Harry had pared his original suggestion of $5 to $10 billion down to the bottom of that range, and Rasminsky successfully urged him to raise it to $8 billion. Second, they wanted more exchange-rate flexibility than was in the White Plan. The Canadian view was that countries should be able to adjust rates by modest amounts without first seeking the approval of the fund. That suggestion made it into the plan and eventually into the IMF Articles of Agreement, which allowed for unchallenged changes of up to 10 percent.

Less successfully, the Canadian team argued for generalizing the fund's powers to borrow from financial markets. Harry was proposing to allow the fund to borrow if necessary to shore up its assets, while the Canadian team thought it would be better to borrow regularly so that the fund could do more lending. The original backup proposal remained in the plan. The Canadians also wanted to eliminate most of the provisions in the plan that would give the United States an effective veto over major decisions. Those provisions, though, were an essential part of Harry's strategy for persuading Congress that the fund would not threaten U.S. monetary sovereignty and would leave the country in charge of how its gold and currency reserves would be used.

More generally, the Canadian plan aimed to bridge the gap between the White and Keynes plans. Canada was especially well placed for that ambition. It was allied with the United Kingdom as a member of the Commonwealth and with the United States as its contiguous northern neighbor. It was trusted by both sides as an unbiased and nonthreatening intermediary. Rasminsky and his team just wanted to be sure that the two dominant countries did not fall out over the details and that some sort of plan for international monetary cooperation would be approved and put into action. Nonetheless, their intervention nearly backfired. Keynes resented the fact that the Canadian plan was essentially an amendment of the White Plan and paid little attention to the structure of his own efforts. The British promptly dubbed Rasminsky's proposals "off-White" and paid them little overt respect. They knew, however, that the Keynes Plan was going to face a difficult uphill climb if it lacked Canadian support.

Sometime after Rasminsky's meetings in Washington, Dennis H. Robertson—a senior adviser at the British Treasury, one of Keynes's close confidants, and a distinguished economist—wrote a note for internal discussion in which he practically ceded the stage to the emerging North American view. "My own impression of the present situation is that the tide of events, especially as embodied in the outlook of the very compact and able Canadian team, is carrying us strongly in the direction of" accepting the structure ["*differentia*," in his phrasing] of the White Plan for a fund without the power to create money. He had, as yet, "no intention of lowering the [clearing union] flag," but he clearly saw the end of the battle.[40]

Keynes did not go to Washington for the meetings in June 1943. Frederick Phillips headed the four-man British delegation, and the other three were all close associates of Keynes: Redvers Opie, Lionel Robbins, and Dennis Robertson. Although they tried valiantly to keep the structure of the Keynes Plan alive as an alternative, they had no discernible success in interesting other countries in it. Perhaps the problem was merely that the meetings were taking place in the U.S. Treasury and were being chaired effectively by Harry. Perhaps it was because Rasminsky and his Canadian colleagues were clearly in the American camp. Perhaps it was because the various delegations were persuaded that such a Fund could succeed only if the U.S. government was fully behind it. Or perhaps most delegates simply preferred the U.S. plan. It is most likely that these influences came together to form an irresistible force.[41]

Keynes probably realized as early as April 1943 that his own plan was doomed. In a letter to Harrod that month, he wrote, "I fully expect that we shall do well to compromise with the American scheme and very likely accept their dress in the long run."[42] The meetings in June then turned out to be decisive. Within days, Keynes threw in the towel. To prepare for further internal discussions in London, he drafted a note that began:

> We accept the substance of White's essential conditions, namely:—
> (i) We agree to the subscription principle;
> (ii) We agree to the limitation of liability;
> (iii) We agree that no country shall be required to change the gold value of its currency against its will.
> We also accept the U.S. formula for quotas and voting power, and the general shape of [White's stabilization fund]. We are prepared to agree, as a condition of the scheme, that the initial exchange rate between pound and dollar shall be £1 = $4.[43]

In public Keynes's associates continued for a time to pretend that the clearing union was still an active option. On August 26, 1943, Dennis Robertson gave a speech in Chicago, at a conference organized by the Federal Reserve Bank of Chicago that Harry also attended, in which he made a case for acceptance of the essential features of the British plan: establishment of an international currency, loans in the form of overdrafts, and unconditional access to credits.[44] Behind the public scene, negotiations would continue for another year, but the debate would be over how to modify the White Plan to make it clearer and more palatable. The end result would be presented as a "synthesis" of the two plans, but the structure of the outcome—the architecture and the scaffolding—would be almost entirely American.

CHAPTER ELEVEN

The Path to Bretton Woods, 1943–44

Prosperity, like peace, is indivisible.

—White Plan, April 1942

THE DOMINANCE OF THE White Plan over the Keynes Plan and the unveiling of the proposal to create new global institutions brought Harry into the media glare for the first time. This formerly obscure federal bureaucrat began to get serious public attention, which was generally admiring.

In April 1944 a profile in the *Boston Globe* noted that he "is affable, never gets sore and has fun . . . except when someone bothers him on Sunday. But he'll spare a little time from his only lazy day to look over his wife's manuscript for the children's books she writes, or to swap wisecracks with his two children."[1] Similarly, a profile in *Newsweek* after the Bretton Woods conference described Harry as a "taker-over" who knew how to get a job done efficiently. It opened with an anecdote about Harry earlier in his life having suddenly stopped his car and "jumped out" while passing through a small town in California because he had spotted a house on fire. He took charge of the effort to save belongings and extinguish the fire and then drove on. Years later at Bretton Woods, the story continued, friends had to force Harry to relax a bit during the conference. They "lured him to the foot of Mount Washington for a wiener roast and then refused to take him back to the conference until after a rest. Once he was sure he could not get back to the hotel, White unbent. He sang barbershop harmony. He danced on the grass. Finally he 'took over' the picnic."[2]

As this anecdote suggests, Harry's natural persona gravitated toward work over relaxation. He could be nudged, but he still had an inner need to take control, and his responsibilities in trying to create a system of global finance seem to have intensified this trait. Even when dealing with mundane family matters at home during the war, he had trouble shedding the cloak of responsibility and control that he wore in the office.

In March 1944, while Harry was immersed in preparations for the Bretton Woods conference, he found time to vent his frustration at what seemed to him to be onerous demands that the Bethesda–Chevy Chase High School was imposing on his daughter Joan, who was then in ninth grade. Given the opportunity to write a "parents' comment" to the school on Joan's report card, he lashed out:

> Why can't the students be permitted one or two periods a day for study periods? Much too much homework is being assigned! You teachers have apparently a distorted perspective of the proper role of algebra, Latin, French, etc. in the life of a growing girl. School hours are too long. Joan leaves home at 8:30 A.M. and returns after 4 P.M. Music, helping with housework (this is *war time*), leaves only evenings for study. She always has from 3 to 4 hours homework. When is she supposed to play, read, and take care of the personal duties a girl of fourteen must fulfill? And when is she to have time to converse with her parents, write letters, go to movies, visit friends, and go shopping? I wonder if your principal is at all aware of trends in modern education, or of the requirements of modern life for adolescents. [Signed] HDW, March 20, 1944.[3]

In his great task at work, however, Harry had to overcome more obstacles before he could fully take control. Winning the battle against the Keynes Plan was only the beginning.

By mid-1943 Harry was making solid progress in winning support for his proposed stabilization fund and world bank. The remaining tasks— aimed at ultimately winning approval and getting the institutions established—were still daunting. First, he had to work closely with the British team to forge a consensus. Second, he had to continue negotiations with other countries to incorporate their interests wherever possible. Third, he had to persuade a skeptical public in the United States that global cooperation was in the country's interest. And fourth, he had to reach out to the U.S. Congress, which in the end would hold the keys to success.

Consensus with Great Britain

Of these four tasks, forging consensus for a synthesis with the British was the most straightforward. Partly this was because the two teams had been interacting already for almost a year, and the successive drafts of the White Plan had become more palatable to Keynes and his colleagues. Partly it was because the whole scheme, whatever its remaining problems might be, was very much in the British interest. Keynes certainly preferred his own plan, which would serve his country's interests even better and would salve his and his country's loss of pride in the wake of American ascendency, but he was not about to let the best be the enemy of the good.

The crucial set of meetings for developing a joint plan took place in Washington from September 13 through October 11, 1943. There were seven formal meetings between the U.S. and British teams, of which six were chaired by White. He was ill at the time of one meeting, which was chaired by Assistant Secretary of State Adolf Berle, and Edward Bernstein served as the senior Treasury representative.[4]

This was the fourth occasion on which Keynes and White had met, dating back to Harry's 1935 trip to London, but it was the first opportunity for extensive face-to-face discussions. Over the course of that month, the two men met either alone or accompanied by their colleagues at least fourteen times to discuss issues related to the design of the proposed fund and bank.

Much has been written about the relationship between Keynes and White, most of which has focused on the immense differences in background, character, and interests, specifically on Keynes's intellectual and cultural superiority to his allegedly brash and crude American counterpart. Such assessments paint an incomplete portrait of a complex relationship (fig. 13).

Keynes's first biographer, Roy Harrod, drew a benign and friendly picture of the relationship. He explicitly denied, on firsthand experience, that Keynes had "no love" for Harry. He also offered a comparable denial of White's supposed dislike for Keynes, which was based on the testimony of "those close to White" with whom he had spoken. Keynes's most recent biographer, Robert Skidelsky, dismisses much of Harrod's testimony

Fig. 13. *Harry enjoying a light moment with Keynes at Bretton Woods, July 1944. International Monetary Fund*

as the hagiography of a devoted acolyte. Skidelsky is not wrong in that general assessment, but in this instance Harrod's account has credibility because it is impartial as well as informed by proximity. Harrod noted that the relationship was "unbalanced" because White represented the superior economic power while Keynes possessed the greater intellect. He found that White had "revered Keynes as the greatest living economist" but had come to view him in more human terms once they began their regular meetings. He quotes White as saying to colleagues, "Don't let that clever fellow throw dust in your eyes," and as casting "doubt on Keynes's motives." Despite the occasional "air of belligerency," though, "they ultimately became great cronies, going off to the baseball game together and having plenty of fun."[5]

The mention of "going off to the baseball game" refers to an incident in Washington, when White took Keynes to a game (probably a Washington Senators' home game) to introduce him to what was then considered the American national pastime. Later, during their time together at the Bretton Woods conference, Harry apparently persuaded the great man to watch a volleyball match that he had organized between the U.S. and Soviet delegations.

We know little about Harry's opinion of Keynes because he seldom expressed it in any form that has been preserved. After his initial trip to London in May 1935, he wrote to his wife, Anne, that "two of the most interesting meetings I've had have been with Keynes and Laski! I'll tell you about them."[6] That Harry found Keynes "interesting" is neither surprising nor informative, and unfortunately Harry chose to convey his more substantive reactions orally when he returned to Washington rather than writing them down.

Harry's mention of Harold Laski is also interesting because Laski was a prominent political scientist. During the Great Depression, Laski was promoting Marxism as an alternative economic system, but he was much admired on the political left for his broader views of economic policy. Bruce Craig interpreted Harry's apparent admiration for Laski as evidence of admiration for the Soviet Union, but the truth is elusive. Harry's respect was not blind, and it was shared by other prominent thinkers. In August 1943 Anne wrote to her daughters that she and Harry had "been reading Harold Laski's new book, 'Reflections on the Revolution of Our Time.' He has some fine things to say and some stupid ones." In 1947 Albert Einstein unsuccessfully proposed Laski to be the first president of Brandeis University.[7]

In May 1944, almost a decade after that initial meeting, by which time White and Keynes had become much better acquainted through numerous meetings in London and Washington, President Roosevelt (who had met Keynes earlier, in 1934 and 1941) asked Harry if the great man was being "friendly." Harry (never a man for a one-word answer) "replied that Keynes was an extremely able and tough negotiator with, of course, a thorough understanding of the problems that confronted us, but when not negotiating or discussing points of differences that he was quite friendly."[8] Otherwise, Harry seems to have kept his personal opinions to himself.

Keynes often expressed frustration and irritation over his interactions with Harry and other American negotiators. His most complete assessment of Harry was given in a letter to Sir Wilfrid Eady (second secretary in the U.K. Treasury) during the extended meetings in Washington in the fall of 1943. He expressed respect and fondness for Harry, but he also described him as what one might call a borderline sociopath.

> Any reserves we may have about him are a pale reflection of what his colleagues feel. He is over-bearing, a bad colleague, always trying to bounce you, with harsh rasping voice, aesthetically oppressive in mind and manner; he has not the faintest conception how to behave or observe the rules of civilised discourse. At the same time, I have a great respect and even liking for him. In many respects he is the best man here. A very able and devoted public servant, carrying an immense burden of responsibility and initiative, of high integrity and of clear sighted idealistic international purpose, genuinely intending to do his best for the world. Moreover, his over-powering will combined with the fact that he has constructive ideas mean that he does get things done, which few else here do. He is not open to flattery in any crude sense. The way to reach him is to respect his purpose, arouse his intellectual interest (it is a great softener to intercourse that it is easy to arouse his genuine interest in the merits of any issue) and to tell him off very frankly and firmly without finesse when he has gone off the rails of relevant argument or appropriate behaviour.[9]

One should not, however, take the negative elements of Keynes's assessment at face value. The insults essentially reflected the widespread contempt of the British upper classes for their supposedly cruder cousins across the Atlantic. He may also have been influenced by his own well-known anti-Semitism. In another, nastier, letter to Eady written the same day and dripping with sarcastic disdain, he hazarded the guess that White's deputy, Edward M. ("Eddie") Bernstein, was the real force behind what he viewed as the overly complicated drafting of the U.S. proposals:

> Both the currency scheme [the IMF] and the investment scheme [the World Bank] are, I think, largely the fruit of the brain not of Harry but of his little attaché, Bernstein. It is with him rather than Harry that the pride of authorship lies. And when we seduce Harry from the true faith, little Bernstein wins him back again in the course of the night. Bernstein is a regular little rabbi, a reader out of the Talmud, to Harry's grand political high rabbidom. He

is very clever and rather sweet, but knows absolutely nothing outside the turns and twists of his own mind. There is, as I have expressed it, a very high degree of endogamy between his ideas. The
chap knows every rat run in his local ghetto, but it is difficult to
persuade him to come out for a walk with us on the high ways of
the world.[10]

What is clear is that, despite their differences, Keynes and White
bonded personally through the whole process of negotiating both bilateral financial aid to Britain and the establishment of the Bretton Woods
institutions. As Keynes was preparing to leave London for Atlantic City,
New Jersey, for the meetings of the drafting committee that preceded the
Bretton Woods conference, he wrote skeptically of Harry's plans for both
sets of meetings. "Dr White's conception of all this seems to get 'curiouser
and curiouser.' . . . [The delegates at Bretton Woods] are not even to have
the semblance of doing any work, since that is to be done before they
meet. . . . It would seem probable that acute alcohol poisoning would set in
before the end." A month later, however, at the conclusion of the Atlantic
City meetings, Keynes wrote approvingly of the process and its results.
"White has proved an altogether admirable chairman. His kindness to me
personally has been extreme. And behind the scenes he has always been
out to find a way of agreement except when his own political difficulties
stood in the way."[11]

In post–Bretton Woods correspondence, they addressed each other
with the salutations "Dear Maynard" and "my dear Harry." Keynes further
showed his affection by sending Harry a copy of a recently published history of the Bank of England, "in memory and token of our collaboration
at Bretton Woods." Later, he sent him a cartoon that mocked himself. In
the months leading up to the inaugural meeting of the IMF and World
Bank governors in 1946, even after President Truman had named Harry
to be the U.S. executive director at the IMF, Keynes lobbied for him to
be nominated also to the higher post of managing director of the IMF. In
return, Harry's sympathy note to Lady Keynes, expressing his "deep personal loss" on learning of her husband's death in April 1946, was no doubt
genuinely felt.

In the fall of 1943, the development of this relationship was still in an
early stage, but Keynes and White were already collegial. One issue on
which they differed strongly but were eager to find a compromise was the
timing of extending discussions beyond their two countries. Harry wanted

to engage at least all four members of the Grand Alliance. On July 24, 1943, he wrote to Keynes, concluding, "If we can secure prior agreement on the basic points *among the four major powers*, I believe that a formal conference would have little difficulty formulating a document that had a good chance of being accepted by Congress."[12] Keynes, however, had no interest in engaging either the Chinese or the Russians at this point in the effort.

After several meetings of their two delegations that left this and other items unresolved, Keynes proposed a way forward. Meeting privately with Harry before a general meeting of the delegations on October 6, he suggested that they "prepare a draft setting forth the principles which we have agreed upon. This draft would be the basis for discussion in each country."[13] Harry had hoped that such a document would emerge only after wider consultation with more countries, but he now agreed to accept Keynes's plan.

Another central issue dividing the American and British negotiating teams was the operational role of "unitas" (Harry's term for a new international currency unit). Harry was arguing that the fund should deal only in gold and national currencies. Otherwise, it might appear that the United States was tying the dollar to an international currency in amounts that it could not control. Economists at the U.S. Federal Reserve Board were worried about losing control over the U.S. money supply, and Harry was also eager to avoid trying to explain the matter to Congress. In Harry's conception, unitas could be a useful yardstick for measuring the fund's accounts, but he was adamantly opposed to using it in fund operations as an international currency. Keynes objected just as strongly to having the fund rely on holding and lending gold and currencies, which he feared would make it too dependent on the U.S. dollar and too much like the gold standard that he had been railing against for two decades. In addition, just as Harry had to worry about reactions in Congress and the Federal Reserve, Keynes had to worry about reactions in the Cabinet and the Bank of England. "Certainly this is the biggest snag so far as our Cabinet directive is concerned," he wrote to Eady from Washington on October 3.[14]

The oddity in this debate was that by the autumn of 1943, the role of unitas no longer had much practical significance. Keynes had already conceded that the fund would consist of gold and currencies deposited by member countries, rather than issuing its own assets in the form of overdrafts. He just wanted the fund to lend an international currency backed by those assets (which Eady and Keynes were calling "monetised unitas") rather than lending the "mixed bag" of the assets directly.

In addition, many people were still spending time and energy agonizing over what to call such an asset. Unitas and bancor were the leading but not the only coinages being discussed. Jacob Viner suggested "mondor," suggestive of a global gold standard. Less seriously, Dennis Robertson, one of the wittiest of British economists, suggested either "Unicorn" or "Winfranks," the latter being a portmanteau of Winston (Churchill) and Franklin (Roosevelt). The ever-diplomatic Canadians just called it "the Unit" in their June 1943 plan. Regardless of name, the functions of the currency unit were going to be strictly limited.[15]

Despite his misgivings, Keynes agreed to draft a statement of principles without an operational function for unitas as a "generalized currency." As a caveat, he warned that this procedure was contrary to his instructions from London and that "it must not be taken as committing London to its acceptance."[16] Even within the British team, however, enthusiasm for the unitas scheme was waning. The Cambridge economist James Meade (Nobel laureate in 1977) warned Keynes that "in insisting on the monetisation of Unitas . . . we are fighting for a shadow instead of for the substance. . . . If we were to break on this point, we should indeed be criminally foolish."[17]

Keynes quickly drafted a statement of principles, the U.S. team made some redrafts, and on October 9 the two teams had a joint draft that they were prepared to begin discussing with other countries. Harry told Vice President Wallace a few months later that the final product was to be a "compromise" with the British, "but perhaps a little bit more like the American plan."[18] That assessment, however, was more diplomatic tact than accurate assessment. As we saw in chapter 10, little of Keynes's original conception remained at that stage.

The American and British teams continued to revise the joint statement repeatedly over the next few months, while discussions took place more widely with delegations from other countries. In March 1944 White told a delegate from China that the use of unitas "was now merely one of terminology, the British wanting to satisfy British public opinion."[19] The final version of the Joint Statement by Experts on the Establishment of an International Monetary Fund was published in April 1944. By that time, unitas had disappeared altogether. Keynes took it out of his final draft, and it passed unmourned on both sides of the Atlantic. As we shall see in the next chapter, however, its removal did cause problems later.

Winning Over the Other Major Powers

For the second task, Harry and his colleagues continued to meet with delegations from other countries simultaneously with their discussions with the British. Several delegations sought to insert provisions that would be favorable to their own countries or would be consistent with their views of monetary relations.[20] The roles of gold and silver were raised in numerous meetings, mostly by countries that were major producers or holders of the metals. France, which held much affection for the stability allegedly associated with the classic gold standard, issued its own plan in May 1943 based in large part on the 1936 Tripartite Agreement among France, Britain, and the United States. The delegation from the Soviet Union expressed concerns about the amount of information it might be compelled to provide, including that about its gold production and holdings. In each case, Harry was able to deal with these proposals and concerns by offering repeated and detailed explanations of what was already in his plan and the Joint Statement or by making minor adjustments to the drafts in progress. In no case did any country threaten to boycott the proceedings because its concerns were not being met.

In theory, the most important meetings were to be with China and the Soviet Union, because those two countries and Britain and the United States constituted the Grand Alliance and were generally considered the "four great powers" in the war effort. In practice, neither country showed much interest in the overall design. Neither country had any major input in the text of the Joint Statement, but both delegations agreed to support it.

Harry and other Treasury officials met regularly with Chinese officials throughout 1943 and 1944, primarily to discuss loans and other bilateral issues. Postwar planning was a secondary issue for the Chinese, but they wanted to ensure that they would have a seat on the "executive committee" (which became the Executive Board) that would manage the operations of the IMF. Accordingly, the Joint Statement declared that the "committee shall consist of at least nine members including representatives of the five countries with the largest quotas." (The inclusion of a fifth country in the assured list was intended to pull in France as well as the four great powers.)

The Soviet Union was initially even less interested in the planning, but in January 1944 it finally sent a delegation from Moscow. That delegation, headed by Nicolai V. Chechulin (deputy head of the central bank), held at least fourteen meetings with Harry's Treasury team over the next few months. They appear to have been interested mainly in hearing what was going on and ensuring that the proposed institutions would be compatible with the Soviet system of central planning and international barter. These meetings resulted in the insertion of several provisions in the Joint Statement to satisfy Soviet concerns about data provision and the integrity of its bilateral arrangements with neighboring countries.[21]

By the time the Joint Statement was published, Harry's team at the Treasury had discussed it in draft form with all the countries that were to be invited to the formal conference at which the charters of the IMF and World Bank were to be put in final form. From that point on, the charters would have to be drafted consistently with the principles in the Joint Statement. Because all participants had been consulted, and because they all would have the opportunity to help draft the final documents, they all would be expected to abide by that simple but powerful rule.

Persuading the American Public

Harry's third front was public opinion in the United States. The proposal to create new international institutions, funded largely by the United States, had the potential to generate a groundswell of opposition. Memories of the Great Depression were still vivid, an immensely costly world war was still under way, and the economic future was highly uncertain. The Roosevelt administration was vigorously and publicly committed to a policy of openness. Harry's slogan that "prosperity, like peace, is indivisible" had become a rallying cry for postwar planning, but bringing the public along on this ride was not going to be easy.

The Republican Party was still in the minority but had gained large numbers of seats in the House and Senate in the 1942 elections. At least some of their number were bound to oppose proposals to move toward more open trade and finance. The 1944 Republican Party platform, while expressing favor for "a great extension of world trade" after the war, promised to "establish and maintain a fair protective tariff on competitive products." The U.S. Chamber of Commerce and the American Bankers Association were also expected to oppose the proposals and lobby against them. In late April 1943 the chairman of Chase National Bank in New York gave a speech to a meeting of the International Chamber of Commerce. He summarized the Keynes and White plans that had just been published and suggested that they both had shortcomings and were, in his view, unlikely to be implemented. He concluded that a better solution would be to reestablish a dollar-based gold standard along with further reductions in trade barriers.[22]

To forestall such criticisms, Harry initiated a public relations campaign to explain the complex and controversial proposals to influential groups in the United States. In January 1943 he presented a paper, "Postwar Currency Stabilization," at the annual meeting of the American Economic Association in Washington. In March the association published the paper in its flagship journal, the *American Economic Review*. Harry continued with a speech to the Council on Foreign Relations in New York City on April 30, 1943. In August he spoke to the same meeting of bankers in Chicago at which Dennis Robertson made his last-ditch effort to save the Keynes Plan. For the next few months, while Harry was preoccupied with his meetings with the British and other country delegations, he dispatched other senior staff—principally his deputy, Eddie Bernstein—to speak on his behalf. In October Eddie gave at least three speeches about the proposed stabilization fund to groups of bankers and business leaders in New York and Philadelphia.

In December 1943 Harry gave a seminar on the fund at his alma mater, Harvard University. In early January 1944 he made the case to a prominent group of labor union leaders. More broadly, he began holding press conferences to explain the proposals to journalists. Eddie and two other Treasury officials met on Harry's behalf with Walter Lippmann, the *New York Herald Tribune* columnist who was then one of the most influential political commentators in the country. By the spring of 1944, when planning for the Bretton Woods conference was under way, the White Plan and its offspring, the Joint Statement, were being regularly covered in the major newspapers and magazines.

Another element of the outreach was to ensure that all the relevant federal agencies were included. Although the substantive work was centered in the Treasury, Roosevelt assigned the task of organizing and running the conference to the State Department. The large U.S. delegation and secretariat at Bretton Woods included—in addition to Treasury and State Department officials—representatives of the White House Executive Office, the Department of Agriculture, the Department of Commerce, the Department of Labor, the War Department, the Office of Economic Stabilization, the Foreign Economic Administration, the Federal Reserve Board, regional Federal Reserve Banks, the Export-Import Bank, the Securities and Exchange Commission, and the Bureau of the Budget, as well as members of Congress, commercial bankers, and academics.[23]

At Bretton Woods, Harry held regular press conferences to explain the plan. At the first meeting, on July 2, journalists were particularly keen to sort out the relationship between the British and American schemes. Harry went to some length to explain that his plan emerged from U.S. history, institutions, and interests, independently from the British. With an exaggeration that revealed a measure of defensiveness, he asserted that "we did not hear of the Keynes plan until many months after ours had been formulated. . . . It has been said so often that the United States gets all its monetary ideas from Keynes that I thought you might like to know these plans are completely independent." He also averred hopefully that once American bankers had more time to review the results of the conference, they would have "a more sympathetic understanding of what we are trying to do."[24]

Forging a Majority in the U.S. Congress

The final preparatory task, the one that would determine whether the IMF and the World Bank would ever become real institutions with money and influence, was to build support for them by a majority in the U.S. Congress. The public outreach program would help build support, but more direct persuasion would also be needed. That effort, too, began in April 1943, when Secretary Morgenthau testified before six different congressional committees, three in the House of Representatives and three in the Senate.[25]

More testimony would follow, along with meetings with individual legislators. Meanwhile, Morgenthau determined that it would help to include a few members of Congress in the U.S. delegation at Bretton Woods. The House and Senate banking committees were expected to hold hearings after the conference in advance of introducing legislation to implement the expected agreements. The Senate Banking Committee was chaired by Robert F. Wagner, Democrat from New York. Its ranking minority member was Charles W. Tobey, Republican from New Hampshire. On the House side, the Committee on Banking and Currency was chaired by Brent Spence, Democrat from Kentucky. The ranking Republican was Jesse P. Wolcott, from Michigan. Roosevelt picked all four to be members of the U.S. delegation. The roles were cast.

Organizing the Conference

As the winter of 1943–44 drew to a close, preparations shifted from the outreach tasks to planning for and holding an international conference. For the U.S. government, inviting all the allied countries to participate in the drafting and approval of charters for an International Monetary Fund and an International Bank for Reconstruction and Development was now an urgent priority. Harry was eager to fix a venue and a date and get the invitations in the mail. He feared, though, that time was running out. He could not act until he got a final agreement with the British on the wording of the Joint Statement. He was almost there, but negotiations were dragging on, and delay could prove fatal.

The Republican convention to approve a party platform and nominate a candidate for president was scheduled to start on June 26. If the conference coincided with the convention, Republican opponents of the conference would be sure to attack. If the convention were to adopt a platform with a plank opposing the proposed institutions, it could tie the hands of some members of the U.S. delegation and scuttle the whole project. Harry desperately wanted his conference to start by the end of May and finish before the Republicans began their work.

On March 21, Harry sent a warning to Morgenthau that they needed to act soon. "We presume that it would be wholly unfeasible for a conference to be held any time between the Republican Convention and the election" in November, he wrote to the secretary. Any help in getting the British to sign off on the Joint Statement would be valuable.[26] He also had to overcome continuing opposition from the State Department, where officials would have been happier waiting until after the war to try to organize such a major endeavor.

On April 1 Harry and two colleagues—Eddie Bernstein and Ansel F. Luxford—went over to Foggy Bottom in response to a State Department request to discuss "whether a conference . . . should be held."[27] Dean Acheson, speaking for the State Department, opened the meeting by making the case once again for postponing. Harry's longtime critic at State, Leo Pasvolsky, weighed in, suggesting that such a conference might interfere with alternative schemes that were already under consideration in the U.S. Congress. A Republican congressman from Illinois, Charles S. Dewey Jr., was scheduling hearings on a plan to create a more limited institution called the Central Reconstruction Fund. Separately, three Democratic senators, including Harry S. Truman—the Missouri senator who would soon be picked by Roosevelt to be vice president in his fourth term—had introduced a resolution proposing an international conference on economic cooperation.[28] Another State Department official, Emilio G. Collado (who would later become the first U.S. executive director at the World Bank), worried that the Treasury proposal might interfere with efforts to get congressional approval for increased funding for the U.S. Export-Import Bank. The prevailing view at State seemed to be that all these alternatives should be given priority.

Harry pushed back hard. Postponement, he argued, might make it impossible ever to get agreement. The congressional proposals could proceed at their own pace, and the Exim Bank had enough money to continue for the time being. These arguments carried the day. Acheson declared himself persuaded, and he concluded that "it would be desirable to hold a conference before the conventions." An end-of-May opening date was beginning to look feasible.

Through the first half of April, Harry discussed plans with the British, the Soviets, and the Chinese. On April 17 he reached final agreement with the British on the Joint Statement. By then, however, the British team was convinced that it needed more time to get ready. Arranging safe transatlantic travel in the midst of the war raised logistic and diplomatic challenges. The conference therefore would have to start later than planned. That delay, in turn, gave rise to a new problem. Keynes pled with Harry not to make him spend the summer in Washington, with its oppressive (pre–air conditioning) heat and humidity. He had a serious heart condition and did not want to risk aggravating it. He made one last plea to hold the conference in London but asked—as a fallback position—that Harry pick "some pleasant resort in the Rocky Mountains."[29]

The crucial meeting for scheduling the conference was held at the White House on May 18. Morgenthau, White, and Ambassador Winant met with Roosevelt to get his approval. Morgenthau had abandoned hope for starting the conference before the Republican convention, and he now proposed to wait until July 6 to give the many foreign delegations time to make plans for their arrival. The president dismissed Harry's concern about the potential conflict with the Republican convention and suggested that holding the two events simultaneously might be amusing. "We ought to provide our guests with some entertainment," he suggested, to some laughter.[30]

The group also agreed not to hold the conference in Washington, but it did not settle on an alternative venue. Morgenthau mentioned that someone had suggested French Lick, Indiana, which had a large, historic hotel suitable for such a gathering, but he had concluded that it would be too hot there in the summer. Perhaps because Winant was from New Hampshire and was a former governor of the state, Roosevelt suggested Portsmouth, which had both a historic grand hotel (Wentworth by the Sea, at which the Treaty of Portsmouth, ending the Russo-Japanese War, had been negotiated and signed in 1905) and a naval base for security.

Around this time, the State Department considered several other sites, including the Roney Plaza Hotel in Miami Beach, Florida; the Claridge Hotel in Atlantic City, New Jersey (which had hosted the United Nations Relief and Rehabilitation Administration World Conference the previous November and which became the site for the preliminary financial meetings in June); the resort hotel in Poland Spring, Maine; and the Grand Union Hotel in Saratoga, New York. These and other alternatives were all deemed unsuitable, owing to summer heat and lack of air conditioning, a shortage of available accommodations, or policies discriminating against racial or religious minorities. Morgenthau reportedly was particularly concerned to avoid the use of a site with a history of discrimination against Jews.[31]

The next week was devoted to fixing plans for the conference. When the technicians investigated facilities in Portsmouth, they discovered that the resort hotel could not accommodate the gathering, which was now expected to draw in several hundred delegates and other participants. Elsewhere in New Hampshire, though, they located another grand but fading relic of the Gilded Age, the Mount Washington Hotel at Bretton Woods. It was available, and it was accessible via a nearby tiny railroad station. It would need a great deal of sprucing up over the next few weeks, but the organizers were optimistic enough to move the starting date of the conference forward again, to July 1. On May 25, Roosevelt agreed, and the stage was set.[32]

Getting Ready in Atlantic City

The decision to hold the conference at Bretton Woods left just over five weeks to prepare, and the effective lead time was even shorter. If the delegates from forty-four countries had to draft charters for the two new institutions with only the Joint Statement to guide them, the chances for success would be slim. Harry had therefore decided to host a preliminary drafting session with a much smaller group before the main conference. To give the State Department time to have the hotel at Bretton Woods prepared for a massive influx, he arranged for this preliminary meeting to be held at the seaside resort of Atlantic City, New Jersey.

Keynes was as unhappy with this plan as he was about most other aspects of the proceedings. In a May 1944 letter to his colleague David Walley, he expressed a fear that the meeting would be a "most monstrous monkey house" full of masses of inept and inarticulate people from all over the world.[33] That derisive "monkey-house" terminology had already been in use within the British delegation for at least a year. Another of Keynes's colleagues, Lionel Robbins, wrote in his diary during the June 1943 meeting of eighteen country delegations in Washington (discussed in chapter 10) that the meeting "was the real test of the monkey-house method. And in the absence of prior agreement between the US and the UK, it was obviously breaking down."[34] The method, of course, did not break down.

It would be much better, Keynes thought, to let the Anglo-American experts draft the documents and then bring everyone else in to approve and sign them. Harry was having none of this British exclusiveness. By June 15 he and much of the American team were encamped at the Claridge Hotel in Atlantic City. The team comprised two of the twelve official delegates (White and Edward E. "Ned" Brown, president of the First National Bank of Chicago and of the Federal Advisory Council of the Federal Reserve System), twenty-two economists and other technical experts, and a fourteen-member secretarial staff. Although the delegates from Great Britain and fourteen other countries would not be arriving until a week later, the U.S. team went straight to work.

The first week of work in Atlantic City was restricted to preliminary meetings, but Harry quickly found that the technical work was overwhelming. He was also being pestered to deal with logistic and public relations questions for Bretton Woods, and it was all too much. He asked Morgenthau to send two Treasury officials, M. Frederik (Fred) Smith and Charles Bell, to help with publicity and logistics, respectively. Morgenthau was also feeling work pressure building up in Washington because Harry was not in the office, but he reluctantly let them go. Bell went to Atlantic City for the first weekend and managed to convince the U.S. team to hold a Sunday afternoon meeting at the beach. Harry was reluctant, if only because he had not even brought a swimsuit. Bell loaned Harry his trunks, and the atmosphere lightened up a little for the moment.[35]

Keynes and other delegates did not set sail from Southampton, England, until June 16, having been held up by security concerns in the aftermath of the massive D-Day landings ten days earlier. The H.M.S. *Queen Mary* carried a sizable contingent in addition to the British delegation: Keynes's wife, Lydia; delegates from Belgium, China, Czechoslovakia, Greece, India, the Netherlands, and Norway; and Lauren W. Casaday, the U.S. Treasury representative at the embassy in London.[36] The group reached Atlantic City on June 23, several days after the Americans and representatives of other countries had begun work.

Once everyone was on hand, the formal proceedings began on June 24 with the election of Harry as chairman. The work ahead was still a little prodigious, even for him. "A three ring circus is tame compared to this sideshow. However, we're making progress," he wrote home to Anne on June 26. He was buoyed by the more important progress being reported from both the Western and Eastern Fronts in post–D-Day Europe. "Those Russians are sure pushing along," he told Anne optimistically. "It won't be long now." The bulk of his attention, however, was on the task at hand and the looming tasks that lay ahead at Bretton Woods. His letter to Anne continued:

> This conference is sure to be a humdinger. More troubles than you could think possible. So many more delegates than expected are coming, & rooms are so few that they'll have to put two ministers of finance in one room! or almost.
>
> The British delegation is a strong one, and so will be the Brazilian, Chinese, Indian, Dutch, and Canadian. Monteros [Antonio Espinosa de los Monteros, the head of the Bank of Mexico] is here and as usual is very helpful.
>
> Fred Smith just arrived, and said the Sec. [Morgenthau] is in a hell of a state. The bond drive arrangement did not go well, and he's tired and nervous and upset. It's going to be great at Bretton Woods. He's taking his wife along, I understand.[37]

In the end, all that the Atlantic City meeting achieved was to enable many of the delegates to meet and take the measure of one another and to catalogue the many points of disagreement or confusion. Early in the proceedings, the U.S. delegation circulated preliminary drafts of the IMF and World Bank Articles of Agreement, the former being keyed to the relevant points in the Joint Statement. As Harry had reported to Morgenthau on June 22: "No attempt is being made to get agreement on these drafts. We are concerned with clarifying questions and finding out where difficulties arise." The delegates were organized into specialized committees to discuss a list of twenty-one "unsettled questions." A "committee on agenda" prepared a draft plan for the Bretton Woods conference.[38] The real work lay just ahead.

CHAPTER TWELVE

The Bretton Woods Conference, 1944

England has . . . gone a long way toward our position, but . . . [she] cannot make too many [more] compromises. If she does, her Parliament will throw it out.

—Harry White at Bretton Woods

ON SATURDAY, JULY 1, 1944, more than seven hundred people from forty-five countries descended into a New Hampshire valley below Mount Washington and about four miles north of the Crawford Depot train station, where most of the delegates arrived. The crowd included 167 official delegates, nearly as many advisers and secretaries to the delegations, observers from international organizations, a large conference secretariat, other staff and hangers-on, and nearly one hundred accredited journalists.[1] Harry's fear that finance ministers would have to share rooms did not materialize, but many lower-ranking officials had to stay in other hotels at some distance from the Mount Washington.

The valley had once been part of a plantation granted by British King George III in 1772 to Sir Thomas Wentworth, who named it Bretton Woods after his Yorkshire estate, Bretton Hall. In the twentieth century, the name had survived only as a postal address, but it was about to become synonymous with international financial cooperation.

The Bretton Woods conference was destined to become one of the most celebrated and certainly the most studied financial events of the twentieth century. It was heavily covered on radio and in newspapers and magazines as it occurred, by the journalists who crowded around the once- and future-magnificent but then fading Mount Washington Hotel throughout the three weeks of meetings. Henry Morgenthau's speech concluding the conference was broadcast live across the United States directly from the hotel ballroom. Since then, countless articles and a great many books have been written about it and continue to be written. Whenever finance officials or even heads of government around the world appeal for reform of the financial system, they often call for a "new Bretton Woods."

An early indicator of how deeply rooted Bretton Woods became in the popular imagination may be found in a 1948 drama, *Ten Blocks on the Camino Real*, by the American playwright Tennessee Williams. In one scene in this one-act play, an American soldier named Kilroy (the generic name commonly used in that era to designate an ordinary soldier) is attempting to seduce the sultry and too easily seduced Latin American beauty, Esmeralda. As the scene progresses, the Bretton Woods conference makes a surprising appearance.

> *(Esmeralda curls up on the low divan . . . yawns, touching her lips delicately with a tiny handkerchief.)*
> KILROY: You don't talk much.
> ESMERALDA: You want me to talk?
> KILROY: Well, that's the way we do things in the States. A little vino, some records on the Victrola, some quiet conversation, and then if both parties are in a mood for romance . . . *(Gesture)*.
> ESMERALDA: Oh. . . . *(She rises indolently and pours some wine from a slender crystal decanter. Starts Victrola playing softly, "Quiereme Mucho." Returns to divan and strikes a voluptuous pose. . . . After a thoughtful pause)* They say that the monetary system has got to be stabilized all over the world.
> KILROY: *(Taking glass.)* Huh?
> ESMERALDA: It has to do with some kind of agreement which was made in the woods.
> KILROY: Oh.

The Bretton Woods conference was also the apotheosis of Harry White's career and is the main reason we should remember him today.

He had primary responsibility for the preparation, conduct, and follow-up to the conference, which ultimately became the only truly successful international monetary conference of the twentieth century. That work occupied him heavily from 1941 until the end of his Treasury career in 1946. Even so, he was never the star of the show.

As we saw in preceding chapters, Harry's role in the preparation and outcomes of the conference was overshadowed by the luminescence of John Maynard Keynes. At the conference itself, although Harry was chairman of Commission I, with responsibility for drafting the charter of the International Monetary Fund, he did not have the status of the other commission chairmen. The best suite at the Mount Washington Hotel, room 119, was reserved for Henry Morgenthau (chair of the U.S. delegation), his wife, Elinor, and their daughter, Joan. The next-best suite, room 219, directly above the Morgenthaus', was occupied by Lord Keynes (chair of the British delegation and of Commission II, with responsibility for the World Bank) and his wife, Lydia.

Years later, the hotel honored its most distinguished guests by placing brass plates on selected doors with the names of people who had stayed in those rooms. In the process, a workman mentally transposed the digits for suite 219 and placed the name of John Maynard Keynes on the undistinguished guest room 129, next door to rather than above the Morgenthau suite. The plate remained on the wrong door for many years, and Robert Skidelsky's biography of Keynes repeated the error.[2]

The lower suite, occupied by the Morgenthaus, was regarded as better because it avoided the need for taking the stairs or waiting for the small elevator down the hallway. It was, however, not without its drawbacks. According to John Morton Blum, "Morgenthau, whose room was just below Keynes's, later remembered most sharply the penetrating rhythm of the exercises of Lady Keynes, a *prima ballerina* who was unaware that her routine practicing could be heard through the ceiling beneath her."[3] The Keyneses' second-floor suite also had its drawbacks, and Lord Keynes slept mostly in another room (number 201) at the end of the corridor above the ballroom, because it was less drafty and had a working fireplace.

Eduardo Suárez (chair of the Mexican delegation and of Commission III, with responsibility for all other matters) had a large room on the third floor, number 331, with a fireplace and a view of the mountain. Harry was on his own and was assigned an ordinary guest room, number 131, down the hall from his boss.

Harry's life at Bretton Woods was a blur of activity. In addition to running Commission I and keeping tabs on all the other meetings that

Fig. 14. *Harry and Eddie Bernstein (center of middle row) at Bretton Woods, surrounded by a very motley crew. Family scrapbook, courtesy of Claire A. Pinkham*

took place simultaneously, he held a press conference almost every day at 3:00 P.M., often for forty or more journalists from news outlets around the world. Witnesses to those events described them as clear and lively expositions of the arcane topics under discussion, for which Harry seemed to draw on reserves of energy and intellect from his years of teaching at Harvard and Lawrence. As one reporter described it, "White, in his afternoon seminars, works up the enthusiasm of a professor, and frequently shakes his finger with the ejaculation, 'That's a very intelligent question. I'm glad it was asked,' etc. and then is off in high speed in a dissertation on the economic facts of international life."[4]

Harry did manage to relax occasionally (fig. 14), as when he organized volleyball and softball games, including a volleyball game between the U.S. and Soviet participants (which the Soviets won). Late in the evening, fueled by alcohol at the hotel's basement bar (generally known to the delegates as "Commission Four") and joined by polyglot delegates, he would sometimes lead rounds of drinking songs.[5] He almost certainly found time to go to a few of the movies that the hotel showed every night.

These occasional respites did little to relieve the strain, on Harry and many others. By the third week of the conference, Morgenthau became worried that the drive to finish by Wednesday, July 19, was affecting everyone's health and abilities. At a meeting with several heads of delegation, Keynes told Morgenthau that "several of my people . . . are quite breaking up under the strain." Harry admitted that the "night before last I blew up at one of Dean [Acheson]'s men and lost my temper. I rarely do that. It was just that I was very irritated." Others on his team were also getting "irritable and a little inefficient." He felt himself "cracking up," but he had forced himself to go to bed at ten o'clock the next night. On other days he had been getting along on some four hours of sleep, and he was still exhausted. Hearing these and other accounts, Morgenthau agreed to extend the proceedings by three days and wrap up on Saturday instead of Wednesday.[6]

On the last day of the conference, Harry pulled out a postcard with a painting of the hotel and the peaks of the White Mountains reproduced on the front. Turning it over, he penned a simple note to his daughters: "Joan and Kutze [Ruth]—I am writing this at a meeting while one of the delegates is making a long speech. From now on—the work being over—the speeches are the order of the day. And the weather looks so lovely through the window! Dad."[7]

Earlier, Harry's first task had been to get to this remote resort in the White Mountains in short order once the Atlantic City preliminary meetings wrapped up. The main work in Atlantic City was concluded on Wednesday, June 28. Harry then returned to Washington so he could spend one night at home, meet with the Latin American delegations and the rest of the U.S. delegation on Friday, and then leave for New Hampshire on a special train with that group and other delegations that had not been involved in the preconference meetings. Most of the other participants in Atlantic City headed north on another special train Friday evening. The two trains were linked together in Philadelphia, and the mass of delegates and technicians arrived in Bretton Woods in the early morning hours of Saturday, July 1, 1944.

The Bretton Woods conference could easily have degenerated into Keynes's "most monstrous monkey-house," with so many people from so many countries speaking so many languages. Instead, in the course of three weeks, the forty-four national delegations disposed of all the outstanding issues and produced the final draft of the Articles of Agreement of the institutions that we know today as the IMF and the World Bank.

Secretary Morgenthau served as president of the conference, and the State Department organized and ran the proceedings through the conference secretariat. The chairmen of the delegations from four other countries (Australia, Belgium, Brazil, and the Soviet Union) were designated as vice presidents.

These nominations reflected both the importance of geographic diversity in conference leadership positions and the qualifications of the individual chairmen. Leslie Melville was a senior official of the Commonwealth Bank of Australia, which at the time was serving as Australia's central bank. He later served as executive director at both the IMF and the World Bank. Camille Gutt was the finance minister in Belgium's government in exile. In 1946 he became the first managing director of the IMF. Arthur de Souza Costa was minister of finance in Brazil, and Mikhail S. Stepanov was deputy commissar for foreign trade in the Soviet Union (fig. 15). The dominant figures, however, were still White and Keynes.

The outstanding issues that the conference had to resolve were not all equally important, and most seem rather technical and pedestrian in retrospect. Moreover, Harry White did not play an important role in resolving every issue. Comprehensive histories of Bretton Woods are available, and what follows here is not intended to replace them.[8] The issues examined here were central for Harry, were critical for the success of the conference, and have had substantial effect on the way the two institutions have functioned.

Perhaps the most central issue, because it divided the U.S. and U.K. positions, concerned the degree of flexibility that countries would have to adjust their exchange rates. Another issue, which seemed obscure and theoretical at the time but turned out to have practical significance, concerned the role of "gold-convertible currencies." More practical issues with political importance included the allocation of quotas among countries, a special rule for allocating voting power to small countries, and the location of the headquarters.

Exchange Rate Flexibility

A fundamental principle in the White Plan was that every member country should agree to fix its exchange rate in terms of gold "or in terms of important currencies."[9] Changes in parities would be made only after obtaining the concurrence of the fund. The goal of this provision was to

Fig. 15. *Members of the U.S. and Soviet delegations at Bretton Woods. Harry is fifth from left in the back row. Other Americans include Morgenthau (seated, fourth from left), his eventual successor, Fred Vinson (seated, third from left), Eddie Bernstein (far left, rear), and Mable Newcomer, the lone female delegate at the conference. The chair of the Soviet delegation, Mikhail Stepanov, is seated next to Morgenthau (fourth from right). His deputy, Nikolai Chechulin, is standing behind him, fifth from right. International Monetary Fund*

prevent countries from engaging in competitive depreciations ("currency wars," in modern parlance), a practice that had done much to reduce international trade in the interwar period and that had been a significant contributor to the Depression of the 1930s.

The members of the British delegation supported the basic idea of fixing exchange rates, but they wanted to have more flexibility to change rates unilaterally in case of need. In the negotiations leading up to Bretton Woods, the U.S. team had agreed to allow changes after consultation with the fund but without requiring fund approval if the change did not exceed 10 percent. Furthermore, the fund was not to object to any proposed change that was "essential to correct a fundamental disequilibrium." That last provision meant that the fund could not require a country with an unsustainable deficit to change its domestic policies when the country preferred to change its exchange rate instead. On the *Queen Mary*, en route to Atlantic City, the British delegation drafted a proposal to allow more flexibility without the need for approval by the fund. This "boat draft" would have allowed a member country to make whatever change in its exchange rate that it deemed "necessary and advisable." If the fund disagreed, its only remedy would have been to suspend the country's right to borrow from it. Harry dug in his heels. As he reported to Morgenthau during the Atlantic City meeting, "We should not budge one bit" on that issue.[10] The 10 percent limit remained in place.

On the opening day of the Bretton Woods conference, Harry was still worried that the British would continue to press for more flexibility. That morning, he led a discussion at a meeting of the U.S. delegation on the key issues that remained to be settled. "One of the major issues between the United States and the U.K.," he explained, was "in the degree of flexibility of exchanges, the conditions under which a country can alter its exchange rate." For several minutes, he gave a tutorial on the issue, in a way that provided the justification for the "fixed but adjustable" system of exchange rate rules that would become known as the Bretton Woods system.[11]

The difference in view between the U.S. and British negotiators, Harry explained, arose in large part because of different experiences in the interwar period. The general perception in Britain was that the economy had suffered primarily because of adherence to the gold standard from 1925 until the government was forced to abandon it in 1931. The perception in the United States was that the U.S. economy had suffered throughout the 1930s in part because of monetary chaos as country after country abandoned the gold standard and engaged in competitive currency devaluations. Looking forward, Keynes and the other British negotiators wanted to avoid the severe restrictions of rigidly fixed exchange rates, whereas White and the other U.S. negotiators wanted to establish a firm basis for setting and limiting changes in exchange rates.

More generally, Harry argued that any set of rules would fail if they were either too rigid or too loose. The key was to insert "a little flexibility" into a firm set of rules. Otherwise, chaos would inevitably follow. Harry concluded that allowing countries to adjust their rates by up to 10 percent and requiring them to seek international approval through the IMF for larger changes was the Goldilocks solution to the problem. He urged his American colleagues to have his back while he refused to yield to any requests for greater flexibility.

As the conference proceeded, the British did not press the point particularly hard. The U.S. team managed to keep the 10 percent limit but compromised by softening the proposed penalty for an unauthorized change in an exchange rate.[12] Article IV of the IMF Articles of Agreement, with its "obligations regarding exchange stability," survived largely intact.

The main casualty of the U.S. insistence on limited flexibility of exchange rates was that the Australians refused to accept it. The Australian delegation signed the Final Act at Bretton Woods subject to a qualification on this point. For that and other reasons, Australia did not join the IMF until August 1947.[13]

The Role of the U.S. Dollar

The Joint Statement issued in April 1944 proposed that several rules governing relations between the fund and its member countries should depend in part on the member's holdings of "gold and gold-convertible exchange" (GCE). It did not define GCE, but the term was understood to refer to official holdings of currencies (or highly liquid securities) that could be freely exchanged for gold. A country's official holdings of gold and GCE were to be considered in the determination of how much of such assets the country would have to pay in its membership subscription, so that poor countries would not be shut out. It also was intended to help determine the country's quota. So that the fund could carry out these functions, each member would have to report its holdings of gold and GCE to the fund. The rule for fixing a country's exchange rate, however, was proposed to be more restrictive: each par value was to be expressed in relation to gold, not to another currency.[14]

When Harry's team at the Treasury circulated a draft of the IMF Articles of Agreement at the outset of the Bretton Woods conference, it noted that the "phrase 'gold and gold-convertible exchange' is subject to definition and to such change in terminology as may be agreed."[15] One problem was that while only the U.S. dollar was interchangeable with gold for official international settlements, some other currencies could be freely exchanged for dollars and thus might meet the implicit criterion. How widely was this net to be cast? Another problem was that even the dollar had only limited convertibility into gold. Keynes repeatedly complained that the GCE phrase was essentially meaningless.

The question lay dormant for nearly two weeks as the conference proceeded, until the fourth meeting of Commission I, chaired by Harry on

July 13. At that meeting, a delegate from India, A. D. Shroff, challenged the U.S. delegate, Eddie Bernstein, to give the commission a definition of GCE. Before Bernstein could answer, Dennis Robertson, of the British Treasury, jumped in to say that it was "not in any way [the United States'] fault that the furnishing of this definition had been so long delayed." Without elaborating on whose fault it was but implying that it had been his own country's, Robertson proposed that the phrase be replaced by the much simpler and clearer phrase, "gold and United States dollars." Bernstein then concurred in a way that suggested that he and Robertson had been discussing the issue and had come to this agreement: "The practical importance of holdings of the currencies represented here is so small that it has been felt it would be easier for this purpose to regard the United States dollar as what was intended when we speak of gold convertible exchange."[16]

As further confirmation that this decision was probably reached jointly by Robertson and Bernstein, Lionel Robbins (another British delegate) noted in his diary on July 7 that "Robertson and Bernstein, who are very good friends, are continually in session. If the Conference comes to anything it will owe a great deal to their unremitting labours." On July 14, he noted, "Last night, Bernstein and Robertson sat up until past three and reached substantial agreement on most of the technical questions still outstanding" regarding the fund.[17]

No one on the commission objected, and so Harry referred the matter to the Special Committee that was charged with introducing amendments into the draft articles. The official minutes of the meeting record the decision: "The query with regard to the definition of gold-convertible exchange was also referred to the Special Committee with the suggestion that it might prove advisable to substitute the phrase 'United States dollars.'"[18]

The proposal to base the IMF financial structure on the U.S. dollar rather than on GCE was important to the British delegation. The next day (July 14), Robertson again insisted that the wording be changed from GCE to U.S. dollars, and he pressed Bernstein and White to promise to incorporate that language in the articles.[19] He insisted on it because Keynes believed that the phrase "gold-convertible exchange" was meaningless and because the U.S. dollar was what everyone understood to be the true meaning of the vague phrasing.*

---

* Some studies have interpreted this exchange quite differently and have suggested that the Americans pulled a fast one on the British, and even that Harry

When the IMF began operations in 1946, it was going to be a dollar-based financial institution no matter what language was inserted into the articles, simply because the United States held most of the world's monetary gold and the dollar was the only currency that was both convertible and widely held in official reserves. It is thus not surprising that no one in 1944 thought that the choice between the more restrictive and the more flexible wording would have any practical effect.[*]

IMF Quotas

A third challenging issue was the allocation of quotas and voting power among the participating countries. Harry had been discussing this issue with most of the potential members in meetings over the preceding year, beginning with the multilateral gathering in June 1943 described in

---

outwitted Keynes while the great man was distracted by his duties on the design of the World Bank. That interpretation began with Armand Van Dormael. His 1978 account (*Bretton Woods*, 200–203) noted that the language allowing countries to express par values in terms of gold or GCE (not just gold, as in the Joint Statement) was inserted by the U.S. delegation, apparently without Keynes's becoming aware of it. Van Dormael acknowledged that the subsequent change in wording from GCE to U.S. dollars was proposed by Robertson, but he asserted falsely that Robertson acted "against Keynes's instructions." More recently, Benn Steil (*Battle of Bretton Woods*, 195, 216) asserted that White engineered the change in wording "on the sly" and that Robertson "walked straight into White's trap" and made his suggestion without knowing what he was doing. Steil's account concluded that the change in wording caused, rather than reflected, the dominance of the dollar in official financial transactions after the war. Edmund Conway (*Summit*, 243–47) was closer to the mark, though he also regarded Robertson's intervention as an error rather than a deliberate attempt to clarify the wording. Kurt Schuler and Andrew Rosenberg, in *Bretton Woods Transcripts* (Kindle location 485–90), stressed the corroborating remark by Bernstein without mentioning Robertson's proposal, thus implying that the suggestion came from the United States rather than from the United Kingdom.

[*] By the late 1950s, as more and more countries were able to accumulate reserves through international trade and to make their own currencies convertible in exchange, the restriction that every country had to peg the value of its currency to gold or to the gold content of the U.S. dollar became a straitjacket for the international financial system. It may also have contributed to the tendency for the dollar to continue to be the dominant reserve currency. By the early 1970s, this dollar-based Bretton Woods system had done much for the world economy but was no longer viable.

chapter 10. The issue had turned out to be a matter of great importance, not so much because of the practical consequences, but, rather, because of the political implications of the ranking. China and India, for example, were rivals for recognition as countries with global influence. Whichever one had the larger quota in the IMF would have a leg up in the competition for recognition after the war. That was a game that Harry did not want to play, and he was determined to pretend that the allocation was going to be made on technical calculations rather than political negotiations.

For the June 1943 meeting with representatives of eighteen countries, Harry asked one of his staff, Raymond Mikesell, to devise a formula that would produce appropriate quota rankings. Although Mikesell does not figure much in the rest of this history, his role in devising the quota formula was important both for translating Harry's vision into practice and for enabling the IMF to function efficiently over several decades. Unlike many of the Treasury economists who helped Harry design the IMF and the World Bank, Mikesell did not subsequently join the staff of either institution. Instead, he had a distinguished academic career, first at the University of Virginia and later at the University of Oregon. He published three accounts of his work on Bretton Woods. When he died in 2006 at the age of ninety-three, he was survived by only one other member of the Bretton Woods delegations and secretariat (Jacques J. Polak, of the Netherlands delegation).

Harry instructed Mikesell that the top four countries had to be the United States, the United Kingdom, the Soviet Union, and China, in that order. He reportedly told Mikesell that this ordering had already been agreed on by President Roosevelt and Secretary of State Cordell Hull. The problems were that there was no objective way to calculate these quotas using economic data and that it ignored the economic importance of France. (As an occupied territory with an allied but exiled government, France was not an official member of the Grand Alliance.)

Even if Mikesell had used only one data series—say, national income—he would have had to select the coverage period arbitrarily. Income data during the war were essentially useless, and prewar data were outdated. Moreover, national income did not adequately measure a country's ability to contribute to the fund's resources, its potential need to borrow, or the legitimacy of its voting power. Harry therefore asked Mikesell to use four different series of mostly prewar data. Mikesell just experimented with different weights, using a desktop mechanical calculator, until he got what looked like a reasonable result.[20]

This tactic seems bizarre until you realize that *any* formula would have been just as arbitrary. Economists are accustomed to writing down functions to be optimized and then estimating, say, the best price for maximizing the profit from selling a product or the best economic policies for stabilizing the level of consumer prices. Mikesell's task was quite different. He had nothing measurable to maximize, but he had to produce an outcome that would minimize dissonance from offended political leaders. Without the pretense of a technical basis for that outcome, no set of quotas could ever have survived the ensuing debates.

The formula that Harry presented to the assembled delegates in June 1943 was detailed enough to look convincing and to resist efforts to object to it. Each country's quota would be determined as:

(1 + the ratio of exports to national income, 1934–38) multiplied by the sum of the following four numbers:

        0.02 × national income in 1940
+   0.05 × official holdings of gold plus U.S. dollars in 1943
+   0.1 × average imports, 1934–38, and
+   0.1 × the maximum variation in exports, 1934–38.

Mikesell had sufficient data only for twelve countries, but within that group some troubling comparisons arose. The top three countries came out ranked as Harry had asked, but China's quota ($350 million) came out below India's ($367 million). Even that figure was inflated. Mikesell's own initial calculations (dated May 25, 1943) gave China a quota of just $260 million.[21] It had taken a fair bit of tinkering just to get to the $350 million figure circulated in June.

Canada was next in line in the table, but Mikesell excluded France altogether. If he had included it, France would have had a calculated quota above both China's and India's. Although this omission left a gaping hole, no country raised a specific objection to its quota at the June meeting. Mikesell then continued to fiddle with the formula and the data to "improve" the resulting distribution.

By January 1944 Mikesell's calculations covered more countries and yielded quite different numbers at the upper end of the distribution of quotas. He calculated a quota of $500 million for France and arbitrarily raised China's quota to $600 million, nearly double the first estimate that Harry had circulated. Canada and India were tied for sixth place with quotas of $300 million each. These numbers continued to fluctuate in subsequent drafts, and when the Bretton Woods conference opened in July 1944, China had been knocked down again to $350 million. France had taken over fourth place, with a proposed quota of $620 million, and India was fifth, back to its initial quota of $367 million.

The difference between being ranked fifth and sixth had become a matter of some importance because the draft Articles of Agreement specified that only the countries with the five largest quotas could appoint their own executive directors. The rest would have to elect directors, mostly by forming coalitions (known as constituencies) with other countries. Why five? Because France was represented at Bretton Woods by the government-in-exile that was based in London and led by General Charles de Gaulle (officially listed as the French Delegation, rather than France). That government was expected to be a major power in postwar Europe and had to be included alongside the Grand Alliance countries.

The idea of setting aside special privileges for these five great powers was not unique to Bretton Woods. It surfaced even more pointedly in 1945, with the creation of the Security Council as the main decision-making body of the new United Nations Organization. In that context, all that was required was to name the five as the permanent members of the council and grant each of them a veto over council decisions. The task for the Bretton Woods conference was more difficult because the delegates also had to agree on the ranking of the five countries and on specific values for their quotas.

Throughout the yearlong negotiations leading up to the conference, Harry fought off suggestions from Keynes, Jacob Viner, and others to have three separate sets of quotas to determine financial contributions, borrowing limits, and voting power independently. He had insisted successfully on having one unified list, on the simple and persuasive grounds that getting to an international agreement on multiple lists would be impossible. Now, as the conference was finally under way, he still seemed to be far from a definitive set of acceptable numbers.

Harry assigned the task of finalizing the list to the Ad Hoc Committee on Quotas, chaired by Fred M. Vinson, the vice chairman of the U.S. delegation. Vinson was a former Democratic congressman from Kentucky and judge on the U.S. Court of Appeals for the District of Columbia. At the time of the Bretton Woods conference, he was director of the Office of Economic Stabilization. He later succeeded Morgenthau as secretary of the Treasury and then served as chief justice of the Supreme Court.

After some two weeks of closed-door negotiations, Vinson reported to Harry's Commission I that his committee had agreed on a list.[22] It included some striking changes to the preconference proposal. The Soviet Union jumped from $763 million to $1,200 million: still in third place, but now cozily close to the United Kingdom ($1,300 million). China was restored to the fourth position, with $550 million, followed by France ($450 million) and then India ($400 million).

Several delegations still had reservations about the committee's list. As Vinson spoke, he became increasingly emotional in appealing to the commission to accept the compromises that had become necessary. "We are met here in Bretton Woods in an experimental test, probably the first time in the history of the world that forty-four nations have convened seeking to solve difficult problems. We fight together on sodden battlefields. We sail together on the majestic blue. We fly together in the ethereal sky. The test of this conference is whether we can walk together, solve our economic problems, down the road to peace as we today march to victory."[23]

Harry then gave each dissenter a chance to explain his objection. Delegates from ten countries—Australia, China, Ethiopia, France, Greece, India, Iran, the Netherlands, New Zealand, and Yugoslavia—each expressed reservations. Delegates from Canada, Norway, and the United Kingdom followed by expressing support for the committee report. Harry himself intervened to suggest that everyone should pause for a moment to reflect on whether the question of "whether or not a particular quota is a little higher or a little lower than expected" was important enough to scuttle the grand overall project. He then called for a voice vote, which appeared to favor accepting the list. When no one challenged him by calling for a show of hands, he declared that the committee's list of quotas was approved.

Aside from politics and national prestige, the intense negotiations on quotas mattered relatively little once the IMF began operations. When the Soviet Union decided not to join, India moved up to fifth place and was able to appoint an executive director along with the remnants of the Grand Alliance and France. The IMF proved to be flexible in deciding how much to lend to countries, without being limited too strictly by quotas. Even the effect of quotas on voting power turned out to have limited effect because IMF operations functioned mainly on consensus rather than formal votes. Nonetheless, national prestige continued to drive quota debates well into the next century. Whenever the quotas came up for review (normally about once every five years), the staff of the Fund churned out lengthy papers with technical discussions about the weights and values in the quota formula (which continued to be based primarily on Mikesell's 1943 calculations), and the Executive Board devised ways to override the calculations to get the "right" relative rankings. In this way, the balance between measurement and political preference that Harry devised at the outset continued to serve the institution through the decades.

Voting Power

Though relative quotas were to be the primary determinant of voting power in the new institutions, Harry understood from the outset that it was crucially important to ensure that small countries would have a significant voice even if their quotas were minuscule. At the extreme, the smallest countries at Bretton Woods—Liberia and Panama—were assigned quotas of $500,000 each, or 0.006 percent of the total. The three largest countries would have quotas totaling about 60 percent of the total: 31 percent for the United States, 15 percent for the United Kingdom, and 14 percent for the Soviet Union. As a basis for voting power, that seemed unacceptable. As Harry noted in a commentary on Mikesell's calculations in June 1943, "To permit such a concentration of control would destroy the truly international character of the Fund and seriously jeopardize its success." He proposed, therefore, that almost 30 percent of the voting power be allocated equally among all members. Specifically, each country would be granted 100 votes plus one vote for each $1 million in its quota.[24]

The Joint Statement issued in April 1944 backed away from this commitment to the smaller countries. It merely noted vaguely that the "distribution of voting power . . . shall be closely related to the quotas." The U.S. Treasury team then put the proposal back into its initial draft of the IMF articles for discussion at the Atlantic City meeting. It was modified, however, to call for each country to have 250 votes plus one for each $100,000 of quota. Although the number of basic votes was raised from 100 to 250, the effect was more than offset by the tenfold increase in the proposed number of quota-based votes. In effect, the real number of basic votes was reduced by 75 percent. That relationship survived intact through the debates at Bretton Woods and was incorporated into the Articles of Agreement as Article XII, Section 5(a).

It seems that no one at Bretton Woods challenged this proposal. As a result, only about 11 percent of the total voting power was allocated to basic votes, based on the quotas approved at the conference. The "truly international character of the Fund" was thus severely watered down compared with Harry's original proposal. Harry's neglect to follow up on his original vision of a significant role for small countries in governing the institution, compounded by his and others' failure to foresee the need to allow for future growth, left the IMF far more in the hands of large and relatively rich countries than he had wished. Over time, the problem was bound to worsen, as world economic growth induced quota increases that severely marginalized the voting power of small countries. Even though it was widely believed that the postwar world economy would be quite different from that in the interwar period, the delegates had no idea that it would be as dynamic as it turned out to be.*

Headquarters: Washington, D.C.

A fifth issue that bitterly divided the Americans and the British was the location of the headquarters of the proposed institutions. As we saw in chapter 10, Keynes's opening salvo was to suggest in February 1942 that his currency union should operate out of offices in London. His revised plan of April 1943 floated the idea of having two sets of offices, in London and New York. He was adamantly opposed to having them in Washington, where he feared (correctly) that the U.S. government would be constantly trying to interfere with and control operations. Harry made no mention of possible locations in his early drafts, but he had no intention of placing the institutions in Europe. The fund and the bank were American ideas and would be largely funded by the United States. To the U.S. government, it seemed right and natural that they should be located at home.

The first mention of office location in an official document was in the U.S. draft of the IMF articles that was circulated in Atlantic City on June 23, 1944. That draft stated simply: "The principal office of the Fund

---

* By the early twenty-first century, the $8.8 billion in quotas approved at Bretton Woods had risen to more than $212 billion, but the number of basic votes per country remained at the level set in 1944. Voting power had become almost entirely a function of quotas; just a trivial amount (about 2 percent) was allowed for basic votes for each member. Eventually (in 2011) the membership amended Article XII to replace the fixed number with a fixed percentage, but the new percentage was set at only 5.5 percent of the total voting power. In 2019 forty-seven countries in sub-Saharan Africa (25 percent of the membership) held 4.7 percent of the voting power in the IMF. If Harry's 1943 proposal for basic votes (30 percent of total votes) had been adopted at Bretton Woods and then retained, those forty-seven countries would have held 14.3 percent of the vote. The U.S. share would have fallen to 12.4 percent, from its actual 16.5 percent.

shall be located in the member country having the largest quota, and
agencies or branch offices may be established in any member country or
member countries."[25] That forced the British delegation to formulate an
alternative proposal and to try to persuade other delegations to support
it. Nothing emerged from the discussions in Atlantic City, but at Bretton Woods the British proposed that the conference make no decision on
where to locate the headquarters. The Special Committee on Unsettled
Problems floated a proposal to leave the matter in the hands of the IMF
governors, allowing the decision to be made at the first governors' meeting. Instead of deciding now that the fund's offices should be in the United
States, this Alternative B proposed only that the inaugural governors'
meeting should take place there.[26]

The Special Committee was unable to reach a consensus for choos-
ing between the two proposals, and it referred the question to Commission I, which Harry was chairing. On July 14 the British delegation received instructions from London "that if pressed we need not insist upon
our amendment with regard to the location of the Fund."[27] By July 18
the British sensed that their alternative was not going to carry the day,
and so they withdrew it. In its place, they argued that it was "premature
to take any final decision on this matter" and that decisions on locations
of the fund, the bank, and other such institutions should be considered
as "interrelated" and should be decided "by governments rather than [by
this] technical conference." At that point two U.S. allies in Latin America
spoke up. The Cuban delegate opined that the United States was the appropriate place for the fund's offices, and he moved the adoption of the
U.S. proposal. The delegate from Ecuador seconded the motion, at which
point the British gave up. The motion carried with no further discussion.[28]

Although the Bretton Woods conference confirmed that the fund and
the bank were to be headquartered in the United States as long as it had
the largest quota, it left open the question of whether they should be in
Washington, New York, or somewhere else. That gave Keynes an opening
to continue to lobby for New York, where he believed political interfer-
ence would be harder to sustain. He carried that fight all the way to the
inaugural governors' meeting, which took place in Savannah, Georgia, in
March 1946.

Having won the battle to place the headquarters in the United States,
Harry was inclined to accept Keynes's fallback position and set up shop in
New York. Harry was also aware that the U.S. banking lobby was adamant
that the headquarters should be in New York. In July 1945 he wrote to

Professor Philip C. Jessup at Columbia University to suggest that Columbia should establish a school to prepare students for careers at international organizations, including the IMF and the World Bank. Columbia, he noted, would be ideally placed because "it is not unlikely that the head offices will be in New York for both the World Fund and World Bank. These institutions alone will require large technical staffs of the highest competence." Although neither the IMF nor the World Bank ended up in New York, Columbia did establish the School of International and Public Affairs for this purpose in 1946.

By mid-1945 Harry no longer had the influence in the Treasury that he had long enjoyed. When Harry S. Truman succeeded Roosevelt as U.S. president after Roosevelt died in April 1945, Morgenthau sensed correctly that Truman did not respect him. (Truman opined that "Morgenthau didn't know shit from apple butter.")[29] Morgenthau resigned in July, and Truman named Vinson to succeed him. Vinson named White to be the first U.S. executive director in the IMF, but the two men did not have the collegiality that was critically important for White's influence with Morgenthau. The banking lobby also had lost influence, since Congress had approved the Bretton Woods agreements over the bankers' objections. Vinson could locate the new institutions wherever he wanted them.

When Keynes arrived in Savannah in March 1946, Vinson told him that the Truman administration had decided that the IMF and World Bank were both to be headquartered in Washington and that this decision was final and was not subject to negotiation. It is unlikely that Harry had anything to do with the choice. Keynes concluded that "it was primarily a personal decision of Mr Vinson supported only by the Federal Reserve Board (which would find itself strengthened against the New York Federal Reserve Bank by the Washington location)."[30]

Keynes was furious because he had been laboring under the illusion that at least the IMF headquarters was to be in New York. He believed strongly that the New York location would facilitate relations with this "great centre of international finance" and with the newly established United Nations headquarters, and that it would help remove the IMF "from the politics of Congress and the nationalistic whispering gallery of the embassies and legations of Washington." In one of the great rhetorical flourishes for which he was justly famous, Keynes used his governor's speech in Savannah to warn of the consequences. In time, he warned, Carabosse—the wicked fairy godmother in *Sleeping Beauty*—could slip in and pronounce a curse on the IMF and the World Bank: "You two brats shall grow up politicians; your every thought and act shall have an *arrière-pensée*; everything you determine shall not be for its own sake or on its own merits but because of something else."[31] Impressive, but unpersuasive. The headquarters were established in Washington at 1818 H Street, NW, a ten-minute walk up Pennsylvania Avenue from the U.S. Treasury.

PART V

Preparing for Peace and Prosperity

CHAPTER THIRTEEN

Finishing the Job, 1944–45

I like him, and I'd like him to have it [promotion to assistant secretary].

—President Franklin D. Roosevelt, 1944

IN JANUARY 1945 HARRY finally got a title that was commensurate with the responsibilities of chief economist that he had fulfilled for the preceding three years. The Treasury organization chart had room for only two assistant secretaries, and both posts had been occupied by men who were not economists. In November 1944 one of those men, John L. Sullivan, resigned to become assistant secretary of the navy. That created the opening that both Morgenthau and White had been waiting for throughout the war. On November 15 Morgenthau told Roosevelt that he wanted to promote Harry to assistant secretary. The president immediately agreed, saying, "I like him, and I'd like him to have it." He also thought that it would be helpful for Harry to have this title when he was responsible for persuading Congress to enact the Bretton Woods legislation. But he asked Morgenthau to notify Robert E. Hannegan (chairman of the Democratic National Committee) as a courtesy. Hannegan objected because he knew nothing about Harry, and he wanted someone in place who would be politically useful to the president. Although Harry was a Democrat and—in Morgenthau's words—"a rip-roaring Roosevelt man," he had not been politically active since he arrived in Washington a decade earlier. That held up the promotion for several weeks, but Morgenthau persisted and badgered Roosevelt until he got what he wanted.[1]

On December 28 Morgenthau sent a note to Roosevelt, formally asking him to nominate Harry to fill the vacant post of assistant secretary and telling the president that Harry "has earned this reward many times over. The Administration needs him in the field in which he has distinguished himself so brilliantly. White has been more than a match for people like Lord Keynes." Roosevelt acted on the request the same day,[2] and the nomination was made public on January 3, 1945. The Senate quickly confirmed the appointment, which became effective on January 24.

Harry now officially had the top economic post in the Treasury. "Assistant secretary" does not sound very elevated today, but it was then. After World War II, the organization chart of the U.S. Treasury expanded greatly. As of 2021, the position directly below secretary is deputy secretary. Two under secretaries fill the next level, followed by eight assistant secretaries. Thus, the approximate modern equivalent of Harry's 1945 title is under secretary for international affairs.

The promotion did not substantially alter Harry's responsibilities. He remained in charge of the division that was now called Monetary Research and Foreign Funds Control. As World War II drew to a close in the months following the Bretton Woods conference, he faced several challenges, both ongoing and new. His first task was to secure the ratification of the agreements, by the U.S. Congress and by many other countries, and to get the IMF and the World Bank established as the linchpins of the postwar global economy. A multitude of other tasks pulled at him during his last year at the Treasury, including the effort to establish the United Nations Organization, but his mind was focused most on the impending birth of his brainchildren from Bretton Woods.

As Harry became more prominent in Washington, he accumulated coteries of admirers and detractors. The president's liking for and positive view of Harry was shared by Eleanor Roosevelt and by some of those who knew him well.[3] Milo Perkins, executive director of the Board of Economic Warfare during World War II, praised Harry for his sense of humor, comparing him to Will Rogers and remarking after one meeting that he "got a considerable kick out of your various wisecracks."[4] Jacob Viner, who supervised Harry's early years at the Treasury, disagreed with him on many issues, particularly because Viner was skeptical about much of Roosevelt's New Deal and about Bretton Woods. Although their relationship became "strained," he reportedly told colleagues after Harry's death that he viewed him "as a person of unassailable integrity and . . . the most brilliant government economist of his period."[5]

This positive assessment was far from universal. Although many people found much to admire, others found him to be unpleasant or worse. Most often, Harry's peers concluded that he was a curious mix of fine and awful qualities. Keynes, who met with Harry many times, forged a strong friendship with him. Even so, as chapter 11 showed, he was bewildered by what he saw as Harry's oppressively bad manners. John P. Young, a State Department official who served in the conference secretariat at Bretton Woods, found Harry to be "extremely competent and very good to his own people in the Treasury," but "a difficult person, a very rude person, and rather slippery."[6]

Emanuel Alexander Goldenweiser, a senior official at the Federal Reserve Board who served as a technical adviser to the U.S. delegation at Bretton Woods and met often with Harry in preparatory meetings for the conference, once told Lionel Robbins that "Harry is doing very well and trying his hardest to be pleasant." When Robbins "raised [his] eyebrows a trifle" at that assessment, Goldenweiser added that "of course, normally, Harry is the unpleasantest man in Washington."[7]

The most unabashedly negative assessments tended to come from people who barely knew him, such as Thomas McKittrick, the president of the Bank for International Settlements, who termed Harry a "totalitarian"; or those who never met him, such as Morgenthau's biographer John Morton Blum, who wrote that Harry was "by all accounts I could find a nasty man."[8]

On the other hand, if one were to rely only on Harry's subordinates, close colleagues, and family, one would get a picture bordering on hagiography. The ill-bred nastiness that many others experienced is airbrushed away.

The "colored . . . messenger boy" who so impressed Harry in the summer of 1934 (see chapter 4) wept openly when Harry died fourteen years later. "Mr. White understood me as only God above understands me," he reportedly told a colleague. That colleague (another subordinate of Harry), Sol Adler, recounted the episode in a 1956 letter to Harry's sister Bessie Bloom. Adler explained further that "in November 1944 when Harry won the office pool on the presidential elections, he gave his winnings to the messenger boy. But such actions alone could not have inspired such a tribute. It was Harry's fundamental humanity to which the messenger, like everybody else who was fortunate enough to come into close contact with Harry, was responding."[9]

Raymond Mikesell, who worked closely under White throughout the war, including the weeks at Bretton Woods, wrote later: "The staff was intensely loyal to White, and he respected us as scholars and strongly supported us even when he thought we had made mistakes. I do not recall White's embarrassing any staff member by dressing him down, but he showed another side when he was involved in negotiations outside the Treasury Department."[10]

When Harry's name was being dragged in the mud in 1953, a reporter in Massachusetts looked up Mrs. Dorothy Hallock, who had been one of Harry's secretaries from 1939 to 1943. She responded with a recollection that stands as probably the most detailed assessment of his character around the office. Harry, she recalled, "was a wonderful person in every way. . . . He was extremely well-liked as he always had time to enquire of one's health, work or everyday problems. He was one of the most conscientious persons I ever knew, never taking time out to think about himself although many times he was forced to lie down and rest because of ill health. Often he had to be reminded to go to lunch. Outwardly he was a very nervous person. He never walked along corridors, always ran down them and was constantly occupied with affairs concerning his work." She also recalled that Harry had encouraged her to take night courses in economics so that she could get ahead in her career, and he threw birthday and other parties for her at the office. "At times like these," she concluded, "he was very witty and seemingly enjoyed doing things for others."[11]

Another subordinate who was totally devoted to Harry was Linda M. Shanahan, who served as his personal secretary throughout his Treasury and IMF careers. The discovery that she carried a clipped newspaper photograph of Harry in her purse caused great distress to her husband, who reportedly concluded that she was having an affair with him. (A rumor to that effect also took hold during the Bretton Woods conference.) The novelist Julian Barnes once wrote that "all biographers secretly want to annex and channel the sex-lives of their subjects," and that must be even more true of readers of biographies. In this case, however, although Bruce Craig guessed that the rumors were "probably true," it is also the case that a long-standing and close working relationship between people who regularly toil together late into the evening is the quintessential source for prurient speculation.[12]

Ratification of the Bretton Woods Agreements

As the conference at Bretton Woods was ending on July 21, 1944, Harry was in a mood both ebullient about the successful outcome and apprehensive about the battles to come. In a rare free moment that day, he took the time to pen a letter to his two teenage daughters. He had been getting by on four hours of sleep each night, he wrote, but it had been well worth the sacrifices. He wrote of "the splendid cooperative spirit" and of how "everybody—or at least almost everybody—had worked terribly hard. . . . It has been on the whole a very happy experience. . . . I've had fun—and best of all the sense of an important task well done." Still, the job was not yet completed. "Both the Fund and the Bank are, so to speak, in the bag. The last hill has passed; the next one is a mountain, i.e., getting Congress to accept both proposals."[13]

When the conference ended the next day, Harry returned home to Washington, but only for a couple of weeks. He then left for England and France, where he accompanied Secretary Morgenthau on an inspection tour, discussed in the next chapter. When they returned to Washington in mid-August, Morgenthau put Harry in overall charge of the campaign to generate public and congressional support for the Bretton Woods agreements, and he assigned specific responsibilities to Eddie Bernstein (Harry's deputy, in charge of the technical economic work and drafting speeches and other materials), Ansel F. Luxford (assistant to the secretary, in charge of legal aspects), and Fred Smith (also assistant to the secretary, responsible for public relations).

On August 20 Harry had lunch with Maynard Keynes, who was about to return to London, where he would shepherd the agreements through the British Parliament. Keynes impressed on him the view that the British (and by extension most other potential participants) would hold back on any decisions until the U.S. Congress granted its approval.[14] Everything hinged on the passage of the Bretton Woods Agreements Act.

Meanwhile, Roosevelt was campaigning to be elected to an unprecedented fourth term as president. Even as the Bretton Woods conference was proceeding in July, he informed Morgenthau that he wanted to delay any consideration of the outcome by Congress until after the November election.[15] That effectively left only a few months for Congress to hold hearings and pass the necessary legislation, if other countries were to have time to act before the end-of-1945 deadline specified in the Final Act of the conference.

To take advantage of the months before congressional hearings could begin, Harry proposed a campaign to generate public support. He suggested a baker's dozen of civic organizations to which the Treasury could reach out for help. Most were groups focused on international affairs, such as the Council on Foreign Relations, the National Foreign Trade Council, and the United Nations Association. Others focused on promoting peace: the World Peace Foundation and the National Catholic Peace Society. Several had been founded to mobilize women in domestic or international affairs, including the League of Women Voters and the Women's Conference on International Affairs. Harry knew that major business groups such as the American Bankers Association (ABA) and the U.S. Chamber of Commerce viewed government involvement in economic affairs with suspicion and had opposed much of Roosevelt's New Deal legislation. Those organizations were likely to lobby against the legislation, and so he proposed to work with labor groups such as the American Federation of Labor (AFL) and the (then separate) Congress of Industrial Organizations (CIO) to counter them. By December he also had the Farm Bureau Federation on board.[16]

Another part of the plan was to neutralize or co-opt some of the expected opposition. That effort had already started with the inclusion of potential skeptics in the U.S. delegation at Bretton Woods. The ranking Republicans on the banking and currency committees of the Senate and House (as well as the Democratic committee chairs) had been delegates, even though Roosevelt regarded one of them—Senator Charles W. Tobey of New Hampshire—as "a little cracked."[17] The chairman and ranking Republican on the House Committee on Coinage, Weights and Measures had been included as technical advisers to the U.S. delegation. Edward E. ("Ned") Brown, president of the First National Bank of Chicago and the lone business executive in the delegation, helped draft the charter for the World Bank and later would testify in favor of both the World Bank and the IMF. Harry and others met with sympathetic members of Congress to get their advice on how best to build support.[18]

In February 1945 the Treasury hired an outside expert, J. H. Randolph Feltus, to prepare and run a public relations campaign. Part of his program was to "secure conservative support first," particularly by persuading well-known and respected people from outside the Treasury to write and speak favorably about the agreements, and by preparing and distributing pamphlets and other materials aimed at conservative audiences.

For his part, Harry gave numerous speeches and made other public appearances, beginning with the nationally broadcast radio program *American Forum of the Air*, on August 22, 1944. Morgenthau also was a guest on the program, as were Ned Brown, Charles Tobey, and three other members of the U.S. delegation. Afterward, Harry gravitated toward the left-of-center organizations that were natural allies of the Roosevelt administration. In September he spoke at a conference of fifty national women's organizations at the National Archives in Washington. Before the end of 1944, he spoke to at least three other groups, including a meeting of the Foreign Policy Association in New York and a meeting of the National Foreign Trade Council in Washington.

In December, stepping a bit out of his comfort zone, Harry addressed a gathering of bankers in Birmingham, Alabama. In January 1945 he explained the purpose of the Bretton Woods agreements to a more natural ally, the People's Lobby, which was advocating U.S. participation in international arrangements. At the end of February, he spoke to a convention organized by Americans United for World Organization, an influential group that advocated principally for U.S. membership in a permanent United Nations. In each of his addresses and in an article published in *Foreign Affairs*, the gist of Harry's message was what he had stressed from the very beginning of his lengthy quest to formalize international financial cooperation: a continuation of U.S. prosperity required the spread of prosperity in other countries, both to strengthen markets for U.S. output and to preserve the peace. As he put the case to the women's organizations in September, "Depressions in one country gradually affect all countries," including the United States.[19]

Congressional hearings began with the House Committee on Banking and Currency, on March 7, 1945, and continued through June 28, when the corresponding hearings concluded in the Senate. Harry testified before the House committee for four days, starting on March 9, and then for a fifth day a month later, on April 19. In addition, Harry answered a few questions on March 7, to assist Morgenthau in his initial testimony.

Morgenthau and Dean Acheson testified before Harry took the stand. They focused on the strategic aspects of the agreements, and Harry then answered the more technical questions from the committee. He was bombarded with questions about whether the United States was ceding its sovereignty to an uncontrollable international organization, whether the technical aspects of the agreements would be workable in practice, why he did not accept the objections expressed by the banking community, and why he had differed from the great Lord Keynes on so many issues. Afterward, upon reading the transcript, Keynes declared that Harry had handled that last line of questions "magnificently," and he declared that he was "very grateful to him for the handsome way in which the whole difficult issue was handled."[20]

When the hearings began, the possibility was very real that the proposal to establish the IMF would fail. The ABA and the Chamber of Commerce were making a sustained public appeal for Congress to vote it down. They did not oppose the World Bank, but they argued that the world did not need a grand scheme to stabilize currencies and that the credit function envisaged for the IMF could be handled more efficiently by the World Bank. Within the Federal Reserve System, the favorable views of officials at the Federal Reserve Board were offset by the vocal opposition of some at the Federal Reserve Bank of New York. More generally, the opposition comprised what the historian Alfred Eckes called a "loose coalition of isolationists, Republicans, bankers, and laissez faire conservatives."[21]

By traveling to Alabama to speak to a bankers' convention, Harry was exploiting and encouraging a split in view between the ABA, which was dominated by the large money-center banks, and the thousands of smaller local and regional banks. The latter were more open to a proposal that they saw as likely to contribute broadly to economic well-being, in contrast to the ABA's concerns about government intrusion in their own area of interest. Shortly before the House committee hearings began, the Independent Bankers Association, a national organization of some two thousand relatively small banks, issued a statement in support of the agreements. In a phrase that is often echoed in our time, the statement noted that although the group could "hardly claim to speak for Wall Street, we do believe we can speak for Main Street."[22]

In the Senate hearings, the main protagonist was Robert A. Taft, Republican from Ohio. Elected to the Senate in 1938, Taft had spent his first term establishing a reputation as one of Roosevelt's strongest and most effective congressional opponents. As a fervent isolationist, he could have faced a diminished role during the war, but he continued to hammer hard on the president's economic policies. In 1945, fresh from reelection to a second term and his success in establishing and now chairing the Republican Steering Committee, he was determined to block Roosevelt from leading the United States into the global financial institutions approved provisionally at Bretton Woods.

Although Taft was not the ranking Republican on the committee, he was the leading opponent of the proposed legislation. He had studied the issues carefully, and he proved to be an effective debater in the freewheeling atmosphere of the open hearings. He and Harry controlled the floor through six grueling days of questioning between June 14 and the 28th. Taft raised, and Harry responded to, seven major issues.

First, Taft claimed that the gold and dollars that the United States would be depositing in the IMF ($2.75 billion) would be "gone. It is no longer available to us. We may someday get it back if the fund is dissolved, I agree, but in the meantime we haven't got it." Harry responded that the United States could draw out those resources any time it needed them, the same as any other member country. Taft then shifted gears a bit and argued that such drawings would be "at the discretion of a board we cannot control."[23] It was a poor argument. The notion that the United States— the principal financial backer of the institution—might be denied the use of its funds by being outvoted by other countries was ludicrous.* Harry just let it ride, but Taft would raise it again later in a different context.

More tellingly, Taft complained that the "stabilization agreements" that the IMF would be entering into were just loans and were no different from loans that the U.S. government or others might be making in other ways. Harry cheerfully acknowledged that "yes, you may call it a loan," but he insisted that "a stabilization agreement . . . doesn't mean a loan. If it meant a loan, we would call it a loan." (In fact, the distinction is primarily legal, not economic.) As an example, he recalled that the Treasury had made stabilization agreements with Mexico through the U.S. Exchange Stabilization Fund. Although Mexico had not drawn on the arrangements, it had benefited by gaining a resource in case of need. (In this testimony, Harry did not call it a line of credit, but that was plainly his meaning.) The proposed IMF would be "a much larger venture, more comprehensive in scope, but the theory is somewhat similar." This reasoning was more fog than answer, but it served to deflect Taft's attack.[24]

Third, Taft suggested that stabilizing currencies around the world, which was to be one purpose of the IMF, was both unworkable and unnecessary. All that was needed, and all that could be done in the short term, was to stabilize the relationship between the two dominant currencies, the dollar and the pound sterling.

Taft's inspiration for this conclusion was a series of papers by one of Harry's former teachers at Harvard, John H. Williams, by then the dean of the Graduate School of Public Administration at that university and the vice president for research at the Federal Reserve Bank of New York. Williams had been promoting a "key-currency plan" since the mid-1930s, and since mid-1943 he had presented it as an alternative to the Keynes

---

* In the event, the United States has drawn on its quota at the IMF on several occasions, most notably in response to a sharp decline in the exchange value of the dollar in 1978. No objections have ever been raised by other countries.

and White plans for Bretton Woods. Related research at the New York Fed suggested that the 1936 Tripartite Agreement, which aimed to stabilize exchange rates among the dollar, pound, and French franc, offered another simple alternative to the Bretton Woods agreements.[25]

The magnitude of the external debt that Britain had accumulated during the war implied to Williams that the world could not expect Britain to move smoothly toward an open and liberal trade and exchange system within the first few years of peace, as envisaged in the Bretton Woods agreements. That problem, he believed, was what really mattered for postwar financial stability; and it had to be tackled through bilateral arrangements, not by a complicated scheme involving more than forty countries.[26]

Taft embraced the key-currency view, and Williams testified at the Senate hearings at his invitation. Taft himself raised the point several times and questioned first Acheson, then Ned Brown, and finally Harry about why one should not just negotiate an exchange rate between the dollar and the pound and let other currencies respond subsequently. Harry replied, "This is the problem that we are faced with: The appropriate level for sterling depends in part upon the level that is fixed for other countries." He then offered a tutorial on the importance of looking at effective rather than bilateral exchange rates. Taft tried to insist that the one key bilateral rate determined all other rates, and that in any event the others were too uncertain to be determined in advance. Harry rejoined that while "the task of determining exchange rates in the coming months is not an easy one . . . [and] there doubtless will be some errors made," nonetheless it "is not an insuperable task . . . , [and] we have provided certain protective provisions . . . to make possible changes where an error has been made."[27] The Americans and the British had discussed the key-currency plan extensively in the negotiations leading to Bretton Woods, and they had rejected it as an inadequate transition to a multilateral system.

Fourth, Taft worried that decisions of the IMF would be controlled by debtor countries and that the United States would be outvoted on issues of vital national interest. The country was "giving our money to a board which is controlled by the debtors, the very fellows who are going to borrow. That underlies the whole fund." Harry replied by emphasizing the basic principle of a multilateral institution: "Senator, one of the very important and extremely desirable features about this fund is that we do not dictate the monetary policy of the whole world. We do not tell other countries what the gold parities of their currencies shall be, and we do not want any other country to tell us what the gold parity of the dollar shall be. That is a matter of agreement among many countries."[28]

The crux of this issue was whether the United States could rely on the cooperation of other members of the IMF. Harry insisted that it could:

> The American representative will have certain ideas as to what the appropriate decision should be. And I assure you that if the American representative has certain views, unless he is wrong, he is going to be joined by representatives of other countries who also have a sense of fiduciary responsibility, who also have an equal desire to see that the fund will work well, who have an equal desire to see that there shall not be monetary disruption, and who have an interest even greater than ours in seeing that the resources of the fund are not unnecessarily dissipated or unwisely used.[29]

A long argument ensued, and both men got a little testy. At one point, Taft complained that "Mr. White . . . makes a speech every time you ask him a question. You never can get through." To which Harry responded, "Probably if I am not interrupted I can make the answers shorter." To bring the debate back to the point, he acknowledged that there were risks but insisted that the system had to be built on a measure of trust: "If you have no confidence in the other countries, if you do not believe that they are entering into this agreement seriously, wholeheartedly, in order to achieve the same objectives that we desire to achieve, if you believe that they have no sense of fiduciary responsibility, that they intend to enter the fund and permit the dissipation of its assets as quickly as possible, then I say you should vote against the proposal. But that was not the spirit of the representatives there. That is not the basis upon which we are seeking international collaboration."[30]

Fifth, Taft objected to the "scarce currency" clause in Article VII of the IMF charter. As we saw in chapter 10, the insertion of that provision was a crucial compromise for getting to an agreement between the U.S. and British teams. If the United States was to run a large and persistent surplus in its current account, the recurring demand for dollars from deficit countries could threaten to exhaust the IMF's supply. That would trigger a series of actions to apply pressure on the exchange rate and on the U.S. authorities to correct the imbalance. Without the clause, the onus for adjustment could fall entirely on countries with deficits. In Taft's mind, this provision was a giveaway to profligate debtors.

In response, Harry explained that the first effect of IMF operations in such a case would be to delay the onset of a general scarcity of dollars by enabling deficit countries to purchase them temporarily from the fund and thus continue buying U.S exports. If dollars became scarce anyway, then a formal procedure would be triggered. But, he asserted, "we do not believe that is likely to happen." Taft pressed on and pointed out that Article VII permitted deficit countries to discriminate against U.S. exports in conditions of scarcity. Harry countered that without the IMF, such discrimination would be inevitable. The availability of the IMF would postpone and, he hoped, prevent that situation from arising. That response led into a lengthy technical discussion, joined by other Treasury officials, on how the IMF could prevent countries from cheating by accumulating gold and dollar reserves off their official books.[31]

Sixth, Taft argued that the provision in Article XIV of the IMF charter for a transition period before countries would have to eliminate exchange restrictions for current transactions was a loophole that would render the whole agreement meaningless. "Well, it seems to me that article XIV . . . is so indefinite and so uncertain that we have no assurance that we are going to get rid of any of these restrictions short of 5 years or perhaps some time after 5 years." On this point, Taft was right, but, as Harry was quick to point out, the loophole was essential. It would have been impossible to take off all restrictions right away, because most countries lacked the gold and foreign exchange to allow their residents to buy imports without restrictions. Phasing in the convertibility of currencies was preferable to the alternatives, such as competitive devaluations, punitive tariffs, or other barriers to trade. Harry then effectively ended the argument with an emotional plea: "We are attempting to do something along these lines for the first time in history. We are attempting to get countries to cooperate together toward the elimination of the type of restrictions which result in general lowering of the level of world trade. Now, that achievement must be a gradual process. If you attempted to do it suddenly, drastically, you would get nowhere. It would simply end in a break-down. You have to do it gradually. You have to recognize the difficulties which other countries are faced with."[32]

Taft's final attempt to derail the bill was to suggest that Bretton Woods was just a return to the gold standard by another name. That opened an opportunity for Harry to expound on the concept of "fixed but adjustable" exchange rates, as one of the central innovations that he and Keynes had devised for the postwar system. The gold standard had produced a rigid system of fixed exchange rates. The new system would be quite different.

I think there is one difference, Senator Taft, which needs clarifica-
tion. There is confusion, very unfortunate confusion, between the
word "stability" and the word "rigidity." Stability does not mean
rigidity. Stability does not mean fixed rates. Stability means that
degree of flexibility which will not upset the economy, which will
not induce major disequilibrium. For instance, I am told that the
tower of the Empire State Building in New York sways something
like 20 inches in the wind. I imagine any engineer would say that
that provides stability; that if you did not provide for that swaying
it would be rigid and the tower might topple. It is the same thing
with exchange rates. What we are interested in is to avoid disruption and decline in world trade. The way to do that is to have
stability and not rigidity. We have tried rigidity in the past and it
has broken down.[33]

None of Harry's explanations convinced Taft to back down, but his
testimony probably did help limit Taft's support in the committee. A few
days after Harry concluded his sixth and final day of testimony, the committee voted in favor of the Bretton Woods Agreements Act, fourteen to
four. Joining Taft in opposition were just three other Republican senators:
John W. Thomas (Idaho), Hugh A. Butler (Nebraska), and Eugene Mil-
likin (Colorado). Three other Republicans voted in favor, along with all
Democratic senators who voted. (One member from each party did not
vote.) The full Senate approved the legislation on July 19; majorities of
both parties were represented in the final tally, 61–16. President Harry S.
Truman then signed the bill into law on August 4.

The United States was the first of the forty-four countries represented
at Bretton Woods to ratify the agreements. That approval unleashed a
flood of other ratifications around the world. The IMF and the World
Bank officially came into being on December 27, 1945, with thirty-six
member countries. Eventually, every country at Bretton Woods joined
both organizations, with the notable exception of the Soviet Union.

Postwar Aid for Great Britain

After Morgenthau resigned as Treasury secretary and was replaced by Fred
Vinson in July 1945, Harry's influence in discussions about postwar financial aid waned, but he continued to press for large but controlled assistance for Britain. The crucible was a round of negotiations in Washington

in response to a request from the British government for a grant of $6 billion to help restart the British economy after the war. That request was the opening gambit of a negotiating strategy. Earlier, Keynes had hoped for total assistance of $8 billion: a $3 billion grant plus a $5 billion long-term loan. More realistically, at the outset of the negotiations Keynes hoped to get a grant of $5 billion, but he expected no additional credit.[34]

Keynes again was to head the British negotiating mission, and the American side was to be led by Vinson and William L. Clayton, the assistant secretary of state for economic affairs. Harry was to serve as an adviser to Vinson, though he had far less authority to shape the proceedings than he had enjoyed under Morgenthau.

Around the beginning of September, as Keynes and his colleagues were sailing to America from England, Harry proposed a negotiating strategy for the American side. The essence of it was that the U.S. team should begin by insisting on much more detailed information on Britain's economic situation and its need for assistance. In the short term, the U.S. government could help Britain by providing loans through the Export-Import Bank. As the economic situation became clearer, consideration could be given to offering more substantial assistance in exchange for concessions on British trade preferences to countries in the sterling area and the Commonwealth. Harry worried that acceding to the British request for a large grant or a long-term loan at zero interest would risk opening the door to similar demands from the Soviet Union, China, and other allies and would be extremely unlikely to be approved by Congress.[35]

Harry's plan was largely ignored. He and Keynes quickly realized that the shift in leadership from Morgenthau to Vinson at the Treasury and from Edward R. Stettinius to James F. Byrnes as secretary of state had shifted the ground under the negotiations. In a report to London on September 10, Keynes explained the shift. "White was emphatic that in the long run it would be the advice of Clayton and Vinson which would determine the President's action. . . . I gather that it is the intention both of Clayton and Vinson to sit in fairly continuously on the main committees in a way in which their predecessors never would. Vinson explained to me . . . that he wants to give close attention to the factual presentation of our case so that he feels he is thoroughly soaked in it."[36]

As negotiations proceeded in Washington, meetings of the so-called Top Committee were chaired by either Vinson or Clayton. When Clayton was in the chair, Vinson usually represented the Treasury. Harry participated as a representative only when Vinson was absent. Other U.S. members represented the Federal Reserve System, the Commerce Department, and other federal agencies. Harry's initial proposal was for the U.S. government to lend Britain $5 billion at zero interest, with a very long (say, fifty-year) amortization. He warned Keynes at the outset, however, that the Top Committee was unlikely to go that far and that Congress would be unlikely to approve such a plan. As a possible fallback, he suggested that the United States might instead assume part of Britain's external debts to countries in the sterling area, but Keynes resisted that approach.[37]

By September 26 the Top Committee meetings produced agreement on aid of $5 billion, but the two sides were far apart on terms. The Americans were convinced that Congress would approve the plan only if the aid took the form of an interest-bearing loan. Keynes's instructions from London were to insist on a grant. Discussions were continuing as well on associated nonmonetary issues, including the future of the sterling area and the timing and other terms for the unwinding of blocked sterling balances. Throughout this period, Harry's role was largely confined to the technical committee that was assisting the higher-level Top Committee.

Behind the proscenium, Harry was trying to cope with the widespread American opposition—in Congress, some government agencies, and the public at large—to further financial aid, now that the war was over. As he had done so successfully with the Bretton Woods agreements, he wanted to devise a scheme that would disguise but not reduce the generosity of the assistance to Britain. Keynes described it as "a rather fascinating contraption of Harry's," the point of which was "to make the whole affair so complicated that the average Congressman has no idea what it amounts to and whether or not interest does or does not truly emerge."[38]

Harry's scheme included having the U.S. government acquire a portion of the claims against the United Kingdom held by sterling-area countries, discounted from a notional maturity date at 3 percent interest. The British government would then undertake to repay the principal on the claims but not the interest. Keynes calculated that this part of the plan could be worth $2.5 billion to the United Kingdom. As a condition for this assistance, the U.S. government would require the sterling-area countries to make interest-free loans to the British. Intrigued, Keynes concluded that the plan was "conceived on extremely generous lines" and that it "might prove attractive to the general public."[39]

Although Keynes convinced himself that Harry's plan had a decent chance of becoming part of the final package, he was overestimating the influence that Harry retained at that stage. On October 12 Harry warned him that he might get a "nasty surprise," because members of the Treasury team were unable to persuade their colleagues in other agencies of the need for a generous offer. Discussions continued until early December, at the end of which Vinson and Clayton effectively forced an exhausted Keynes to accept a loan of just $3.75 billion at 2 percent interest; repayments were to start after five years.

The outcome of the negotiations was unsatisfactory. The desire of U.S. officials to help Britain was not strong enough to overcome popular resistance, and the final terms were too onerous to overcome the precarious state of British finances. Harry was among the participants who failed to achieve a better result, and some of the blame must be laid on his shoulders. He had a tendency throughout the war to underestimate Britain's financial needs and to overestimate the strength of the British economy. He saw that Britain's economic distress was less severe than Russia's, and he concluded that Russia had at least as compelling a case for assistance as Britain.[40]

Although there is no compelling reason to doubt the sincerity of Harry's efforts to secure a $5 billion loan to Britain on generous terms, he may not have devoted himself to the cause with the same fervor and skill that characterized his wartime efforts. The combination of his waning influence in the Treasury and his lack of conviction regarding both the need for a large grant element and the feasibility of persuading Congress to approve it may well have emasculated his drive to achieve a better outcome.*

More generally, Harry concluded that his own institutional offspring, the IMF and the World Bank, were more appropriate conduits for postwar assistance than a continuation of bilateral aid. He made that case most clearly in a January 1945 article in the journal *Foreign Affairs* and in a second article published the following year in the *Young Democrat*. In *Foreign Affairs*, he argued that the case for large-scale bilateral assistance was off the mark. "To facilitate the restoration of balance in her international accounts Britain needs an expansion of world trade. A loan to Britain . . . will not of itself help significantly with Britain's problem, or with the world's problem of establishing a sound postwar pattern of international pay-

---

* Robert Skidelsky greatly exaggerates the situation when he claims that Harry "stabbed [Keynes] in the back, and he [Keynes] never realized it" (*John Maynard Keynes: Fighting for Britain*, 423). Richard Gardner's assessment that "some of the blame . . . must be placed on Harry White, who still had some of the power he had acquired under Secretary Morgenthau" (*Sterling-Dollar Diplomacy*, 195), is closer to the mark, but it exaggerates the extent of Harry's influence with Vinson.

ments. Such a loan might burden Britain with dollar debt while making no real contribution toward balancing Britain's international payments. On the other hand, the Fund and the Bank, by providing the favorable conditions necessary for expanding world trade and investment, would be of real help."[41]

On the other side of the pond, Churchill understood the constraints on American largesse, and he viewed the glass as far more than half full. Both as prime minister and later, he famously and repeatedly called Lend-Lease assistance to Britain the "most unsordid act in the whole of recorded history" (a characterization that is often misattributed as a reference to the postwar Marshall Plan).[42] Farther down the hierarchy, however, those in the British government who had to find ways to live within the limits of the available funds and then try to recover past economic glories naturally resented the assignment. That resentment, in addition to the wartime tensions between the U.S. Treasury and the State Department regarding the degree of sympathy toward Britain's economic problems, gave rise to a controversy that has never quite died down. As Morgenthau's "numbers man," Harry continues to be blamed for being anti-British, tightfisted, and at least partly responsible for the postwar secular decline in British economic and financial strength.

Postwar Failure of U.S.–Soviet Relations

Toward the end of 1945, after the death of Roosevelt, the end of World War II, and the establishment of the United Nations, Harry became alarmed as the tensions and conflicts between Russia and the United States—largely suppressed but never quite dormant during the war—resumed overtly in both countries. As chapter 8 recounted, he had tried and failed throughout 1944 and the early part of 1945 to promote financial cooperation in the form of a postwar loan. That loan was intended to enable Russia to help rebuild its largely destroyed economy by buying U.S. exports. Despite that failure, Harry quietly began planning to make a public case for continued cooperation in the postwar era. Keeping that alliance alive, he believed, was both necessary and sufficient to prevent the onset of the third major war of the twentieth century. "No major war is possible in the next couple of generations at least with these two countries at peace with each other," he wrote in an unfinished note. No matter how much Germany or Japan might want to try again, no matter what England might do or fail to do to forestall conflict, such developments would matter little if the United States and Russia could resolve the "points of conflict" that divided them.[43]

After drafting four pages in this hopeful vein, Harry stopped without setting down a plan for bridging the divide. Perhaps he got too busy with immediate tasks and deadlines. Perhaps Stalin's decision that month not to join the IMF demoralized him. Perhaps he lost confidence that his hopes could ever be realized. Whatever the motivation, he had reached the end of that journey.

Despite the collapse of his hopes, Harry never lost sight of the goal. In March 1946, for example, when U.S. Senator Claude Pepper (Democrat from Florida) delivered a speech on the Senate floor calling for cooperation rather than conflict in relations with the Soviet Union, Harry wrote a passionate letter to Pepper, thanking him for having "the courage to speak out in the face of powerful and ruthless opposition."[44]

Was this failure to establish a sound economic and diplomatic postwar relationship between the two remaining superpowers a missed opportunity, or was it a Quixotic adventure from the outset? Soviet intransigence, excessive demands, and unilateral dominance of liberated territories in Eastern Europe made the project unlikely to succeed, but there is reason to believe that the Soviet leadership understood how much they had to gain from a deal. From Moscow, Ambassador Averill Harriman cabled that Foreign Minister Vyacheslav M. Molotov had told him that his government placed "great importance . . . on a large postwar credit as a basis for the development of relations between the United States and the Soviet Union."[45] Perhaps so, but Stalin obviously attached greater importance to establishing control over contiguous countries in Europe.

Harry had begun to promote cooperation with Russia in 1939 in the belief that Russia would be too tied down with domestic problems to venture into territorial expansion. When, in 1945, that proved to be wildly optimistic, the plan was doomed, and the onset of the Cold War was foreordained.

CHAPTER FOURTEEN

Dangerous Diversions, 1944–46

The major task that confronts American diplomacy . . . is to
devise means whereby friendship and military alliance can be
assured between the United States and Russia.

—Harry White, 1945

WHILE HARRY WHITE WAS engaged in the efforts to ratify the Bretton
Woods agreements and secure postwar financial support for Great Britain and the Soviet Union, he was also drawn into major controversies
involving Germany and the Soviet Union. One was a scheme devised by
his boss, Treasury Secretary Morgenthau, to pastoralize Germany after
the war. The other was an interagency decision to share the printing of
banknotes for the occupation of Germany with the Soviet Union. The
third was a quiet effort to sustain the Grand Alliance that had joined the
interests of the United States and Russia throughout the war.

The Morgenthau Plan for Germany

Almost immediately after the Bretton Woods conference ended in July
1944, Morgenthau turned his attention to postwar planning for Germany.
Until then, Cordell Hull's State Department had effectively controlled the
U.S. government's planning. As was the case on most international issues

throughout the FDR presidency, Hull and Morgenthau were at odds. Hull and his associates wanted to help Germany rebuild itself into a robust but demilitarized economy and to require it to repay the victorious Allies over time through a reparations program. The State Department developed a plan—to be issued through the interdepartmental Executive Committee on Economic Foreign Policy (ECEFP)—for the allies to occupy and partition Germany, extract large reparations payments (as they had after World War I), and oversee the rebuilding of the German economy. Morgenthau feared that the plan would enable Germany to rearm gradually and initiate a third major war, perhaps as soon as twenty years after the end of the second.

An extensive literature has evolved on Morgenthau's obsession with Germany in 1944 and 1945, much of which includes attempts to psychoanalyze his motives. The historian John Lewis Gaddis, for example, concluded that "Morgenthau's plan . . . is understandable as a reflection of irrational wartime hatred for a cruel and stubborn enemy." Michael Beschloss suggested that Morgenthau "was an original believer in collective guilt for German war crimes." Contemporaneous observers chimed in as well. According to Bruce Craig, Assistant Secretary of War John J. McCloy believed that the plan "could be directly attributed to [Morgenthau's] deep personal need to serve as the avenging angel for world Jewry." Similarly, Craig quotes Secretary of War Henry L. Stimson as attributing the plan to Morgenthau's being "biased by his Semitic grievances."[1]

The Allies' advancement through German-held territory in the months following the D-Day landings in Normandy revealed to the world the horrors of the Holocaust. Morgenthau had been working quietly ever since Hitler came to power in 1933 to use his influence to help alleviate the plight of Jews and other refugees trying to escape from Europe. As an empathic human being, as a Jew (albeit completely secular), and as the father of a son serving in the army in France, Morgenthau had every reason to despise Nazi Germany and to fear the country's recurring tendency to wage war on its neighbors. As the genocide of European Jewry became clearer, his emotions would naturally have been elevated and may have amplified his conviction that Germany had to be prevented from ever regaining the ability to wage war. Whatever the mix of rational analysis and emotional fervor might have been, the result was an indisputably ill-advised and excessive plan to emasculate Germany.

Harry's role in the gestation of the plan is unclear. Neither the politics of postwar reconstruction nor the practicalities of reparations planning were in his remit, and he was otherwise engaged with the effort to win ratification of the Bretton Woods agreements. He was, however, drawn into abetting the development of the plan to an extent that he later came to regret. In August 1948, during Harry's last public appearance, testifying before the House Un-American Activities Committee, Representative John McDowell (Republican from Pennsylvania) confronted him: "I have been told that you were the author of the famous Morgenthau Plan. I presume that is true; is it?" Harry first tried to deflect the question with his customary bite: "Did you also hear that I was the author of the famous White Plan, by chance?" He then answered the question more directly: "No; I would not quite say that. I would say that I participated in a major way in the formulation of a memorandum which was . . . given to the President." He tried to comment further, but McDowell realized that he was charging up the wrong hill, and he cut Harry off and changed the subject.[2]

The Morgenthau Plan aimed to prohibit Germany from rebuilding its industries and force it to convert its economy primarily to agriculture. This "pastoralization" scheme was controversial for two reasons.

First, it was clear to almost everyone who thought about it for more than two minutes that forcing Germany to become an agricultural rather than industrial economy would endanger the economic viability of the whole of Europe and would create an unstoppable backlash both within Germany and throughout its extended neighborhood. However well-intentioned Morgenthau was, his plan was unworkable. Keynes summarized the problem succinctly in a letter to the chancellor of the Exchequer shortly after he received a copy of the plan from Morgenthau. The pastoralization plan, he wrote, "looks quite hopelessly impractical, creating intolerable conditions of a kind which world opinion could not conceivably allow, without any hint as to how they can be ameliorated."[3]

Second, it was clear to some analysts at the time, and it became more evident later, that emasculation of Germany would create an opportunity for the Soviet Union to extend its influence in Eastern and Central Europe. Morgenthau, however, was not alone among senior U.S. officials in believing that the Soviets would have neither the will nor the ability to take advantage of that opportunity.

Once the Cold War began and the Soviet Union successfully established control over East Germany and other countries behind what Truman branded the Iron Curtain, it became fashionable to suggest that Morgenthau must have known that such a disaster was coming. When Harry came under attack for an alleged role in Soviet espionage, his association with the Morgenthau Plan became an excuse for some to argue that the plan was a deliberate attempt to create a vacuum that Soviet forces would rush to fill. A detailed report in 1967 by the U.S. Senate subcommittee on internal security made that case explicitly. Despite the absence of evidence for that speculation, the hypothesis continues to be advanced to this day.[4]

The inspiration for the plan began on a transatlantic flight to Europe in August 1944. Morgenthau had first suggested making the trip while he was taking a break from the Bretton Woods conference on July 6. In conversation with President Roosevelt that day, he asked if he could go to France after the conference "to see how the currency was getting along."[5] Roosevelt agreed, and Morgenthau began preparing for a trip to England and France, to take place the following month. Meanwhile, separately, a committee led by the State Department was completing its report on Germany for the ECEFP. Harry was officially on the committee, but he was busy at Bretton Woods and delegated his role to subordinates. Whether he read the report before the trip is unclear because firsthand recollections are not fully consistent. Nonetheless, Harry's proximity at the moment of gestation has enabled speculation that he could somehow have been a Svengali to a susceptible Henry Morgenthau.

The journalist Charles Whipple stirred up speculation in 1953 by writing, "The story goes that White had written the so-called Morgenthau Plan to make post-war Germany an agrarian nation, and sold it to his boss, who bypassed the State and War Departments and took it to the Quebec conference." In a more recent example, Bruce Craig described a discussion between White and Josiah Ellis ("Joe") DuBois (assistant general counsel for the Treasury) in which White criticized the State Department report as being contrary to Morgenthau's views. Craig's account implied that this conversation took place before the trip to England and therefore constituted evidence that Harry was the inspiration for Morgenthau's thinking. DuBois's account, however, did not indicate whether the discussion took place then or later. (DuBois elsewhere described a meeting before the trip, but that account did not include any suggestion that White told him the State Department report conflicted with Morgenthau's views.) On this slender reed, Craig argued that the Morgenthau Plan developed "under the tutelage of Harry White," and he cited magazine articles and other secondary sources that had drawn similar conclusions.[6]

The most authoritative and detailed accounts of the origin of the Morgenthau Plan were written by E. Francis Penrose and Fred Smith, both of whom were present when Morgenthau first discussed it during

this trip. Smith, an assistant to the secretary of the Treasury with responsibility for public relations, accompanied Morgenthau and White on the
journey. Penrose, an adviser to the U.S. ambassador in London, participated in some of the meetings in England. Other snippets are available
from recollections by Morgenthau and another participant in the trip,
Joe DuBois.

Morgenthau, White, Smith, and DuBois left Washington on August 6
with the expressed purpose of assessing the functioning of the occupation
currencies that the Allied Expeditionary Force was issuing to its troops
as they occupied a widening swath of territory across Europe. After a refueling stop at Presque Isle, Maine, the party crossed the Atlantic on a
military transport plane bound for Prestwick, Scotland. Harry sat next to
Morgenthau, and DuBois and Smith sat directly behind them. When they
headed out over the ocean that morning, as Morgenthau recalled events
three years later, "one of my assistants pulled out of his briefcase a copy
of a State Dept. memorandum on reparations in Germany. I settled back
to read it, first with interest, then with misgivings, and finally with sharp
disagreement."[7]

Many years later, in an oral history in 1973 and in conversation with
Morgenthau's son Henry III in 1981, DuBois recalled overhearing snippets of conversation about Germany between Harry and the secretary, sitting in the row in front of him on the plane. "And by the time we arrived in
England, there was no question in my mind that [Morgenthau] was at this
point completely convinced that the approach that the State Department
had suggested was the wrong approach."[8]

The accounts of Morgenthau and DuBois are mostly consistent. Morgenthau read the State Department report for the first time on that flight.
He disagreed with it vehemently and immediately set about to develop a
much harsher proposal for dealing with the German economy after the
war. What is less clear is what role Harry played in this process other
than possibly handing the report to Morgenthau. Morgenthau's account
gives no indication of his having needed or received any encouragement
to move forward as he subsequently did. Similarly, nothing in DuBois's
accounts suggests that he overheard any of the conversation well enough
to determine who was making which points. In the 1973 oral history interview, DuBois stated explicitly that he did not know whether White expressed any opinion to Morgenthau about the report.

What is even less clear is how much of the report Harry had even
read before the trip. By his own account a few days later (as reported by

Penrose), he did not read the report until a break in a meeting in England on August 12.[9] DuBois, however, in his oral history interview, recalled that he and Harry had discussed the report in Harry's office at the Treasury several days earlier. The truth may well lie in the middle: the various accounts are roughly consistent if Harry gathered the gist of the report before the trip, gave it to Morgenthau on the airplane, and then read it more fully once they were in England.

Regardless of whether Harry first read the State Department report in Washington or later in England, Joe DuBois's account helps clarify what in the report may have upset Harry. The State Department was proposing to demand that Germany make substantial reparations payments to the victorious Allies after the war. Harry was quite familiar with the debate about the wisdom and viability of such reparations after the First World War. In that debate, Keynes had argued that excessive reparations would ruin the German economy and threaten European civilization. In 1929 Keynes amplified the point by emphasizing the "transfer problem": the only way Germany could pay reparations was to generate a trade surplus and earn the foreign exchange to be transferred. That requirement could impose serious costs on the recipients as well. As we saw in chapter 2, Harry aligned himself with Keynes on those issues and argued as early as 1932 that reparations were unnecessary and counterproductive.

In August 1944, upon reading the State Department proposals, Harry realized that the plan would require the Allies to rebuild the German industry that they were systematically destroying in the drive to win the war. He reportedly told DuBois that "it means we're just going to be rebuilding Germany. How are they going to supply us with goods if we don't rebuild their factories?"[10] It is likely that Harry made a similar point to Morgenthau when he showed him the report. Morgenthau needed little convincing. He took the objection further and concluded that Germany must not be allowed to rebuild its industry at all, ever.

An irony in this sequence of events is that Keynes's opposition to reparations derived from his favorable view of the importance of Germany to European prosperity, whereas Harry's opposition derived from an anti-German view. Robert Skidelsky noted that World War I "had not caused [Keynes] to renounce the view, common to his generation, that an economically dynamic Germany was an asset, not a liability to Europe."[11] For Harry, almost a decade younger than Keynes, World War I was the crucible in which he had formed a hatred of Germany while serving in the U.S. Army in France. His opposition to reparations after World War II was based on his objection to the cost that the Allies would bear to enable the payments, not on the likely cost to Germany.

At the end of the flight on August 6, the Treasury party landed in Scotland around midnight and immediately boarded a private train that Eisenhower had sent to meet them. The train took them to a secret destination in southern England where Eisenhower had his headquarters. At noon, they met Eisenhower for lunch.

The lunch meeting was immensely consequential. In a 1947 article based on notes taken "directly after the meeting" in question, Smith began his account in dramatic fashion: "On August 7, 1944, at approximately 12:35 P.M., in a tent in southern England, the Morgenthau Plan was born. Actually, it was General Dwight D. Eisenhower who launched the project."[12]

Over lunch, Harry expressed concerns about the military's planning for the occupation of Germany, which involved bringing in the Civil Affairs Division to repair infrastructure and reestablish the civilian economy as efficiently as possible. Harry suggested that since the European war would be over as soon as the Allies occupied Germany, it would not be necessary to move that quickly. "What I think is that we should give the entire German economy an opportunity to settle down before we do anything with it." Eisenhower, in Smith's recollection, "became grim" and replied, "I am not interested in the German economy and personally would not like to bolster it if that would make it any easier for the Germans. . . . The ringleaders and the SS troops should be given the death penalty without question, but punishment should not end there." He wanted to "see things made good and hard for them for a while." The desire in some quarters to rebuild Germany quickly was motivated by the goal of preventing Russia from expanding the territory under its control. In Eisenhower's view, that was unnecessary because Russia "has problems of her own which will keep her busy until long after we are dead."[13]

Morgenthau's own recollection of the discussion confirmed its essence but differed somewhat on the sequence. Debriefing his staff after the trip, he stated that he (not Harry) opened the discussion by asking Eisenhower where he stood on the treatment of Germany. The general "was very positive that he was going to treat them rough. He was perfectly willing to let them stew in their own juice at the beginning, which is quite contrary to the plans of G5, which General Holmes has been making."[14] Morgenthau's 1947 newspaper article, however, acknowledged that Eisenhower's reaction was prompted by the arguments of "one of my assistants."

The G5 was an allied military committee set up by Eisenhower to develop plans for the return of Europe to civilian life after the war. Brigadier General Julius C. Holmes was the ranking American, serving as deputy to the Canadian head of G5.

Eisenhower's bitter firmness and underestimation of Russia's intentions and capabilities were all the inspiration Morgenthau needed to develop the plan that evidently had been percolating in his mind for some time. After some sightseeing around the nearby docks, a visit with wounded soldiers at a U.S. Army hospital, and a second night's sleep on the train, the Treasury team flew to Cherbourg, France, with a fighter escort the next day and transferred to General Omar N. Bradley's headquarters. There, just thirty or so miles from the front line where the Allies were still pushing German troops out of Normandy, they met with Bradley and other senior officers and viewed Omaha and Utah beaches and other liberated areas. They spent some time on their ostensible purpose, assessing the functioning of the occupation currency issued by the Allied military to its soldiers. The secretary also was able to meet with his son, Henry Morgenthau III, who was serving in the Third Army under Bradley. As soon as they could, however, the foursome returned to England, where they were billeted at Red Rice, a large estate in Hampshire that the U.S. Army was occupying.[15]

By the time Morgenthau reached England again, he was focused fully on the German issue. As he excitedly debriefed his staff upon his return to Washington, "I didn't go over for that, but I made that my business." First, he went into London, where he met with John Anderson, the chancellor of the Exchequer. When he told Anderson that he had "an idea which is purely my own, . . . [to] divide Germany into a number of smaller provinces, stop all industrial production and convert them into small agricultural landholders," the chancellor responded with "dead silence." Morgenthau then met with Winston Churchill and came away convinced that the prime minister was more supportive.[16]

The most important meeting of the trip was held at Red Rice on Sunday, August 12. Morgenthau invited U.S. Ambassador John Gilbert Winant, who brought Penrose along, together with two more aides from the State Department, Walter Radius and Philip Mosely; Colonel Bernard Bernstein, a lawyer who had previously served as legal counsel under Morgenthau at the Treasury and who was now serving under Eisenhower in the Civil Affairs Division; and Robert Sherwood of the Office of War Information. In addition to DuBois, Smith, and White, the Treasury was represented at the meeting by L. C. Aarons and William H. ("Bill") Taylor.

In Smith's account of the meeting, Morgenthau opened the discussion by laying out his vision of converting Germany into an agrarian society. Next, Bernstein explained the current state of thinking in the Civil Affairs Division, which was focused on how to take control and administer Germany efficiently. Winant then described how little information his office had received about the strategic thinking of either the U.S. or the British government. Harry wrapped up the discussion by saying, "What we want from Germany is peace, not reparations," as had been the disastrous policy following World War I. If that meant weakening the economy, then that would have to be done.

Penrose's account is more detailed, and it differs from Smith's in important respects. He wrote that he (not Winant) began the lunch discussion by explaining his understanding of British views on postwar planning for Germany. He omitted any reference to Bernstein's intervention, and he described Harry's remarks as a "purely descriptive summing up" of what had been said so far. After lunch, the group took a recess, during which Penrose asked Harry if he had read the papers that the interagency committee had prepared in Washington. Harry replied that someone had given him a copy in his briefing book, but he had not read it. Penrose concluded that there "was nothing to indicate that up to this time he had studied the subject or formulated even the barest outlines of any 'plan' on it." When the group reconvened in the afternoon, on the lawn of the estate so that they could enjoy a bit of the August sunshine, Morgenthau set out his plan in some detail for the first time. Harry then followed with what Penrose characterized as "transforming the Secretary's sketchy and spasmodic exposition . . . into a clear, amplified, and well-organized restatement." Penrose determined that Harry had come "as nearly as possible to clothing a bad thesis with an appearance of intellectual respectability."[17]

Winant, Penrose, and the other participants from the State Department were appalled at Morgenthau's adamant advocacy for an unworkable policy. Penrose's psychoanalysis of the affair was that both Morgenthau and White were "so deeply aroused over the unprovoked aggression and the horrifying crimes of the Germans in occupied countries that they were not open to reason when it came to postwar German questions."[18] Possibly, but Harry at least was usually not one to fall prey to emotion in policy discussions. Alternatively, he might have seen the futility of opposing his boss on an issue that was rapidly becoming a personal obsession. For whatever reason, he allowed himself to become one of the principal drafters of the conversion of Morgenthau's obsession into a specific proposal to President Roosevelt.

Back in Washington, Morgenthau apparently asked his legal staff to recommend a process to advance his plan. On August 21, John Pehle, the lawyer in charge of Foreign Funds Control, recommended that the secretary name a drafting committee to prepare a preliminary report. The group would comprise himself (Pehle), Ansel Luxford (assistant to the secretary), and Harry. It would report to a committee headed by the secretary, which would also include Under Secretary Daniel W. Bell, Assistant Secretary Herbert E. Gaston, General Counsel Joseph J. O'Connell Jr., Pehle, and Harry. Morgenthau did as Pehle suggested, but he specifically asked Harry to "carry the ball."[19]

On August 22 Harry and Bill Taylor met with Major General John H. Hilldring, the head of the Civil Affairs Division of the U.S. Army. Hilldring's reaction was supportive and similar to Eisenhower's. Taylor's minutes of the meeting reported that Hilldring "agreed entirely with Mr. White that the prime concern in treating with Germany was not reparations or other such matters, but rather the fact that we must be sure we are not doing anything to put Germany into a position where she can wage war again in our time."[20]

On September 2 Harry represented the Treasury at an interdepartmental meeting at the White House, in the office of Roosevelt's adviser Harry Hopkins. He presented Morgenthau's ideas to representatives of the State and War departments, all of whom pushed back against the more extreme elements of the plan. The State Department then produced its own milder alternative, calling for the conversion (in some unspecified way) of "German economic capacity . . . in such manner that it will be so dependent on imports and exports that Germany cannot by its own devices reconvert to war production."[21]

As drafting proceeded within the Treasury for a memorandum to submit to Roosevelt, Harry's group tried to tone down several items on Morgenthau's wish list, but the secretary kept insisting on as tough a set of measures as possible. Notably, Harry wanted to replace Morgenthau's idea of destroying the industrial base in the Ruhr with an international overseer. On September 4 he told Morgenthau, "You might think of the alternative, a very different one, of making the Ruhr an industrial area under international control which will produce reparations for twenty years." Morgenthau was having none of it. "Harry, you can't sell it to me at all," he replied, "because you have it there only so many years and you have an

Anschluss and the Germans go in and take it. The only thing you can sell me, or I will have any part of, is the complete shut-down of the Ruhr."[22]

Discussions continued throughout the day, but Harry was left with no choice but to accept the secretary's "shut-down" proposal. By the end of September 4, he and his team had produced the revised memorandum that became the core of the Morgenthau Plan. It called for the demilitarization of Germany; partitioning the country into two states and an international zone, portions of the original territory being ceded to France and Poland; steps to destroy German industry to an extent that the Ruhr area, "the caldron of wars," should be "so weakened that it can never again become an industrial area"; renunciation of periodic reparations in favor of confiscation of certain German assets and other measures, including "forced German labor outside Germany"; the immediate closing of all educational institutions and media outlets until they could be restructured to prevent their use for propaganda; and other measures to prevent the reintroduction of any militarization.[23]

Harry's major involvement in planning for postwar control of Germany ended there. He continued to participate in some discussions, and he tried occasionally without success to persuade Morgenthau to soften his insistence on deindustrialization. The negotiations, however, took place at higher levels. The first key event was a meeting between Roosevelt and Churchill in Quebec City, which Roosevelt asked Morgenthau to attend. Morgenthau took Harry along because both the future of Lend-Lease aid to Britain and postwar planning for Germany were to be on the agenda. The two leaders agreed to implement procedures in line with the Morgenthau Plan, so that "the metallurgical, chemical, and electrical industries . . . in the Ruhr and in the Saar would . . . be . . . put out of action and closed down."[24]

After the Quebec conference, everyone outside the Treasury started backtracking. Roosevelt's enthusiasm was dampened by the continuing opposition from the State Department and elsewhere. Similarly, Churchill was dissuaded by his advisers, including the foreign minister, Anthony Eden. Morgenthau responded by seizing every opportunity to drum up support among the British. In a meeting in his office on October 17, he pressed Keynes on the matter. Keynes had read the memorandum drafted by Harry's committee, and he diplomatically declared himself to be "in agreement with most of the points made . . . [and] the general approach." Elaborating, however, he averred that he "didn't know quite how far we could go in eliminating industries in Germany." When Morgenthau responded "that he was very happy to learn that Keynes was in sympathy with the general approach," Keynes reminded him that he "didn't think his opinion on this matter made very much difference."[25]

By the time Roosevelt met with Churchill and Josef Stalin at Yalta in February 1945, the Allied directives on Germany were being watered down. The summit communiqué included only a vague statement authorizing the three countries to "take such steps, including the complete disarmament, demilitarization, and the dismemberment of Germany as they deem requisite for future peace and security." Over the next several weeks, negotiations among the Treasury, State, and War departments produced a final agreement designed to decentralize and control the German economy, but without the wholesale destruction of German industry.[26]

Morgenthau declared himself to be satisfied with the outcome, but he never wavered from his conviction that it exposed the world to the risk of a resurgence of German militarism. With Roosevelt's reluctant approval—given practically on the president's deathbed in April 1945—Morgenthau proceeded to produce a book, *Germany Is Our Problem*, published after he left government service, making a public case for the more extreme measures for which he had fought so hard with Harry's help. He elaborated further two years later, in a series of articles in the *New York Post* in which he recounted the inside story of how his plan was developed, discussed, and largely discarded. For his part, Harry remained loyal and never publicly renounced the plan that he had tried to soften. The closest he came was in his attempt to deflect attention from his own role when pressed by Congressman McDowell in 1948, as noted at the beginning of this section.

When *Germany Is Our Problem* was published, in 1945, Morgenthau gave Harry a copy of the book and inscribed it, "For my good friend Harry White, who helped me greatly in getting this book underway, and who assisted me with the original plan for President Roosevelt, with affectionate regards. From Henry Morgenthau Jr." Only later, after Harry's death in 1948, did Morgenthau suggest that "Harry and his associates . . . worked . . . on my book." One such associate, Joe DuBois, recalled in 1973 that he had written "several" chapters himself.[27] Harry's substantive role was probably confined primarily to "getting [it] underway," as Morgenthau wrote in 1945.

Occupation Currencies and the German Plates

As the Allied militaries began to liberate territory from Axis control in the autumn of 1942, they needed a plan for managing the local economies that they would be occupying. Part of the plan had to be to provide currency for the troops to use to buy goods and services locally. Using the country's own currency was not practical in the early days after liberation because the prewar monetary systems were disrupted and degraded, and the invading armies would have had difficulty acquiring enough usable currency. Using U.S. dollars or pounds sterling also raised problems, as it could lead to a flood of redemption requests after the war. Additionally, in cases where the American and other Allied militaries were jointly engaged, they had to coordinate, either by using a common currency or agreeing on exchange rates for separate currencies.[28]

The first test case came in French North Africa, when an Allied force under General Eisenhower invaded in Operation Torch to liberate the region from Nazi rule in November 1942. The army issued specially marked "yellow-seal" (sometimes called "gold-seal") dollar notes as a "spearhead" currency to be used until a viable local currency could be organized. Harry was not yet involved, as he was focused on planning for his international stabilization fund. Daniel W. Bell oversaw this process for the Treasury, working with the Departments of State and War and with British officials. Bell sent Bill Taylor from Harry's division to embed with the invading army and observe how the policy was being implemented.

Taylor reported back that the system was rife with black-market activity. Soldiers had the right to redeem yellow-seal notes for regular U.S. currency when they returned home, and it was not uncommon for them to redeem even more money than they had been paid while on duty. The army command, however, had bigger problems to worry about, and no one was prepared to do anything about it. Separately, Allied European officials, including those in Belgium's government in exile in London, were warning the U.S. government that they would object strongly if the Allies tried to use dollars or pounds in the anticipated liberation of their territory.[29] To Harry and other Treasury staff, it was apparent that as much effort as possible should be devoted in the future to advancing the transition out of spearhead currency and into local denominations.

In February 1943 Bell asked Morgenthau to relieve him of his work on occupation currencies because he was overwhelmed with other tasks. Morgenthau agreed and named Harry to take charge of *all* the Treasury's interactions with the armed forces. Over the next month, Harry reviewed developments in North Africa and then turned his attention to preparations for the next major operation: the invasion of Sicily.

Harry faced two main issues: what sort of currency the U.S. Army should use in the occupation, and what exchange rates should be established between that currency and the U.S. dollar and the normal local currency, the Italian lira. Both issues had to be resolved through negotiations within the U.S. government (principally the Departments of Treasury, State, and War) and with the other Allies, chiefly the British. Although Morgenthau viewed both issues as on Treasury turf, Harry suggested to him that the choice between U.S. and local currencies had an important political dimension in which the State Department would have a strong interest. The Treasury, in Harry's view, should weigh in on both topics but should insist on its prerogatives only on the exchange rate.[30]

On March 30, 1943, Harry put forth a secret memorandum setting out the Treasury position on these issues. It called for two steps: an "invasion stage," in which the U.S. armies would use yellow-seal dollars, followed by an "occupation stage," in which the dollar notes would be replaced by notes denominated in local currency and then by actual local currency "as quickly as possible." The British were to be encouraged to adopt the same procedure and issue pound-denominated "British Military Authority" (BMA) notes in the invasion stage, valued at the prevailing exchange rate ($4 per pound). Other Allied governments should be invited to submit recommendations on exchange rates against their local currencies, but decisions on rates should be made by the American and British governments.[31] These procedures were essentially what was implemented when U.S., British, and Canadian armies liberated Sicily and then the Italian mainland a few months later.

Fixing an appropriate exchange rate between the spearhead currency and the lira proved to be controversial. The official rate was 20 lire to the dollar, but the black-market rate in Italy was at least 100. Roosevelt told Morgenthau he wanted to be "benevolent" to the Sicilian population, but Harry wanted to have a realistic and thus appropriately depreciated rate. In an interagency meeting in April, representatives from State and War argued for a rate in the range of 50 to 75 per dollar. Morgenthau, who seems not to have understood the technical issue very well, told Harry the next day to tell the other agencies that "I wash my hands of it. Let them go ahead and do it just the way they do everything else. I am not going to agree to it, so let them go ahead and do it as they damn please."[32]

Harry had no intention of letting anyone outside the Treasury set the rate as they damn please. He set out to get a rate as close as possible to the black-market rate. He gained the upper hand at the beginning of June when Roosevelt set up an interagency committee for coordinating the "economic operations of United States civilian agencies in areas liberated from enemy control." Roosevelt's plan specified that the "Treasury Department is responsible for fixing exchange rates." Morgenthau designated Harry to carry out that directive. When the army went into Sicily in July, it was instructed to exchange the spearhead currency for lire at the rate of 100 per dollar.[33]

A more serious problem arose toward the end of 1943, as planning was gaining steam for the invasion and occupation of Germany. If all went well, British and American troops would be moving in from the west, while Soviet troops—the Red Army—would be invading from the east. The two forces would then occupy separate regions or zones of the defeated country, but they would need to coordinate their work if they hoped to administer the German economy efficiently. It would be a much more complex and longer-lasting situation than had arisen elsewhere.

On November 24, 1943, the day before the Thanksgiving holiday, Harry met in his office with officials from the British and Soviet embassies (David Whaley and a Mr. Fedotov, the latter probably Anton Nikolaevich Fedotov, who served as an attaché at the Soviet embassy in Washington at that time) to discuss coordination of currency circulation in Germany during the expected occupation. Whaley had agreed to Harry's proposal to issue specially marked notes ("V-Marks" or something similar) to be used by troops from all Allied countries. Fedotov could not agree until he consulted with Moscow, but Harry decided to proceed in the meantime.[34]

The case for the Allies to issue a single occupation currency to all troops, including the Soviets, was strong. Having two separate currencies would raise substantial difficulties, including the need to establish and regulate the exchange rate between the two and the adverse political effects if the two military forces could not present a united front in the administration of the German economy. In January 1944 the U.S. ambassador in Moscow, W. Averell Harriman, discussed the matter with his British counterpart and cabled back to Washington that the "British Government considers most desirable all occupying forces so far as possible use same currency. . . . British Government attach great importance to participation Soviet Government in this scheme."[35] The two Anglophone allies were in full agreement on this principle, and the Soviet government would soon signal its agreement as well.

It quickly became clear, however, that the U.S. Bureau of Engraving and Printing, which would be responsible for the western-zone currency issue, was already stretched well beyond its wartime ability to print and distribute currencies around the world. It had already outsourced the printing of other non-dollar currencies to a private firm, which was working flat out to meet the demand. For two or three months in late 1943 and early 1944, discussions continued within the U.S. government and between the western Allies and the Soviet government on how best to proceed.[36]

As the several U.S. agencies involved in these discussions tried to develop a workable strategy, the Soviet government asked the Americans to provide them with a set of printing plates, which they would use to print identical currency for their own troops. That threw Alvin W. Hall, the director of the Bureau of Engraving and Printing, into a tizzy. (In John Morton Blum's words, Hall was "passionately unhappy.")[37] One of the cardinal rules of the printing press was that the plates had to be guarded more closely than gold, to prevent counterfeiting and abuse. Hall raised strong objections and tried to prevent the government from acceding to the Soviet request.

Treasury officials were divided. Morgenthau was inclined to trust the Soviets and agree to provide the plates, but Bell was opposed. On March 7, 1944, Harry pointed out to them that because the plates could not be used to print U.S. currency, there was little to fear. Nonetheless, he tried to mediate the dispute by persuading the Soviets to withdraw their request. On the evening of March 18, he and Morgenthau met with the Soviet ambassador, Andrei Gromyko, at the secretary's Washington home, to try to talk him out of it. After further discussion among U.S. agencies, Harry met with Gromyko again at the Soviet embassy on March 22, but the request stood.[38]

What none of the U.S. officials knew at the time was that a Soviet intelligence agency, the People's Commissariat for Internal Security (NKVD), was making a clandestine effort to get Harry onto their side of the argument. As the American spy Elizabeth Bentley later described the effort to a Senate subcommittee, her Soviet handler approached her with a request that she ask friends and colleagues of Harry to try to get him in favor of transferring a set of plates. She claimed to have conveyed the request, and she believed that she was personally responsible for the transfer.[39]

Jerrold and Leona Schecter uncovered a cable (cited vaguely as from "Soviet intelligence archives") sent from New York to Moscow on April 15, 1944, reportedly stating that "LAWYER following our instructions passed through ROBERT attained the positive decision of the Treasury Department to provide the Soviet side with the plates."[40] "Lawyer" and "Robert" were code names referring to Harry White and Gregory Silvermaster. That cable provides some confirmation of Bentley's story: the NKVD did ask Bentley to ask Silvermaster to ask White to try to get the Treasury to support transferring the plates. When the U.S. government did agree to the transfer, word quickly got back to Bentley, and she apparently told her handler that she had succeeded in this assignment. To paraphrase an old saying, the sun rose in the morning, and the crowing rooster took the credit.

It is impossible to know whether Silvermaster ever raised the issue directly with Harry, but in any event, there is no evidence that Harry ever changed his mind throughout the internal discussions or even that he had any effect on the outcome beyond serving as a liaison to Gromyko. As Bruce Craig summarized his findings from a thorough review, "White's views already had been formulated and meshed with those of the Soviet Union, and they already were in accord with the overarching American policy objectives." Moreover, the involvement of the Treasury Department was minimal. The State Department view was that it was "essential that we make every effort within our possibility to furnish the plates to [the Soviet] Government."[41] Morgenthau supported the decision, but his main duty was simply to inform Gromyko and to have the Treasury deliver the plates.

What the Schecters' cable also reveals is that the NKVD had a source somewhere inside the government with knowledge of secret interagency decisions. Assuming the date to be correct, the April 15 cable was sent just one day after the Allied Combined Chiefs of Staff, with the support of the U.S. Departments of State and War, decided to provide a duplicate set of currency plates to the Soviet Union. It is possible that Harry mentioned it to Silvermaster, but many other possibilities are just as likely.

The decision to provide the plates to the Soviet government was highly controversial, and it became the subject of much criticism at the height of the postwar anti-Communist hysteria. Both Harry and Bill Taylor were accused of undermining U.S. interests, promoting those of the Soviet Union, and imposing unnecessary costs on the U.S. Treasury. To understand the decision, however, it is necessary to examine the available options. Critics of the decision to provide the plates—including Senate investigators in 1947 and 1953 and an extensive literature on the matter—have implicitly assumed that the alternative was to insist that the U.S. government retain control over the entire currency issue and provide the requisite banknotes to the Soviets.[42] That option, however, was never on the table. First, it would have been technically impossible to print enough banknotes on schedule.[43] Second and more definitively, the Soviets steadfastly refused to consider the idea. (To see the issue from their perspective, consider how the U.S. and British military would have responded to a suggestion that they depend on the Russians to print and distribute all the currency to be used by Allied troops in the western sector.)

The only realistic alternative would have been for the Russians to print a separate and distinct currency for their own troops. That in fact is what the Soviet government threatened to do if their request was denied.[44] Throughout the occupation, at least in its initial stages, two currencies would have circulated in Germany. The Allied Combined Chiefs would have had to establish an exchange rate between the two and oversee their interchange, which they feared could have been chaotic and disruptive. The potential for abuse would have been similar to what it was with the chosen option of having a single currency produced by two sets of printing plates. In either case, if the Russians had wanted to force Britain and the United States to shoulder a greater share of the cost of administering the country, they could have flooded the country with their own output of banknotes and let the western Allies absorb the excess.

In the event, fears of adverse effects proved to be exaggerated. The economist Charles Kindleberger, who was working in the Office of Strategic Services at the time, later dismissed the economic importance of this affair. In his 1991 autobiography, he suggested that the worry came from a "simple-minded view . . . that the Russians could not be trusted not to print a great deal of extra money—despite controls—and use it for their own ends." He concluded that even if they had, the cost to the United States would not have been great. Absorbing occupation currencies did add to the costs incurred by the U.S. Army and the Treasury, but that cost arose primarily from decisions by military commanders not to limit soldiers' redemptions so that they could not redeem more than they had been paid by the army.[45]

Bystander at the Creation: The United Nations

The creation of a United Nations Organization was a long-standing pet project of Franklin Delano Roosevelt. As the Democratic candidate for vice president in 1920, he spoke out often (but unsuccessfully) in favor of U.S. membership in the League of Nations, which was just taking form. By the time he assumed the presidency in 1933, the inadequacy of the League for promoting peaceful cooperation had become all too clear. Roosevelt soured on the institution, but he continued to hope for an effective successor in which the United States would play a leading role. The wartime Grand Alliance served as a stepping-stone. The "Declaration by United Nations" issued by the Grand Alliance was eventually signed by a total of forty-seven countries. The Bretton Woods conference and other multinational wartime conferences were held under the auspices of those United Nations.

In September–October 1944, Roosevelt convened a conference of the four great powers at the Dumbarton Oaks mansion in Washington, D.C., to draft a statement of principles for a permanent successor to the League. Among its stated purposes was to "achieve international cooperation in the solution of international economic, social and other humanitarian problems."[46] He assigned the task of organizing and running the conference to the State Department. The Treasury was to have no substantive role, although Secretary Morgenthau—who never trusted State very much—wanted to have a say in the design of an institution that would have a role, as noted above, in "the solution of international economic . . . problems." As the time of the conference approached, he asked Roosevelt if the Treasury could at least send an observer, but the president decided against having any observers, in order to achieve a degree of intimacy for the discussions.

The Dumbarton Oaks conference succeeded in generating agreement among the four leading allies on a set of principles for establishing the United Nations Organization. After further negotiations with Stalin and Churchill at the February 1945 Yalta summit meeting, Roosevelt planned to convene and personally attend a conference in San Francisco, which would begin in late April and be charged with drafting the charter for the organization. On April 12, during the planning for the conference, Roosevelt died suddenly, leaving the final tasks to Secretary of State Edward Stettinius and his own successor as president, Harry S. Truman.

Preparations for the San Francisco conference were undertaken primarily by a State Department task force headed by Leo Pasvolsky, again without an active role for the Treasury.[47] It was to be a massive undertaking attended by fifty national delegations. Intimacy was no longer an option, and so Morgenthau finally was able to win the president's approval to have a Treasury official present as a technical adviser to the U.S delegation. On March 24, 1945, Morgenthau nominated Harry White to be his man on the scene.[48]

Harry's main responsibility at San Francisco was as one of seven advisers to the U.S. delegation on economic issues. The document issued at Dumbarton Oaks called for the creation of an Economic and Social Council (ECOSOC) under the auspices of the UN General Assembly. The structure and role of ECOSOC were to be determined in San Francisco, and Harry had a special interest in ensuring that the council not impinge on the functions of the IMF or the World Bank, which the U.S. Congress still had to ratify. He knew, however, that he would have a tough time if he tried to influence the proceedings directly. The State Department—especially Pasvolsky, Harry's nemesis and a critic of the Bretton Woods agreements—was not about to share power any more than necessary.

On April 11 Stettinius sent Harry a memorandum detailing a severely circumscribed role for the technical advisers. He would be asked to advise the delegates "on matters in which you are particularly experienced." He would be invited to attend delegation meetings only when "your assistance is required," and he might be assigned to attend some meetings of the conference committees or commissions. He would be expected to work with experts from the State Department "who have been for a long time intimately in touch with every phase of the work." He was not to make any "public or private" comments on the work of the delegation or the conference without the express authorization of the delegation. He was not to bring along any "professional assistants," although he could bring a secretary if he wished.[49]

Harry must have found the tone galling, and he ignored the injunctions as much as he could. He took one of his professional staff, Ludwig Ullmann, with him to San Francisco and met occasionally with other delegates and journalists while the conference was under way. The experience left him with a mixed view of the new secretary of state. During the conference, Harry wrote to his wife, Anne, that Stettinius "behaves a little too much like the president of a Lions convention. The reporters regard him with a fishy eye and tolerant smile. I've heard several say that without Roosevelt behind him, he reveals himself as a zero. However, he had a great build-up and will I believe emerge from this conference with an enhanced reputation."[50]

The Role of the Soviet Union

In addition to the economic issues, Harry had a long-standing interest in one of the most important political matters to be settled at San Francisco: how far the United States should be prepared to compromise to entice the Soviet Union to join. The political structure of the UN was outside Harry's professional expertise and mandate. It did not technically fit the State Department criterion of being a matter on which he was "particularly experienced." It was, however, a matter to which he had given a great deal of thought while working on financial assistance to the Soviet Union throughout the war.

Stalin was insisting on voting rights in the UN General Assembly for at least two Republics within the Soviet Union: Belarus (then known as the Byelorussian Soviet Socialist Republic) and Ukraine. That would effectively give the Soviet Union three votes. That idea did not sit well with the U.S. Congress, but those who were inclined to accept it acknowledged that Britain (whose voting power would be augmented by the Commonwealth countries) and the United States (with economically dependent allies throughout the Americas) had limited space on the moral high ground on which to stake their objections. The issue had little practical importance, but it was a sticking point in the negotiations. In addition, Stalin wanted to be able to veto any decision in the Security Council. That issue had more practical significance. If the U.S. delegation refused to go along, it could jeopardize the goal of creating a universal institution with the ability to help sustain world peace. If the delegation compromised too much, the outcome could potentially render the council impotent.

Harry had faced this controversy throughout the war, including its influence on the negotiations leading to Bretton Woods. Even now, in 1945, he was being questioned extensively by members of congressional committees on whether the Soviet Union would have special privileges in the IMF. (Not until December 1945 did Stalin decide to forgo Soviet membership in the IMF.) Harry was fervent in his belief that cooperation between the United States and the Soviet Union, despite their different political and economic systems, would be the key to preserving the peace. If the Grand Alliance was to collapse after the successful conclusion of World War II (as it did), the prospects for another conflagration would be much higher. Helping persuade the Soviet Union to join the IMF, the World Bank, and the United Nations was Harry's way of perpetuating the alliance.

In the White Plan of April 1942, Harry made the case plainly:

There are certain to be some persons or governments who, either out of fear or prejudice or dislike, would wish to exclude countries with socialist economies from participation in an international undertaking of [this] character. . . . Yet to exclude a country such as Russia would be an egregious error. Russia, despite her socialist economy, could both contribute and profit by participation. To deny her the privileges of joining in this cooperative effort to improve world economic relations would be to repeat the tragic errors of the last generation, and introduce a very discordant note in the new era millions everywhere are hoping for.[51]

Harry spent much of the first half of 1944 holding at least fourteen meetings with the Soviet delegation to the Bretton Woods conference, negotiating what became a few provisions in the Articles of Agreement to accommodate the unique aspects of the Soviet economic system. Having apparently succeeded in that effort, he now was hoping to influence the design of the UN in a similar direction. At some point in the process, late in 1943 or in 1944, he began writing down the case for inclusion, but he may have run out of time, as he never finished the handwritten manuscript.[52]

The earliest the undated draft could have been written was in mid-1943. It refers to the "large sales" and "favorable reviews" of "Walter Lippmann's recent book 'U.S. Foreign Policy.'" The book was published in 1943; the *New York Times* published a review on June 13. The last likely date would be in the third quarter of 1944. The manuscript discusses the possibility of creating a successor to the League of Nations, in a way that suggests clearly that a decision to do so had not yet been made. That decision was made at Dumbarton Oaks in October 1944.

The essence of Harry's case for continued cooperation among the four major allied powers (the United States, the United Kingdom, the Soviet Union, and China) was that if that could be done, a third world war would be virtually impossible: "No combination of powers outside these four would have the slightest chance of victory against them." He recognized, however, that public opinion in the United States was, at best, reluctant to accept such an alliance outside of wartime. He therefore set out to examine the reasons that were being advanced for opposing it.

In the most contentious passage of his manuscript, Harry argued that although the Soviet economic system was quite different from that of the United States, that difference need not preclude the two countries from

forging commercial and financial ties. The Soviets had a socialist economy with some elements of free enterprise and market forces. The United
States, along with almost every other country, had a capitalist economy
with some elements of state ownership, control, and regulation. The differences, he argued, were not so stark as to preclude a working relationship. Similarly, Harry argued that, although much of the Soviet political
system was antithetical to American democracy and repugnant to American values, the United States had found ways to work in peacetime with
many other countries with dismal political histories and practices.

In the middle of the manuscript, Harry noted that the focus of "this
paper" was to examine the requirements for preserving the alliance once
the postwar lull in tensions would be over. That wording suggests that
he intended the manuscript to become an article for publication. He did
not follow up, perhaps because the decision to create the UN organization with the four great powers (and France) as permanent veto-wielding
leaders rendered his argument moot, or perhaps because he decided (correctly) that the paper would need a great deal of reworking before it would
be worth sharing.

The problem with the manuscript was not just length and repetition.
It included instances of jarring language, such as a reference to opposition
emanating from "the very powerful Catholic hierarchy." That was probably an oblique reference to the pernicious influence of the anti-Semitic
Catholic priest Father Charles E. Coughlin and his "America First" campaign, but Harry obviously would have had to jettison the phrase for publication. This first draft also underplayed the horrors of Stalin's rule, referring only in passing to his "purges."

What is most worth noting is that the manuscript shows again that
Harry's belief in the value of the Grand Alliance—first expressed publicly in his 1942 plan for the IMF—was a continuing theme in his work
throughout the war. In a recent book, Benn Steil construed that theme
negatively, arguing dubiously that White's manuscript was actually an emphatic endorsement of Soviet economic policies. Three times in his book,
Steil conflated two separate phrases from the final pages of the manuscript
to make it look as if White had written, "Russia is the first instance of a
socialist economy in action, and it works!" In fact, those last three words
appear all alone in the middle of an otherwise blank and unnumbered
page after the end of the text, followed by a squiggle that could have been
an exclamation point but also may have been a question mark. It was not
connected in any way to the preceding text. The sentence about Russia

was a statement of fact on the previous page. It concluded with a period
and was not the last sentence on that page.

In November 1945 Harry took another stab at explaining his position
on U.S.–Soviet cooperation, and he again dropped the pen without finishing the job. By then, World War II was over, but the destructive force
of the atomic bomb that had brought about the final victory had kindled
fears of the horrors that would inevitably follow if another such conflict
was to arise. Harry set out to draft an argument that would assuage "the
terrific fear engendered by the unknown potentiality of atomic destruc-
tiveness." He noted, as he had earlier, that "no major war is possible unless
[the United States and the Soviet Union] are on opposing sides. . . . The
major task that confronts American diplomacy—and the only task that
has any real value in the major problems that confront us—is to devise
means whereby friendship and military alliance can be assured between
the United States and Russia."[53]

When Harry tried to finish this argument, he ran out of steam. He
wanted to "evaluate precisely what are the points of conflict between" the
two countries. The last sentence that he wrote, however, left the case unspecified: "What Russia is doing outside in the international sphere that
we object to: 1." The rest of the page was left blank.[54]

What these manuscripts do *not* suggest is that Harry believed that the
Soviet economic and political system was superior or preferable to that
of the United States or any other country. His point instead was that the
two systems could coexist in the postwar era and that their coexistence
would be essential to the attainment and preservation of the peace. The
San Francisco conference might afford him an opportunity to make the
case where it most mattered, if only he could get past the gatekeepers in
the Department of State.

At the San Francisco Conference

When Harry arrived in San Francisco in April 1945, near where he and
Anne had spent some of their most carefree years while he studied at
Stanford University some twenty years earlier, he had to reconcile himself
to his limited role. He apparently was content just to hang around the
margins of the grand conference and try to foster a positive process and
outcome. His influence, if any, would come mostly through conversations
with delegates rather than in the formal meetings to which he was only
selectively invited.

One of Harry's first activities upon arriving in San Francisco was to see a few men from the Soviet delegation at Bretton Woods who were also participating in the UN negotiations. He had lunch with Professor (of economics) Amazasp Avakimovich Arutiunian and then took Arutiunian and a few other delegates sightseeing in a Treasury car for the afternoon. ("Remember him?" Harry wrote to Anne from San Francisco. "He was one of the delegation which was at our home.")[55]

Later he took time to visit one of the orphans whom he and Anne had helped raise while they were in Palo Alto in the early 1920s. Dave Everall was now married with a family and was a professor of philosophy at City College of San Francisco. Harry wrote enthusiastically to Anne to describe the reunion. Dave had become "a bit heavy and academic," but he and his wife had "made every bit of furniture in [their] house." Harry was a little overcome by the adulation that Dave still had for him and Anne. "He seems terribly eager to please us and have our approval," Harry wrote. "For a time he was almost tongue-tied in my presence."[56]

As he expected, Harry had no real opportunity to influence the negotiations related to ECOSOC or other economic matters. He stayed in San Francisco only for the first two and a half weeks of what turned out to be a two-month conference of fifty country delegations and some 3,500 participants. By May 10, with at least six weeks left in the deliberations, he was back at the Treasury working on assistance to Britain, China, and the Soviet Union, and—most of all—the ratification process for the Bretton Woods agreements.

Harry captured his frustration with being largely sidelined at San Francisco in a gently ironic letter that he wrote to his teenage daughter Joan a few days after he arrived:

Joanie,

This conference would provide you with material for wit for many a year to come. The milling around of delegates and hangers on, all looking for acquaintances to greet and bow to, makes an amusing spectacle that only the youngest member of our family could do adequate justice to. There are hundreds of reporters trying desperately to squeeze out something of news value when the only news consists of arrivals and carefully guarded statements of various officials. The first real bit of news coming out of this conference will be headlined, worried, nursed, amplified, and analyzed to a fare-you-well. A man with a good tidbit of gossip here can name his own price.

The town is colorful. Sailors, sailors, sailors everywhere (some of them sober). Millions of 'em and there is a bar or cocktail lounge for each of them. Crowds stand outside the hotel where the Russian delegates are quartered and just look and sit.

I have a small room, but I'm kept in constant touch with the outside through my window which looks out on a busy thorough-fare. I hear no dogs in the morning, only city noises, but sleep well. I'm getting a good rest and plenty of sleep, in preparation for the round of big lunches, bigger dinners, and late bull sessions. Here's hoping something more than thousands of belly-aches and hang-overs comes out of this conference.

Daddy[57]

On a more serious level, Harry seems to have found enough oppor-tunities to help the State Department delegation. After Harry returned to Washington, Stettinius wrote to Morgenthau to thank him for nominat-ing Harry to help the delegation, and he expressed the hope that Harry might be able to return before the conference ended. Morgenthau re-sponded that he needed Harry in the office, and he persuaded Stettinius to promise not to ask for his return unless it was really necessary.[58] Harry remained in Washington.

Whatever his help might have been, Harry had no role in the delib-erations on key issues, which took place mostly either at higher political levels or after he left San Francisco.[59] The Soviet Union got its two extra votes through the admission of Belarus and Ukraine as original members, but it agreed to accept a limited version of veto power in the Security Council under which the permanent members could not veto proposals to discuss matters if at least nine of the thirteen members voted in favor. (The veto issue was settled in Moscow on June 6, at a meeting that Averell Harriman and Harry Hopkins, representing the United States, had with Stalin and his foreign minister, Vyacheslav M. Molotov.)

The matter that Harry regarded as most vital to peace and security was that the Security Council be established and that it be structured in a way that would enable postwar cooperation between the two leading pow-ers. When that effort succeeded without his involvement, he could turn his attention back to his main interest, the founding of the International Monetary Fund.

CHAPTER FIFTEEN

The Attack Begins behind the Curtain, 1945

Prosecutor to Elizabeth Bentley: "You never met Harry White?"

Bentley: "No, I didn't."

—Grand jury transcript, April 1948

WHILE HARRY WHITE WAS occupied with disparate tasks for the U.S. Treasury, refugees from the Communist underground were invoking his name in secret meetings with the FBI and other government agencies. Thus began a campaign that ultimately would severely damage his posthumous reputation.

March 1945: Whittaker Chambers Makes a Vague Accusation

Jay Vivian Chambers, who went by many names in the course of his life but was most commonly known as Whittaker, was a onetime member of the Communist Party of the United States (CPUSA) who renounced his former activities and became a fervent crusader against Communism. He would eventually become an iconic hero to anti-Communist fanatics because of the sensationalism of the charges he raised against Alger Hiss, Harry White, and many others.[1] The line between truth and fiction in the stories he spun is never clear, and much of what he claimed is impossible to verify.

Chambers testified multiple times under oath that he left the Communist Party at the end of 1937. In the fall of 1948, however, that dating conflicted with his claim that he had received classified documents from Alger Hiss in the spring of 1938. He then changed his testimony to say that he had left in April 1938.[2] After leaving the party, he began informing on former colleagues and acquaintances, both those whom he knew to have been Communists and those whom he had met around the margins of activities involving the party or its members. He first took his story to Adolf A. Berle Jr., the assistant secretary of state dealing with internal security, in September 1939. Meeting at Berle's home, Chambers ran through a list of names of government officials whom he believed to be party members or engaged in espionage. Some of those names would later be among the most prominent people attacked during the McCarthy era and beyond for alleged links to Communism. One person whom Chambers did *not* name to Berle was Harry Dexter White.[3]

Although Chambers was subsequently interviewed on several occasions by officials from the State Department, the FBI, and other agencies, the first time he ever mentioned White's name was some five and a half years later, in March 1945. By this time, hysteria about Communism was rising in the United States, and the State Department was undertaking to investigate reports of Communists in the federal government. The department's chief security officer, Raymond Murphy, interviewed Chambers on March 20. After naming several other people who he claimed were important figures in "the underground" in the period 1934–37, Chambers mentioned Harry White. Murphy's notes on the meeting read: "Harry White of the Treasury was described as a member at large but rather timid. He put on as assistants in the Treasury Glaser a member of the underground group and an Adler or Odler another party member. The two Coe brothers, also party members, were also put on by White."[4]

The somewhat garbled names Murphy recorded refer to Harold Glasser, Solomon Adler, and Frank and Robert Coe. In context, the phrase "member at large" that Chambers seems to have attached to Harry appears to imply a loose association with the "underground" groups with which Chambers had interacted in the mid-1930s. The phrase "rather timid" is particular striking, because "timid" is just about the last adjective that anyone who knew Harry would have applied to him. For Chambers to have qualified his description in this way probably meant that White did not actually attend meetings in Chambers's presence, but his name had been mentioned by others who were there. In particular, Chambers seems to have picked up talk of Harry's having appointed people in the underground groups to Treasury positions. Whether Chambers ever even met Harry, as he claimed but Harry denied, is impossible to know.

Much of what Chambers told Murphy was untrue, probably because he had heard it all as secondhand rumors. Harry was not responsible for hiring *any* of the men mentioned by Chambers. Frank Coe was already working as an economist at the Treasury when Harry arrived there in 1934, although Harry did play a role in his return to the Treasury in 1939. Adler and Glasser were hired, also as economists, by Harry's forerunner as division chief at the Treasury, George C. Haas. By 1937 they were reporting to Harry and working closely with him. Robert Coe (Frank's brother) did not work for the Treasury at all.[5]

If, as Chambers alleged, Adler, Frank Coe, and Glasser were participants in underground groups around 1937, they may well have invoked Harry's name as someone sympathetic to the causes that the groups supported. The notion that Harry was a "member at large" of such a group though too "timid" to attend its meetings could easily have been inferred by a fertile mind such as Chambers's.

Another question arising from this episode is why Chambers brought up Harry's name in March 1945 but not earlier. In his 1948 public testimony and in his 1952 memoir, Chambers justified the discrepancy by claiming that he earlier had been trying to protect Harry. He wrote in his book that in 1939, "I still hoped that I had broken [him] away from the Communist Party."[6] Since neither Chambers nor anyone else ever claimed that Harry was a party member, and since Chambers had no knowledge of Harry's possible activities after 1937, that claim can only have been a belated effort to paper over a major inconsistency in his varying accounts.

As we shall see in chapters 18 and 19, Chambers made further and more specific charges a few years later, after other accounts had become public.

November 1945: Elizabeth Bentley Spreads Hearsay

From the early 1930s, Harry and Anne were friends with Greg and Helen Silvermaster. (Nathan Gregory Silvermaster normally used only his middle and last names and was generally known as Greg. In testimony before a grand jury, Harry recalled that he had been friends with him for several years before he even knew that his first name was Nathan.) That friendship had entangled Harry in an investigation of Silvermaster in 1942 (see chapter 8), and it came to haunt him again in 1945. That November a woman named Elizabeth Terrill Bentley drew on her contacts with the Silvermasters to become the first person to allege a direct connection between Harry White and Soviet espionage.

Substantial evidence is now available indicating that the Silvermasters were regular hosts to a group of Soviet sympathizers who collected information, including, notably, military data, from various sources and passed it on through couriers to Soviet intelligence operatives. This "Silvermaster group," as it came to be called, met at the Silvermasters' house on 30th Street in upper northwest Washington until the Soviets shut down the operation in 1944. Bentley was a member of the group and apparently served as a courier. By her own account, she was a protégé and, for a time, the lover of a Soviet spy named Jacob Golos, who led her into the practice of espionage for the Soviet Union. After several years of increasingly dangerous underground activity, she broke with the Communist Party in 1945 and went to the FBI to tell her story.[7]

The details of Bentley's story are murky because she told different versions over the years. Although many accounts, including a well-researched biography by Kathryn S. Olmsted, have quoted liberally from Bentley's own writings as if they were true accounts, Bentley herself admitted that her 1951 "autobiography" was "fiction."[8] The mere fact of being a notorious liar does not imply that everything one says is false, but it does mean that the only parts that can be taken seriously are those that can be definitively and independently corroborated from other sources. The main problem, though, is simply that Bentley's allegations against Harry were merely hearsay and revealed nothing incriminatory.

The essence of the story is that a few members of the group worked at the Treasury and would come to the Silvermasters' house with documents that they claimed "came from Harry." Bentley never met Harry herself, and she had no information on whether he had any direct contact with the activities of the group. The question, then, is whether Harry deliberately gave copies of Treasury documents to his employees to pass on to the Soviets, or whether the employees obtained the documents surreptitiously or even in the normal course of their duties.

This kernel is best illustrated by the sworn testimony that Bentley gave before a grand jury in March and April 1948. Grand jury proceedings are confidential and are usually sealed permanently, but this one was declassified in 1999 in response to a federal court case brought by researchers. The grand jury was investigating espionage charges against federal officials, and the prosecutor posed questions concerning witnesses' knowledge of those whose names had been mentioned.

On March 30, the prosecutor asked Bentley about documents that she had conveyed to her Soviet contacts. At one point he asked her, "Did you ever see any of these documents in the possession of Harry Dexter White?" She replied, "I never met Mr. White, so I couldn't tell you."[9] A week later, on April 6, Bentley testified that she had seen copies of letters sent to Harry White from Treasury staff in China and Portugal. She believed that White had provided these letters to her network of spies with the knowledge that they would be conveyed to Soviet intelligence. That led to the following exchange:

Q. How did you know that it came from Mr. White?
A. Because whoever had picked it up from Mr. White would tell me, whether it was Lud Ullmann or Greg Silvermaster.
Q. Did he say that Mr. White had turned it over to him?
A. Yes. Or else I would be sitting in the kitchen and they would say that Harry White had been there an hour before, or something like that.
Q. Did they say that Harry White brought material to the house?
A. Oh, yes. It wasn't a usual procedure, but he did bring some things to the house.
Q. Do you recall what documents he did bring to the house?
A. No, I don't know.
Q. You never met Harry White?
A. No, I didn't.
Q. And the information you received concerning Harry White you received from either Greg Silvermaster or Ullmann?
A. Or Helen Silvermaster.[10]

She never saw Harry at the Silvermasters' house, but she heard talk of his having been there. In fact, Harry and Anne did occasionally visit the Silvermasters, with whom they were long-standing friends. Moreover, someone was conveying Treasury documents to the group, some of which were either to or from Harry. Her testimony here points most clearly to William Ludwig ("Lud") Ullmann as involved in some way.

Ullmann was born in Springfield, Missouri, in 1908. After graduating from Harvard with a degree in business administration, he worked for various government agencies in the 1930s. At some point in the late

1930s, he met Harry White, probably through their mutual friend Greg Silvermaster. In 1939 Harry hired Ullmann for the Treasury, where he worked until he enlisted in the army in October 1942. For the next three years, Ullmann was stationed at the Pentagon, but he continued to assist the Treasury occasionally, and he participated in both the Bretton Woods and the San Francisco conferences. He rejoined the Treasury staff after the war and worked there until he resigned in 1947.

Ullmann's presence at the Silvermasters' house was not just that of a friendly visitor: he lived there and jointly owned the house with the couple.[11] Assuming that the essence of Bentley's story is true, it still remains to be determined whether Ullmann was merely part of the transmission process in conjunction with the Silvermasters or was the source of Treasury documents.

Most of the material transmitted by this group has never been identified, but some of it has. Ignoring all the unsubstantiated tales, only one Treasury document associated with Harry White has been identified as having been conveyed to Soviet operatives. It thus must serve as a stand-in for all the other documents that are imagined to have been similarly transmitted. No one, it seems, has ever bothered to try to link the original document to what the Soviets saw in order to assess its context or relevance. This document, however, is readily found in the National Archives in College Park, Maryland, and in the Morgenthau Diaries.[12]

Soviet access to the document in question is discussed in a book by Allen Weinstein and Alexander Vassiliev, which is based on the second author's privileged access to KGB archives in Russia (discussed in chapter 20). The book does not describe the actual document, but it does discuss a Soviet cable that mentions it. In the authors' account, Pavel M. Fitin (head of foreign intelligence for the NKVD) wrote to a superior in Moscow, complaining that the New York office had been slow in translating and transmitting information from the Silvermaster group. As an example, he noted that New York had received in February or March 1944, but had forwarded only on May 25, material including "a three-page draft memorandum composed by White for Morgenthau about amendments to the Soviet-American agreement on Lend-Lease and about granting a loan to the Soviet Union for reconstructing the national economy, etc."[13]

On January 5, 1944, Harry gave a three-page memorandum to Morgenthau with the title "Memorandum for the President: Ten Billion Dollar Reconstruction Arrangement with Russia." It was a draft for a proposal for Morgenthau to send to Roosevelt, setting out alternative methods for lending $10 billion in goods to the Soviet Union to help with postwar reconstruction. The memorandum (also discussed in chapter 8) noted that the simplest method would be to use the existing Lend-Lease Act to augment the resources already being lent to Russia to help with the war effort. Alternatively, the president could ask Congress for a new loan appropriation. Because public support would be essential for the success of the effort, Harry recommended the latter course. The timing, the content, and the length of the memorandum match the description in the cable cited by Weinstein and Vassiliev.

The Weinstein-Vassiliev account indicates that someone in the Silvermaster group obtained a copy of this memorandum (or a draft of it) and forwarded it to a Soviet contact a month or two after it was written. The New York office then took another three or four months to translate it into Russian and forward it to Moscow. Although the reference in the NKVD reaction is only to a "three-page memo," the original document comprised a dozen pages: the three-page memorandum plus a four-page appendix and a five-page attachment. It appears, then, that whoever passed it on either had access only to the memorandum itself or chose not to disclose the more detailed information in the attachments.

The absence of the attachments in the transmission to Moscow is significant because they contained information that would have been far more useful to Soviet officials. All that the memorandum contained was the basic argument for making the loan and an explanation of the two methods between which the president could choose. The appendix to the memorandum set out in detail the anticipated benefits to the United States—economic, military, and political—for engaging in deeper economic cooperation with the Soviet Union. The second attachment described in detail the possible strategy for negotiating with the Russians and then with Congress. Both attachments described how such a loan might help draw the Soviet Union into joining the war with Japan in addition to its ongoing efforts in the war with Germany. Conveying that information would have been especially sensitive, but there is no evidence that anyone did so.

It is of course possible that Harry gave his copy of the three-page memorandum to someone such as Ullmann or Silvermaster, knowing that he would pass it on to Russian contacts. That is what earlier assessments have generally assumed. If so, then the intermediary would have had to make another copy (possibly by photographing it) and return it to Harry, because Harry's copy did not disappear. His secretary filed it in the usual way, and it eventually passed on to the Treasury files at the U.S. National Archives.

Before jumping to such a conclusion, it would be appropriate to consider alternative, less convoluted explanations. In particular, the source of the document given to the Russians may very well have been someone else in the Treasury with access to it. The memorandum at College Park includes two helpful notations in this regard.

First, the drafting history of the memorandum is listed at the bottom of the last page: "HDW/HG/ISF/WHT/EMB/efs."[14] That notation means that the first draft was by Edward M. Bernstein (EMB) and that it was then revised successively by William H. Taylor, Irving S. Friedman, Harold Glasser, and Harry White. (The lower-case initials "efs" denote the typist, possibly Elsie Sharf.) The appendix gives the same drafting list, and the other attachment indicates that it was drafted only by Glasser.

Second, the first page of the memorandum includes a notation that the original was to be given to Morgenthau at a 3:30 P.M. meeting on January 5, 1944, and that carbon copies were to be given to seven staff members: the four who helped draft it before giving it to Harry, and "Paul, Luxford, [and] DuBois"—that is, Randolph Paul, Ansel F. Luxford, and Josiah Ellis DuBois. All these men were Treasury officials who were invited to attend the meeting with Morgenthau. Six days later, a copy was given to "Miss Dickenson [*sic*]," presumably Jane Dickinson, a staff member who assisted at the Bretton Woods conference later in 1944 but who otherwise does not figure in this story.

Three of the eight people (in addition to White and Morgenthau) known to have legitimately possessed copies of the memorandum were mentioned, or may have been mentioned, in Soviet cables that were subsequently partially decrypted, translated, and interpreted by U.S. agencies: Josiah DuBois, Harold Glasser, and Ansel Luxford. DuBois and Luxford were mentioned only because they were friends of Glasser and may have held views sympathetic to Russia. A fourth person, Bill Taylor, was smeared by Bentley, who never met him but told the FBI that she heard his name mentioned at the Silvermasters' house. After a long battle, Taylor was formally cleared of wrongdoing in 1956. That leaves Glasser as a possible conduit.

Harold Glasser was born in Chicago in November 1905. Like Harry, he was the son of Jewish immigrants from Lithuania, and he studied economics at the Harvard graduate school in 1929–30. Although Harry was studying there at the same time, there is no record of their having met. George Haas, who was Harry's division chief at the Treasury, hired Glasser for the division in 1936. When Harry was promoted to head his own division in 1938, he took Glasser with him as his deputy. During the war, the Treasury posted Glasser abroad on three occasions, during which Frank Coe replaced him as the deputy chief under Harry. In January 1944 Glasser had recently returned to headquarters from Algeria.[15]

Direct evidence that Glasser was involved in Soviet espionage rests primarily on a tentative identification of him as an individual mentioned in several Soviet cables under the code name "Rouble" and on a detailed autobiographical sketch that was reportedly lodged in NKVD files in Moscow.[16] The FBI investigated him in 1941 after receiving a report that he had been an organizer for the Communist Party when he lived in Chicago and that he was a member of the Washington chapter of Americans for Democratic Action. An agent in Chicago interviewed Professor Paul H. Douglas, one of the leading economists of his generation, who remembered Glasser well as having been one of his students at the University of Chicago. Douglas—implicitly alluding to the number of people who voted for Roosevelt in the 1940 presidential election— told the agent that Glasser was "a liberal, along with twenty-eight million loyal Americans."[17] In Washington, extensive interviewing of Treasury employees, their neighbors, and their other acquaintances turned up no incriminating information, and the FBI closed the file until Bentley and Chambers mentioned Glasser some four years later.

Glasser was never charged with a crime, and he continued to work at the U.S. Treasury until 1947, by which time Treasury Secretary John Snyder had promoted him to chief of the division that Harry had once run. The long-running investigation by the FBI eventually compelled Snyder to force Glasser to resign. In closed-door testimony to a grand jury and public testimony to the U.S. Senate Judiciary Committee, Glasser refused to answer questions about his or others' connections to the Communist Party. The notoriety that ensued from his public testimony ended his professional career. He died in Laguna Hills, California, in 1992, a week short of his eighty-seventh birthday.

Rouble does appear to have been an active supplier of official documents to Soviet intelligence, at least as indicated by a set of documents allegedly conveyed to the Soviets by Rouble in June 1945. A Soviet cable dated June 21, 1945, describes a telegram from the U.S. ambassador to Moscow (W. Averell Harriman) to the State Department assessing the magnitude of Soviet material losses in the war. Another on the same date conveys the text of a letter from an employee of the U.S. Office of Strategic Services (OSS, the forerunner of the CIA) to the Treasury's office in London, concerning the transfer of Nazi funds through Switzerland. A cable dated June 23 discusses a telegram from a Treasury representative in Helsinki regarding the laundering of Nazi funds, and one of June 28 describes an internal Treasury memorandum on the prosecution of war crimes. The random nature of these documents suggests that their transmission to Moscow was probably the work of someone who just gathered up whatever he or she could find around the office and passed it on. It clearly is not the result of a systematic effort to convey relevant information.

If the code name Rouble does refer to Glasser, then he would seem to be the most likely suspect as the source of the "Memorandum for the President" described above. He helped write it, and he had at least one copy of the final draft. Ullmann was working at the Pentagon, not the Treasury, at that time, but he might have visited his old Treasury offices on occasion, particularly in the months leading up to Bretton Woods. The Treasury building was not secured, as it is today. Anyone could enter during business hours and walk around. Gathering up a copy from someone's desk would not have been difficult, especially since some weeks seem to have elapsed after the January 5, 1944, meeting before the memorandum was transmitted through the Silvermaster group. In any event, there are at least two people (Glasser and Ullmann) who might have conveyed the document in this manner.

In sum, the pieces of Bentley's testimony that can be corroborated merely showed that information about Treasury activities was being transmitted through a spy ring and that some of that information originated from Harry. Her testimony did not provide supportable evidence that he was personally involved in that process. She did, however, set in motion events that seemed to be more damning.

The FBI Responds

As soon as Bentley alleged that Harry was involved with the Silvermaster group, FBI Director J. Edgar Hoover wrote to President Truman's military aide, Brigadier General Harry Hawkins Vaughan, informing him that a "highly confidential source" (Bentley) had made allegations against a dozen individuals, including Harry White. The report noted that the Bureau could not yet determine the "complicity" of any of the named individuals or whether they "had actual knowledge of the disposition being made of the information they were transmitting." The Bureau therefore was initiating an investigation.[18]

Hoover then ordered both electronic and physical surveillance of Harry and everyone else whom Bentley had accused. On November 28, 1945, the FBI placed a wiretap on Harry's home phone, which it continued to monitor for almost eighteen months (until May 16, 1947), even after the Whites had moved from their house in Bethesda to an apartment in Washington, D.C. The Bureau apparently used listening devices in his home, and it intercepted his mail. The Bureau also began watching his home and tailing him regularly to record his movements and find out whom he was meeting.[19]

This extensive and intensive surveillance turned up nothing illegal and revealed no connection with Soviet espionage. As an internal FBI report summarized the results of its surveillance of Harry, "It has not been possible to locate independent information that White was involved in espionage activities during this period."[20] The surveillance did, however, suggest to the FBI that Harry had many contacts with individuals who were similarly suspected of having Soviet or Communist sympathies. The Bureau's agents correlated these contacts with their old file on Anne's left-wing activities and thus reinforced their conclusions that the pair was up to no good. They confirmed facts that had never been secrets but that the Bureau thought to be highly suspect. Yes, Harry was friends with the Silvermasters and Ullmann. And yes, he saw various other people with leftish views socially and at work.

As this surveillance continued, the FBI compiled an extensive report on Soviet intelligence activities and sent it to Vaughan, Attorney General Tom C. Clark, and an official in the State Department in early December 1945. It included a brief summary of Bentley's allegations, and it also mentioned that a woman named Katherine Wills, who was suffering from "a paranoid form of schizophrenia" and a "hazy recollection," had included Harry in a list of names in "the fall of 1944."[21]

There is no record indicating that Truman saw either the preliminary report on Bentley or this more general report on Soviet activities. In a telephone call on November 14, 1945, Hoover and Truman discussed the general issue of Soviet espionage, but Hoover's note on the call does not indicate that he mentioned any names. Hoover then met with Secretary of State James Byrnes the next morning. In that meeting, Hoover did name names, but he told Byrnes that the "allegations . . . had not as yet been fully corroborated."[22] In any case, none of the recipients took the vague allegations seriously enough to act on them.

On January 23, 1946, Truman announced that he was appointing Harry to be the U.S. executive director at the IMF, subject to confirmation by the U.S Senate. For more than two months before this date, the FBI had been analyzing what it had learned from Bentley and from its surveillance of Harry's movements and phone calls. The possibility that Harry would move from the Treasury to the newly created IMF galvanized the Bureau into further action. It did not know how seriously to take Bentley's accusations, but it seems that it wanted to avoid being accused later of not alerting the White House to a potential embarrassment.

On February 1 Hoover drafted a letter to General Vaughan, with a carefully hedged (and frequently inaccurate) description of what his agents had learned and with the stated intent of discouraging Truman from proceeding with the appointment of White to the IMF post. He wrote that an unnamed source (Bentley) had alleged that Harry was "a valuable adjunct to an underground Soviet espionage organization operating in Washington, D.C." Even before Bentley's revelations, the FBI had learned that White was meeting with Soviet officials, notably the Soviet ambassador, Andrei Gromyko, and members of the delegation to the Bretton Woods conference. The fact that White was supposed to be meeting these people as a regular part of his duties at the Treasury did not factor into the agency report. Although the letter was dated February 1, an FBI official delivered the letter and the report to Vaughan only on February 4.[23]

Although the substantive information about Harry's alleged involvement with Soviet espionage was still based on Bentley's hearsay, this second FBI report dropped the qualification about its being unverified. Instead, the report asserted incredibly that "in no instance is any transaction or events related where the reliability of the source of information is questionable." How Bentley's information went from unverified to unquestionable in two months in the absence of any new incriminating evidence was unexplained. The transformation suggests a measure of desperation in Hoover's effort to block Harry's appointment. Vaughan apparently sent the report to the State Department rather than directly to Truman, because Truman eventually received it from Secretary of State James F. Byrnes.[24] The slow and indirect routing of the letter, despite the urgency presented by the Senate confirmation calendar, suggests that Vaughan and Byrnes retained a degree of skepticism about the allegations.

As noted earlier, the FBI's surveillance of Harry had revealed that Harry was in contact with several individuals whom the Bureau suspected of having Communist sympathies. Although all those individuals were either long-standing friends of the Whites or people with whom Harry would normally be meeting in the course of his Treasury duties, in the anti-Communist fervor of 1946 these associations were enough to warrant sending a lengthy (twenty-eight-page) description to the White House.

The first example of nefarious activity that the FBI highlighted in its report was a visit of friends to the Whites' home in Bethesda. On November 22, 1945—which was Thanksgiving Day, although not noted as such in the FBI report—the agent who was watching the house observed a car pulling up in front and two individuals getting out and going into the house. He tracked the ownership of the car to Frances L. Edelstein, the wife of Harry M. Edelstein, who worked for the government in the Interior Department. The agent assumed (no doubt correctly) that the two visitors were in fact the Edelsteins.[25]

Frances Edelstein was alleged to be a member of the Washington Committee for Democratic Action, as was Anne Terry White. The Whites and the Edelsteins were friends, and the obvious interpretation of this event was that the Whites had invited the couple over to celebrate Thanksgiving. The problem was that the committee in question was on the attorney general's secret list of organizations thought to be subversive. This list, which was made public in 1948, included both organizations thought to be dominated or influenced by the Communist Party of the United States and those thought to have overlapping membership with Communist-dominated groups.[26] The Washington Committee for Democratic Action was active in causes related to the protection of civil liberties. Because it attracted a wide array of Washington liberals during World War II, it caused much distress during the McCarthy era when past membership in it became an excuse for being blacklisted from employment.

Harry Edelstein, according to the FBI report, "at one time was interested in Commonwealth College in the state of Arkansas, an institution which on many occasions has been criticized for its propagation of Communist ideals." He was also "listed in the active indices" of two other organizations "reported by numerous sources to be under Communist domination and influence." Having such people as social visitors was evidently cause for serious concern by the FBI in 1945.

The FBI's three-step chain of connections from Communism to the Whites was patently absurd, and it illustrates the illogical thought processes that entrapped thousands of American citizens in the years after World War II. A college had been "criticized" for propagating "Communist ideals." Harry Edelstein "at one time was interested in" that college.

Edelstein was a friend of Harry White. Therefore, White might be a Communist. Even the initial allegation was grossly exaggerated. Commonwealth College was established in 1923 to promote socialist ideals in education and support the growth of labor unions. In 1926 an official of the Arkansas Chamber of Commerce attacked the college for allegedly promoting Communist ideology and taking money from the Soviet Union. The official claimed that the U.S. Department of Justice had produced a report to that effect. The Chamber of Commerce launched an aggressive investigation. Eventually, J. Edgar Hoover, then the director of the forerunner of the FBI, issued a denial that such a report had ever existed. No links between Commonwealth College and the Communist Party or the Soviet Union were ever established.[27]

The report continued with an account of Harry's going to New York in early December "for the purpose of having certain dental work done." He stayed with another dentist, Dr. Abraham Wolfson, in Newark, New Jersey, and he "took this opportunity to view certain real property in New Jersey with a view to its purchase." The FBI considered Wolfson to be suspect because he belonged to the Washington Committee for Democratic Action and other social and political organizations, had once signed a petition calling for the abolition of the Committee on Un-American Activities, and was alleged (by "a highly confidential source") to have been a member of the Communist Party.[28]

Abe Wolfson was the ex-husband of Anne's sister and was treated as an ongoing member of the family by Anne and Harry. He was an orthodontist in New Jersey. He apparently recommended that Harry see a dentist in New York for treatment of a serious problem. In an undated letter, Harry wrote to Anne from New York reporting on this trip. "The dentist outlined my program. In an hour or two I'll have four or six teeth out, and he's going to work on me tomorrow so I'm afraid I may not have time to look for farm—but I'll try."[29] (The reference to a farm in New Jersey was undoubtedly an early foray in the search that led to the purchase in 1946 of their country home in New Hampshire.)

After making several more such insinuations based on conversations and meetings with government officials, newspaper reporters, friends, and family, the report concluded by noting that the FBI had listened to a conversation between "one of [Harry White's] daughters" and a friend. Although the agent, who must have been listening to the wiretapped telephone, did not know which daughter was speaking, it was the eighteen-year-old Ruth.[30] The FBI summarized the conversation to indicate just how suspiciously it believed the family behaved:

In a discussion of their aims and likes, Miss White stated that a large portion of their "friends" called close friends believe in the same political ideas—the same as their family. Further that all of the family had been engaged in politics and so the friends they have in the house are the ones they can speak freely with and not just say "What lovely weather we are having." Continuing, Miss White stated the belief that when one is an adult, he must stick with his convictions that she thinks her parents have arrived at a correct understanding of political and religious beliefs and other basic things.

One can only marvel at the mind-set that would lead someone to consider such a conversation between two teenage girls as worthy of inclusion in a report to the president of the United States.

Five days after Hoover sent the report to Vaughn, Truman forwarded the report on February 6 to Fred M. Vinson—the secretary of the Treasury, who had recommended Harry for the job at the IMF—with a request for a meeting with him and Secretary of State Byrnes, to "discuss the situation and find out what we should do." It was a bit late, however, as the Senate confirmed Harry's appointment that same day. The three men met briefly in the oval office before lunch on February 7. With the appointment already confirmed, and with the allegations against Harry still of an ambiguous nature, the three men apparently decided to do nothing at all.[31] The president signed and issued the formal commission that afternoon.

CHAPTER SIXTEEN

At the International Monetary Fund, 1946–47

For the Americans, Dr Harry White, as [Managing] Director of the Fund . . . could not be improved upon.

—John Maynard Keynes, 1946

THE DEATH OF FRANKLIN D. Roosevelt in April 1945, the resignation of Henry Morgenthau as Treasury secretary in July, and the end of World War II in August meant that Harry White's job at the Treasury was effectively completed. Although he got along with Morgenthau's successor, Fred M. Vinson, and with Roosevelt's successor, Harry S. Truman, the excitement and drive were gone. Soon Harry developed a negative view of both Truman and Vinson. As he told Vice President Henry A. Wallace while they were being driven between meetings one day in November 1945, he found that Truman "always uses good words but never does anything, or if he does act he acts weakly or on the wrong side." From other remarks that Harry made that day, Wallace concluded that Harry "apparently is not [a] great admirer of his present chief, Vinson. Apparently he feels he is quite opportunistic."[1]

In the spring of 1946, the American journalist I. F. ("Izzy") Stone came to see Harry at his office in the Treasury building on Pennsylvania Avenue. Stone, who had just returned from an extended trip through Eastern Europe and Palestine documenting the plight of Jewish refugees, was an admirer of Harry and his work. (When Harry died two years later, Stone wrote to Harry's widow, Anne, to say, "I don't think I ever met a more brilliant person in my life.")[2] On this occasion, he just wanted to get a sense of the atmosphere in Washington. What was it like, now that Truman had succeeded Roosevelt? Harry replied in a way that Stone felt could "sum up the Truman years." Under Roosevelt, Harry mused, "We'd go over to the White House for a conference on some particular policy, lose the argument, and yet walk out the door somehow thrilled and inspired to go on and do the job the way the Big Boss had ordered. [Now], you go in to see Mr. Truman. He's very nice to you. He lets you do what you want to, and yet you leave feeling somehow dispirited and flat."[3]

Truman was, indeed, very nice to Harry and was eager to support the Bretton Woods agreements. Two weeks before the war ended with an unconditional victory for the Alliance in August 1945, Truman signed the Bretton Woods Agreements Act, ratifying U.S. membership in the multilateral institutions that all the Allies had approved *ad referendum* at Bretton Woods. Harry's wartime work was over, but he turned immediately to the next phase: getting the IMF and the World Bank up and operating.

In January 1946, as discussed in chapter 15, Truman named Harry to serve as the U.S. executive director at the IMF. Since the United States had by far the largest voting power, its director was the number-two official, after the managing director.* At the first meeting of the Executive Board, in March, Harry chaired the opening session until the board elected Camille Gutt as managing director. Gutt, from Belgium, had served as the minister of finance in his country's government in exile during the war. He would be the first of an unbroken string of at least twelve Europeans heading the IMF over the next nearly eight decades.

Harry and his family also underwent substantial lifestyle changes in 1946. Both of their daughters were now away from home, studying at Barnard College in New York City. That summer, Harry and Anne sold their house in Bethesda and moved much closer to the IMF and the Treasury, renting a two-bedroom ground-floor apartment (no. 114-B) with a view of

---

* The post of IMF deputy managing director was not established until 1949, but the number two official at the IMF has always been a U.S national. From 1949 to 1994, the deputy managing director was always a U.S. national and was designated as the number two official. The U.S. executive director no longer had any special status or management function. Starting in 1994, the number of deputies was increased and the first deputy—again, always from the United States—was assigned the lead role among them.

gardens and a fountain, in the Center Building of the elegant Westchester Apartments on Cathedral Avenue, in northwest Washington.* They also finally found a country home that they could afford (at $7,500) in their beloved New Hampshire. The house was a simple one-story building with a well and a septic tank and had only just been connected to the electric grid, but it was set in rolling and verdant hills and had plenty of space for children and adults to play. Now the family could spend their summer vacations on their own twenty-eight acres, near Fitzwilliam and not far from Hancock, where they had spent several happy holidays at Lauchlin Currie's house.

This little New Hampshire farm, aptly named Blueberry Hill by the previous owners, would be the White family retreat for the rest of Harry's life and into the 1980s (fig. 16). The pursuit, preparation, and consumption of the farm's namesake fruit became a favorite pastoral pastime of the family for three generations.

Preparation

The Bretton Woods Agreements Act, enacted on July 31, 1945, established the National Advisory Council on International Monetary and Financial Problems (NAC). One of its major tasks was to oversee U.S. participation in the IMF and World Bank. President Truman named Vinson to chair the NAC. Vinson in turn named Harry to serve as his alternate on the NAC and as chairman of the Technical Committee on the Fund and the Bank, which was charged with organizing the activities necessary to get the new institutions up and running.[4]

The IMF officially came into being on December 27, 1945, when the requisite number of countries had ratified the Articles of Agreement. That kicked the work of the NAC into high gear. Harry's technical committee focused on drafting bylaws for the Fund and the Bank and preparing for the inaugural meeting of the Boards of Governors. The main issues concerned the selection of a headquarters site, setting a place and date for the inaugural meeting, and defining the role of executive directors. On each

* The Westchester is a complex of five residential buildings, but only four were built when the Whites lived there. It opened in 1931 as rental apartments and converted to cooperative ownership in 1953. For more on the Westchester, see Goode, *Best Addresses*, 300–306.

Fig. 16. *Blueberry Hill, the Whites' summer home in New Hampshire from 1946. Family scrapbook, courtesy of Claire A. Pinkham*

of these nominally open questions, the U.S. authorities—and therefore Harry—were able and resolved to impose their will.

As discussed in chapter 12, once Keynes gave up on building support for locating the Bretton Woods organizations in London, he argued adamantly that the IMF should be headquartered in New York. Although Harry was amenable to that suggestion, Vinson wanted the Fund to be close at hand. Harry's technical committee left the matter open for a decision by the governors. As late as February 20, 1946, just two weeks before the inaugural governors' meeting, Vinson still had not announced a decision. On that day, Frank Coe, who was serving as secretary to the NAC, wrote to Vinson that "Clayton . . . prefers New York. So probably will the bankers and nearly all foreign countries. We have told foreign countries that no American position has yet been determined on this issue."[5] (Coe was director of the Division of Monetary Research at the Treasury, having replaced Harry in that position. William L. Clayton, assistant secretary of state, was the alternate to Secretary James F. Byrnes on the NAC.) That gave Keynes a platform to make one more appeal, and he tried to compromise by suggesting Philadelphia: halfway between Washington and New York. By then, however, Vinson probably had already made up his mind to place both institutions in Washington.

A second issue, seemingly trivial, was to set the time and place of the inaugural meeting. It had to be in the United States, since it was the country with the largest quota and financial contribution. The meeting also had to take place before the end of the winter of 1945–46, or at the latest in early spring, so that the IMF could begin its work. Meteorologically, it made sense for the venue to move from the now-frozen White Mountains of Bretton Woods, New Hampshire, to a milder southern state. Harry's committee found a suitable site in the General Oglethorpe Hotel on Wilmington Island, just outside Savannah, Georgia. Keynes had no objection to the site, but he strongly wanted to delay the meeting until early April to give himself and his British colleagues time to prepare and avoid a conflict with the preparation of his government's annual budget. April, however, was unsatisfactory to the U.S. Treasury, as it would conflict with the preparation of a tax bill. Treasury representatives in London informed Keynes in January that the meeting had to be held in the first half of March.[6]

Savannah: Inaugural Meeting of Governors

The role of executive directors was the most important of the decisions that had been deferred at Bretton Woods and left to be decided by the governors at the inaugural meeting. As the U.S. executive director, Harry was to be the number-two official at the IMF, but his role—and that of the other directors—was yet to be determined.

The articles provided for the IMF to be managed by a board of twelve executive directors, of which at least five (possibly six or seven) would be appointed by their national governments. The rest were to be elected to two-year terms by one or more constituent member countries. Two seats were set aside to be elected by countries in Latin America (technically, by the "American Republics not entitled to appoint directors"). Directors were to be officers of the IMF, meaning that their loyalty and obligations were supposed to be to the institution, not narrowly to the countries that appointed or elected them. They were to be "responsible for the conduct of the general operations of the Fund" and were to "function in continuous session" at Fund headquarters.

Beyond these general descriptions, much had been left open. If the IMF wanted to attract senior government officials with influence in their home countries, it could scarcely expect them to work full-time in Washington. Nor could it expect them to concern themselves with daily decisions such as approving exchange rate changes or requests to borrow. Conversely, if member governments wanted to keep tight control over IMF financial operations, they could scarcely hope to do so unless the executive directors were actively and continuously engaged. Keynes had argued long and hard for a minimal and intermittent role, so that the IMF could function as a quasi-automatic mechanism for providing financial assistance. Harry had fought for more control and for full-time engagement, and he had won a partial victory with the phrase "in continuous session" in Article XII, Section 3, of the Articles of Agreement. The meaning and significance of that phrase still had to be determined by the governors at their inaugural meeting.

The Savannah meeting was a grand occasion at which many of the world's leading financial officials gathered to give their blessings to the birth of the IMF and the World Bank. It was also a reunion of many of the same officials who had labored mightily at Bretton Woods. Most of the heavy lifting had already been done, and few in attendance were prepared to do more than relax and pat each other on the back for a tremendously challenging job well done.

Behind doors, and far from the dining and drinking, Savannah provided the backdrop for the last debate between the leading founders, Keynes and White, and the only one for which a verbatim transcript exists.[7] Summary minutes were recorded for most of the pre–Bretton Woods meetings between Keynes and White in Washington and London. Transcripts are available for many of the meetings at Bretton Woods, but the two men were in different commissions (Keynes dealing with the World Bank, and White with the IMF). The Savannah meeting stands alone as a record of how the two men interacted.

The debate took place in the Beach House of the General Oglethorpe Hotel, where the Committee on Functions and Remuneration held its meetings. Keynes, as the governor for the United Kingdom, was on the committee, as was William Clayton, the alternate governor for the United States. Harry attended the meetings as Clayton's backup.

The central question before the committee was the interpretation of the phrase "in continuous session" as it applied to the Executive Board of the IMF. Clayton opened the debate for the American side by making what was essentially a pedantic argument: What could the phrase possibly mean other than that executive directors were expected to be full-time employees? Keynes responded with a lengthy discourse on what he thought the directors should be expected to do and what sort of person that would require. "One of the most important purposes of the Fund," he suggested, "is the interchange of views by people who are forming high policy in their own countries. . . . We think that if the Executive Directors are . . . people in high positions they will be men of high caliber, more so than if they have to be seconded by their government with all their time [spent] elsewhere."[8]

After a further fruitless argument in which Clayton repeatedly sought to clarify the meaning of *continuous*, Clayton realized that he was out of his depth in a debate with Keynes. He asked to be relieved by Harry, who "was at Bretton Woods and . . . is much more familiar with [the subject] than I am."

Harry did not shy from confronting Keynes. "I think," he began, "there is much that he said that we should find ourselves in complete disagreement with in respect of the management of the Fund." He then set out a vision of the executive directors as "men of high competence in the field in which they deal," who would be capable of making a deep analysis of the diverse problems of the many member countries. Those problems, in his view, could not be solved "merely by sitting down in a few days and having somebody bring you the material and make a decision." The high-level officials that Keynes preferred would be likely to know only the problems of their own country. The "cardinal point" was that the "thoughts and energy and vitality" of each executive director should be directed primarily at "the problem of the proper operation of the Fund."

After a few participants from other countries spoke on the issue, Harry expounded further. Suppose that a "small cloud" appeared on the horizon in the economic fortunes of a member country. Could the Fund expect a man (and men were what everyone imagined as being relevant) from that country's government to "go to the Managing Director of the Fund and say, 'This troubles us'"? And if he did, what would the managing director "do about it" without first getting a full discussion in the Executive Board?

Keynes eventually tried another tack. It might be true that the appointed directors, who represented only their own countries, could function more or less independently in Washington, but the elected directors would have to travel frequently to keep in touch with the several countries in their constituency. That thought led him to suggest that alternate directors could be full-time, while their principals spent more time at home. At that point, the chairman decided to give the committee members a chance to reflect overnight before resuming. As the Indian delegate noted, "When two gladiators like Lord Keynes and Mr. White differ, it is very difficult for some of us to enter the fray or come to decisions."

The following evening, the U.S. delegation met and agreed to present a compromise formulation in which the executive director *or* his alternate would be expected to be "continuously available at the principal office of the Fund." The next morning, March 14, Harry explained to the committee that the United States intended to appoint both an executive director *and* an alternate as full-time employees of the IMF. He acknowledged, however, that other countries might wish to make different arrangements. Clayton added that he expected that once governments gained experience in dealing with the fund, they would find after a year or two that having both men present full-time would be the optimal arrangement. He and his U.S. colleagues were willing to let that situation emerge gradually, rather than forcing it from the beginning.

That settled the matter, but the Canadian delegate pointed out that the compromise solution created another delicate problem. The committee still had to agree on a proposal for compensating directors and their alternates. If only some were full-time, what formula could the committee devise for their salaries?

The salary question gave Keynes another opportunity to plea for a smaller scale of involvement. He opened the discussion by proposing that the bylaws allow for a total compensation of the two men that would be the equivalent of one full-time and one part-time official. He also wanted to have duties shared between the Fund and the Bank. Otherwise, the twelve director seats could end up being allocated to a total of forty-eight individuals, and the total expense would certainly be criticized. In any event, the United Kingdom intended to share the duties of its representatives rather than send so many top people abroad when they were needed more at home to help with plans for reconstruction.

Harry objected and argued that the IMF would need as many good men as could be made available. The only way that outcome could be achieved would be to provide for adequate compensation for both the director and the alternate. To this Keynes found a quite clever response. The articles stated that each director was to appoint his alternate. That meant, in his view, that the alternate worked for the director, not for the Fund. To ask the Fund to pay the alternate a salary would be a "very serious abuse."

Harry mocked that reasoning and responded that the alternate had to be an active and well-informed participant in meetings, not just "a man who comes to a meeting . . . and votes according to instructions" in the absence of the director.

At that point, the chairman appointed a subcommittee, comprising Keynes and a few others and chaired by Clayton, to propose a salary structure. The next day, they proposed to pay directors and alternates net-of-tax salaries of $17,000 and $11,500, respectively (roughly equivalent to $240,000 and $164,000 in 2021). Keynes abstained from the vote to endorse that solution because it conflicted with his previous instructions from London, and he had not yet received a new authority.

The next evening, at a plenary meeting of governors, Keynes stated that, after consulting with the chancellor of the Exchequer, he was "unable to support" the decision on compensation. That prompted Harry to take the discussion to a deeper level. After noting that he was rising to speak "with no small sense of embarrassment" (because, as the U.S. executive director, he was set to benefit from the generous salary level), he sought to explain the underlying cause of the opposing views.

Ever since Harry first sketched out a plan for a stabilization fund in 1941, his vision had been for an institution that would restore and transform multilateral finance for the global good. That vision was far broader than anything Keynes had in mind. As he now summarized his view:

> It has been our belief from the very beginning that the Fund constitutes a very powerful instrument for the coordination on monetary policies, for the prevention of economic warfare, and for an attempt to foster sound monetary policies throughout the world. . . . The British view . . . was based more on the concept . . . that the greater emphasis should be on the provision of short-term credit, . . . whereby a country, when it felt the need of foreign exchange, would be able to acquire it. A concomitant of that view was the view that the more nearly the Fund approached an automatic action the more nearly did it fit into their concept of the sort of organization that was necessary.[9]

The broader vision, he argued, could be achieved only if the Fund had the resources to attract a group of leaders who could analyze the difficult problems that would come before them and then represent their views and those of their colleagues from around the world to their home countries. Any attempt to weaken those resources would be a threat to the purposes of the Fund and would reduce the institution to "little else than a source of credit and an automatic source."

Keynes demurred: he did not disagree with the purposes as Harry had set them out. His only concern was with "the most efficient working of the Fund and Bank and the confidence and respect with which these new institutions would be viewed throughout the world." In that concern, however, he stood alone. The chairman put the question to a vote, and the proposal was approved; Keynes was the lone dissenter.

Once again, a compromise had been reached, albeit one that retained the essence of the U.S. position over that of the British. By setting the salary of the alternate at two-thirds that of the executive director, the governors respected the British view opposing the payment of full salaries to both, while the salary levels were still high enough to attract officials to work full-time. The "two gladiators" had completed their final battle without either one having to land a fatal blow.

The last loose end that the Savannah meeting had to tie up was the selection of the leaders of the two institutions: the managing director of the IMF and the president of the World Bank. Harry would have been a natural choice for managing director, but Vinson had other priorities. Of the two institutions, the World Bank was the more important to the United States in 1946. The Bank would be providing or facilitating the financing to rebuild the economies that had been devastated by the war. To raise funds, it would be selling bonds, primarily in the New York capital market. Vinson and others in the Truman administration were convinced that having an American with a strong reputation in U.S. financial markets as president would be an essential element in the prospects for the Bank's success, particularly considering the skepticism that many U.S. bankers had shown regarding the Bretton Woods institutions. Vinson planned to find and nominate such a person, and he seems to have understood that for him to try to place U.S. nationals in both of the top leadership positions would create a counterproductive backlash from other governments. Hence, in January he had awarded Harry the consolation prize as the U.S. executive director.

Harry's confirmation as executive director had not stopped the speculation or the campaigning for him to be managing director. On January 24, 1946, Bill Taylor, who was serving as the Treasury representative at the U.S. embassy in London, met with Keynes to convey a message from Harry regarding plans for the inaugural governors' meeting. During the meeting, Keynes noted that he had read in the newspapers about Harry's nomination to be executive director. He remarked to Taylor that he "hoped that the nomination . . . would not rule out [White's] standing for the position of Managing Director." He continued that "unless the Fund had a really good manager it would not make very much difference whether the Executive Directors were good or just mediocre."[10]

On February 20 Frank Coe suggested to Vinson that he "should tell [the State Department] and others that it is both possible and desirable to have White made Managing Director of the Fund. We could 'politic' with the British and others about a British or small country President of the Bank."[11] Who else might have been behind this appeal is impossible to judge. There is no evidence that Harry ever campaigned directly for the job, or that he ever expected to be put up for it. Whatever the background, the appeal was futile because Vinson had no intention of "politicking" over the presidency of the Bank.

Shortly after Harry arrived in Savannah, he wrote to Anne that "it looks certain that the managing director of the Fund will be a Canadian, and some unknown (as yet) American President of the Bank. Clayton does not want the job. Vinson is playing quite a dominant role here but . . . as yet nothing definite has been taken up."[12] (After Clayton and possibly others turned down the offer to run the World Bank, Truman eventually settled on Eugene Meyer, a former investment banker who was then publisher of the *Washington Post*.)

Harry's reference to the likelihood of a Canadian being selected to head the IMF is of historical interest, because a mythology emerged later that an implicit agreement was made that the managing director should always be a European. The real understanding was merely that the job should not be awarded to anyone from the United States. Vinson's first choice was Graham Towers, the governor of the Bank of Canada. Towers, however, preferred to remain in his job, and he turned down the offer even after Truman asked the prime minister of Canada to persuade Towers to accept. Vinson next asked Donald Gordon, a former deputy governor of the Bank of Canada, who also declined. Only then did he decide to leave the choice to others, who coalesced to select Camille Gutt. Five years later, the British authorities tried unsuccessfully to generate support for another Canadian, Louis Rasminsky (then Canada's executive director in the Fund). The European lock on the position evolved only because of Canada's lack of interest and its failure to put forth candidates with widespread support from other members.[13]

Executive Director

The work of the IMF began with the inaugural meeting of the Executive Board at 11:00 A.M. on May 6, 1946. Directors were meeting in mundane temporary quarters rented for the occasion: Room A of the Washington Hotel, across 15th Street from the U.S. Treasury. As the director from the host country, Harry opened the meeting as temporary chairman. For him, as for everyone present, it was an exciting but also a solemn occasion. He began with words intended to convey a heavy responsibility: "We have the honor to meet as the board of Executive Directors of an organization new in the annals of international monetary practice. I am sure that we are assuming the responsibilities of our office in that spirit of humility which our difficult task and our profound obligations to the world evoke. The opportunity we have for helping to promote monetary stability, a high level of international trade, and world prosperity is very great. We want to meet that challenge." He added that the problems before them were "very complex" and that directors would be "pioneering" and have "much to learn." He welcomed his colleagues "on behalf of the American people." He then nominated Gutt to be managing director. The Board of Governors had already approved Gutt for the job at the Savannah meeting, and the Executive Board completed the process in a unanimous vote.[14]

Two days later, Harry presided over one more meeting, and then Gutt took over. (The managing director serves also as chair of the Executive Board.) Harry moved aside to the U.S. seat, which would be his perch for the next eleven months.

Much of the work of the Executive Board through the rest of 1946 concerned internal arrangements for hiring and paying staff and moving into more permanent offices. More substantively, the Board had to assess the exchange rate parities requested by each of the thirty-nine countries that had joined the IMF in that first year. It was a controversial and consequential task, which Harry called "a revolutionary step in international monetary development." It had the potential to avert conflicts between countries, reduce gaps in international payments, and avoid a return to the disastrously autarkic exchange rate policies of the interwar years. Unfortunately, as Harry explained on multiple occasions afterward, it was also an impossible task. Despite a daunting effort at analysis by Eddie Bernstein (who had become director of the IMF's research department) and his staff, neither the IMF nor anyone else had any way to determine the ideal equilibrium rates. Although many of the proposed rates were expected to be overvalued, for Harry and his colleagues on the Board to try to dispute a country's proposal would have tied up the Fund in a series of fruitless debates.[15]

After weeks of discussion, the IMF announced that for most countries, it was just accepting the proposals.[16] In a futile effort to minimize criticism of the decision, the announcement played down the internal debates that had preceded it. Although Harry publicly defended it, he summarized his private view in a letter that he wrote to his daughter Joan, sitting in his Washington apartment on a Saturday morning the day after the last Executive Board meeting on the subject of initial parities: "Dear Joanie, . . . I've finished a hard week at the office topping off a very busy two months there in preparation for the Fund's first major step . . . the establishment of initial exchange rates. They will be announced about the 16th [of December] with a simple statement that 12 good men 'rasselled' over for several days. It went through 12 drafts and was finally boiled down from 10 pages to two! The importance of the statement lies chiefly in what was left out."[17]

The Executive Board also had to devise policies for its further interactions with member countries, particularly for handling requests to borrow. Aside from the approval of exchange rates and requests by several countries to become members, most of this work was preparatory and preliminary. The IMF received no requests from members to borrow from it until April 1947, after Harry had resigned from the Board.[18]

Harry devoted some time to writing an exposition on applying the provisions of the articles in practice. The articles reflected many compromises to accommodate the concerns of the forty-four countries that had participated in the Bretton Woods conference. That left much room for interpretation by the Executive Board once the Fund was operating. The eleven other directors naturally looked to Harry to take the lead in that endeavor. He was, after all, the main author of the articles. Privately, he began drafting a detailed interpretation with suggestions for how the Board should take control in its dealings with members. As examples, he wrote that the Executive Board should be prepared to determine whether each member country was conducting its economic policies to promote stability, orderly relations with other countries, and the avoidance of competitive devaluations; whether a country requesting to borrow from the Fund would be using the resources consistently with the purposes of the articles; and whether a country should impose controls on capital outflows.[19]

Like so many other manuscripts that Harry wrote in spare moments throughout his professional career, his more than one hundred pages of

"Notes on the Articles" remained unfinished and abandoned at the end. The draft evoked a decidedly activist approach that was consistent with the vision he had promoted at Bretton Woods over the far more passive role envisaged by Keynes and the other British negotiators. Although he never delivered it to the Fund, he obviously used it to inform his arguments before his fellow executive directors.[20] For better or worse, his appeal for an activist IMF became the basis for the Fund's role in the world economy: a role that continued to grow in scope and importance throughout the rest of the twentieth century.

On January 15, 1947, Harry and Anne took an overnight train (because dense fog in Washington forced the cancellation of their scheduled flight) to Coral Gables, Florida, so that he could give an after-dinner speech and a luncheon address at the University of Miami (and so they could go fishing and relax for one weekend, staying in the Lord Tarleton Hotel in Miami Beach). In the evening speech at the Coral Gables Country Club, he set out his vision of a shared global prosperity: "We are still very far from the goal of *world* prosperity and *world* stability that we are after. For, like peace, prosperity and stability are indivisible. To have them for ourselves we must achieve them for the rest of the world—or, at least, for a very large portion of the rest. *American* prosperity and *American* stability will be built on sand if they are not built on the prosperity and stability of most of the countries of the world." He continued by dividing the world into several categories, depending on how seriously they had been affected by World War II. The North American economies had been relatively unscathed, but others—he singled out Britain and the Soviet Union—had been "grievously" damaged and needed substantial economic assistance. The IMF and World Bank had been created to make a shared prosperity and sustained reconstruction possible.[21]

In February Harry had his only opportunity to travel outside the United States on behalf of the IMF. This trip, which nearly proved fatal, came about through a series of unusual events. Three months earlier, the ambassador from Ecuador to the United States had invited an IMF staff member, Robert Triffin, to lunch and asked him to take on a consultancy as an adviser to the Ecuadoran government. Since 1942, Triffin—a Belgian-born, naturalized U.S. citizen—had worked on Latin America as an economist at the Federal Reserve Board in Washington and had developed a solid reputation as an expert on the economy of the region.[22] In 1946 he had transferred to the IMF as one of its first professional staff members in the Research Department. Becoming a consultant to the Ecuadoran government would have been incompatible with his responsibilities at the

IMF, and he declined the offer. As an alternative, he promised to explore the idea of participating in an official mission for the IMF.

On January 14 Triffin's boss, Eddie Bernstein, proposed to the Executive Board that the Fund send Triffin and two other staff economists to Ecuador to assess economic conditions and policies. For reasons that were not explained in the minutes of the meeting, the Executive Board decided instead to organize a higher-level visit headed by two executive directors; Triffin would serve as the senior participating staff member.[23] Managing Director Gutt asked Harry to head the mission.

Over the next three weeks, this plan was expanded to cover ten countries, from Mexico in the north to Brazil in the south, and to last well over a month. Harry would be accompanied by the executive directors elected by these countries, as well as one or two members of the staff. Rodrigo Gómez, the director from Mexico, participated in the first part of the trip. Francisco Alves dos Santos-Filho, from Brazil, joined the mission in Panama and continued from there. Triffin would join them in time for the visit to Ecuador.

The notion of sending executive directors to lead missions to countries will seem odd to anyone familiar with current practices in the IMF. For most of the Fund's history, senior staff members have led country missions. The executive director for the country, or someone from that office, normally accompanies the mission, but only as an observer. In 1947 the Fund was still "feeling its way," in the words of its first historian, Keith Horsefield. Moreover, it did not yet have enough experienced staff to handle such duties. Only in January 1948 did the Board decide that mission chiefs should be staff rather than executive directors.[24]

Harry's mission was practically unprecedented. Until then, the executive directors had been working as a group in Washington. Contacts with member countries had been primarily through correspondence. In January 1947 the Board was galvanized into becoming more proactive, and not only because of the request from Ecuador. The Fund had received a request from the World Bank for information on economic conditions in Denmark, which was asking for a reconstruction loan. The Fund responded to that request on February 6, by agreeing to send the executive director for Belgium, Hubert Ansiaux, and the alternate executive director for Egypt, Mahmoud Saleh El Falaki, to Copenhagen on a fact-finding mission. On the same day, the Board gave its formal approval to Harry's mission to Latin America, where he would investigate and advise on economic conditions, policies, and plans for monetary and institutional reform.

Harry began his trip by flying to Mexico City on February 7. He continued on to San José, Costa Rica (which he loved), on the 11th; to Managua, Nicaragua ("this awful capital city"), on the 13th; to Guatemala City, Guatemala ("clean little city" with a perfect climate and interesting people), on the 16th; and then back to Mexico on the 17th, where he found time for his favorite pastime, watching a movie, even though the film was in Spanish and he could not understand a word of the dialogue.[25] Four days later, he flew to Panama for a day of meetings at the finance ministry while awaiting his scheduled onward flight. He then continued to Quito, Ecuador.

The stop in Ecuador was the centerpiece of the mission. The economy was in crisis: there were large deficits in the balance of payments, a rapid depletion of foreign exchange reserves, and a banking system on the verge of collapse. As Triffin reported afterward, "It would be impossible to exaggerate the urgency of concrete action with respect to the exchange problem and the banking crisis." Moreover, the government and the central bank seemed to have finally begun to focus on the need for that action. In the other countries that Harry visited, the primary objective was to gather information and develop contacts for future relations. In Ecuador, the goal was to assess the prospects for immediate assistance from the Fund.[26]

Unfortunately, Harry had to leave the completion of this urgent task to others, particularly Triffin. In Quito's rarefied air, almost two miles above sea level, he became seriously ill. Unable to participate much in the meetings, he nonetheless continued to Lima, Peru (a "prosperous city" in a very poor country), in an attempt to carry on with the mission. There he was diagnosed as having suffered a heart attack and was hospitalized. After a week of care and some rest, he was able to fly to La Paz, Bolivia, on March 3. Making that stop was extremely hazardous to his health, since La Paz, at nearly 12,000 feet, is about a half mile higher than Quito. He managed well enough to return closer to sea level in Santiago, Chile, on March 6.[27]

After a month of grueling travel, Harry's damaged heart was in danger of failing. He was scheduled to fly next across the Andes—the second-highest mountain range in the world—to Brazil, but doctors who treated him in Santiago advised strongly against taking that risk. (Full cabin pressurization was not initiated in passenger airplanes until later that year.) After ten days in Chile, he aborted the trip and returned to Washington via Panama and Miami, on a route where the plane would fly at a lower altitude of around 5,000 feet.

Harry was determined to keep secret the extent of his health problem because he did not want to be perceived as unable to work as effectively as he always had. In his letters home for the rest of the trip, he made no mention of becoming ill. He persisted with this reticence for the rest of his life. Testifying privately before a grand jury in March 1948, he referred casually to "my first attack a year ago in the spring, but not a serious attack."[28] In August 1948 he complained bitterly when a congressman publicly outed him as ailing (see chapter 18).

Harry had to face the fact that he could no longer meet the pace of work that setting up the IMF required. Two weeks after returning from Chile, he wrote to President Truman and Managing Director Gutt to submit his resignation, to become effective as soon as Gutt returned from a trip to Europe.

In recognition of the central role that Harry had played in conceiving, designing, and running the IMF, the Executive Board persuaded him to remain engaged informally with the title of Honorary Adviser. Gutt cabled from Paris:

> It is with deep regret that I learn of Harry White's resignation as Executive Director. As his colleague of many years I know at first-hand how important his work has been in the field of international finance. The fact that the World Fund and Bank are now in operation is in a very large measure due to his imagination and foresight and his steadfast devotion to the principle of international financial cooperation. It is good to know of the action of the Executive Board appointing him honorary Adviser to the Fund. I am gratified that as we proceed with our work of realizing the high ideals of Bretton Woods we can count on his help and advice.[29]

On April 7 Truman wrote with similar generosity:

> With sincere regret and considerable reluctance I accept your resignation as U.S. Executive Director of the International Monetary Fund, effective on Mr. Gutt's return from Europe.
>
> I know you can view with a great deal of personal satisfaction your career in public service, crowned as it has been by your ceaseless efforts to make a real contribution to the stability of international trade through the International Bank and the Inter-

national Monetary Fund, which hold so much promise to a world desperately anxious for a lasting peace.

You have filled with distinction your present assignment as United States Representative on the Board of Executive Directors of the International Monetary Fund, and your unfaltering efforts have been a source of great pride to me.

I wish you the very best of luck and will feel free to call upon you from time to time for assistance in dealing with problems we will be continually facing in which your background and abilities make you peculiarly able to help us.

Very sincerely yours,

[signed] Harry Truman[30]

CHAPTER SEVENTEEN

Freelance Consultant, 1947–48

We live so monotonous an existence that if we did any less we'd
be dead.

—Anne Terry White, November 1947

HARRY WAS JUST FIFTY-FOUR years old when his health forced him to
retire from the International Monetary Fund in April 1947. His damaged
heart was still a secret, but his rapidly thinning hair and decaying teeth
revealed a body ravaged by overwork, prematurely beyond its peak, and
no longer vigorous. His reputation was at its apex, but he had to start over
professionally and try to lead a quieter and less stressful life.

Having begun late and finished early, Harry's entire career to that
point had spanned just fourteen years. His government and IMF pen-
sions would keep him and his family afloat financially, but to maintain
a comfortable lifestyle would require him to find some form of employment consistent with his newly limited physical fitness. He soon decided to hang a shingle as an independent consultant to governments,
offering advice on economic and financial policies. As he wrote to New
York City Mayor William O'Dwyer that month, "I intend to make
my headquarters in the world's financial center—your fair city—and
be a doctor to the world's monetary ills. And there sure are plenty of
such ills."[1]

Setting Up Shop

To maximize his opportunities and contacts, Harry quickly opened two offices. One was in the center of Washington, at 1024 Connecticut Avenue, NW, just north of the K Street lobbying corridor and within a few blocks of his former offices at the Treasury and the IMF. The other, which he found with help from O'Dwyer, was in downtown Manhattan, at 65 Broadway, around the corner from the New York Stock Exchange and not far from the Federal Reserve Bank.* Until he could complete the arrangements, Bernard Bernstein—a former Treasury colleague—offered to let him use his Manhattan office and apartment whenever Harry needed to be in New York. These various arrangements also enabled him to work near other former colleagues and friends such as Oscar Cox and Randolph Feltus.

In Washington, Harry continued to rent his apartment in the Westchester complex on Cathedral Avenue. He also rented an apartment on the Upper West Side of Manhattan (at 334 W. 86th St.), just three subway stops from where his two daughters were studying at Barnard College.

As he left the IMF, Harry wrote to several prominent officials with whom he had dealt over the years, requesting autographed portraits that he could display in his new offices as symbols of his status in Washington (fig. 17). Those who responded positively included President Truman ("Kindest regards to Harry D. White, Harry Truman"); former Vice President Henry Wallace ("For Harry D White for whom I have long had the greatest admiration. Henry A. Wallace"); Secretary of State Dean Acheson ("To Harry White for whom many years of work together and some battles have constantly increased my regard and respect. Dean Acheson"); Federal Reserve Chairman William McChesney Martin Jr.; and other cabinet members, senators, and members of Congress.[2]

Although Harry had labored in obscurity throughout much of his career, he had gained a measure of fame and a high degree of credibility through his advocacy for the Bretton Woods agreements and his service as executive director at the IMF. He was particularly admired in the countries

* The office building in Washington no longer exists. That street address is now occupied by a men's clothing store. In Manhattan, 65 Broadway, also known as the American Express building, is a twenty-one-story neoclassical structure, built in 1917 as the headquarters for the eponymous company. American Express sold the building in 1975. It continues to function as an office building.

Fig. 17. *Gifts from former Vice President Henry Wallace and President Harry Truman, 1947. Family collection, courtesy of Claire A. Pinkham*

that he had done so much to help in his public career. Soon after he left the IMF, the government of France offered him one of its most prestigious awards, naming him an Officer of the French Legion of Honor "for the eminent services that you have always rendered for the French cause in the United States."[3]

Closer to home, the American Economic Association invited Harry to deliver "one of the main papers" at the group's annual meeting, which was to be held in Chicago during the last week of December 1947.[4] Harry agreed, but in the event he had to cancel after he suffered a second heart attack.

Throughout this time, Harry stayed in touch with Henry Wallace and reportedly was Wallace's preferred choice for Treasury secretary, in the most unlikely event that Wallace's quest for the presidency should succeed. Wallace was the candidate of the Progressive Party for president in 1948, but he won no electoral votes. In a speech at a party rally the week after Harry's death, Wallace described Harry as "a man of peace . . . my friend and old associate . . . [whose] genius cut the cost and the length of the war."[5]

Harry had no difficulty finding clients, especially in Latin America, where he had extensive hands-on experience and had made many friends both for himself and for the United States. Several years later, Harry's former Treasury colleague Sol Adler wrote that officials in Latin America had regarded Harry "as a real brother because he was one of the few Americans with whom they came into official contact who responded to them as a human being, that is, in the highest American tradition. Needless to say, in so doing he was being a loyal and good American, since he was winning friends for his country as well as for himself."[6] Though Harry did not speak Spanish or Portuguese, he had made official visits to Cuba, Brazil, and Mexico while at the Treasury, and to Mexico and eight more countries in the region while at the IMF. Letters that he wrote to his daughters in 1947 suggest that he intended for his consulting practice to focus on the region.

One of Harry's first clients, in May 1947, was the government of Chile, which invited him to head a mission to Santiago. That mission took place either later that month or in June. The central bank of Chile reportedly also considered hiring Harry as a consultant, but that initiative seems to have been scuttled by the U.S. State Department for unexplained reasons.[7]

In October, Cox invited him to become a member of the Board of Directors of a new company, Trade Abroad, Inc. A few months later, Harry considered accepting an offer for a visiting professorship in the Economics Department at the University of Michigan, but other pressures intervened.[8]

Harry's main client throughout this final year of his life was Banco de Mexico, the central bank of Mexico, which paid him a retainer of $18,000 a year (equivalent to about $202,000 in 2021) to serve as a consultant and adviser. He spent a few weeks in Mexico City for that purpose in July 1947 and again in June 1948. In January 1948 he submitted a report that set out a draft program for Mexican-American cooperation on economic affairs.[9] For most of that winter, however, he was out of commission because of continuing health problems.

In September 1947 Harry suffered a second heart attack while in New York. The damage this time was more serious than the effects of his first attack some six months earlier in Ecuador. For several weeks he was confined to his bed. His doctor then recommended that he take an extended break from work and spend the winter somewhere in the south, where warm sunshine could help him recover. Dutifully (and not very happily), the Whites decided to spend November 1947 through February 1948 in St. Petersburg, Florida, where they rented accommodations in the Lexington Arms, a three-story apartment building not far from Tampa Bay.

The forced rest was not to the taste of either Harry or Anne. As Anne described it in a letter to their daughter Joan shortly after they arrived: "It is our routine to go for a short walk morning and afternoon and to end up [with] a long read on . . . our special bench under a palm tree. . . . We live so monotonous an existence that if we did any less we'd be dead."[10]

By January 1948 Harry was beginning to regain his strength and do a bit of work. They left St. Petersburg at the end of February and returned to their Manhattan apartment. In March he was back at work in New York and Washington. Publicly, Harry still kept his heart decay secret, out of concern that potential clients would hesitate to hire him if they knew how precarious his health really was. Extended travel was out of the question. Unable to provide much direct advice to Banco de Mexico or other clients, he turned instead to developing a proposal for amending the IMF Articles of Agreement.

Amending the IMF Charter

Harry made what amounted to his last contribution to the IMF more than a year after he had resigned from his post. In April 1948 he was feeling guilty that he had not been able to do much work for Mexico. More fundamentally, he was concerned that the IMF was not living up to its potential in an increasingly challenging world economy. The postwar surge in growth in some countries, the economic setbacks in others, and the onset of political tensions in the form of the Cold War were, he believed, soon going to strain the limited resources of the IMF and the World Bank. Less than four years after Bretton Woods, he regretted that he had not created a more dynamically flexible system to deal with these unforeseen developments. The IMF, in particular, was going to prove to be inadequate: "We cannot expect a boy to do a man's job. As drawn up at Bretton Woods, the institutions were to have man's capacity for a man-sized job. Since then the job has grown to giant size, while the man to handle it has, figuratively speaking, shrunk to a mere boy."[11] Harry decided to kill both of his concerns with one effort: writing a proposal to amend the IMF Articles of Agreement, which he would give to the Mexican authorities in the hope that they would present it to the Fund for action by the Executive Board.

The proposed amendment was a complicated scheme to create an "international medium of exchange" that national governments could use for the strictly limited purpose of increasing international trade. The essential idea was that the IMF would set up "trade dollar (TD)" accounts for each member country.[12] If the IMF staff determined that a country would be able to increase its imports if it were less constrained by the availability of foreign exchange, the Fund would allocate TD credits to that country. If the staff determined that a country would be able to increase its exports if other countries were less constrained, then it would allocate TD debits to that country and require it to accept TDs in exchange for its goods. TDs could be used only to increase imports above the level of the user's imports in a designated base period. Countries accepting TDs would earn interest on their holdings, and countries using them would pay interest.

In writing the manuscript, Harry tried to anticipate the many objections that would be raised against his proposal. He acknowledged that countries might disagree with the staff's analysis of their needs and circumstances and would ask for additional credits or a lower requirement to accept them. He proposed to deal with that situation by establishing a review committee comprising staff from the IMF and the UN Economic and Social Council (ECOSOC), as well as technical experts from the country. He further proposed that the whole scheme should be wound down after fifteen years, on the assumption that the postwar pressure on IMF resources would prove to be temporary.

Separately, Harry produced a "rough draft of a statement that might be used to introduce the proposed amendments on the agenda." In it he argued that the "contributions of both [the Fund and the Bank have] been much less than anticipated." Part of the problem was the rise of "world tensions," a veiled reference to the onset of the Cold War and the consequent expenses of the arms race. Most people, he recalled, had expected the end of World War II to be followed by "a degree of unity and good will in international political relations among the victorious allies never before reached in peace time. It was expected that the world would move rapidly—to use the phrase Wendell Willkie made famous—toward 'One World.'" Instead, "the tensions between certain of the major powers" had produced "almost catastrophic" economic pressures.[13]

Another factor was the surge in price inflation, which had already reduced the real value of the Fund's resources almost by half. But Harry argued that the problem also arose because of shortcomings in the "policies and resources" of the institutions. Unless improvements were made, he concluded that the Fund and the Bank would "continue merely to nibble at the edges of the problems. They will continue to produce a maximum of façade and a minimum of results." He was particularly critical of the management of the World Bank, which had been parsimonious with its lending. "Had the Bank pursued a policy more in spirit with that laid down in the Charter . . . , the difficulties facing the Fund would have been less and a greater contribution would have been made by both institutions."[14]

This was a strikingly harsh indictment of his own intellectual children, which he had worked so hard to conceive and bear. He now believed that neither he nor anyone else involved in the process of creation had anticipated how the world would evolve after the war. The institutions created at Bretton Woods were not up to these unanticipated challenges.

Harry drafted this proposal in some haste, and he sent the manuscript to the Mexican ambassador in Washington (Antonio Espinosa de los Monteros) on April 21. He doubtless discussed it with Mexico's central bankers during a visit to Mexico City in June, but those discussions would have been only of a preliminary character. No one acted on the proposal during the summer months, and the manuscript became an orphan when Harry died suddenly in mid-August.

In October officials in the Mexican central bank decided to offer the manuscript to the IMF as a sort of posthumous tribute to Harry. When they introduced it at the Executive Board, the Mexican executive director, Raul Martinez-Ostos, noted that they "had not taken any position either supporting or opposing any of the recommendations therein, and were putting the paper forward at this time as a valuable technical study which might contribute to the eventual solution of a difficult and important problem."[15]

The neutrality with which the Mexican authorities presented Harry's proposal enabled the IMF to avoid taking up his manuscript as a formal proposal for action. The Executive Board asked the staff to prepare an analysis of it, and the Research Department did so over the next several months.[16] That analysis was drafted with a slightly negative slant. The proposal was then laid to rest. In retrospect, however, it was a remarkably prescient forerunner of what became the First Amendment of the articles two decades later.

The staff analysis of Harry's proposal naturally looked back in time for comparisons. It noted that the proposal was closer to the Keynes Plan for an international clearing union than to the White Plan that had superseded it. The biggest difference was that Harry's proposal was intended to be a supplement to the existing structure of the IMF, not a substitute for it. Also, instead of working with fixed quotas for each country, access to the scheme would be based on a country's trade position and prospects relative to a base period that would be updated each year. Because countries would be required to use most of their drawing rights under the original articles before gaining access to the supplementary scheme, actual access to it was likely to be limited in scale. From these considerations, the staff concluded that it did not expect the scheme to contribute substantially to an increase in world trade and could worsen the distribution of trade and the scale of trade imbalances.[17]

Apart from the details of the scheme, which Harry doubtless would have revised greatly if he had lived to discuss it with his former colleagues and react to a public debate, the underlying conception was an appropriate response to a major problem that was just then emerging—and that was far from temporary, as Harry thought. With the perspective of someone living in 1948, he saw the issue as being caused by a shortage of foreign exchange reserves in many countries that had been devastated by the war. Moreover, the demand for reserves was being driven up by the advent of the Cold War and the corresponding need for many countries to strengthen their defense capabilities. If these shortages could be overcome by the growth of trade, the problem would gradually fade away. With the perspective of hindsight from the twenty-first century, one can see that the inadequacies of the original Bretton Woods institutions were only to get worse.

The international financial system that Harry had created was bound to be dependent on the supply of U.S. dollars to support cross-border trade, combined with the firm dollar price of gold in support of cross-border finance. One of the keenest observers of the problems with this dependence in the postwar economy was Robert Triffin, whom we met earlier as a member of Harry's mission through Central and South America in 1947. White and Triffin's interactions may well have helped inspire each man's thinking about the practical shortcomings of the system.

At heart, Triffin was an academic who—like Harry—had begun his career teaching at Harvard. In 1951, after his service in the Federal Reserve Board, the IMF, and the Organization for European Economic Cooperation, he began his main vocation as an economics professor at Yale University. Toward the end of that decade, he formulated the theory that became known as the Triffin Dilemma. He saw that the Bretton Woods system of fixed exchange rates linked to gold and the U.S. dollar was generating growth in international trade that could not be sustained in the long run. Countries outside the United States would continue to accumulate dollars as reserves in excess of the rate at which the United States could accumulate gold to serve as a backing for the stock of dollars. Eventually, that would induce governments to demand gold in exchange for their holdings at a rate that would cause the system to collapse.[18]

Within a few years of Triffin's statement of the dilemma, the Bretton Woods system began to unravel much as he had predicted. Discussions among the major advanced economies, between those countries and a group of developing countries, and within the IMF led in 1968 to an agreement to amend the Articles of Agreement and create the Special Drawing Right (SDR) as a new international financial asset. The SDR was defined initially as equivalent to the gold content of the U.S. dollar. Beginning in 1970, SDRs were issued ("allocated") to all participating countries in proportion to their IMF quotas. Rules governing the use of those allocations were designed to ensure that the SDR would serve as a supplement to official foreign exchange reserves. Over the succeeding decades, the SDR was redefined and restructured, but it continued to serve as a supplementary reserve in support of the growth of international trade.[19]

The SDR scheme differed from Harry's 1948 proposal in many technical respects, but its essence was similar. The SDR, like the proposed TD, was designed to act as a specialized line of credit to supplement U.S. dollars in countries' official reserves. Participating countries could draw on that credit line temporarily to settle net balances with trading partners, and they would have to replenish ("reconstitute") their holding every few years. In both schemes, countries with strong payments positions could be required ("designated") to accept the special asset on demand.* Both schemes aimed to preserve the Bretton Woods system of fixed exchange rates, although by 1968 the strains on the system had become so great that the Band-Aid of the SDR could not save it. Perhaps Harry's TDs could have saved the system if they had been introduced in the late 1940s, but that is just speculation.

The main interest of this episode is that Harry recognized that the design of the system that he had fought so hard to create was going to be inadequate to serve the unexpectedly challenging postwar world economy. It was only four years after Bretton Woods, three years after the end of the war, and one year after the beginning of IMF financial operations, but the world had changed. Had Harry not died so young, he would have

---

* This description applies to the original form of the SDR and the original rules for its use. In 1974 the SDR was redefined as a basket of currencies. The reconstitution requirement was abrogated in 1981. The designation requirement is still in effect but has not been invoked since 1987.

seen the Bretton Woods era become the most dynamic quarter century in history, measured by the extent and breadth of global economic growth.[20] But he did not live to make an effective case for modifying the system so that it could adapt to the evolving challenges. The financial system created at Bretton Woods sailed on unchanged through the 1950s and 1960s until it sank in the 1970s, in the wake of the growth that it had made possible.

Jewish Causes and the Creation of Israel

Beyond these spinoffs from his Treasury and IMF career, Harry made time to pursue a new personal passion. Although not a religious man, he had come to care deeply about the plight of the Jewish people, especially as the horrors of the Holocaust emerged in the later stages of the war. Assisting his boss in the development of the Morgenthau Plan for Germany had intensified his awareness of and sensitivity to the dangers that still awaited the refugees and other survivors of the Nazi onslaught. More broadly, Morgenthau, as head of the War Refugee Board beginning in January 1944, was a leading figure in an effort by officials in the Roosevelt administration to shift government policy toward helping Jewish refugees escape from German-held territory and relocate in the United States, over strong objections from the State Department.

At a meeting with Morgenthau on January 13, 1944, Harry and six Treasury colleagues persuaded the secretary to ask Roosevelt to overrule State Department objections to helping Jewish refugees who were trying to flee the Axis forces. Harry made a strong emotional appeal that U.S. policy to date was even worse than Hitler's because it was "covered up by a species of hypocrisy in which men are deterred from doing what they wish to do." Morgenthau complained, "I can't take too much pounding today," but he did take the process forward. In February Harry and the others sent a letter thanking the secretary for his efforts in behalf of European Jews who were being threatened with extinction.[21]

The reader will recall from chapters 1 and 2 that one of Harry's early passions in life was the education of boys, which he pursued in part by helping Jewish orphans. He put that ambition aside to focus on economic policy, but he never lost sight of it. In 1946, while serving as an executive director in the IMF, he seized an opportunity to gain a new foothold in Jewish education. The Albert Einstein Foundation, led by the industrialist S. Ralph Lazrus and aided by Einstein's strong support, was in the early planning stages of an effort to establish the first university in the United

States to be founded by Jews. Through an intermediary, Lazrus asked Harry to prepare a proposal for bringing that vision into practice.[22]

Harry undertook the project enthusiastically. He and Anne hosted several sessions with other participants in their Bethesda home, and they both participated in the drafting.[23] Over the next two years, the Einstein Foundation built on that beginning to establish Brandeis University as an institution named after Louis D. Brandeis, the first Jewish justice of the U.S. Supreme Court, open to all students regardless of religion or ethnicity.

In February 1947 Lazrus invited Harry to become a member of the Board of Trustees of the Einstein Foundation. Harry accepted the invitation in late March, after returning from his trip through Latin America, but by then the foundation was riven with dissent. Einstein and Lazrus both withdrew from supporting the project to establish the university, and Lazrus reneged on his intention to put Harry's name forward for election to the board.[24] That ended the prospect, but Harry soon moved into an even more promising endeavor.

While Harry was at the IMF, the movement to establish the state of Israel began in earnest. Great Britain had sovereignty over Palestine under the terms of a mandate issued by the League of Nations in 1922 following the 1917 overthrow of the Ottoman Turkish Empire. The League mandate specified that the territory should be governed so as to lead to "the establishment in Palestine of a national home for the Jewish people," while not prejudicing "the civil and religious rights of the non-Jewish communities in Palestine." In February 1947 the British government referred the question of the governance of Palestine to the League's successor, the United Nations. From that point on, the likelihood of the creation of a Jewish state continued to rise. President Truman endorsed the idea in May, and the UN approved it in November. Six months later, on May 14, 1948, Israel became a state.

As soon as the move won UN approval, Eliezer Siegfried Hoofien, the head of the Anglo-Palestine Bank (APB), organized an effort to develop a new financial system to replace the one based on British practices and the pound sterling. He began by asking Eliezer Kaplan—the treasurer of the Jewish Agency for Palestine, who was slated to become Israel's first minister of finance—to set up a meeting of Jewish experts in London. That group was to comprise Sir Jeremy Raisman, Oscar Gass, and Harry White. Raisman (whose first given name was Abraham) was a retired British civil servant who had directed wartime finance in India and had led the Indian delegation at Bretton Woods. By 1947 Raisman was serving as an independent consultant to governments in several countries. Gass also was a freelance consultant. He had worked in the U.S. Treasury from 1933 to 1942, including a stint as an economist in Harry's division for the last few years. He would go on to serve as an economic adviser to the state of Israel from 1948 until his retirement in 1955.[25] Both men knew Harry well. Gass had been asked by the Jewish Agency to assemble a group of American advisers, and he naturally included Harry as the foremost monetary expert.

The proposed London meeting could not take place. Harry was recuperating in Florida for the winter and was in no condition to travel overseas. Undeterred, Gass called Harry to persuade him to provide advice on the design of new financial institutions for Israel. Harry could not resist the opportunity to do some useful work. He agreed to provide advice pro bono, but the group insisted on paying him a retainer of $1,000 a month. That seems to have amused Harry. "I was certainly under the impression that I was helping you boys out personally," he wrote to Gass on November 13. "It never occurred to me that any remuneration to me was involved." He concluded by expressing his delight at the progress being made in the UN Security Council toward the partition of Palestine into Jewish and Arab states. "I still have my fingers crossed, as you boys have, but it already looks so much better than I had anticipated that I feel real optimistic about the outcome."[26]

Harry advised Gass on an initial proposal for a monetary system, but he soon became disillusioned. Early in January 1948, Harry wrote to Gass to express serious concerns about the direction that the Jewish Agency for Palestine was taking in the planning for a new currency. In what can be described only as a hopeless naïveté about the prospects for cooperation between Jews and Arabs, their plan was based on the assumption (explicit in the UN proposal) that a Joint Monetary Board would run the Jewish and Arab financial systems. The two states would issue separate currencies, but they would be tied together by a fixed exchange rate. That rate would be maintained by a currency board arrangement similar to the one that was already in place, backed by the board's holdings of reserve currencies. Trade and finance between the two states would be open and free.[27]

For the moment at least, Harry accepted the likelihood of a joint board, but he did not believe that open trade and finance could be made compatible with a firmly fixed exchange rate. Eventually, the national interests of the two states would diverge, and something would have to give way. Harry did not mince words in his letter to Gass. "I did not think that anyone familiar with monetary problems could have believed that it was possible for each of two countries in a monetary union to possess complete sovereignty in monetary policy and administration, yet be certain of maintaining indefinitely a fixed *de facto* exchange rate between their currencies."[28] Instead, the plan should assume a "fixed but adjustable" exchange rate, as in the Bretton Woods system.

In March 1948, shortly after Harry returned to New York from his winter's exile in Florida, Gass arranged for Harry and Hoofien to meet for the first time, over lunch (Gass also attending) while Hoofien was visiting the city.[29] A few days later, Harry sent Gass some critical comments on the ideas that Hoofien was putting forward for establishing a currency for the Jewish state. (The name of this new state—Israel—was not chosen until May 14.)

Part of Hoofien's plan involved setting up a currency board in Palestine, composed entirely of local residents and independent from the British authorities that had been issuing the currency for the past three decades. The resulting system, however, was to remain patterned on the one set up and controlled by the British since 1917. Hoofien apparently envisaged that the local board would hold pounds sterling (or U.S. dollars) as a reserve against the currency issue but would have the authority to choose a backing ratio of less than 100 percent. (At one stage, the plan called for a 30 percent backing.)

On February 22, 1948, Britain unilaterally expelled the Palestine pound from the sterling bloc, announced that it would no longer issue the currency, and froze most of Palestine's deposits held in London. That threw planning into chaos. In a March 18 letter to Gass, Harry warned that the British would never accept any arrangement unless the Palestinian currency was unequivocally distinct from the pound sterling and unless the independence was total and unambiguous. Moreover, maintaining a currency board arrangement would be an expensive way to use scarce foreign exchange, which might be needed to acquire vital imports in the early years of the new state. He suggested that it would be better to impose effective "legislative restraints against the undue note and credit expansion" instead of a fixed ratio.[30]

Harry's letter also drew on his "experience with getting new currencies prepared in short time," a reference both to his work in Latin America and to his involvement in the design and production of occupation currencies for Allied troops during World War II. It was already the middle of March, and the withdrawal of British authority was being planned for

May. Hoofien, Harry warned, had to get the process under way without delay, or the UN would have little choice other than to continue British control.[31]

As the mid-May date for the handover approached, Kaplan and Gass hired Harry to prepare "a draft of permanent, basic monetary and banking legislation for the Jewish State."[32] The earlier hope for an economic union between the Jewish and Arab states had vanished in the wake of Arab opposition. Looking now at the prospect for a new independent state with no experience in independent monetary affairs, Harry saw the situation as practically unique. In some respects, monetary arrangements would have to be tailored to the fact that the new state would be small and heavily dependent on external trade and support. In that respect, it would be a developing country, not unlike the smaller Latin American countries on which he had worked in previous years. In other respects, however, it would be more like a small but more advanced developed country. Its well-trained financial leaders and their experience with the British system of colonial finance meant that he could prescribe a more sophisticated system than if the initial conditions were more constrained. On that basis, he went to work and quickly prepared a blueprint.

Harry submitted a detailed plan for a central bank and a national currency at the end of May 1948, two weeks after the new state came into being. As a stopgap, Israel was still using the banknotes issued by the Palestine Currency Board. The gist of Harry's argument was that Israel would need a transitional arrangement for at least six months, but it should try to move to a permanent system within a year. (Hoofien's plan called for the APB to serve as the bank of issue for up to five years.) The system should be flexible enough to provide for the economy's monetary needs during its initial struggle for existence and then during an expected period of economic growth. Currency credibility and price stability should be established through sound management, initially by the APB (which would be the currency-issuing bank during the transition) and then by the central bank. Reserves of gold and foreign exchange would help, but the government could not expect to rely on a gold-exchange system in the difficult circumstances that it would face. Continuing some elements of the British system might also help in the transition, but Israel would have to move quickly to establish the independence of its currency and its monetary policies.[33]

Harry proposed that the Israeli government should begin by devising "a new currency unit (with a name in keeping with the dignity of Israel)" and having an adequate supply of banknotes printed abroad, either in the United States or in Switzerland. It then should move quickly to establish a central bank, provided that the government had "the authority to set up a Central Bank by decree." (He seems to have feared that the UN might still exercise some control.) Until the central bank was established, the government would have to exercise strict control over the amount of currency that the APB could issue. Because the country would be "fighting for its existence," the government would have to secure adequate financing for its operations, which initially would have to come primarily in the form of loans from the APB. If the bank proved unwilling to make loans in large enough amounts, then the creation of a central bank would have to come even more quickly.

Harry closed with a stark warning. "If hostilities continue long, it will be little short of a miracle if the Government can prevent prices from rising sharply." Preventing runaway inflation had to be a high priority, and the only way to stop it in these circumstances would be to take difficult and harsh measures, including "stringent methods of price and credit control, wage freezing, and widespread rationing, and possibly even a properly drafted program of forced loans to the Government by individuals." Experience showed that countries always "acted much too late."

As minister of finance, Kaplan was prevented by circumstances from following Harry's advice. Intense fighting continued between Israel and several neighboring countries until well into 1949. Israel then had to undertake an enormous buildup of housing and other infrastructure as it absorbed millions of European refugees and other Jews returning from the diaspora. Faced with these challenges, Kaplan decided to rely on the APB for the currency issue (initially still called the Palestine pound; later, the Israel pound), and he placed other central banking functions within his own ministry. The Bank of Israel was finally established as the country's central bank in December 1954, six and a half years after the creation of the state.

PART VI

Death and Defamation

CHAPTER EIGHTEEN

Dealing with the Red Scare, 1947–48

Behold . . . him who . . . was a man most masterful;

not a citizen who did not look with envy on his lot;

see him now and see the breakers of misfortune swallow him!

—Sophocles, *Oedipus the King*

IN 1947 THE ALLEGATIONS made by Whittaker Chambers and Elizabeth Bentley about Communist affiliations and espionage activities of federal government employees were still a closely held secret. As recounted in chapter 15, the FBI responded by investigating the named individuals, including Harry White, with electronic and physical surveillance. In Harry's case, the investigation revealed nothing illegal, but it did confirm his social and professional association with several other people who were under suspicion. The last year of Harry's life was to become increasingly consumed by the fallout from these allegations and findings.

March 1948: Harry Testifies before a Grand Jury

At the end of July 1947, Harry went to New York from Blueberry Hill, his summer home in New Hampshire, getting ready for a trip to Mexico City, where he would be seeing his main consulting client, the Mexican central bank. Leaving his temporary New York office one day, he encountered

Frank Coe, a colleague throughout Harry's long tenure at the U.S. Treasury who was now the secretary of the IMF, one of the most senior posts at the fledgling institution. Coe was agitated because he had been subpoenaed to testify before a grand jury. As Harry would later recall, Frank "was all in a dither and didn't know what it was all about." Frank asked Harry if he had any idea what they might want to ask him, but Harry knew nothing about it. Coe feared, though, that there was "a witch-hunt on of all the New Deal people."[1]

Some time later, Harry saw Frank again and asked him how it had gone. Mysteriously, Frank replied, "Well, I'm not supposed to tell you about anything." Harry was naturally curious. "Well, what . . . why? Could it be a secret?" "Well," Frank replied, "they [the prosecutors] asked me not to say." To which Harry could only say, "Under those circumstances, then, don't tell me."[2]

The mystery was cleared up somewhat a couple of weeks later. On August 15, 1947, two FBI agents interviewed Harry at his New York apartment for almost two hours, asking him what he knew about several people who had been alleged to be Communists or to have engaged in espionage for the Soviet Union. They asked him about Lauchlin Currie, Sonia Gold, A. George Silverman, Nathan Gregory Silvermaster, William H. Taylor, and William Ludwig Ullmann. Harry certainly knew all of them. Currie, Silverman, and Silvermaster were all old friends of his; and Gold, Taylor, and Ullmann had all worked at the Treasury at various times. But he told the agents that he had no knowledge of any of them being either a Communist or a spy.[3]

Harry had no reason to suspect Frank Coe, either, and he probably assumed that the grand jury prosecutors had questioned Frank similarly about people he had known. More ominously, at some point Frank told Harry that he had also been interviewed by FBI agents, and that they had asked him specifically about his relationship with Harry: "why [Harry] had hired him and why some other people had been hired under [him]." Harry gave this account little thought at the time. The existence of the grand jury was public knowledge, as was the fact that witnesses were being asked whether they knew certain prominent people, including the financier Bernard Baruch and William J. Donovan (the head of the oddly named Office of Strategic Services, the forerunner of the CIA) as well as Morgenthau and White. The leading speculation was that the investigation had something to do with the aborted Morgenthau Plan for Germany. After the FBI interviewed Harry in mid-August, however, "it assumed a quite different significance to me."[4]

The FBI interview was a prelude to a plan to obtain Harry's testimony before the grand jury that was investigating various allegations of Soviet espionage by employees of the federal government, including most notably the case against the State Department official Alger Hiss. The grand jury began interviewing witnesses on or before July 22, 1947, including (on July 31) FBI agent Francis D. O'Brien, who then telephoned Harry to request the meeting described above.[5] On September 10, the U.S. District Court in New York issued a subpoena for Harry to appear before the grand jury on October 22.

The timing turned out to be problematic. On September 6, four days before the subpoena was issued, Harry suffered his second heart attack, and his physician strongly recommended that he take time off and spend the winter in Florida, where the mild climate might help him recover. Harry requested a postponement, which the court granted. After two more postponements, and after spending much of the winter in St. Petersburg, Florida, Harry finally arranged to testify over two days, March 24 and 25, 1948. Even then, he was still greatly weakened by his heart condition. Every half hour or so throughout his lengthy testimony, he had to ask for a brief recess so that he could regain enough strength to continue.

Two assistant U.S. attorneys, Thomas J. Donegan and T. Vincent Quinn, did the questioning. Donegan opened the proceedings, and Quinn joined in subsequently, though only on the first day. Jurors also occasionally asked questions. After reviewing Harry's educational and employment record, Donegan asked a variation of the now familiar and infamous question, "Have you ever been or are you a member of the Communist Party?" "No, of course not," Harry replied. "Have you ever been associated with any groups which were known to you as having been affiliated in any way with the Communist Party? [Answer:] Not to my knowledge. As a matter of fact, I haven't been affiliated with any group outside of the university alumni, so I couldn't have been."[6]

Donegan continued by asking Harry what he knew about various people who were under investigation. In addition to the people about whom O'Brien had asked seven months earlier, Harry was now questioned extensively about Frank Coe and was also asked about Helen Silvermaster and two Treasury officials, Harold Glasser and Victor Perlo. Donegan also asked Harry about meetings with Coe and Silverman in July 1947, in an apparent attempt to trap him into giving testimony that might conflict with theirs. Harry almost fell into the trap inadvertently when he initially forgot about a second meeting with Coe; but he remembered it later, and he voluntarily corrected his answer the following day.

The historian Athan Theoharis speculated that Donegan knew more than he was letting on because he had information obtained from an illegal wiretap on Harry's telephone. Bruce Craig repeated that speculation and added, "Donegan revealed that he already knew that White had called Silverman." In fact, Donegan asked Harry if he had called Silverman, but he did not say that he knew that the call had taken place. According to the FBI file on its surveillance, the Bureau ended the wiretap on May 16, 1947, a month and a half before the events in question. It therefore seems more likely that Donegan's line of questioning was based on earlier testimony or on surveillance of someone other than Harry. Theoharis also speculated that Harry's meetings with Coe and Silverman were a deliberate attempt to "concert his testimony" with theirs, which could have led to a charge of attempted obstruction of justice.[7] Certainly, that is what Donegan believed and was trying to establish, but there is no evidence to support the charge. It is more likely, as would have been perfectly natural, that Harry discussed the matter with Coe and Silverman simply to get a sense of what to expect if he were questioned.

During the second day that Harry was on the witness stand, a juror (or jurors) seemed puzzled by the distinction that Harry was drawing between being a Communist and being engaged in espionage. As soon as Harry had heard that the grand jury was interviewing Coe and other officials, he had understood that the government was interested in determining whether they had been members of the Communist Party. After all, that line of inquiry—although not yet in full McCarthy mode—was very much in the atmosphere. Only after the FBI interviewed him did Harry realize that some individuals were also suspected of spying for the Soviet Union. On hearing that, a juror wanted to know, "Isn't there an implication by the inquiry into one [i.e., being a Communist] that it could also refer to the other [i.e., being a spy]?" Harry volunteered this reply: "I don't think I would assume that a Communist was necessarily engaged in espionage, no. I would feel . . . that he shouldn't work for the Government, but I certainly wouldn't feel that he was engaged in espionage activities in the way in which the FBI indicated to me that they thought some of them were. No."[8]

As the questioning continued, Donegan made it clear that the government suspected Ludwig Ullmann of taking Treasury documents out of the office, photographing them, and giving the photographs to the Silvermasters to pass on to the Soviets. Ullmann (a bachelor) lived with the Silvermasters. He was an accomplished amateur photographer and kept a darkroom in the basement of their house. By the time Harry was testifying to the grand jury, the FBI had heard Elizabeth Bentley's story alleging that the Silvermasters and Ullmann had regularly conveyed material in this way. On March 30, 1948, five days after Harry's testimony, she would repeat the story to the grand jury. Donegan now (on March 25) was preparing for Bentley's appearance by getting Harry to tell the jurors what he knew or did not know about what seemed to have been going on under his nose.

> Q. Mr. White, have you any knowledge or did you at any time have any suspicion that Mr. Ullmann was taking home documents from the Treasury Department for the purpose of photographing such documents or abstracting the information contained thereon?
>
> A. No, not only did I [not] know that, but if you will pardon me I can say that I find that very difficult to believe even now. . . . I don't believe that he did. I know that he took documents home, of course.
>
> Q. Now, was that in the course of his regular duties, to take out—
>
> A. Oh, yes, all the men took night work home. Not all, but I would say 80 percent of them. . . . Top secret documents nobody took home, to my knowledge. They were not supposed to. Confidential, yes.

Continuing, Harry acknowledged that the systems in place at the Treasury relied more on trusting staff to follow the rules than on securing the physical documents. Top secret and "eyes only" documents—mostly those that contained information on impending exchange rate changes and other time-sensitive data—were kept securely in an office safe under the watchful eye of his private secretary, but others could easily have been removed and then brought back the next day without raising suspicion. Nonetheless, he trusted his staff and refused to believe that anyone had acted wrongly. And was he "aware of" the Silvermasters or Ullmann "being Communistically inclined, as a result of any conversation? No," he replied, "I would say definitely not."

Finally, Donegan and others questioned Harry about his interactions with Soviet officials, starting with Anatole Gromov. Bentley had mentioned that name to the FBI and to the House Un-American Activities Committee (HUAC) as a Russian spy who received stolen documents from her and others. Although Gromov reported to Soviet intelligence in Moscow, his cover job was as a senior official in the Soviet embassy in Washington. Since Harry was the U.S. Treasury's principal liaison with the embassy, he could have met Gromov in the normal course of his work. Donegan, in an apparent effort to link Harry to Bentley, asked if he had ever met Gromov, "either officially or unofficially." It took Harry a minute or two to try to connect his experiences with the name, but he then replied that an individual who might have been Gromov had "occasionally sent for material . . . to transmit formal messages to somebody else whose name I don't remember but who was a part of the Embassy. But we had a number of discussions with both the Ambassador [Andrei Gromyko] and the first secretary [possibly Gromov] who acted as financial counselor." When shown a photograph of Gromov, however, Harry said it was not the same man. He had never seen this person.

Donegan then wanted to know if Harry had ever seen any Soviet officials socially, outside his official duties. That question brought back happy memories of the men with whom he had met often in 1944 and 1945 regarding Bretton Woods and the founding of the United Nations in San Francisco. The "four or five" Soviets who had helped negotiate terms for the IMF and World Bank at Bretton Woods had "entertained me and I had them all down [to] the house one afternoon. . . . There was another occasion in which two or three of that commission came to call" in connection with the negotiations. He volunteered that he had also had dinner on one occasion with a "Professor Bistroff, if it is of any importance."

That last point, with its phonetic misspelling by the court stenographer, was a reference to Fedor Bystrov, who was professor of finance at the Institute of Foreign Trade in Moscow and who had served as a technical expert advising the Soviet delegation at Bretton Woods. That Bretton Woods experience gave rise to a continuing acquaintance. In December 1944, five months after Bretton Woods, Bystrov—still in Washington and working out of the Soviet Purchasing Commission—sent Harry a Christmas present from the Soviet embassy consisting of five bottles of wine and five boxes of cigarettes. Bizarrely, the present was delivered by mistake to a carpenter in northeast Washington who was also named Harry D. White.

This was not the first time the carpenter had received Harry's misdelivered mail. Some four years earlier, a friend of Harry had sent him a book by the Hungarian sociologist Karl Mannheim (probably the 1940 English translation of *Man and Society in an Age of Reconstruction*). It went instead to the same-named carpenter, who no doubt was greatly puzzled.

He kept the book (but presumably did not read it) until the arrival of the wine and cigarettes finally enabled him to guess what had happened. Harry eventually got the presents, thanked Professor Bystrov, and offered to split the wine and cigarettes with the carpenter—but not until the story of the mix-up had been published in the *Washington Times-Herald*, complete with a photograph of the carpenter and his wife admiring the Soviet wines.[9]

A bit more than a year later, the Soviet Union had declined to join the IMF, but it had agreed to send a delegation to the inaugural meeting of IMF and World Bank governors in Savannah, Georgia, in March 1946. This delegation, with the role of observers, was to be headed by Professor Bystrov. As the date for the meetings approached, Harry and Anne invited the Bystrovs to join them for an informal dinner at their home in Bethesda. That was the occasion to which Harry alluded in his grand jury testimony two years later. In his mind, and in reality, nothing in his social interactions with Bystrov or any other member of the Soviet delegations carried any nefarious or untoward connotations. By 1948, however, the onset of the Cold War had become a horror-house mirror that distorted every image of such connections. And as we shall see in the next two chapters, the distortions were only going to get worse.

Toward the end of the second day of testimony, Donegan asked Harry about the 1941 episode (described in chapter 8) in which the FBI questioned him about his and his wife's alleged involvement in what Donegan called a "communist-front" organization. Harry's memory was a little vague after the passage of more than six years, but he explained once again that the FBI had confused him with another Harry White. His wife had indeed belonged to one or two social service organizations, but he had no reason to believe that those groups were Communist-oriented. "I have known—I won't say hundreds, but scores—of very fine persons who were members of that organization [the League of Women Shoppers] at that time, and I would certainly say [now], and I would say categorically then, that they were not, these persons I have in mind, were not" Communists. Moreover, Harry insisted, his "wife is an authoress and writes books and is not much interested in politics."[10]

Under questioning from a juror, Harry explained again in detail how his office filing system worked. Anyone who was working on a topic could obtain a document from one of the secretarial staff, without going through Harry, unless the document was labeled "Top Secret" or "Eyes Only." Frank Coe, Gold, Glasser, Taylor, and Ullmann were among those who had such access, along with Solomon Adler when he was not on overseas assignments. Silverman presumably had similar access, but he worked in a different part of the Treasury.

Finally, Donegan ran through a list of names—even longer than the list he had started with the day before—and asked Harry which ones he had known "socially, that is, outside of being employed by the Government and under your supervision." Harry replied affirmatively for Adler, Frank Coe, Currie, Alger Hiss, and Irving Kaplan ("a lousy [volleyball] player, but a funny guy"). He had also met Victor Perlo and Donald Wheeler but did not know them very well. Several others on Donegan's list he either had never heard of or knew of only by reputation.[11] Harry doubtless understood that these were people who were being investigated as possibly involved in espionage for the Soviet Union, but he did not believe that any of those who were his friends or colleagues were guilty of that charge.

Harry certainly did not imagine that he himself was suspected in any way. Two days later, he wrote to a friend, Oscar S. Cox (an attorney who had formerly worked for the Treasury), describing how well the process had gone. Although the questioning had often turned to matters that he thought were trivial ("What the devil such details had to do with their inquiry, I don't know"), everyone had been courteous to him, and he had done his best to tell them whatever he could remember.[12]

When Harry was excused after this testimony, it was obvious that the prosecutors had no basis on which to ask for an indictment. Bentley's testimony that he had been the source of official documents conveyed to her ring of spies had been shown to be based only on hearsay. Not only did Donegan have no evidence to corroborate it, but Harry had unwittingly provided him with the names of several people who also had ready access to Treasury documents and who therefore could easily have been the original source. Even if someone had mentioned to the group that a document had come from Harry, that need not imply that Harry had knowingly conveyed it for an illicit purpose. A few days after Harry's testimony, Bentley appeared before the grand jury. When asked if she had ever seen documents "in the possession of Harry Dexter White," she replied, "I never met Mr. White, so I couldn't tell you."[13]

On July 20, 1948, the grand jury issued indictments for the top twelve officials in the Communist Party of the United States, alleging that they were engaged in a conspiracy to overthrow the U.S. government. None of the individuals mentioned in the questioning related to Harry White was ever indicted, except for Alger Hiss, whom White knew only through official contacts and who was mentioned in this context only in passing. (Hiss, by far the most famous of the espionage suspects, was indicted for perjury in December 1948 and was convicted of the charge in January 1950.)

August 1948: Harry Testifies to HUAC

The story might have ended with Harry's grand jury testimony, except that some members of Congress who were serving on HUAC decided to take the allegations public. First to be brought up was Bentley, who testified before the committee on July 31, 1948. She repeated her story about hearing people alleging that Harry had been the source of materials brought to her spy ring. "He gave information to Mr. Silvermaster which was relayed on to me," she asserted.

This was the first time that such a claim had ever been made publicly or conveyed to Harry's ears in any way. Informed of her testimony by a reporter from United Press International, he was taken aback. After all, he had never even heard of Elizabeth Bentley. "This is the most fantastic thing I have ever heard of," he told the reporter. "I'm shocked."[14] He set out immediately to ask HUAC for the opportunity to testify so he could refute the charges.

The committee quite rightly dismissed Bentley's charges as hearsay but followed up a few days later with public testimony from Chambers. Having now heard Bentley's accusations, Chambers proceeded to embellish his previous quite limited description of what he knew about Harry. He now claimed that he had met Harry personally in the 1930s and had discussed involvement in the "Communist movement" with him. He claimed that the only reason that he had never mentioned Harry to investigators until 1945 was that he was trying to protect Harry's reputation. (Chambers asserted that he had first mentioned Harry White to the FBI "about four years" after his September 1939 meeting with Berle, which was about a year and a half before he actually did so in March 1945.) Moreover, he claimed that when he quit the Communist Party in 1937, he had asked Harry "to break away from the Communist movement," and he thought that he "had succeeded." But "Miss Bentley's testimony and certain things I heard from other sources assured me that I had failed."[15]

The questioning was astonishingly unfocused. No one asked Chambers what he meant by "certain things I heard." Nor did anyone ask how Bentley's testimony in 1948 could have convinced him three years earlier, in 1945, to stop protecting Harry's reputation and name him to the FBI.

Several committee members seem to have been more interested in establishing their anti-Communist bona fides than in hearing Chambers's account of his alleged contacts. The presiding member, Karl E. Mundt, Republican from South Dakota, tried unsuccessfully to talk Chambers into defining Communism and Nazism or fascism as equivalent forms of totalitarianism. Then John E. Rankin, Democrat from Mississippi, suggested that the "basic principles" of Communism included "the wiping out of the Christian church throughout the world" and making "a slave of every American man, woman, and child." To his credit, Chambers demurred to agree to this suggestion. The chief investigator for HUAC, Robert E. Stripling, had to work hard to get the questioning back to the subject at hand.

Chambers went on to describe Harry as someone who had participated in an underground "cell" in the mid-1930s but who later was merely regarded by the party as a useful supporter because he was destined to become a high government official. Asked by a committee member whether Harry was "considered as a source of information to the Communist cell," Chambers replied, "No." Lumping Harry together with other officials such as Alger Hiss, Chambers stressed that "these people were specifically not wanted to act as sources of information. These people were an elite group, an outstanding group, which it was believed would rise to positions as, indeed, some of them did—notably Mr. White and Mr. Hiss—in the Government, and their position in the Government would be of very much more service to the Communist Party."

No one on the committee seems to have noticed the lack of logic in this account. Harry's rise through the ranks in the Treasury did not begin until well after Chambers had left the party. For a group of underground spies to have anticipated that rise and to have deliberately farmed him out to act independently on behalf of the party within the government as a kind of Manchurian candidate defies credulity.

Logical or not, Chambers's claims regarding Harry and other senior officials were bombshell news. The next morning, the front page of the *New York Times* ran the headline "Red 'Underground' in Federal Posts Alleged by Editor." (Chambers was then an editor at *Time* magazine.) The story detailed much of the testimony and appeared to take it seriously. Harry now was forced into full defensive mode as he prepared to make a public rebuttal.

During the next few days, Harry—who was vacationing with Anne and their daughters at Blueberry Hill in New Hampshire—corresponded with friends who were sympathetic and who had been similarly shocked by the accusations. Randolph Feltus, an attorney and public relations consultant who had helped the Treasury persuade Congress to ratify the Bretton Woods agreements, wrote to offer his help in clearing Harry's name from this "outrageous smear attack." Robert Patterson, who had served as under secretary of war under Roosevelt and as secretary of war under Truman, wrote to express his trust and support. To another friend, Harry wrote that he was looking forward to being able to "hit back. . . . I want to answer those god-damn charges as soon as possible."[16]

Harry's opportunity came on August 13, 1948, just ten days after Chambers's testimony. The hearing was held in the large, ornate Caucus Room in the Old (later renamed the Cannon) House Office Building. Freshly arrived back in Washington from New Hampshire, Harry stood behind a bank of myriad microphones, wearing a dapper three-piece striped gray suit and a bright paisley tie, and swore to tell nothing but the truth.

The committee had nine members, of whom five were present that day: the chairman, J. Parnell Thomas (Republican from New Jersey); three of the other four Republicans (Karl E. Mundt from South Dakota, John McDowell from Pennsylvania, and Richard M. Nixon from California); and one of the four Democrats (F. Edward Hébert from Louisiana). Questions addressed to Harry came entirely from the Republican members and from the committee's chief investigator, Robert E. Stripling.

Facing the five congressmen, with row upon row of reporters and observers behind him, Harry was in a feisty and combative mood. He delivered a bravura performance, declaring both his innocence and his outrage and denouncing the charges as "unqualifiedly false." He showed none of the docile deference to authority that members of Congress typically expect. When McDowell commented, "Dr. White, I am almost ashamed to say that up until Miss Bentley mentioned your name I had never heard of you," Harry replied, "Well, it is nothing to be ashamed of. May I ask your name?"

As a report in the *New Yorker* magazine put it, Harry "handled the Committee men like a Border collie maneuvering sheep." The *New York Times* editorialized against the whole proceeding, noting that the committee "can be charged with having denied [White] the due protection of the law, with having allowed witnesses to make unsubstantiated statements of which the accused learned only through public sources, and by so doing ignoring the Bill of Rights and outraging our American sense of justice."[17]

Harry's opening statement, with its dramatic assertion that "my creed is the American creed," expressed his general belief in American democracy, freedom of choice, and the absence of "arbitrary and unwarranted use of power" against individuals or groups, his opposition to "discrimination in any form," and his more specific belief in the goal of "an increasing measure of political, economic, and emotional security for all." Later in the hearing, he seemed to equate HUAC's proceedings with the infamous Star Chamber court in England before the English civil war, in which the accused could be found guilty in secret hearings with no opportunity to defend themselves. The comparison naturally irritated some committee members, especially Nixon. Harry backed off only slightly and emphasized that his key point was to object to the public airing of unsubstantiated accusations without the "protective devices which our fathers felt were necessary to surround an individual who was accused of a crime."[18] His vivid testimony generated frequent loud applause from the many spectators in the hearing room.

No one was accusing Harry of being a Communist. When HUAC issued its report on the hearings, it acknowledged that "no charge of Communist Party affiliation was made against either Lauchlin Currie or Harry Dexter White. Both denied such affiliation."[19] Still, Chambers had asserted that he had known Harry during the period when he (Chambers) was a member of the Communist Party; that is, up to about the end of 1937. A central issue in the HUAC hearing was therefore whether Chambers had in fact known White personally. Testifying under oath more than a decade after the alleged encounters, Harry stated, "To the best of my recollection I remember no such name," alluding to Chambers. Since Chambers had also testified that he was known within the "Communist apparatus" only as "Carl," Stripling asked Harry if he had ever known anyone by that name. "I have no recollection," Harry replied. "I doubt very much whether I would have known any man by just the first name. It would have been very peculiar."

The committee's other substantive questions focused mainly on Harry's knowledge or suspicion of possible Communism or participation in espionage by his friends or colleagues. At least some members had obviously concluded that anyone who knew so many people who had come under suspicion must be guilty in some way. Thomas expressed his belief in guilt by association in the starkest terms. "Mr. White, of all the persons who have been mentioned at these hearings to date, 9 or 10 have worked in your Department, and in addition to that, two others are friends of yours, and one is a very close friend. Now, how do you account for that?" Harry's response, in its essence, was that his friends and colleagues were exceptionally good economists, and that those who had worked under him had all been subjected to standard loyalty investigations by the Secret Service before they could work at the Treasury. Moreover, he did not believe that any of them were guilty of the charges that had been made against them.

The fact that some of the accused had refused to answer questions from HUAC by invoking their rights under the Fifth Amendment of the U.S. Constitution was mentioned several times. Harry, who was freely answering all their questions, refused to either condemn or defend others who had chosen to take that option. Had Harry lived, he no doubt would have enjoyed the spectacle of seeing Parnell Thomas "plead the Fifth" in his own behalf before being convicted and sent to jail in 1950 for defrauding the government.

For a man suffering from a serious heart ailment, the stress of the public hearing was enormous. Before it began, Harry sent a private note to Thomas, stating: "I am recovering from a severe heart attack. I would appreciate it if the chairman would give me 5 or 10 minutes rest after each hour." Thomas agreed, but when Harry mentioned in his testimony that he had occasionally (several years earlier) played Ping-Pong at the home of a friend whom the committee suspected of being a spy, Thomas interrupted him sarcastically: "For a person who had a severe heart condition, you certainly can play a lot of sports."[20]

Thomas's statement was the first time that Harry's heart disease had been mentioned publicly, and it blew the cover that Harry had developed carefully to preserve an illusion of good health. He objected strenuously. "I did not intend that this note should be read aloud. I do not know any reason why it should be public that I am ill, but I think probably one of the reasons why I suffered a heart attack was because I played so many sports, and so well." This objection earned a round of applause from the spectators in the room, but it did not elicit any apology from the chairman.[21]

After the HUAC hearing, Harry returned to New York. The next day, he saw his doctor, who advised him to rest. Instead, he went immediately to New Hampshire by train, experiencing chest pains on the way. The country air and the friendly surroundings of the family vacation home might have provided him the opportunity to relax for a time before returning to Washington in the fall to answer the charges more fully. The stress of the hearing and the travel, though, had been too great. When

Anne met him at the train station in Greenfield, New Hampshire, she was terrified to see how much his condition had worsened. His face was almost blue. She took him home to Blueberry Hill and called a local physician, Dr. George S. Emerson.[22] Neither Emerson nor a second physician who attended him the next day could help him. On that second day, August 16, Harry suffered his third heart attack. He died peacefully at home, in the presence of his wife and children, in the fading light of the late afternoon.

CHAPTER NINETEEN

Afterlife

The Attack Continues, 1948–54

Democrat . . . [is] a political label . . . corrupted by the red slime
of a White.

—Senator Joseph McCarthy, February 1954

HARRY WHITE'S FATAL HEART attack in August 1948 did not end the
assault on his character. Instead, his departure from the stage provided
an open forum for his accusers. He was never without his defenders, but
their voices were drowned out by the rise of McCarthyism in the five
years after his death. The *New York Times* declared accurately in an editorial on August 18, 1948, that Harry's "death was due to a heart condition
brought about by years of arduous government service and aggravated by
the ordeal through which he had to pass during the committee hearings."
Harry's critics, however, started spreading a rumor that he had committed suicide. Appalled, the physician who had tended to him the afternoon
before he died issued a statement setting out the true circumstances. Red-
hunting fanatics nonetheless have continued to repeat the rumor well into
the twenty-first century.

The most egregious repetition of the disproved suicide story came
in December 1967, when the Internal Security subcommittee of the U.S.
Senate issued a document asserting falsely that White had died "the

apparent victim of suicide by sleeping pills." The *New York Times* then repeated the claim in a story on December 10. In response to a protest from Harry's daughter Joan White Pinkham, the *Times* and the Associated Press subsequently corrected the record. The author of the Senate report (an academic historian at the University of Dallas) refused to withdraw his claim, and the Senate document stands uncorrected.[1]

Overall, the immediate aftermath was positive. In addition to public tributes in the *New York Times* and other major newspapers, the IMF Executive Board honored him with a eulogy, and many public figures as well as friends and colleagues sent scores of condolence letters and telegrams to Harry's widow, Anne. Henry Morgenthau wrote to Anne: "Harry had a keen, original mind. I threw many tough problems at him but sooner or later he always came up with the answers. . . . Harry was a top flight public servant who served his country well. If I get around to writing the real story of my life in the Treasury, Harry will occupy an important place in the book." Harry and Anne's old friend from Harvard, Lauchlin Currie, who had testified before the House Un-American Activities Committee on the same day as Harry, dashed off a handwritten letter:

Dear Anne,

I've been horribly shocked and depressed over the news of Harry's death. Ever since Randolph [Feltus] called me this morning I've been thinking of Harry and how our lives were interwoven. I met Harry at the first meeting of [Economics] 11 in 1925. Thereafter our lives crossed and recrossed and our careers were roughly parallel, even to our appearing together last Friday to answer the same charges, almost exactly twenty-three years after our first meeting.

Altho, unfortunately, we saw little of each other in recent years we had shared so many experiences over such a long period that I feel a great sense of personal loss. As you know at one time I leaned on him heavily and drew strength from his courage and self reliance. Even last week I derived comfort from the conviction that he would be a vigorous, competent and courageous witness, which, of course, he was.

I hope that Harry himself, or someone thoroughly conversant with his work, has written out in some detail his amazing record of inventiveness. As I think back, the variety and range of the difficult problems he mastered and the variety of the subjects on which he worked were truly astounding—and all this under most difficult circumstances. If and when you have the job done, I shall be only too happy to help in every way I can.

Deo and the boys join me in extending to you, Ruth and Joan our most profound sympathy.

Sincerely,

Lauch[2]

The more general reaction, however, was and continues to be ferociously negative. For more than six decades, Harry White's posthumous reputation has been defined largely by a mythological belief that he led a double life: openly as a Treasury and IMF bureaucrat and secretly as a spy for the Soviet Union. On November 23, 1953, more than five years after his death, he was on the cover of *Time* magazine with the headline, "The Strange Case of Harry Dexter White . . . How much did President Truman know?" That same day, *Life* magazine ran a lengthy story about him, with a cover headline, "Who Was Harry Dexter White?" Those and other stories were prompted by a sensational charge by the attorney general of the United States that President Harry S. Truman had appointed White to his post at the International Monetary Fund despite having been warned beforehand by the FBI that White was engaged in espionage. The spy allegations have persisted to the present and have been magnified by additional evidence made public in the 1990s. The conflict between the apparent evidence and the reality of White's career calls for a close examination.

November 1948: Chambers Begins to Embellish His Story

The Pumpkin Papers

Most immediately, Harry's death freed Whittaker Chambers from the risk of having his stories directly challenged, and he took full advantage of the opening. Chambers was under fire from the defense team in the legal case against Alger Hiss. Since Chambers and Hiss had made conflicting claims under oath, one of them had to be guilty of perjury. In November 1948, to support his claim that Hiss had given material to him to convey to a Soviet agent, Chambers retrieved several documents from a personal stash that he claimed to have kept hidden for more than ten years. Most were purportedly from Hiss, but the trove also included a set of notes, mostly handwritten by Harry White, on four sheets of lined legal-size yellow ("foolscap") paper. A few weeks later, Chambers produced microfilms of other documents, which he had hidden in a pumpkin on his Maryland farm. Journalists loved the drama, and the whole collection became known popularly as the "pumpkin papers."

In the anti-Communist hysteria of 1948, it was easy to convince a credulous public that Harry had in fact given these notes to Chambers in the late 1930s for the alleged purpose. The government even called in handwriting experts to verify that Harry had written the notes. Their verification added to the aura of guilt surrounding them. Chambers justified not revealing their existence for a decade by calling the whole collection a "life preserver" to be saved for just such an emergency as this. Two years later, while the hysteria was still in the ascendant, Representative Richard M. Nixon read excerpts of this so-called White Memorandum on the floor of the House of Representatives, and it entered the lore and the lexicon of the public case against Harry.[3]

It is worth a close look to examine the nature and context of the notes. Although many public accounts referred to them as an eight-page memorandum,[4] they were not a memorandum at all. They were seven pages of notes on both sides of four sheets of paper, made over the course of several weeks beginning in January 1938. On the back page of the fourth sheet, someone else had written "65 big sheets 4 little slips," apparently referring to the total amount of material that Chambers claimed to have retained. The eighth page was otherwise blank. The handwriting experts seem not to have noticed that the handwriting on the last page was quite different from that on the preceding pages. Moreover, no one at the time seems to have noticed that White could not have known how many pages of material Chambers eventually accumulated.

To anyone who has ever worked in a large bureaucracy like the U.S. Treasury, the nature of Harry's notes will be readily apparent. He regularly attended several meetings each day, in various offices at the Treasury and in other departments around Washington. He would have carried a pad of lined paper with him to take notes on whatever topics were being discussed. At some point when he no longer needed the notes to jog his memory, he would have discarded them. Anyone in the building who was so inclined could easily have retrieved them from a desk or trash can and conveyed them to Chambers. If Harry had wanted to convey information to the Soviets (or anyone else), these disjointed and sometimes cryptic notes would have been an extremely odd and ineffective way to do so.

The notes begin on January 10, 1938, with an account of how "Taylor" (Wayne C. Taylor, an assistant secretary at the Treasury) had persuaded Herbert Feis in the State Department to get Cordell Hull (secretary of state) to try to get Secretary Morgenthau to accept a partial settlement of Hungarian debt to the U.S. government. Morgenthau had declined to go along, and Harry's notes indicated his perplexity both at the proposal and the "surreptitious" way it had been taken to Morgenthau.

The background to this note is that Harry attended a meeting at Morgenthau's home on a Saturday evening, January 8, 1938, at which Morgenthau showed exasperation at being pressured into making a hasty decision on the settlement of Hungarian debts. Taylor—somewhat of a renegade in the Treasury—pushed the State Department on the issue, apparently without clearing his action with Morgenthau. On Sunday, Harry probably participated in drafting a report that his division chief (George Haas) sent to Morgenthau on Monday providing background information on the Hungarian economy, after which Morgenthau called Taylor to instruct him to do nothing until he (Morgenthau) returned from a two-week trip.[5] Harry's note to himself that day (January 10) was a natural reaction to the discussions taking place in the office that morning.

The next section of the notes, dated January 19, 1938, summarizes various points regarding Japan. Tensions were high between Japan and the United States in the aftermath of Japan's sinking of an American warship, the U.S.S. *Panay*, in China. A navy captain, Royal E. Ingersoll (spelled "Ingersol" in this instance in Harry's scribbled notes), had been stationed in London to act as liaison with the British (or "English," in Harry's notes) government about a possible economic boycott against Japan. It was being reported that Japan had new oil storage facilities and that it was not expected to declare war on China "for some time at least." These notes also are likely to have been based on regular meetings at the Treasury. Morgenthau was away from Washington at the time, but the Treasury was actively looking into options for responding to Japan, short of going to war. Incongruously, Harry's note includes the observation that "Sec. reading Red Star Over China and is quite interested." *Red Star over China*, Edgar Snow's account of the rise of the Communist movement led by Mao Zedong, was published toward the end of 1937 and was favorably reviewed in the *New York Times* on January 9, 1938, just ten days before this meeting.

The next few pages are undated. The notes, which cover events relating both to Japan and to Europe, could be a continuation of the meeting on January 19, but the context is unstated. One paragraph on the fifth page seems to be an aide-mémoire either to help him prepare to make a statement about the navy captain in London, or perhaps to summarize what he had just said at the meeting. ("I have heard nothing as to Capt. Ingersoll's mission in England beyond my earlier explanation.")

The sixth page contains a single sentence, "The Van Zeeland report was not taken seriously here." On January 9, 1938, Paul Van Zeeland—a former prime minister of Belgium—issued a report calling for an international monetary conference to stabilize currency values. The proposed conference was to have included the fascist powers Germany and Italy, and none of the major Western powers showed any interest in it. Even before the report was released, Morgenthau told reporters that the response of the U.S. government would be "definitely no."[6] The reaffirmation of this rejection was probably the last item mentioned at the January 19 meeting, as the rest of that page is blank.

The seventh and final page, written some weeks later, is headed "(via Cochran)," meaning that Harry is noting a report by Merle Cochran, who was serving as the Treasury liaison at the U.S. embassy in Paris. Cochran returned to Paris on February 15, 1938, from the regular monthly governors' meeting at the Bank for International Settlements in Basel, Switzerland. He then sent a cable to Washington reporting on discussions he had had with some of the governors and other officials. Harry's notes summarized a few brief incidental points from Cochran's twelve-page report.[7] He noted that Cochran had met with "Bachman" (Gottlieb Bachmann, then a senior official at the Swiss National Bank and later its president), who had told him that Japan was trying to get Swiss banks to lend them money for industrial development, but no Swiss bank was interested. Cochran also reported that "Schacht [Hjalmar Schacht, president of the German Reichsbank and a former economy minister in the Nazi government] impressed me—and some of my friends also—as finding some hope in the Van Zeeland report as a basis for a possible approach between Germany and the British and the French."

Although parts of these notes might have been of interest to the Soviet Union in 1938, it would not have made sense for Harry to write up a series of random notes in this way over the course of at least five weeks and then give it to Chambers to convey to his Soviet contacts. The fact that the notes somehow came into Chambers's possession, to be squirreled away for more than a decade until Harry had died and could no longer dispute Chambers's account, tells us nothing more than that someone in the Treasury managed to take them away and pass them on.

The revelation of the notes' existence in Chambers's possession stirred a renewed interest in the alleged activities of the late Harry White. Chambers testified again in December 1948: to HUAC in executive session on December 6, to the still-active grand jury over several days starting on December 7, and publicly at a HUAC hearing on December 8. This series of meetings produced new, more detailed accounts of Chambers's supposed interactions with Harry in the 1930s, of which two—despite, or because of, their bizarre details—proved to have an enduring influence in the story: one involving a report on Soviet monetary policy, and one regarding an Oriental rug.

The Alleged Report on Soviet Monetary Policy

At the public HUAC hearing and on many later occasions, Chambers told a detailed story about driving from Washington to Peterborough, New Hampshire, in August 1937, accompanied by Alger and Priscilla Hiss. The ostensible purpose of the trip was for Chambers to meet with Harry for about twenty minutes to pass on a request from the Soviet Union for him to write a report on how to reform Soviet monetary policy. After Harry agreed to do so (or so Chambers claimed), Chambers and the Hisses then supposedly drove back to Washington. No evidence has ever turned up that Harry wrote such a report, and much of the story was debunked during the trial of Alger Hiss for perjury. Notably, the Hisses were vacationing on the Eastern Shore of Maryland at the time, and the proprietor of the New Hampshire inn where the three travelers supposedly stayed produced evidence that they had not been there. More than half a century later, however, the story is still being purveyed as if it were true.[8]

The Bokhara Carpet

The story of the rug is slightly more credible but still far from conclusive. Chambers's story was that in December 1936, his Soviet handler, Boris Bykov, gave him six hundred dollars with instructions to use it to purchase gifts for four Americans in thanks for their clandestine services. Chambers purchased four Bokhara-style Armenian carpets at a good price through an acquaintance and sold two of them at a lower price to George Silverman, telling him to keep one for himself and give the other to his friend Harry White. Silverman apparently did as he was asked, but the circumstances were not necessarily as Chambers wished people to believe.

One of Harry's close friends in Washington, George Silverman was born in Poland in 1900. After his family emigrated to the United States, he enlisted in the U.S. Army in 1918 but had the good luck to enroll just two days before the armistice was signed, on November 11. He became a U.S. citizen in 1921 and later worked in a variety of positions in the federal government. During World War II, he served as a civilian adviser to the assistant chief of the Air Staff. He left the government in 1945 and worked in a variety of other positions, mostly in the private sector. He testified twice before HUAC, in 1948 and 1950, denying charges raised against him and refusing to answer questions about Communism. As happened to others, the notoriety of those hearings made it very difficult for him to obtain work. He moved to Montclair, New Jersey, where he died in 1973.

After hearing Chambers's testimony about the rugs, the grand jury called Silverman in to testify on December 15, 1948 (the same day on which it issued an indictment against Hiss). The prosecutors subjected him to very extensive and detailed questioning about the rugs. Silverman testified that in 1936, Harry and Anne had invited him to stay in their home for two months while his wife was away. They had refused to let him pay rent, and so in December he seized the opportunity to give them the carpet as a New Year's present to thank them for their kindness. He had obtained the rug as part of a shipment of four that Chambers had asked him to take delivery of at his home in Washington. He had returned two of the rugs to Chambers, had kept one, and had given the other to the Whites.[9]

No evidence ever turned up to contradict Silverman's testimony about the way he gave the rug to the Whites. Although Harry was no longer alive and able to confirm the account, Anne did so in 1949. Neither Harry nor Anne ever showed any embarrassment about the gift, and they kept the rug in prominent locations in their house for many years.[10]

The overall thrust of Silverman's account of himself as uninvolved with the circle of Americans who were passing information to the Soviets is less clear. He knew Chambers and interacted with him during the period in the 1930s when Chambers was a member of the Communist Party and acting as a conveyer of documents. In any case, he seems not to have been active in espionage himself. Evidence from Soviet cables and archives generally describes him as an indirect source of gossip rather than a conduit of official documents. One cable stated that Silverman "is very cautious and . . . doesn't know that he is working for us." Another noted that the Soviets had no direct contact with him and relied on a complex network of American contacts to obtain very limited information from him. None of what they learned pertained to his work.[11]

When Bentley first told her story to the FBI in November 1945, she asserted that "the Russians had in the past given White presents including a Persian rug." Thus, the story was already circulating within the ring of spies, but the original source was never revealed. As is the case with so many other facets of the story, the truth remains elusive.

The only clear conclusion from these muddy stories is that Chambers was adept at making up stories to fit whatever narrative he wanted to construct at the moment. In December 1948, to bolster his account of how he obtained the seven pages of Harry White's notes in 1938, he told HUAC that the notes were just an example—the only one that he had kept—of material that he had received from Harry over a period of several years in the 1930s. On January 18, 1949, in testimony to the grand jury, he stated that "Harry Dexter White used to give us handwritten material from time to time, and may have occasionally given us a typed copy."[12] In testimony a week later, however, a juror pressed Chambers to say more precisely how he had obtained such material.

> JUROR: These papers that Mr. White gave you for transmission—how did you get them?
> CHAMBERS: How I got the papers from White?
> JUROR: Yes. Did you meet him, and what were the facts about them?
> CHAMBERS: I don't think that White ever personally gave me material. He gave it to George Silverman, who gave it to me; and I think that in that case Silverman sometimes returned the material the next morning.[13]

In other words, although Chambers claimed to have had a years-long personal relationship with Harry, all the papers that he supposedly obtained from him were passed through an intermediary, allegedly George Silverman, although at one point in his testimony on January 20, 1949, he cited Frank Coe as the "go-between." On that date, Chambers told the grand jury that Frank Coe had introduced him to Harry. Somewhat later, he claimed to have received a "transmission . . . by way of Robert Coe [Frank's brother, whom Harry did not know at all], which took place some time in 1935, I think." He then contradicted himself by telling the jurors that Silverman had introduced him to Harry.[14] Silverman testified on December 15, 1948, that he never transmitted any unauthorized information, either on his own behalf or from anyone else, to Chambers or any other person. Without any corroboration, Chambers's account cannot be credited.

The McCarthy Era, 1950–54 and Beyond

For the next few years, the allegations against Harry were overshadowed by the sensational trials of Alger Hiss and by the multifarious, mostly unsubstantiated allegations by Senator Joseph McCarthy (Republican from Wisconsin) and his supporters against Communists who were supposedly still working in the federal government. McCarthy and colleagues did drag Harry's name into the mud that they were stirring up, but without any evidence of espionage or wrongdoing. Their main charge was that they suspected that certain policy decisions made by the Treasury during World War II had been influenced by Communist subversives within the government, including Harry. This demagogic campaign culminated in a speech that McCarthy delivered in Charleston, West Virginia, in which he declared that the Democratic Party had been guilty of "twenty years of treason" and that the party label had been "stitched with the idiocy of a Truman, rotted by the deceit of an Acheson, corrupted by the red slime of a White."[15]

The three principal policy issues raised in Senate hearings in relation to Harry were the unimplemented Morgenthau Plan for destroying Germany's industrial base, the interagency decision to provide plates to the Soviet Union for printing currency to be used by Soviet troops during the occupation of conquered German territory, and the Treasury's reluctance to make unconditional loans to the Chinese government during the war.

As discussed in chapter 14, the Morgenthau Plan, on which Morgenthau solicited Harry's assistance, is explained entirely by both men's abhorrence of German militarism and the Holocaust. And as discussed in the same chapter, though Harry and his staff had an important role in planning and implementing the provision of currencies for U.S. troops occupying liberated territories during the war, they had little substantive role in the decision to provide printing plates to the Soviet Union. The notion that each of these actions was instead driven by sympathies to Communism or the Soviet Union was always based purely on speculation.

As chapter 8 discussed, the U.S. insistence on a tight leash on financial assistance to China during the war is explained entirely by concerns about corruption and incompetence within the government of Chiang Kai-shek. Nonetheless, after the establishment of the People's Republic of China in 1949, U.S. conservatives took up "Who lost China?" as a rallying cry for attacking Harry and others who had implemented that policy.

The Senate Intelligence Committee held hearings on the subject in 1953. The attack focused mostly but not entirely on actions of the State Department during the Truman administration, when the Communists won the civil war and drove the Nationalists off to Taiwan. The committee chair, Senator Pat McCarran, publicly charged that Harry had been responsible for withholding disbursements and thus undercutting Chiang's ability to hold on to power. Three years later, in July 1956, Senator John M. Butler of Maryland—a protégé of McCarthy—held a "one-man hearing" to solicit testimony from a former Treasury official, Arthur N. Young, claiming that Harry's reluctance to provide gold shipments to China and then promoting a loan to the Soviet Union demonstrated "a strong anti-Chinese and pro-Russian bias."[16]

A good indication of Harry's real view on this subject is suggested by a note that he sent to Morgenthau's successor as Treasury secretary, Fred M. Vinson, in August 1945. The note—sent on the very day that Japan surrendered but presumably written before that event—covered a copy of a newly published book by Edgar Snow, *The Pattern of Soviet Power*. "The chapter I should like to call your especial attention to," Harry wrote, "is Chapter 8, pages 121–142."[17] That chapter, titled "The Two Chinas," sets out Snow's conclusions on how the United States should react to the struggle between Chiang's government and the Communists. It starts from the premise that U.S. policy throughout the war was to get China to focus on fighting the Japanese, preferably through joint action by the Nationalists and the Communists, and to avoid getting bogged down in a civil war. Chiang, however, had become obsessed with keeping the Communists out of the way and destroying their forces if possible.

Snow concluded with a prediction that as the war wound down and China was liberated from Japanese control, the unification of Chinese forces would become even more important. Russia's interest was in having a secure eastern border, preferably with a Communist government in place. In Snow's view, Russian and U.S. interests coincided. His book did not explicitly advocate a Communist takeover, but he did not bemoan that prospect, either, as long as the focus of Chinese military efforts remained directed at Japan. Referring to the top U.S. military leaders and diplomats in China, he observed, "Obviously General [Joseph W.] Stillwell is no

Communist, nor is General [Patrick J.] Hurley, and neither is taking orders from the Kremlin; yet it is now well known that both of them, as well as other spokesmen of American policy, urged in Chungking precisely the same political reconciliation, as advocated by the Soviet press."[18]

All the available evidence indicates that the pace of U.S. financial assistance to China was not determined by a supposed sympathy toward Mao.[19] Throughout the twelve-plus years of Roosevelt's presidency and Morgenthau's tenure as Treasury secretary, the U.S. government tried to balance China's demands for aid against the need for prudence in providing it. Harry had a major influence on the tactics of providing that aid, but he had relatively little to do with the major decisions on strategy. The top-level political judgments were that China was an essential bulwark against Japanese aggression in the Pacific and that Chiang was the essential but highly unreliable conduit for shoring up that bulwark. Decisions on the provision of aid flowed directly and inexorably from those judgments.

Guilt by Association

McCarthy and his supporters and sympathizers created nodes of association among the people they attacked. Because Harry was suspect, his friends and colleagues were also suspect. Because some of those associates were also suspect for other reasons, the suspicion against Harry was intensified. That in turn tightened the screws on everyone in the nexus. Four cases may help illustrate the complex of relationships between Harry and associates who were not members of the Communist Party but who came under suspicion for a variety of reasons. None was ever found guilty of any crime, but McCarthy's attacks upended their lives.

In one especially tragic example, we saw in chapter 14 how William H. (Bill) Taylor was caught in this spider web because he had worked for Harry on designing and implementing the currency for Allied troops to use in occupied Germany in the late stages of World War II. Taylor, a naturalized U.S. citizen born in Canada, met Harry when he visited the Treasury on a research project in 1940. With Harry's encouragement, he moved to Washington and worked for the Treasury throughout the war. He had no substantive role in the controversial decision to provide duplicate printing plates to the Soviet Union in 1944, but he did attend meetings and write minutes summarizing the deliberations.

Taylor joined the IMF staff in 1946 and built a successful career. By 1953 he was assistant director of the Fund's Middle Eastern Department.

Then, in December 1953, McCarthy initiated an investigation into the handling of the currency plates, on the basis of the proposition that it benefited the Soviet Union at the expense of the United States. Announcing the probe, McCarthy called Taylor a "protégé" of Harry and noted that Taylor knew several other people, including Gregory Silvermaster, who were under suspicion. McCarthy cited those relationships as an excuse for questioning him.[20]

The Republican members of McCarthy's Subcommittee on Investigations (Democratic members refused to participate) held hearings, first in executive session and then in public. Taylor testified in a closed-door hearing but was not called on for the public hearing. Under intense, hostile questioning, mostly from Senator Karl Mundt (Republican from South Dakota) and General Counsel Roy M. Cohn, Taylor patiently explained what really happened. He also firmly denied ever having been a Communist or knowing—or even suspecting—that any of his friends or Treasury colleagues was a Communist or had engaged in activities supportive of Communism. The worst that anyone else testifying at the hearing had to say about Taylor was that they recalled him making favorable remarks during the war about the successes of the Red Army.[21]

Taylor's rebuff of McCarthy's attack did not end the saga. Following the hearings, the International Organizations Employees Loyalty Board launched an investigation. The loyalty board operated under the auspices of the Civil Service Commission. It was set up in January 1953 by an executive order signed by President Truman in the wake of the Frank Coe debacle described below. Its purpose was to investigate the loyalty to the United States of U.S. citizens working at the United Nations and other international organizations. Its rulings were advisory and were not binding on the organizations, but they had a chilling effect.

As the investigation dragged on, Taylor demanded the right to a public hearing, and he asked for the right to cross-examine Bentley. He eventually got the public hearing but not the cross-examination. In July 1955 the board issued a ruling that it was "convinced that [Taylor] has engaged in espionage and subversive activity against the United States . . . and that he was and possibly still is an adherent to the Communist ideology." Taylor appealed, and the board agreed to hear additional evidence. After further hearings, the board reversed its decision, vacated its original statement, and concluded that "on all the evidence there is not a reasonable doubt as to your loyalty to the Government of the United States."[22]

The official clearance seemed to be a happy ending, and Taylor was able to keep his job at the IMF. IMF management, however, remained nervous about his status and the possibility of repercussions from the U.S. authorities. His superiors ceased giving him any meaningful work to do. His effective duties were reduced to writing minutes of Executive Board meetings. Many of his colleagues shunned him as a pariah, and he grew increasingly isolated and bored. In 1965, outside the IMF building where he had worked for nearly two decades, Bill Taylor collapsed and died from a heart attack.

Virginius Frank Coe has made several appearances in the preceding chapters as one of Harry's most senior staff at the Treasury and later as secretary of the IMF. His story is worth recounting in some detail because it is complicated and because it has not been told fully until now.

Born in 1907 in Richmond, Virginia (hence his first given name, which he eventually stopped using), he studied economics under Jacob Viner at the University of Chicago in the late 1920s and early 1930s. There he helped Viner in the preparation of his book *Studies in International Trade*. Before joining the Treasury staff along with Harry as a member of Viner's Brain Trust in 1934, he worked as a scholar at Johns Hopkins Institute of Law, the University of Chicago, and the Brookings Institution. He bounced around several jobs in Washington and Toronto in the later 1930s and then returned to the Treasury to work in Harry's division in 1939. The following year, Harry promoted him to be his deputy, replacing Harold Glasser.

A few months after the United States entered World War II, Frank moved first to the Board of Economic Warfare and then to the Foreign Economic Administration (FEA), where he became assistant administrator. In 1945 he returned to the Treasury to replace Harry as division chief following Harry's promotion to assistant secretary. In June 1946 he obtained his last official post: the potentially powerful position of secretary of the IMF (effectively, at that time, the chief operating officer).*

Chambers mentioned Coe in a list of his contacts that he gave to Assistant Secretary of State Adolf Berle in 1939, but Berle did not take such a vague allegation seriously. The more serious charge conveyed to the FBI

---

* In the modern IMF, one of the deputy managing directors serves as the chief operating officer, in charge of administering the institution. The secretary is the liaison between management and the Executive Board and the head of the department that organizes and conducts meetings of the Executive Board, the governors, and other senior groups. The original organization chart was far more compact.

was from Bentley in November 1945, when she named Coe as someone whom she believed to be a member of the Silvermaster group. (Later, testifying before a grand jury in February 1949, Bentley admitted that she had never met Coe.)[23] The FBI placed Coe under surveillance and interviewed him in 1947. He testified before HUAC on the same day as Harry (August 13, 1948) and denied being a member of the Communist Party or participating in espionage.

Although Coe was an official of the IMF and was expected to travel internationally as a normal part of his job, the U.S. government revoked his passport in 1951 "for security reasons." On October 27, 1952, Senator McCarthy gave a speech with a slur on Coe aimed at linking him to Adlai Stevenson, the Democratic candidate for president, and thereby damaging Stevenson's chances in the November elections.[24]

McCarthy's speech set in motion a disastrous sequence of events. In December 1952 Frank was called to testify before a grand jury that was investigating "subversive activities and espionage by U.S. citizens employed by the United Nations." (The IMF is a specialized agency in the UN system.) By this time, government officials investigating Communist influence had developed the practice of questioning witnesses about whether they knew other people who might be Communists or sympathizers. To avoid being drawn into such a line of inquiry, one had to rely on the right not "to be compelled . . . to be a witness against himself," in the language of the Fifth Amendment to the U.S. Constitution. On this occasion, Frank refused to answer questions about his own or anyone else's political activities, even though in 1948 he had explicitly denied under oath that he was a member of the Communist Party. On December 1, testifying before the Senate Subcommittee on Internal Security led by Senator Pat McCarran (Democrat from Nevada), he again invoked his constitutional rights and refused to answer questions. The next day, under strong pressure from the U.S. government, the IMF managing director, Ivar Rooth, called Frank into his office and demanded his resignation.

The loss of his position at the IMF was not the end of the persecution. As Frank—just forty-five years old—set out to try to find another job, he soon discovered that FBI agents were still following him. When he left job interviews, an agent would show up at the potential employer's office and tell him that Coe was a risk to national security and should not be hired. With employment in the United States effectively closed off, Frank was forced to look overseas. Although he still had no passport, he left the country in April 1953 on a job search that took him to Canada, Cuba, the

Bahamas, and Mexico. It seems that the authorities in each of these countries were more sympathetic to his plight than was his own government, and he had no difficulty crossing any borders. He returned by train to Laredo, Texas, again without difficulty but still without a job.[25]

While Frank was abroad, the infamous Roy Cohn—a Senate staff lawyer who served as an attack dog for McCarran and McCarthy, among others, and who was eventually disbarred for unethical conduct—publicly accused him of blocking a devaluation of the Austrian schilling in 1949 to further the interests of the Soviet Union. The charge was absurd and was quickly disproved by the IMF. Cohn also called Coe a fugitive from American justice, which was similarly absurd because no one had even asked Coe to testify at that time, much less subpoenaed him. To clear his name, Frank returned from Mexico City as soon as he read in a newspaper that Cohn had attacked him. He testified in executive session on June 3, 1953, and in public on June 5 before a Senate subcommittee. The hearings were chaired by Mundt on June 3 and by McCarthy on June 5. He answered questions about the Austrian devaluation and other matters, but he again refused to answer about anyone's participation in the Communist Party.

The Senate hearings were a fishing expedition aimed at public shaming. The investigators had no idea of what Frank might have done to jeopardize national security, beyond the vague accusations made years earlier by Chambers and Bentley and Cohn's patently false charges. Even so, much later the FBI was able to draw a tentative link using information from Soviet cables partially decoded through the Venona project (discussed in chapter 20).

The Venona project produced a translation of a Soviet cable from New York to Moscow dated August 31, 1944, that included the sentence "ROBERT hopes to influence PAGE through PEAK." In annotations dated May 27, 1968, the FBI analyst noted that "Robert" was Silvermaster; "Page" was "possibly" Lauchlin Currie; and "Peak" was "possibly" Frank Coe. More seriously, a cable dated December 29, 1944, included the sentence fragment "we are sending five films of PEAK's materials on the progress of the talks between the COUNTRY and the ISLAND about DECREE in the second phase of the war." In annotations with the same date as those for the earlier cable, the analyst interpreted the subject as "talks between the United States and Great Britain about Lend-Lease." Again, "Peak" was identified as "possibly" Frank Coe.[26]

The information in the December 29 cable was innocuous because the Phase II Lend-Lease agreement with Britain had been made public a month earlier. Also, the cable did not indicate whether the Soviets received those materials directly from Peak or through an intermediary such as Robert.

Coe, as assistant administrator of the Foreign Economic Administration, represented the FEA in the interagency meetings (led by Morgenthau) on Phase II.[27] Why did the FBI pick him as "possibly" being Peak, rather than any of the other agency representatives who had access to the same information? It seems likely that it was simply because he was the only one who had been named by Bentley, other than White and Currie, both of whom had different code names in the Venona traffic. A clearer identification appears in the Soviet files known as the Vassiliev Notebooks (see chapter 20), which became available only in the 1990s, long after the events chronicled here. There a 1949 Soviet cable details the "failures" of Soviet intelligence resulting from depending heavily on unreliable Americans such as Chambers and Bentley. Among Bentley's contacts, the writer lists "Peak" and identifies him as Frank Coe.[28]

If the Vassiliev Notebooks are accurate, it thus appears likely that Coe was at least an indirect source for materials being transmitted to the Russians through Bentley, even if those materials were few in number and relatively anodyne by the time they were conveyed. Since Bentley was the conduit for those materials and she admitted that she had never met Coe, it is evident that Coe did not transmit documents directly to her or to the Soviets. Perhaps he gave documents to someone else to give to her. If so, perhaps he knew that the material was intended for the Soviets; perhaps not. As is most likely in Harry's case, perhaps someone else in Coe's office took documents and passed them on. The full story is elusive.

Whatever the truth might be regarding Coe, he paid a heavy price. He moved to New York, where he hoped to escape persecution and find a proper job. For the next five years, though, the FBI continued to prevent him from getting any employment other than menial jobs. His relationships with his two children became strained, and his marriage ended in divorce. Eventually, he found a new relationship, remarried, had a third child, and set out again to try to resume his broken career. In 1958 he heard from a Chinese friend named Chi Chao-ting, whom Frank had known since they were students together at the University of Chicago. Chi had become a senior economics official in the Chinese government, and he invited Frank to come to Beijing.

In June 1958 the Supreme Court overturned the U.S. government's right to deny passports for political reasons.[29] That enabled Frank to travel freely and more widely again. After one last effort to find a new life in the West, which took him to London and to Bromma, Sweden, Frank left for

China with his wife Ruth and baby daughter, Katy, in August. Once in Beijing, he never left.

In China, Coe worked for the government, mostly at home, writing reports and speeches in English. He met Mao Zedong on several occasions, as did other Western expats and visitors, who were generally treated as honored guests. Still, Frank apparently found the work incredibly boring, and he began drinking heavily. On a happier note, the couple had a second daughter, Ling Ling (Frank's fourth child), and the family settled into an expat life. In 1961 his friend and former Treasury colleague Solomon ("Sol") Adler joined him in Beijing. For a time, they lived next door to each other, in a complex of small houses on the grounds of the Peace Hotel. Like the Coes, the Adlers (Sol and his wife, Pat) would spend the rest of their lives in China. Frank also became friends with Sidney Rittenberg, an American expat who had been stationed in China with the U.S. Army during World War II and who had decided to stay. The American journalist Anna Louise Strong also lived in Beijing from 1958 and became part of this social group. Frank served as the executor of her estate when she died in 1970.[30]

Aside from the boredom, the downside of living in China was a sense of isolation, especially after the Cultural Revolution began in 1966. Frank never learned the language, although his wife and children did. At first, relief from isolation came through interactions with their expat friends and senior Chinese officials, including Mao Zedong. When U.S. President Richard Nixon made his historic trip to Beijing in February 1972, Frank was invited to attend a reception, but he refused to go to meet a man who had played such a prominent role in the persecution of suspected Communists in the McCarthy era. That visit, however, enabled a steadier flow of Western visitors in its aftermath, several of whom made a point of meeting with Frank and Ruth. Prominent Westerners who visited over the next several years included the Marxist scholar Paul Sweezy, formerly of Harvard University; the English economist and long-standing friend of China, Joan Robinson; the Harvard historian and China scholar John King Fairbank; John Kenneth Galbraith, another Harvard economist; and the playwright Arthur Miller and his wife, the photographer Inge Morath.[31]

In August 1979 Fairbank, while on a trip to China with Vice President Walter Mondale, made his second visit to see Frank and found him to be "living in fine style." A few months later, however, Frank—a heavy smoker as well as a drinker—wrote to Fairbank to say that he had been diagnosed with lung cancer. Six months later, in June 1980, Frank died in Beijing of a pulmonary embolism.

Harry's great friend from their days as graduate students and then instructors at Harvard, Lauchlin "Lauch" Currie was attacked in ways strikingly similar to those against Harry. A Canadian by birth, he was naturalized as a U.S. citizen in 1934 and spent the next eleven years in the service of the federal government. As the chief economist in the White House during World War II, he interacted regularly with Soviet officials. That made him an attractive target for Soviet efforts to try to glean information about U.S. policies and intentions. Like Harry, he also was friends with both George Silverman and Greg Silvermaster. Silverman probably mentioned Currie to Chambers, who described him to Adolf Berle as a "fellow traveler" in 1939. Bentley added a secondhand report in 1945. When HUAC made those allegations public in 1948, Lauch—like Harry—responded by testifying fully in his own defense in a public hearing. The release of the Venona cables in the mid-1990s confirmed that the Soviets had sought to profit from Currie's openness to them.[32]

The exposure from the HUAC hearings made it difficult for Currie to work in the United States at jobs commensurate with his education and experience. In 1949 he began working in Colombia on a project for the World Bank. That led to additional assignments for the Colombian government, and before long he married a Colombian and settled there. He testified voluntarily again, before a Senate committee, in 1952. The U.S. government's harassment of him culminated in 1954, when the State Department revoked his passport. Currie eventually became a citizen of Colombia, where he lived and worked for the rest of his life. He died in Bogotá in 1993.

Harry first met Solomon ("Sol") Adler in 1936, when Adler was seeking employment at the U.S. Treasury. Adler was born in the northern English city of Leeds in 1909 and studied economics at New College in Oxford University and then at the London School of Economics. After teaching at LSE for a couple of years, he moved to the United States in 1935. He applied for U.S. citizenship the following year and completed the process in 1940.

George Haas hired Adler to work in the Division of Monetary Research. When Harry got his own division in 1938, Adler transferred there and worked for Harry until 1945, when Coe took over the division. During roughly the second half of that period, Adler was stationed mostly in Chungking as the Treasury's wartime representative in China.

Chambers mentioned Adler to Adolf Berle at their meeting in September 1939, and Bentley named him in 1945 as a member of the Silvermaster group. In the Vassiliev Notebooks, the 1949 "failures" report mentioned above in the discussion of Frank Coe also listed Adler with the code name "Sachs" as one of the people from whom Bentley was supposed to be getting information. In the Venona decryptions, a January 1945 cable to Moscow alleged that Sachs wanted his material to be given to Earl Browder (head of the Communist Party of the United States) as well as to Moscow. The FBI did not determine who Sachs might be.[33] If the two people are the same, then this cable would serve to corroborate Bentley's allegation. That is, however, rather speculative evidence, because the Soviet code names were not uniquely assigned, and they frequently changed.

The case against Adler is also complicated by the way Bentley tried to inflate her claims about him. She first told the FBI that all she had seen had been "harmless" letters sent by Adler from China, but she later asserted that she knew Adler to be a member of the Communist Party because her group collected party dues from him. As Bruce Craig has pointed out, Adler was not even in the United States during the period when she claimed that he was making those payments, and there is no evidence that he sent any such payments from China.[34] In 1949 Bentley admitted under oath to a grand jury that she never met Adler until a Loyalty Board hearing long after the war.

In the McCarthy era, congressional investigators examined the regular reports that Adler sent to Washington from Chungking during the war and concluded that they seemed sympathetic to the Communist forces and hostile to Chiang's Nationalist government. A more objective description would be that Adler was reinforcing the prevailing view in the Roosevelt administration that China's ability to fight Japan was being undercut by infighting between the Communists and the Nationalists, and he was advising on ways to try to get them to work more effectively together. His analyses were not substantively different from those of many other observers of the wartime situation in China.

Although Adler denied being a member of the Communist Party and the evidence against him was quite shaky, an extensive governmental investigation of his loyalty to the United States led eventually to the revocation of his citizenship. In the meantime, he resigned from the Treasury and returned to England and occupied himself by writing a book on the Chinese economy, published in 1957. In 1961 he moved to Beijing, where he joined Frank Coe as an adviser to the government. Unlike Coe, he continued to travel outside the country for professional events in the United States and Britain, but he lived in China for the rest of his life. He died there in 1994.

Effects at the IMF

Aside from these personal consequences, the McCarthy persecutions had long-lasting institutional effects. Beginning in January 1953, U.S. citizens working at the IMF and other international organizations were routinely subjected to loyalty investigations as a condition of employment. Truman's executive order directed the U.S. State Department to investigate each such employee or applicant for employment and report any "derogatory" information indicating that the individual might be likely to engage in "espionage or subversive activities against the United States." The IMF managing director, Ivar Rooth, protested this procedure to the U.S. secretary of state, but to no avail. He was informed that the U.S. government expected the Fund not to employ anyone "demonstrated to be, or likely to be engaged in subversive activities against the United States." If the IMF did not cooperate, "continued support to [the IMF] by the United States cannot be assured." The FBI then proceeded to fingerprint, question, and investigate U.S. citizens working for the IMF. At least three staff members were subjected to a particularly intensive investigation, but all were eventually cleared.[35]

Of more direct interest to this story, the IMF had to grapple with how to honor the memory of its principal founding father. In 1947, while Harry White was still alive, the Fund commissioned the German sculptor Benno Elkan—who had recently made a bronze bust of the late John Maynard Keynes for King's College, Cambridge University—to create a similar bust of Keynes for the IMF. In February 1950 the Fund commissioned a famous American sculptor, Malvina Hoffman (who had studied under Auguste Rodin in Paris), to do a bronze bust of Harry as a companion piece (fig. 18). Both busts were placed initially in the IMF–World Bank joint library but were soon moved to the office of the managing director to avoid giving Harry's image such prominence. At one point in the next few years, some senior officials at the Fund suggested putting the bust of White into storage. The highly influential executive director from Egypt, Ahmed Zaki Saad, insisted that the busts of both founders be treated equally. He was unable to block the transfer to a basement storage room, but the result was that the busts of both Keynes and White were put away, where they remained for some thirty years.

The bust of Keynes was taken out of storage in the 1980s and moved back to the managing director's office. In 1987 it was placed in the office of the director of research, Jacob Frenkel. When Stanley Fischer joined the IMF as first deputy managing director in 1994, he had Keynes placed

Fig. 18. *Busts of Harry White, by Malvina Hoffman, and of John Maynard Keynes, by Benno Elkan. International Monetary Fund, IMF Photo/Stephen Jaffe*

in his own office and later had White rescued from the basement and placed on a pedestal in his conference room. Shortly before Fischer left the Fund in 2001, while he was acting managing director, he directed that both busts be placed prominently in the meeting room of the Executive Board, where they remain as of this writing.[36]

November 1953: The Eisenhower Administration Uses Harry to Attack Truman

Harry's relative obscurity to the public ended, briefly but spectacularly, in November 1953. In a speech on November 6 to some 1,200 people at a meeting of the Executive Club of Chicago, President Eisenhower's attorney general, Herbert Brownell, directly levied a charge of espionage: "Harry Dexter White was a Russian spy. He smuggled secret documents to Russian agents for transmission to Moscow. [He] was known to be a Communist spy by the very people who appointed him to the most sensitive and important position he ever held in government service."[37]

What made the charge even more sensational was that Brownell went on falsely to accuse former President Truman of appointing White as executive director at the IMF while "knowing" that Harry was a spy. "White's spying activities were reported by the FBI to the White House by means of a report delivered to President Truman through his military aide, Brig. Gen. Harry H. Vaughan, in December of 1945. In the face of this information, and incredible though it may seem, President Truman subsequently on Jan. 23, 1946, nominated White, who was then Assistant Secretary of the Treasury, to the even more important position of executive director for the United States in the International Monetary Fund."

Brownell concluded by echoing the alarmist language used by McCarthy for the preceding four years about the threat of Communists in government: "When no attention was paid to so great a danger as the espionage activities of Harry Dexter White you can imagine how little notice was given to Communist party members, Communist propagandists and Communist fellow-travelers in Government. That is the reason why the problem of weeding out from the ranks of Government employees persons who are dangerous is so great a problem today."

Even in 1953, news could be disseminated quickly and effectively. In addition to daily newspapers, radio and television broadcasts, and the newsreels that preceded movies in theaters, weekly magazines were still a major part of American life. Before the month was over, Harry was on the cover of *Time* and was the subject of a lengthy, unflattering profile in *Life*. Chambers wrote an article for *Look*. Also, Harry's hometown newspaper, the *Boston Globe*, ran a twelve-part series on Harry's life. These stories all contained many inaccuracies, and the tone was indicative of the snark that the anti-Communist paranoia of the early 1950s so easily fostered. *Life* simply made up a personality and a biography for Harry: "White was . . . not exactly an unwitting dupe, but a man whose basic inferiority complex and lust for recognition made him as eager to serve the Communists as his own government." Similarly, *Time* described him as a "stocky little man with a cropped brush mustache that twitched when he was nervous. . . . He lunged around the corridors with a jerky gait . . . a ruthless martinet . . . intolerant . . . worked and schemed constantly, slept and played little." Chambers called him a "fidgety, often irritable, rather unimpressive, but ambitious little man."[38]

Throughout his adult life, one of Harry's favorite leisure activities was going to the movies. Several of his letters to family members mention movies as a way of relaxing in the evening. On occasion, he would lament that he had been so busy in a particular week that he had found time for "only two" movies. Once, on vacation, he and Anne went for a walk around Buffalo, New York, until Harry "was smitten with a desire to see a newsreel." Around 1940, he compiled a lengthy list of "outstanding movies," either for his own edification or (more likely) as recommendations for his daughters.[39] He later appended several more films issued during the war years. The list reveals a wide range of tastes, from musicals such as *One Hundred Men and a Girl* to historical dramas such as *Battleship Potemkin*. Hollywood fare made up the bulk of this list, but it also included several French films and a handful from Russia, Germany, and other European and Asian countries.

A bizarre facet of the posthumous attack on Harry was that even his love of movies became a source of suspicion about him. The 1953 profile in *Life* magazine speculated that instead of going to the movies, he was using the story to cover up nefarious activities. The article quoted Harry as telling a reporter in 1944: "I love the movies, any kind of movies at all. I go at least twice a week, even if I have to go by myself." The *Life* writers then drew a totally unsupported conclusion with the clear intention of conning readers into believing the worst: "A man who is known as a solitary moviegoer, a man said to sit alone through a couple of double bills a week, can gain himself a half dozen hours or so to pursue any secret inclinations he might have."[40] Or not.

Having been an obscure economist throughout his adult life, Harry was suddenly—more than five years after his death—one of the most famous and notorious men in America. As we saw in chapter 15, what really happened in 1946 was that on January 26 Truman nominated Harry to be the inaugural U.S. executive director at the IMF. On February 6 the Senate confirmed Harry's appointment, the same day that Truman received an FBI report that an unnamed source had alleged that Harry was involved with an espionage operation in Washington. After meeting the next day with his top two cabinet secretaries (Treasury Secretary Fred M. Vinson and Secretary of State James F. Byrnes), Truman decided to take no action. His reasons for that decision are opaque, but the most reasonable explanation is that he attached little credence to the report—at least, not enough credence to withdraw an already confirmed appointment.[41] Since the report was based on hearsay evidence that an earlier FBI report had already discounted as unverified, and since the FBI and then Truman's staff took five days to convey the report to him, it seems that skepticism was both logically derived and widely shared. For Brownell to turn this episode into an unalloyed attack on Truman for being soft on Communism was irresponsible.

Truman's response to this attack was muddled; he reacted quickly without verifying the archival record of events. He first denied ever receiving a report on White, and then he told a reporter (falsely) that he had fired Harry as soon as he had learned what was going on. HUAC then tried to subpoena the former president to testify. Truman refused to acknowledge the subpoena, and a constitutional crisis was averted only because the congressional committee withdrew it. Eisenhower, who had approved Brownell's speech in advance, tried to distance himself from it when the speech came under heavy criticism. He also denied ever meeting Harry, even though White and Morgenthau met with him at least twice: once in Algiers in October 1943 to discuss the finances of the Allied occupation of North Africa, and then over a working lunch in England in August 1944 to discuss the Morgenthau Plan for the demilitarization of Germany, during which White participated actively in the discussion. Everyone involved—two presidents, the House committee, the attorney general, and the ghost of Harry White—was tarnished. Much later, Brownell reportedly concluded that "the only thing he regretted in public life was delivering the Harry Dexter White speech."[42]

After this episode, a myth developed that Truman had intended to nominate White to be managing director of the IMF (the top job at the institution) but decided to keep him in a lower-profile job (the number-two position) once the espionage charges emerged. Truman himself encouraged that interpretation, probably because it helped minimize the fallout from Brownell's attack. Since Truman learned of the allegations only after publicly announcing Harry's nomination to the lower position, the story does not hold together. The only semifactual basis for it was that Keynes, who was the driving force behind efforts to persuade Truman to make Harry the managing director, kept up his advocacy even after Harry was confirmed as executive director. Keynes did not give up until the Board of Governors selected Belgium's wartime finance minister, Camille Gutt, as managing director in March 1946 (see chapter 16).

CHAPTER TWENTY

Second Afterlife

The Attack Resumes, 1955 to the Present

For my part, I, as probably the only living participant in Operation Snow, can testify: Harry Dexter White was never one of our agents.

—Vitaly Pavlov, retired NKVD agent, in *Operation Snow*, 1996

Senate Hearings in 1955

Brownell's 1953 attack on Truman and White rekindled interest in Harry for a brief time and led to further investigations by state officials in New Hampshire, the FBI, and the Senate Subcommittee on Internal Security (led initially by Pat McCarran of Nevada and later, after McCarran's death in September 1954, by James Eastland of Mississippi).*

Prompted by Brownell's speech, the newly elected attorney general of New Hampshire, Louis C. Wyman, sent two officials to Blueberry Hill in

---

* McCarran and Eastland were both Democratic senators. In 1953–54 the Republican Party controlled the Senate, and the subcommittee was chaired by William E. Jenner of Indiana. Under his chairmanship, the subcommittee published a report in July 1953, *Interlocking Subversion in Government Departments*, which summarized the investigations of numerous individuals, including Harry White, up to that time.

November 1953, where Anne still lived in the summer. They took away some suspicious-looking items, including several Russian songbooks, which Anne had collected since at least the 1930s. Wyman turned this material over to the FBI, which copied it to add to its file on Harry. Almost two years later, in July 1955, Senator Eastland wrote to Wyman to ask if he knew of any additional material that might be kept at the White home in New Hampshire. That induced Wyman to make a second raid on Blueberry Hill, in which his agents took away the bulk of Harry's personal papers. (The material taken in both raids was eventually returned to Anne and is now in an archive at Princeton University.)[1]

The denouement of this activity was a pair of subcommittee hearings that Eastland held in June and August 1955, primarily to introduce into the record excerpts from the Morgenthau Diaries, the two batches of documents taken from Blueberry Hill, and papers that Anne had donated to Princeton University beginning in 1950. The June hearing dealt exclusively with the Morgenthau Diaries, which contained no information relevant to possible espionage but which included many excerpts detailing Harry's influential role in the U.S. Treasury. The subcommittee's general counsel, J. G. Sourwine, introduced each excerpt with a short statement aimed at making Harry seem like a dangerous infiltrator. To him, the transcript of one of Morgenthau's regular senior staff meetings revealed Harry to be a "wisecracker" and a "court jester" with an "anti-big-business attitude." When Harry conveyed to Morgenthau a report from the wartime Treasury representative in Lisbon, Portugal, Sourwine claimed that it proved that Harry had "a worldwide commercial espionage system reporting to him."[2]

At the hearing on August 30, 1955, Eastland was the only senator present. The principal witness was Wyman, who introduced excerpts from the Blueberry Hill and Princeton documents. The printed record of the hearing included, in addition to the transcript and the introduced documents, a sixty-page foreword explaining Eastland's understanding of the context. The foreword took pains to infer hidden meanings from items that in normal times would have been considered innocently personal. Anne's Russian songbooks, for example, were described as evidence of Harry's "ardent obsession with matters pertaining to the Soviet Union."[3]

Most of the foreword consisted of summaries of various associates of Harry whom Eastland considered to be engaged, along with White, in a "conspiracy of strategically placed individuals in government to subordinate the interests of the United States to the imperialistic designs of the Soviet Union."[4] In fact, however, none of the material presented to Eastland and entered into the record revealed any evidence of such a conspiracy other than confirmation that Harry had numerous and regular contacts with Soviet officials as part of his official duties and with friends and colleagues who had varying degrees of connection to progressive, left-wing, and socialist causes. These Eastland hearings did not result in any charges or even substantive revelations.

July 1995: The Venona Cables Are Declassified

After the mid-1950s, the McCarthy era ended, and interest in Harry generally subsided. The U.S. Senate censured Joseph McCarthy in December 1954 for, among other misdeeds, his irresponsible bullying tactics ("conduct . . . contrary to senatorial traditions"). Shortly afterward, the FBI closed its file on Harry, and the Senate committee moved on to other topics. This quiescent period ended in 1995, when the National Security Agency (NSA) began declassifying and releasing decrypted Soviet cables from the 1940s.

In 1939 the Signal Intelligence Service (SIS) of the U.S. Army began intercepting encrypted cables sent to Moscow by Soviet diplomatic offices in the United States. In 1943 the SIS initiated a program to try to decode and translate the cables. That program, which was later code-named Venona, continued until 1980 under the SIS and its successor, the NSA. The cables made copious use of code names, regardless of whether the person in question was a Soviet agent, a target for attempts to glean information, or even a prominent public figure. (Cables referred to President Roosevelt as "Kapitan.") Code names changed frequently, and in some cases the same code name referred to more than one individual. The output of the Venona project was a large set of "decrypts": Soviet cables decoded by SIS and NSA staff, usually with substantial gaps in what could be decoded, translated from Russian to English by other staff, and annotated by FBI agents who attempted to decipher the identities of code-named persons.

In 1995 the NSA agreed to declassify the translated decrypts—but not the Russian originals—and release them to the public. Over the next few years, some three thousand of these reconstructed fragments were published by the NSA. Fifteen cables, dating from April 1944 through May 1945, refer in some fashion to Harry White.[5]

Although the NSA website asserts that the Venona project exposed Harry White as a "major KGB espionage agent," the evidence is far more ambiguous. A close examination of the decrypts shows that the information being conveyed from Harry may well have been obtained in the normal course of diplomatic or social contacts. Unless one is willing to accept the uncorroborated accounts of Soviet officials and spies at face value, the documents are subject to a wide range of interpretation. The ambiguity is heightened when one considers that in most cases, decryption of the original text has been only partial. Large gaps exist in the most crucial cables. Moreover, in some cases the translation seems odd, but it cannot be checked against the original Russian, which remains classified.

Most of the cables with references to Harry mention him just in passing or convey secondhand information from other sources. For example, a cable dated January 18, 1945, summarizes a report from Greg Silvermaster, who believed that he could get Harry to appoint someone with the code name Rouble to take over as head of the Monetary Division at the Treasury when he (Harry) took up his new post as assistant secretary. An FBI analyst later suggested that Rouble was "probably" Harold Glasser. Silvermaster reportedly wanted to use this possibility as leverage to get Moscow to transfer Rouble into his spy network. While this report, if accurate, is rather damning evidence against Silvermaster, it offers no evidence against White, who did not promote Glasser as his successor. Instead, Frank Coe replaced Harry in 1945. In turn, when Coe left the Treasury a year later to join White at the IMF, Coe managed to get Glasser promoted as *his* successor. By a complicated logical chain, one could argue that Harry was being manipulated into helping the spies. One could argue more credibly, however, that Coe was the orchestrator of the succession, or that both appointments were made independently of any outside pressure and that Silvermaster was exaggerating his own influence to gain favor with Moscow.

The modern case against Harry rests largely on four sets of cables from the Venona project: one from April 1944, one from August 1944 (a lengthy report sent in three consecutive cables), one from November 1944, and one from May 1945 (again a single report sent in three cables).

Cable Sent in April 1944

On April 29, 1944, the New York office sent a cable to Moscow that included this fragment: "According to JURIST's data, HEN HARRIER in a conversation with CHANNEL PILOT touched upon the question of giving us a 5 billion loan. The idea appealed to CHANNEL PILOT and he

[C% discussed] it with . . .".[6] (C% indicates some uncertainty about the description.) Substituting in the analyst's guesses regarding code names, the fragment becomes "According to Harry White's data, Cordell Hull in a conversation with Henry Wallace touched upon the question of giving us a $5 billion loan. The idea appealed to Wallace and he discussed it with . . ."

Discussions of a possible loan of that magnitude to the Soviet Union had been under way within the U.S. administration and between Treasury and Soviet officials for several months. The State Department opposed the idea because of secret reports that the Soviets were establishing brutal police states in areas that they were liberating from German control. Morgenthau and others in the Treasury did not learn of those reports until 1945.[7]

What the cable seems to suggest is that Soviet intelligence had somehow obtained a report from Harry about a discussion of the proposed loan between the secretary of state and the vice president. Whether Harry might have learned about the conversation first- or secondhand, whether the curious phrase "White's data" refers to a memorandum or an oral report, and whether the information was conveyed to the Soviets directly from Harry or through an intermediary cannot be determined.[8] Since Harry was meeting regularly at that time with the Soviet delegation to the Bretton Woods conference, the most likely explanation is that he mentioned it to one or more of them, and they passed on the information to their superiors. Although the cable has been interpreted by some as evidence of espionage, a discussion of that nature would not have been problematic or even unusual under the circumstances.

Cables Sent in August 1944

In January 1944 a delegation of Soviet officials arrived in Washington to hold an extended series of meetings at the U.S. Treasury to prepare for their participation in the Bretton Woods conference. Harry led the talks for the Treasury and met with the delegation at least fourteen times through May. By the time the delegations all convened in New Hampshire in July, Harry knew the Soviets well enough to view them not only as helpful colleagues but also as people with whom he could play softball or volleyball and socialize from time to time.

The number-two official in the Soviet delegation was Nicolai V. Chechulin, the deputy head of the Soviet central bank. In the Venona traffic, he has been identified as the Soviet official with the code name "Kol'tsov." Chechulin apparently developed a particularly good relationship with Harry, and the Soviet intelligence agency (the NKVD) sent him to see Harry in Washington shortly after the end of the Bretton Woods conference. Chechulin reported back that they met on July 31 and discussed plans for Lend-Lease and other financial aid to the Soviet Union; postwar planning for Germany, Poland, Finland, and the Baltic countries; tactics for regenerating international trade after the war; Harry's plan to accompany Morgenthau to Europe in a few days; and Harry's opinion that Roosevelt would win a fourth term in November. They planned to meet again in mid-August, after Harry returned from Europe.[9]

The fact that Harry met with Chechulin for a frank discussion, possibly outside his office, should not raise any eyebrows. That would have been perfectly normal between senior Allied officials. (Where they met is unclear. The translated decrypt states that they met at Harry's "apartment." The Whites were living in their house in Bethesda at that time and did not have an apartment until 1946.) If Harry speculated about what the U.S. postwar policy toward Finland or the Baltics might be or discussed other aspects of postwar planning, one could have a spirited argument about how appropriate such a discussion would have been at the time. To call it espionage, however, would be rather bizarre.[10]

The more disturbing part of Chechulin's report comes at the end, where he claims that he and Harry talked about "the technique of further work with us." The cryptographers worked hard to decipher this final paragraph and eventually issued an amended text, which they rendered as follows:

> As regards the technique of further work with us JURIST said that his wife was [B% ready] for any self-sacrifice[;] he himself did not think about his personal security, but a compromise [PROVAL] would lead to a political scandal and [B% the discredit] of all supporters of the new course[c], therefore he would have to be very cautious. He asked whether he should [5 groups unrecovered] his work with us. I [C% replied] that he should refrain. JURIST has no suitable apartment for a permanent meeting place[;] all his friends are family people. Meetings could be held at their houses in such a way that one meeting devolved on each every 4–5 months. He proposes infrequent conversations lasting up to half an hour while driving in his automobile.[11]

"Jurist" was a code name for Harry White. The notations B% and C% indicate degrees of uncertainty about the decryption; C suggests more doubt than B. The phrase "5 groups unrecovered" indicates that a block of text (probably about five words long) could not be decoded. The Russian word провал (*proval*) would reasonably be translated as "failure" in this context. The choice of "compromise" probably refers to the possibility of discovery. In any case, the meaning of the paragraph is plain enough. Chechulin is characterizing Harry as an active supplier of information who knows that what he tells Chechulin is being conveyed secretly to Moscow. Moreover, Harry is said to be willing to take great risks to continue to meet with him regularly.

If taken at face value, this report looks damning. But should we take it at face value? One problem is that no evidence has turned up in subsequent Venona cables or elsewhere that such follow-up meetings ever took place. Another is the contradiction between this conversation possibly taking place at White's home and the claim that the location was not "suitable" for further meetings. After all, Harry never made any secret of his readiness to meet with Chechulin and other members of the Soviet delegation either at work or socially. Nor would there have been any reason for him to do so. Harry might well have offered to meet him again, and even to pick him up and drive him to work occasionally. (The Soviet embassy was on 16th Street, NW, just a short walk from the Treasury.) The notion that they would meet "while driving in his automobile," however, is most unlikely. Harry reportedly complied scrupulously with the gas rationing that was then in effect, and he normally carpooled to work instead of commuting alone in his 1940 Chrysler.[12]

Chechulin had been ordered to meet with Harry to try to learn as much as he could and set up further meetings if possible. That he would try to put the best face on the outcome is more than a mere possibility. As the historian Amy Knight has reminded readers, when assessing reports from Soviet agents, one should "read between the lines, and always consider the source."[13]

Cable Sent in November 1944

Later in 1944, an NKVD operative in New York (identified by the FBI as Pavel Ivanovich Fedosimov, the same man who forwarded the report from Chechulin in August) forwarded a report to Pavel M. Fitin at headquarters in Moscow. The report was from an agent in Washington, tentatively identified as Iskhak Abdulovich Akhmerov.[14]

The cable uses code names for all the people mentioned in it and even for the place name Washington ("Karfagen," Russian for Carthage). The FBI analyst identified "Richard" as Harry White; "Robert" as Silvermaster; "Pilot" as Ludwig Ullmann; "Victor" (the addressee) as "possibly Lieut.-General Pavel M. Fitin"; and "Maj" as Fedosimov. Anne Terry White is not mentioned by name; the reference is only to "Richard's wife." The code name "Albert" is not identified in this cable, but other cables link that code name to Akhmerov. For example, a cable dated October 1, 1944, initially listed Albert as unidentified, but the analyst later changed the identification to Akhmerov.

If one accepts the identification of code names, the cable reported a conversation between Akhmerov and Greg Silvermaster. According to Fedosimov, Silvermaster had told Akhmerov about a discussion he had with Harry White's wife, "who knows about her husband's participation with us."

Although there are two large gaps in what the NSA was able to decode, the cable seems to indicate that Harry's wife told Silvermaster that she was worried about their financial situation because they would soon have expenses of "up to two thousand a year" for their daughter's education. This news apparently prompted Silvermaster to worry that Harry might take a more lucrative job outside Washington, which would deprive him (Silvermaster) of access to a valuable source of information. Silvermaster then informed Akhmerov that he had told Harry's wife that "we"—apparently meaning the Soviets—"would willingly have helped them" stay in Washington.

The NKVD response to this report from Silvermaster was conflicted. Akhmerov is said to have told Silvermaster that the NKVD would "agree to provide for Richard's daughter's education" and to have "definitely advised Robert [Silvermaster], Pilot [Ullmann] and PA . . . against attempting to offer Richard [White] assistance." Fedosimov then concluded his report by writing that while he shared Akhmerov's "opinion about the necessity of assistance," he wanted to draw Moscow's "attention to the fact that Richard has taken the offer of assistance favourably."

Although the cable (as decoded and translated) referred only to a single daughter, Harry and Anne had two daughters. Ruth was eighteen at the time and studying at Barnard College of Columbia University. (Ruth eventually also got a law degree from Columbia.) Joan, fifteen, was in high school. Three years later, she too studied at Barnard. It would not be surprising if Anne had told Greg (a family friend) that she was worried about expenses. It would also have been consistent with other reports about

Silvermaster that he would have panicked at the thought that Harry might leave town and deprive him of regular access to the friend who was viewed by the Soviets as his main asset. The rest of what he told Akhmerov, about Harry's willingness to accept financial assistance and about Anne's knowledge of Harry's "participation," may well have been an effort on his part to persuade his Soviet contacts to help him keep Harry in town.

The Venona decrypts include no record of a response from Moscow to Fedosimov's request for money to give to the Whites. Documents uncovered much later (discussed below) revealed that the suggestion to give money to Harry originated with Greg Silvermaster, that Soviet operatives then gave $2,000 to Silvermaster for this purpose, and that Silvermaster apparently got cold feet and never tried to give it to Harry or Anne.[15] No evidence has surfaced that the Whites ever asked for or received any outside money—either directly or through Silvermaster—to help pay for their daughters' tuition, or for any other purpose.

Cables Sent in May 1945

The fourth group of cables that has been cited as indicative of Harry's guilt reported on a meeting between him and a reporter for the Tass news agency during the April–May 1945 meetings in San Francisco to establish the United Nations.

As described in chapter 14, Harry represented the Treasury at the San Francisco meeting. For at least several months leading up to the event, he was worried that the resurgence of anti-Soviet sentiment in the United States would block the agreement to create the Security Council with all the Grand Alliance as permanent members. Without that agreement, the risk of a third world war would be much higher.

The Soviet Union was also eager to have a successful conclusion of the conference. To that end, it sent agents out to collect as much background information as possible. On April 6, 1945, two weeks before the conference, a cable was sent from Moscow instructing the New York office to tell an unidentified agent (code-named Albert) "to make arrangements with 'Robert' [Silvermaster] about maintaining contact with 'Richard' [White] and 'Pilot' [Ullmann] in Babylon [San Francisco]."[16]

Contacting Harry was not difficult, as he was already on friendly terms with several of the Soviet delegates, who had also participated in the Bretton Woods conference the previous summer. Shortly after arriving at the Sir Francis Drake Hotel in San Francisco, Harry had lunch with Amazasp Arutiunian, a Soviet delegate from Bretton Woods who, in the interim, had dined at the Whites' home in Bethesda along with several of his colleagues. Later, Harry and Lud Ullmann commandeered a Treasury car and took Arutiunian and a few other Soviet delegates out for a Sunday afternoon of sightseeing around San Francisco. None of this activity, of course, was in any way untoward or secretive.

Some days later, Harry was interviewed by Vladimir Pravdin, a reporter for the Soviet news agency Tass. After the interview, Pravdin (who was secretly working for Soviet intelligence) reported his findings to the NKVD in a series of cables.[17] The NSA was able to decipher only a small part of the cables, and most of what was published in the Venona traffic was just sentence fragments. From those fragments and a number of more complete segments, one can piece together a few salient points.

One of the key issues that the conference aimed to iron out concerned the rules for conducting the work of the Security Council. At the Yalta summit, in February 1945, Roosevelt, Stalin, and Churchill had agreed that each of the five permanent members of the council would have veto power, but they left open part of the interpretation of that power. The Soviet Union wanted to have the right to veto whether any issue would even be discussed by the council, while the United States and Great Britain wanted to have free and open discussion of all issues and limit the veto to council decisions. Several smaller countries remained opposed to the whole idea of granting veto rights to a few great powers.[18]

Pravdin was especially eager to discover how strongly the U.S. delegation would oppose the Soviet proposal for a comprehensive veto. He apparently thought that he got what he wanted, and he reported to his bosses in New York and Moscow that "Richard stated: 'Truman and Stettinius want to achieve the success of the conference at any price. In [19 groups of code unrecovered] in relation to the USSR and [26 groups unrecovered] will agree on the veto."[19] There is no way to tell what the last twelve words—interrupted by perhaps forty-five words that could not be deciphered—meant, but it would be reasonable to infer that Pravdin was reporting that White had told him that the United States was prepared to cave in to the Soviet position on the veto. If so, then either White or Pravdin was mistaken. Truman had given the U.S. delegation instructions not to yield on this point, and in fact it did not.

More generally, Harry was still worried that conflict between the United States and the Soviet Union was going to undermine the whole effort to create a viable United Nations Organization. It was his cherished dream to perpetuate the Grand Alliance after the war and thereby stimulate both peace and global prosperity. Shortly after arriving in San

Francisco, he wrote to Anne that the "American delegation has some members whose sole claim to notice is their virulent anti-Russian bias, and apparent passion for old Poland." That concern was echoed in Pravdin's report of his interview some days later, when he wrote that some unidentified proposal "could be an effective method of counteracting the attempts of the USA to put the USSR in a disadvantageous position."[20]

Piecing these various fragments together, it appears that Harry's views were in sync with Truman's but not with those of some key members of the U.S. delegation. Harry may have been particularly worried about Senator Arthur H. Vandenberg (Republican from Michigan), a former isolationist who by 1945 was supporting a bipartisan foreign policy but was viewed with some suspicion in Democratic circles. Pravdin reported that he had learned, apparently from Harry, that "if something prevents a successful conclusion of the conference, Vandenberg will declare that the Democratic party of Truman and Stettinius is to blame."

Harry obviously would have known that whatever he told Pravdin would find its way to the Soviet delegation in San Francisco. He may well have made similar comments to the delegates on his Sunday outing with them the week before. Whether this sort of back-channel diplomacy was well aimed is certainly a topic that could make for a lively debate. To argue that it constituted espionage, as some writers have suggested, is a far more dubious proposition.[21]

To summarize: the release of the Venona cables verified that Harry met freely with his Soviet counterparts, which was perfectly normal and open and which he always happily acknowledged. It also verified that Silvermaster and a few others—probably Glasser, Silverman, and Ullmann, and possibly Coe—were engaged in espionage and in some cases were eagerly invoking Harry's name. It verified part of Bentley's account that was based on her direct observation rather than hearsay: there was an active group of government officials in Washington leaking information to the Soviets. It showed how active and extensive was the Soviet effort to co-opt Harry and obtain information from him and others around him. But it showed very little, and nothing definitive, about Harry's alleged direct engagement with his spying colleagues.

1996: Operation Snow Is Revealed

Another revelation that occurred about the same time as the release of the Venona cables was the publication of a memoir by Vitaly Pavlov, who had been an NKVD agent during World War II. His book, published in Russian in 1996, described his participation in "Operation Snow," which called for him to meet with and try to co-opt Harry White.

Throughout the 1930s, the Soviet Union grew increasingly concerned about the possibility that Japan would invade, attempt to occupy, and disrupt Russia's eastern provinces. Japan had invaded and occupied Manchuria since 1931, and it invaded eastern China in 1937. When Japanese forces launched attacks into Mongolia (which was then under Soviet dominance) in 1939, the Soviet concerns greatly escalated. Stalin and his advisers began looking for ways to secure help from the United States in preventing further Japanese aggression. Japan clearly posed a threat to the United States as well as to Russia, but Soviet leaders were worried that the Roosevelt administration would be loath to intervene until it was too late.

According to Pavlov's memoir, the NKVD hatched a plan in 1939 to approach Harry and assess whether his attitude toward Japan was compatible with Soviet views. The NKVD knew of Harry through one of its American agents who worked in the Treasury. Pavlov either did not know the American agent's name or declined to reveal it. He described the person only as "agent X." X had described Harry (accurately) as an official who was "especially capable," who held strongly "anti-Fascist" views, and who "enjoyed a special position with" Secretary Morgenthau. The NKVD had X set up a social event at which White could be innocently brought into contact with Iskhak Akhmerov, who was using an assumed name, Bill Greinke, and posing as a "Sinologist working on the problems of the Far East."[22] Harry apparently found "Greinke" to be an interesting person, and he reportedly expressed an interest in talking to him again.

Two years later, the Soviets decided that it was time to follow up. Akhmerov, then based in Moscow, tapped Pavlov for the task of traveling to Washington to try to meet with Harry and urge him to persuade his superiors to take a tougher stance against Japan. As a young and relatively inexperienced agent, Pavlov was understandably nervous, but he claims to have carried it off successfully. He arrived in Washington from Moscow via New York on a Monday in mid-May, probably the 19th, telephoned Harry at the Treasury the next day, and invited him for lunch on Wednesday.

Pavlov's account of the timing does not quite hold together. After describing his arrival as happening in mid-May, he goes on to write that the "cherry trees that the American capital is so famous for were in bloom." Those cherry trees bloom in early April, or even late March, and are always finished before the middle of April.

Pavlov's excuse for calling Harry unexpectedly was that he was a friend and protégé of Bill Greinke. Bill, he claimed, was still in China but had asked him to convey some ideas. Harry was responsive and agreed to meet Pavlov for lunch at the Old Ebbitt Grill, a famous restaurant a half block from the Treasury on F Street. (In 1983, after a sale to new owners, the restaurant was moved around the corner to 15th Street, directly facing the Treasury building across the street.) After the usual icebreaking chat, Pavlov handed Harry a note, ostensibly from Bill the Sinologist, setting out the need for resistance against Japanese aggression in the Pacific. Harry reportedly said that he agreed with the analysis, returned the note to Pavlov, paid for lunch, and went back to the office. That was it. Operation Snow was complete.

What struck Pavlov years later as indicating the great success of the operation was that U.S. policy did evolve in the way that the Soviets had hoped. From July through November 1941, the Roosevelt administration took increasingly strong measures to dissuade Japan from territorial expansion in East Asia, culminating in demands from Secretary of State Cordell Hull and from the president for Japan to withdraw its forces from China and Vietnam. Japan's attack on Pearl Harbor on December 7 brought the United States into World War II.

Though it may have seemed natural to Pavlov to claim credit for this series of events, the real effect of Operation Snow was almost certainly nil. Harry had been expressing concern about Japan for years before his lunch with Pavlov, and nothing that he wrote between May and December was substantively different from what he had been writing earlier. From the time of the outbreak of war between China and Japan in 1937, Harry had been calling for more economic and financial support for China. At his urging, the Treasury had been acting as a countervailing influence against the State Department, which wanted to avoid being drawn into the conflict.

In October 1938 Harry drafted a memorandum for Morgenthau to send to Roosevelt, which warned that "Japan at first wanted only Manchuria; then North China; now she will not be content with less than the whole of China." In a thinly veiled swipe at the timidity of the State Department, the memorandum complained: "All my [i.e., Morgenthau's] efforts to secure immediate substantial aid for China have proved of no avail against the adamant foreign policy of doing nothing which could possibly be objected to by an aggressor nation."[23]

Throughout 1940 and 1941, as discussed in chapter 7, Harry looked for ways to use the vast economic and financial power of the United States to forestall a war with Japan. In the weeks before Pearl Harbor, he pushed the idea of offering trade and financial assistance to Japan in exchange for a military withdrawal from China. He also pushed for increased assistance to Latin America to counter the threat of dependence on Germany and Italy, and to Russia to help it sustain its war with Germany. The consistency of Harry's views and actions before and after his lunch at the Old Ebbitt Grill demonstrates that, while he agreed with the Soviet position as set out by his Sinologist acquaintance, he was not influenced by it.

Despite the innocuous and completely passive nature of Harry's involvement in this episode, despite Pavlov's explicit denial of any agency relationship (quoted at the beginning of this chapter), and despite the confirmation of that denial by Pavlov's superior at the KGB (Major General Julius Kobyakov), the revelation of Operation Snow was eagerly seized on by Harry's detractors as further evidence of culpability. In a particularly illogical example, a book by the journalist John Koster suggested that Harry's meeting with Pavlov led directly to the Japanese attack on Pearl Harbor. Jerrold and Leona Schecter also drew that bizarre conclusion and added that the meeting "contributed to the Berlin crisis of 1948" as well.[24]

KGB Archives

The collapse of the Soviet Union in 1991 brought an end to the espionage agency known in the west as the KGB (literally, the Committee for State Security). The KGB was replaced by multiple, less comprehensive agencies in the various former Soviet Republics. The Russian Federation created two agencies, the Federal Security Service (FSB) and the Foreign Intelligence Service (FIS). The KGB archives covering foreign intelligence are held mostly by the FIS, which guards them closely and has not yet made them generally available for research.[25] A few windows have opened into their contents, albeit with only a narrow field of vision. Two sources are relevant for investigating possible links between Harry and Soviet intelligence: the so-called Mitrokhin Archive and the Vassiliev Notebooks.

The Mitrokhin Archive

Vasili Mitrokhin was a disaffected KGB officer who secretly made notes on files that he examined in the organization's archives over a period of some twelve years, beginning in 1972. He defected in 1992, smuggled his notes out of Russia, and eventually became a British citizen. Together with a British historian, Christopher Andrew, he wrote a series of books about his findings, beginning with *The Sword and the Shield*, which was published in 1999. In 2014 Cambridge University made an edited Russian-language version of the archive available to the public. Although the books include numerous references to Harry's alleging that he was a Soviet agent, almost none of what it reports is based on information obtained by Mitrokhin.

The 1999 book reports only one fragment of information about the NKVD's efforts to obtain information from White, based on Mitrokhin's notes. As is known from other sources described above, including the Venona cables and Vitaly Pavlov's memoir, Soviet intelligence used Iskhak Akhmerov, an "illegal" who lived in the United States under a variety of cover names, nationalities, and occupations in the late 1930s and again from 1942, to try to glean information from Harry. From Akhmerov's reports to Moscow, Mitrokhin found that Akhmerov used two code names for White: "KASSIR, later JURIST."[26] (In the foreword to the book, Andrew acknowledges that the assignment of a code name does not mean that a person was involved in espionage.) Jurist also appears in the Venona traffic, but Kassir was a revelation.

Other references to Harry throughout the book were based on other sources and are not always accurate. Instances noted above include the authors' false assertion that Chambers named Harry in his list of contacts in 1939 and their characterization of Nicolai Chechulin as Harry's "handler."

The Vassiliev Notebooks

Alexander Vassiliev is a Russian journalist and former KGB agent. In his capacity as a journalist, he worked with the American historian Allen Weinstein to get exclusive access to certain files from the KGB archives in exchange for payments to the organization of retired Soviet intelligence officers. That collaboration resulted in a 1998 book by the two men, *The Haunted Wood*. The book was based in part on eight handwritten notebooks, totaling some 1,100 pages, that Vassiliev compiled as summaries of and verbatim excerpts from the files that the FIS allowed him to see. In 2009 the authors deposited these "Vassiliev Notebooks" with the History and Public Policy Program Digital Archive of the Manuscript Division in the Library of Congress. The Wilson Center in Washington, D.C., subsequently published the notebooks online in three forms: the original notebooks, handwritten in Russian; a Russian transcription; and an English translation.

As a historical source, the notebooks are secondary to the primary KGB files, which are in Moscow and not generally accessible to researchers. Vassiliev was allowed to see only a selection of the files, which were first vetted by the Press Bureau of the FIS. One also has to trust that the KGB documents are accurate descriptions of the meetings and communications that they report.[27] Subject to those caveats, the notebooks provide a detailed look inside the process of Soviet penetration of the U.S. government, including the period of alliance during World War II.

The notebooks describe several instances of the Soviet effort to collect information from Harry during the war. The main conduit for that effort was Harry's friend Greg Silvermaster, usually referred to by a code name (Robert or Pal, both of which also appear in the Venona cables). His identification with those code names is clearly established by correlation with known facts about him, including references to his affliction with severe asthma attacks. (Silvermaster was assigned by the U.S. Department of Agriculture to serve as a technical secretary to the U.S. delegation at the Bretton Woods conference, but he had to return to Washington after the first several days because of an asthma attack.)[28] Soviet agents and officials in the Communist Party of the United States had him convey to them whatever gossip or other information that he could get from Harry.

According to the notebooks, the use of Silvermaster in this way began in 1940. Vassiliev's note states: "So. established contact with Robert in late 1940 by arrangement with Helmsman. Soon thereafter 'Pilot,' 'Richard,' and 'Peak' were turned over to Robert as contacts through the CP line."[29] Replacing code names with the alleged real names, this sentence becomes: "Jacob Golos established contact with Silvermaster in late 1940 by arrangement with Earl Browder. Soon thereafter Ludwig Ullmann, Harry White, and Frank Coe were turned over to Silvermaster as contacts through the Communist Party line." Earl Browder was the head of the Communist Party of the United States. Golos was a Russian-born naturalized U.S. citizen who ran a travel agency as cover for his underground activity providing fake passports for Soviet operatives. Ullmann, as we have seen, was a U.S. Treasury official who lived with the Silvermasters in Washington. Frank Coe was also working at the Treasury and probably knew Silvermaster through his friendship with Harry.

To fulfill his assignment, Silvermaster reported anything Harry or others told him in conversations that might be of interest to the party. In August 1941, for example, he conveyed a story that Weinstein and Vassiliev thought was "especially timely and . . . directly from the top." In the notebook, the report stated: "At lunch on July 31 Knox proposed a wager that the Germans would occupy Moscow, Leningrad, Kiev and Odessa by 1 September." This was nine days after German troops began the invasion of Russia in the drive known as Operation Barbarossa. The report continued, "Morgenthau took the wager. On 1 August he announced this to his colleagues. Sullivan (Morgenthau's deputy, a conservative) backed Knox. General Counsel Foley sided with Morgenthau." In *The Haunted Wood*, Weinstein and Vassiliev inferred that Morgenthau had "shared this news with Silvermaster and other key staff members."[30]

Morgenthau almost certainly did *not* share this information with Silvermaster, whom he probably never met. Silvermaster was working at the Bureau of Economic Warfare and had never worked in the Treasury. What actually happened is described in detail in the Morgenthau Diaries.

On the morning of July 31, Morgenthau telephoned the secretary of the navy, Frank Knox, and invited him to have lunch with him at the Treasury. Knox had another commitment, but he reciprocated by inviting Morgenthau to have dinner with him that evening on his official yacht, the former presidential yacht *Sequoia*. Morgenthau accepted.[31] The next morning, Morgenthau presided over his regular daily "Group Meeting" with fourteen members of his senior staff. As was usually the case, the meeting opened with several minutes of jocular banter before the secretary got down to business.

A few minutes into the discussion, Morgenthau remarked: "I made a good bet last night with Frank Knox. Ten dollars. . . . He said that before the first of September that Leningrad, Moscow, Smolensk and Odessa would fall." That produced a lively exchange in which Harry agreed with Morgenthau that the Germans would have a harder time conquering the Soviet cities, while John L. Sullivan (assistant secretary) sided with Knox. General Counsel Edward H. Foley did not express any view. Jacob Viner joked that Knox had been wrong to commit to the fall of all four cities, because the Germans "might not want one of those." After the laughter died down, Peter H. Odegard (special assistant in charge of the War Bonds campaign) sparked a discussion about whether Morgenthau's expected ten-dollar winnings would be taxable. The group then moved on to serious matters.[32]

Some time in the next few days, Harry—or possibly someone else at the meeting, if anyone else knew Silvermaster personally—relayed the gist of this exchange to his friend. Doing so could not have been intended to convey useful and timely information to the Communist Party or to Soviet intelligence officers. If that had been the purpose, he would have told Silvermaster about the substance of the meeting, which included a discussion about the controversy over whether to allow the Japanese ocean liner *Tatsuta Maru* to sail back to Japan from San Francisco despite a presidential order to seize Japanese assets. Instead, he just told an amusing and harmless story about the bet. Somewhere along the way, several details got garbled: dinner became lunch; Smolensk became Kiev; and Foley got injected into the debate. All of which was just normal conversation from one friend to another.

Morgenthau won the bet.

The following year, in January 1942, it seems that the Soviets decided to try to develop a more direct means of getting information from Harry, probably because Silvermaster was not able to get very much that was useful. The notebook includes a lengthy report dated January 10, 1942, from headquarters in Moscow to Vasily Zarubin, the head of the NKVD section in New York. The relevant statement is that "'Pal' . . . should continue to work with 'Jurist' on his further development in order to prepare the 'Jurist's' transfer to direct communications with our operative." (As mentioned earlier, Jurist was another code name that the Soviets used to refer to Harry, and Pal referred to Silvermaster.) After describing similar directives regarding other sources, the report continues, "The work . . . should be oriented toward obtaining information that is accessible to them through their jobs and toward studying their capabilities, as well as educating them in a probationary direction."[33]

In Russian spy-speak, a "probationer" was an agent. The term *probationary direction* means that the NKVD wanted to try to turn Harry and others into Soviet agents instead of their being merely blind sources of information. The implication of this report is that Harry—at least in early 1942—was not an agent, but the Soviets clearly wanted him to become one.

In March 1942 Silvermaster reportedly told Zarubin that he (Silvermaster) was being investigated by the FBI for three reasons: he had been active in the California labor movement in the 1930s, he was on a list of suspected people developed by Martin Dies (the head of the House Committee on Un-American Activities), and his wife was active in "various Spanish and Chinese organizations." As discussed in chapter 8, Harry was also on the Dies list because Anne was involved with the League of Women Shoppers and the Washington chapter of the Committee for Democratic Action. (The Vassiliev Notebooks describe it as a list of one

hundred people, but the actual list contained about 1,100 names.) In neither case did the FBI investigation reveal any wrongdoing, but while the
investigation was under way, Moscow ordered a temporary halt in Zarubin's contacts with Silvermaster.[34]

The Haunted Wood describes this incident, but it strays from the notebook account that is its primary source and makes multiple errors. It repeats the assertion that the Dies list was just one hundred names. It asserts
that Silvermaster was "discharged from the Treasury Department in June
1942"; Silvermaster worked at the Board of Economic Warfare (BEW),
not the Treasury. More seriously, it claims that, as part of the FBI investigation in March 1942, an agent contacted Harry, "who promptly informed
Silvermaster."[35] What the notebook actually states is that Silvermaster's
supervisor at the BEW, whose name happened to be White, informed
Silvermaster that the FBI was investigating him.[36] That Mr. White was
not Harry. Only after the FBI acknowledged its mistake and closed its
file on Harry did an agent question him about Silvermaster. As noted in
chapter 8, that interview took place in June 1942.

The next entry pertaining to Harry is from a cable that Zarubin sent
to headquarters on October 12, 1942. The NKVD was still trying to get
information from Harry through Silvermaster, but without much success. Zarubin wrote (with alleged real names inserted here in brackets):
"According to 'Sound' [Golos], 'Pal' [Silvermaster] continues to draw information from 'Jurist' [White] while engaging in a friendly relationship
with him. 'Jurist' is a very nervous and cowardly person and is not getting
very close to 'Pal' politically. He is more interested in matters of domestic
policy and his job."[37] Since "nervous and cowardly" is far from the mark
as a description of Harry's personality, and since Harry was engaged entirely in international, not domestic, policy, it appears that Silvermaster
(or possibly Golos) was just making excuses for not being able to convey
anything useful.

On November 26, Moscow cabled back to Zarubin that he had to
do better. Headquarters had received information from some unnamed
source that "'Jurist' at one time was a probationer for the neighbors,"
meaning that Harry was reported to have been a source for the military
arm of Soviet intelligence, the GRU. Since Whittaker Chambers claimed
to have been serving as a courier for the GRU in the 1930s and to have
conveyed information from Harry, this report, on cursory examination,
could appear to be a confirmation of part of Chambers's account.

As discussed in chapter 15, much of what Chambers told investigators after he broke from the party was either exaggerated or demonstrably

false. The allegation that Harry was reporting to the GRU in the 1930s has not been otherwise corroborated, and without some background on what information the NKVD office had received and from whom, it is impossible to verify the meaning of the "probationer" reference in the notebook. Since by Chambers's own sworn testimony, everything that he obtained from White came indirectly through intermediaries, the most likely explanation is that Harry was a blind source in the 1930s, as he was during the war. What is clear is that in 1942, Moscow was using the suggestion that Harry had once been a source to encourage Zarubin to be more aggressive in trying to recruit him. "He should, at last, be properly recruited for work and taken on for direct communications. In view of 'Jurist's' value and the necessity of adhering to the rules of covert work, we consider it advisable to assign a special illegal to work with him. . . . Wire us your suggestions."[38] (*Illegal* was a term used by the Soviets to denote a Soviet agent planted in a Western country under cover of a false identity and occupation.)

The frustration continued. On February 9, 1943, Zarubin cabled to Moscow that Silvermaster was no longer able to get *any* information from Harry. "Re: 'Jurist'—'Sound' reports that in recent months he has begun to visit 'Pal' less often, obviously out of fear for his career, and has almost completely forgotten about his leftist attitudes in the past. According to 'Sound,' 'Pal' says there are no opportunities to approach 'Jurist.'"[39] Either Harry had soured on his friend Greg for some reason, or he was simply too busy to keep up with his earlier social activities. He was fully engaged in drafting his plan for what would become the Bretton Woods agreements, and he was also responsible for overseeing Lend-Lease aid to various Allied countries. It was an early stage of an extremely intense work schedule that would persist for the next four years.

As late as the summer of 1945, Silvermaster was still making excuses for not being able to get any useful information from Harry. Toward the end of July, according to Vassiliev's notes, the Silvermasters went to New York to meet with Akhmerov. Three weeks later, Akhmerov reported to Moscow that the meetings were "unpleasant" and made him "uneasy." At one point, Helen Silvermaster (code-named "Dora") began "slander[ing]" Harry (code-named "Richard"). (Akhmerov's report also mentions Greg Silvermaster, code-named "Robert," and Ullmann, code-named "Donald.")

> [Dora] talked about Richard, trying to slander him any way she could. She said that he did not understand politics, that he did not share our polit. views at all, that on many occasions he has

revealed hostility toward our country, that she did not trust him, and that she was not convinced that he wouldn't betray us. Once more, as I had before, I explained to her that, unfortunately, we could not expect all our friends to provide the same level of loyalty and active service as Robert, Dora, and Donald, that we had to take our friends just as they were, with all their flaws, and to do everything we could to get the best possible results out of them.[40]

On September 3, 1945, the New York office of the NKVD sent a report to Moscow dealing with the ineffectiveness of the ongoing attempt to get information from White through Silvermaster. Silvermaster was suffering from his chronic asthma, but the larger problem was that no one was telling him anything. Using "Robert" to refer to Silvermaster and the new code name "Reed" to refer to White, the report claimed that the "reason that Reed doesn't pass along information or documents is not that he doesn't want to help us, but partly because he is extremely absentminded and forgets his promises, but mainly because he considers such work secondary. According to Robert, Reed feels that his main calling is to provide advice on fundamental political and econom. issues."[41] In other words, Harry (who was not otherwise alleged to be absent-minded) was not providing information because he was too busy to pass on the sort of gossip that he and Silvermaster had exchanged on earlier occasions.

The Soviets eventually found ways to reach Harry without having to rely on Silvermaster. As the Venona traffic revealed, in 1944 they used Nicolai Chechulin, the deputy head of the delegation at Bretton Woods, to become friendly with Harry, report back on whatever he could learn, and try to co-opt and recruit him as an agent. They also sent Vladimir Pravdin to the United States in the guise of a correspondent for the Tass news agency. In April 1945 Pravdin interviewed Harry during the UN conference in San Francisco and filed a lengthy report with his superiors, who forwarded it to Moscow. From Harry's personal correspondence and other sources, we know that he enjoyed the company of several of the Soviet delegates at Bretton Woods and entertained them at his home and elsewhere. They no doubt also reported whatever they heard.

What the Vassiliev Notebooks add to this account is that Pravdin interviewed Harry again in Washington on a few occasions, beginning in July 1945, around the time that Harry was concluding his successful campaign to shepherd the Bretton Woods Agreements Act through Congress. During an interview on August 8, Pravdin solicited the information that

Pilot (Ullmann) planned to resign from the air force and return to work at the Treasury. An economist in Harry's division, Sonia Gold, was about to go on maternity leave, and that appeared to create an opening for Ullmann to join the division. Pravdin claimed that he told Harry that the Soviets wanted him (Harry) to stay at the Treasury, where he could be a useful source, and he wrote that Harry was "flattered" by the attention.[42]

It is at least possible that Pravdin exaggerated much of this account. It seems more likely that he told Harry that he, as a Tass reporter, hoped that Harry would stay at Treasury and continue to be available to him as a source. The reference to Sonia Gold makes little sense, since she was in a lower position than what Ullmann would have been seeking, and Harry had almost no contact with her.

Pravdin's garbled account of Gold's status probably came from a source other than his interview with Harry. He was not alone in his confusion. To the FBI in 1945 and to the grand jury in 1948 and 1949, Elizabeth Bentley claimed that people in the "Silvermaster group" had persuaded Harry White to hire Sonia Gold as his secretary, and that Harry had then given her documents to pass on to the group. In fact, Harold Glasser arranged for her to be hired as an economist (not a secretary) in Harry's large division, and she worked under Glasser's supervision. The only known instances of Harry's having any contact with her were when he saw her in his office as part of the standard vetting procedure for new hires, on July 21, 1943, and incidental contacts while she was working in the division. Some authors have repeated Bentley's lie as if it were true.[43]

The FBI also was confused by the misidentification of her as a secretary. In the Venona traffic, the translation of a decoded cable from New York to Moscow dated January 18, 1945, included this report: "Some months ago Robert [Silvermaster] complained that Rouble ["probably Harold Glasser"] was hiding important documents from Zhenya (his secretary)." The FBI analyst annotated the cable with this assessment: "Zhenya: Sonia Gold, nee Steinman, employed in the Treasury Department from 24 August 1943 to 21 August 1947. If she was in fact Glasser's secretary at the time of this message, the statement here is a strong confirmation of the identifications of Rouble and Zhenya; if she was not, it strongly suggests that one or both identifications are incorrect."[44] (The Vassiliev Notebooks, however, appear to confirm that Zhenya and Rouble were Gold and Glasser.)

In any event, Harry had no intention of staying at Treasury. He was focused entirely on moving to the IMF and guiding its initial decisions and actions.

Pravdin reportedly did meet with Harry on other occasions in 1945, and he evidently did succeed in gaining Harry's confidence to some extent. On August 13, Harry gave him copies of two of Anne's books and asked him to try to get them published in Russia. That puzzled Pravdin's bosses in Moscow, who could not envisage trying to market the books to a Russian audience.[45]

Another source that the Soviets used to try to get information from Harry was Harold Glasser, who was Harry's deputy in the Division of Monetary Research for the latter part of the wartime period. One of the Vassiliev Notebooks describes a report dated December 31, 1944, from Anatoly Gorsky, a state security officer operating undercover as an official at the Soviet embassy in Washington. The report describes a lengthy interview with Rouble, who is identified as Glasser.

During the meeting, Glasser reportedly told Gorsky that he and Harry had been friends for a while, and that Harry had been instrumental in getting him his job at the Treasury. He claimed that Harry knew at that time that Glasser "was a fellowcountryman," meaning that he had some relationship to Communism. (The definition of *fellowcountryman* in the Vassiliev concordance is "local Communists, members of the CPUSA or other fraternal Communist party/organization.") Glasser further claimed that "on several occasions, [White] let [him] familiarize himself with certain documents that had no direct bearing on [his] work and told him certain things. At the same time, they never once explicitly discussed [Glasser's] belonging to the fellowcountrymen."[46] A reasonable interpretation of this report is that Harry knew when he hired Glasser at the Treasury that Glasser had left-wing views and belonged to an organization of the sort that was being investigated by HUAC and the FBI. Moreover, he trusted Glasser enough to share sensitive information with him at work. To go further and conclude that Harry was knowingly passing information or documents through Glasser to the Soviet apparatus would go well beyond the available evidence.

Epilogue

The Legacy Redux

A man of peace . . . [and] the most brilliant monetary economist
in the world.

—former Vice President Henry Wallace, 1948

HARRY WHITE'S WASHINGTON CAREER was brief but intense. His prescient view of the potential benefits of an active economic role for the
federal government brought him to the attention of senior officials in
Washington. Once secured in the corridors of the U.S. Treasury, he made
his mark by advocating effectively both for anti-Depression activism and
a concerted effort to support potential allies against the growing threats
from the Axis powers. Having become a senior official himself by the onset
of World War II, he was in a strong position to prepare the United States
to assume the dominant role in postwar political and economic affairs.

In a little more than twelve years as a professional economist, Harry
White directed and oversaw four major achievements.

First, he was the principal designer and founder of two multilateral
financial institutions that continue to play important—and controversial—roles today: the International Monetary Fund and the World Bank.
In the popular imagination, he shares the accolades with the far more
celebrated British economist John Maynard Keynes. In truth, though

371

Keynes and White had similar visions of the institutional structure that the world needed to restore international trade and multilateral finance, the end products were largely as White first conceived them. In addition, he played a central role in persuading other countries and the U.S. Congress to approve the plans and establish what became known as the Bretton Woods institutions.

Second, he was responsible for creating a system and a forum for international financial cooperation, which also still exists within the IMF and other institutions that have evolved in its wake. The Depression of the 1930s and then World War II had undermined the previous arrangements, based on fixed values for currencies in relation to the price of gold, that had enabled export-led economic growth in the late nineteenth and early twentieth centuries. The Bretton Woods system effectively restored the necessary level of trust between countries by establishing a regular dialogue and mechanisms for resolving financial disputes.

Third, White's Bretton Woods system incorporated a worldwide agreement to reestablish multilateral financial settlements and eliminate restrictions on the exchange of currencies for international trade. Reliance on bilateral trade and settlements throughout the 1930s and early 1940s had been a substantial drag on economic growth. Removing that obstacle led to a sustained resumption of economic growth throughout much of the world.

Fourth, the Bretton Woods agreements included specific commitments by participating countries to stabilize exchange rates and anchor currency values on the price of gold expressed in a fully convertible U.S. dollar. The genius of this agreement was its emphasis on stability with enough flexibility to avoid rigidity. The system was dissolved in the early 1970s, but only after it had contributed importantly to a widely shared explosion of export-led growth.

The underappreciation of White's role in these accomplishments is attributable in part to the natural inclination of many analysts to credit the great Keynes with the predominant role. White overcame this apparent greatness gap both because he had the U.S. government—which was financing most of the initial operation—at his back and because he brought a broader vision of multilateral cooperation to the table.

White won many skirmishes against Keynes. The Bretton Woods conference was a broad international project, not the bilateral big-power ("founder-state") deal that Keynes preferred. The IMF was not to be based on a new international currency, as Keynes (and, at least at first,

Henry Morgenthau) had wanted. Instead, the IMF lent gold or U.S. dollars and eventually other national currencies. Its financial size was limited by the amount of member countries' subscriptions. Its financial structure was based largely on U.S. banking practices, rather than the British use of overdrafts. Members had to accept limits on their right to change exchange rates without the concurrence of the IMF. All IMF lending was overseen by a resident Executive Board, not extended automatically in response to members' requests. In addition, to ensure political oversight and reassure skeptics in Congress, U.S. officials insisted that the new institutions would be headquartered in Washington, close to the U.S. Treasury.

As we saw in chapter 10, Keynes wanted the Bretton Woods institutions to be purely technical automatons, lending to countries upon request, whereas White wanted to keep their activities under tighter political control and oversight. Keynes was bitter about the outcome, and he had good reason to be. Over the decades that followed, both the IMF and the World Bank became increasingly involved in politically important issues. Rather than being passive suppliers of credit to finance international payments deficits (the IMF) and neutral suppliers of credit to finance economic development (the World Bank), the Executive Boards of both institutions began to make decisions about the appropriateness of countries' economic policies and investment decisions.

In the twenty-first century, the IMF defines its mission as "working to foster global monetary cooperation, secure financial stability, facilitate international trade, promote high employment and sustainable economic growth, and reduce poverty around the world." The World Bank defines its mission as "ending extreme poverty and promoting shared prosperity."[1] While these are worthy objectives, they have—for better or worse—embroiled both institutions far more deeply in the domestic politics of borrowing countries than either Keynes or White could have imagined.

Harry also had a stronger hand in the effort to create global institutions because his vision was more broadly internationalist and comprehensive than that of the British team. Keynes was constrained by Britain's circumstances, but he also was less internationalist by nature.

One constraint was that Britain had very large external debts, mostly in the form of blocked sterling balances owned by India and other Commonwealth countries. Keynes had to fight for a lengthy period to unwind those blockages, which prevented him from favoring a rapid move toward currency convertibility. To Harry, restoring convertibility as soon as possible was key to postwar prosperity. As he put it in his April 1942 plan for the IMF: "Balances owned by residents of another country which have been blocked because holdings of gold and other liquid foreign exchange assets are inadequate . . . will constitute after the war one of the danger spots to monetary stability, and to resumption of liberal trade policies. If the Fund can eliminate that danger spot it will have justified its existence—even were it to accomplish little else."[2]

A second constraint was that Keynes had to try to preserve the system of trade and currency preferences that was fundamental to the economics of the British Empire in the post–gold standard era. Colonies and dominions within the empire were encouraged to link their currencies to the pound sterling and were granted lower tariff rates on exports to Britain. That system clashed with Harry's vision of establishing free and open trade around the globe. The U.S. Congress was unlikely to accept any proposal that would promote growth in imports unless it equally enabled growth in U.S. exports. That put the two sides in conflicting positions.

In addition to these constraints, Keynes was limited by being more skeptical about the stabilizing role of financial markets than White was. Both men advocated controlling the flow of capital to prevent private capital markets from undermining the stability of trade flows, but Keynes saw that proposal as more fundamental to the system. Britain, he argued, had already "gone a long way towards perfecting" capital controls, and his proposal for an international currency union would help promote international cooperation in that direction. In Harry's view, when a country was facing an unsustainable payments deficit, it had to find a way to avoid controlling imports or repeatedly depreciating its exchange rate. In such circumstances, capital controls were "the best of the bad choices."[3] That view carried over into the charter of the IMF, which promoted multilateral finance but empowered the Fund to require a country to impose capital controls if it would otherwise have to take more destructive measures.

Both because Britain was deeply dependent on U.S. financial assistance and because internationalism was in an unusual ascendancy in the United States as World War II was drawing to a successful conclusion, Keynes had no chance to win any of the major battles. The best that he could achieve was to talk the U.S. team out of a short fixed term for the transition to full currency convertibility for trade-related transactions. That bought several more years for Britain to reestablish convertibility for the pound and unblock the accumulated sterling balances at the Bank of England. Not until 1958 did Britain and many other European countries become fully compliant with the Bretton Woods system.

The dominance of the United States and Harry White should not obscure the universal agreement that the fundamental purpose of the IMF was Keynesian.[4] Harry's economic philosophy was essentially Keynesian, and that philosophy carried over into the IMF Articles of Agreement. A purpose of the IMF, expressed in Article I, was (and is) to "facilitate the expansion and balanced growth of international trade, and to contribute thereby to the promotion and maintenance of high levels of employment and real income and to the development of the productive resources of all members as primary objectives of economic policy." Moreover, the IMF was designed to encourage countries to use Keynesian policy tools: pursue active fiscal and monetary policies and reduce reliance on trade barriers and autarkic or mercantilist economic policies.

Yet another reason for the obfuscation of Harry White's legacy has been the persistence of a suspicion that he was a nefarious character with a shady secret life. Purveyors of that legend have made much of three interrelated facts. Harry was sympathetic to Russia. Harry had close friends and colleagues who were or may have been Communists, and some of them were engaged in espionage on behalf of the Soviet Union. Harry hired, promoted, and protected those associates. Therefore, the story goes, he must have been guilty of the same or similar crimes, and he must have betrayed his country.

On closer examination, that conclusion appears much less convincing, for several reasons.

First, the logical chain was extremely weak. Harry certainly found it to be ridiculous. When he testified before the House Un-American Activities Committee in August 1948, the committee chairman, J. Parnell Thomas, tried to construct a case based on Harry's associations. Harry batted the argument away with a derisive syllogism: "(a) There are Communists; (b) I have friends; (c) those friends might be Communists. I mean, that is silly."[5] In the eight years that Harry ran a large division at the Treasury, he hired, worked with, and promoted hundreds of people. Finding later that three or four of them betrayed that trust tells us nothing about Harry's possible culpability.

More generally, it is essential to recall that in the Red-hunting era of the late 1940s and early 1950s, it was common practice to identify suspects by associating them with other people who were also suspected in the same way. The charges had a circularity that was as frightening as it was vacuous. In one typical example, George A. Eddy—an economist at the U.S. Treasury for much of the period after 1934—was suspended from his

job without pay in September 1954 and was charged with a Bill of Particulars to which he had to respond if he wished to be reinstated. The first
charge in the Bill of Particulars was this: "You have listed as references,
in your applications for Federal Employment, the names of Lauchlin B.
Currie, Harry Dexter White and V. Frank Coe, all of whom were publicly
identified as involved in a Soviet espionage group."[6] Nowhere in the list of
charges was any allegation that Eddy was a Communist or had engaged in
espionage. He was stripped of his employment because he had worked and
associated with people against whom unsubstantiated charges had been
brought. (Eddy successfully defended himself against the charges. He was
reinstated, but he then resigned.) In at least some cases, the charges against
those people were based primarily or entirely on their own associations.

The case against Harry White rests largely on his association with
numerous people who were thought to be engaged in activities linked to
the Communist Party, Soviet intelligence agencies, or "subversive" (as that
term was understood at the time) organizations. As Supreme Court Justice
William O. Douglas wrote in 1974, Harry's "great 'crime' was knowing
people the investigators thought were communists."[7] Accusations that he
was directly engaged in illegal or disloyal activities were based on self-
serving and unreliable accounts, hearsay, or speculation. Both in contemporaneous discussions and in the later extensive literature, the notion that
Harry "must have known" or "probably suspected" that his friends and
colleagues were up to no good was a regular feature of the conclusions
that were drawn, even by authors who have otherwise shown sensitivity to
the ambiguity of the evidence.[8]

None of White's associates—his friends or employees—was ever
charged with a crime as a result of the espionage and disloyalty investigations, but many of them led ruined or forcefully altered lives after they
were attacked in the Red-hunting era. Many were immigrants and naturalized U.S. citizens. Almost certainly, some of them were guilty of espionage. Others were valued targets and blind sources of Soviet espionage.
Still others were undoubtedly innocent.

We have encountered many of these individuals in the course of this
narrative. Leaving out those whom Harry barely knew, and only through
occasional work contacts, such as Sonia Gold, Alger Hiss (assistant secretary of state), and Victor Perlo (an economist who joined the Treasury
staff to work under Frank Coe toward the end of Harry's tenure in the
department),[9] we are left with nine people who were linked in some way
to Harry in the investigations. The clearest and most compelling charge

is that Greg Silvermaster, his wife, Helen, and their housemate, Lud Ullmann, were host to a group of people who provided documents and other information for conveyance to Soviet intelligence operatives. Harry's friend George Silverman and his Treasury colleagues Harold Glasser and Frank Coe may have been active participants in that scheme, although the evidence is mixed. Other associates who came under suspicion were probably liberals with varying degrees of activism in left-leaning organizations and possibly a measure of sympathy with Communism and the Soviet Union. The reputations of people such as Solomon Adler, Lauchlin Currie, and William Henry Taylor were—and still are—attacked, but the evidence does not show that they were involved in any form of espionage.

Second, Harry and his associates were only a small portion of the cohort of economists working in the Roosevelt administration who came under attack in that era. Several New Deal economists, including Treasury officials such as George Eddy, Irving Friedman, and Charles Kindleberger—and those in other agencies such as the agricultural economist Mordecai Ezekiel—were investigated by the FBI because of their associations with others who were suspected.[10] Some economists, such as Irving Kaplan and William Remington, both of whom worked at the War Production Board; Paul Sweezy, who worked at the Office of Strategic Services during the war; and Michael Greenberg (Board of Economic Warfare and Foreign Economic Administration) were investigated primarily because of suspected involvement in the Communist Party or affiliated organizations, not because of suspected illegal activity. Charles Kramer, who worked for a time at the Office of Price Administration, was investigated because of testimony from the unreliable Elizabeth Bentley.

Although none of these individuals was ever prosecuted for espionage, some, such as Kramer and Remington, might have been if the evidence from the Venona project and the Vassiliev Notebooks had been available at the time. Remington was convicted of perjury for denying his connections to Communism. In prison, he was murdered by fellow prisoners, led by a fanatical anti-Communist. Greenberg, a British citizen, returned to England in 1947 after being investigated by the FBI and the Civil Service Commission for having Marxist views. Sweezy was convicted of contempt for refusing to cooperate with an investigation of his Marxist views, but the Supreme Court overturned his conviction in 1957. Many others, of course, were completely innocent.[11]

Third, the fact that these attacks were so widespread and indiscriminate naturally created skepticism and a backlash among people who otherwise might have responded more helpfully. When the FBI investigated Greg Silvermaster in 1942, all that it knew was that he had been active in the movement to organize agricultural workers in the 1930s and had joined an organization in which Communists were active. It was not a charge that Harry was likely to take seriously. Neither did the other officials who had to respond, right up to Under Secretary of War Robert Patterson, who made the decision not to take any action. Harry similarly dismissed allegations against Harold Glasser, George Silverman, and others. After all, he himself had been investigated because of his wife's involvement in "charitable enterprises" such as the League of Women Shoppers. He knew or at least suspected that the FBI had tapped his telephone. He regarded Martin Dies and the other congressional investigators with utter contempt. It is perfectly understandable that he would dismiss the allegations that were presented to him.

Fourth, Harry's sympathy for Russia was not even a legitimate cause for suspicion, much less for a finding of guilt. His view of social policy was anchored firmly on the left, and he was living in an era when the old economic systems of the West were no longer working. The U.S. economy imploded in the 1930s and suffered through several years in which the unemployment rate hovered around 25 percent. Harry joined the Roosevelt administration as it was trying to save capitalism from itself by creating a mixed economy with a much heavier government component than the country would have tolerated earlier. Internationally, Roosevelt extended diplomatic recognition to the Soviet Union in 1933 and embraced it as a wartime ally in 1942. The tragic ugliness of the Soviet regime burst into the open when Stalin signed a nonaggression pact with Hitler in 1939, but the German invasion of Russia in 1941 enabled Roosevelt to forge the alliance that was of crucial importance for the fight against Nazi Germany. Throughout that era, from 1933 through 1945, Harry's views were to the left of center for the country but were well within the mainstream of Washington under Roosevelt. Viewed through the prism of the Cold War, that sympathy looks dangerously naive, but Harry died before that view emerged.

To return to the point that began the prologue to this book: Harry White's life was indeed a paradox, but not the one that has often been posed in attempts to explain him. The prevailing narrative has been that he appeared to be a hardworking, loyal civil servant throughout his career in the U.S. government and the IMF but in fact lived a secret life as a spy for the Soviet Union. As a logical proposition, that narrative does not hold together. It lacks a convincing motive, because Harry was not a Communist and no evidence has surfaced to suggest that he ever received any unexplained or illicit compensation. His personality was antithetical to the suggestion that he would have done the bidding of bad actors. As the Harvard economist John Kenneth Galbraith once wryly observed, "The only socialist or communist state that Harry White would have been associated with was one that he fully controlled himself."[12] The whole espionage narrative leaves one with a sense that much of his life and work simply cannot be explained.

When subjected to a close look at the historical record, the empirical basis for that narrative collapses. The evidence is clear that Soviet agents tried to co-opt him, tried to milk him for as much information as they could glean, and used a variety of methods to do so over a period of several years. The evidence is also clear that those efforts occasionally succeeded. In direct contacts with Soviet officials and with agents posing as journalists or executives, and by sharing information in the normal course of his work, Harry became a valuable, albeit uncertain and unreliable, source for Soviet intelligence. To extend that conclusion and argue that Harry conveyed information knowingly and that he did so to promote Soviet over American interests requires one to speculate without the support of any reliable data. The resulting stories do not hold together.

The real paradox is that Harry White approached his life's work with tenacity of purpose, intellectual rigor, and extremely hard work, but he approached his personal life with a naive romanticism that left him vulnerable to the machinations and manipulations of those around him. There was a touching sentimentality to much of his personal life: playing the mandolin; getting married in a religious ceremony to please his and Anne's relatives; enlisting in the army so he could fight the "Boches" (but he ended up in France far from battle, teaching English to a young girl); making the "education of boys" his first career goal; working at home with the radio on, children playing, and the dogs barking; watching MGM musicals at the local cinema; enjoying the cities of Central America with the wide-eyed amazement of a typical American tourist.

Harry had, as he said, "many friends," often with backgrounds similar to his own: the offspring of Ashkenazi Jewish immigrants from Russia or Eastern Europe, eschewing their religious heritage but holding strongly progressive views on economic and social policies. In the anti-Communist fervor of the 1940s, they constituted a beleaguered community, increasingly persecuted and distrustful of authority. Harry trusted and was loyal to his friends, and that in the end was the source of his downfall.

The charge of espionage does not fit into this narrative. The inescapable conclusion is that if Harry Dexter White was a spy, he was very bad at it. He almost certainly never conveyed a confidential document, and he left the Soviet agencies constantly frustrated at their inability to learn anything from him. As a source, by their own accounts, he was practically worthless. For a man who was so good at everything he applied himself to doing, to accuse him of such an agency would be the unkindest charge of all.

Notes

Prologue

1. "Due Process for Harry White," *New York Times*, August 18, 1944, 24.
2. Boughton, "The Case against Harry Dexter White: Still Not Proven."
3. Skidelsky, *John Maynard Keynes: Fighting for Britain*, 260–62.

Chapter 1. Who—Really—Was Harry White?

1. Harrod, *Life of Keynes*, 537–38; and Skidelsky, *John Maynard Keynes: Fighting for Britain*, 424.
2. The newspaper account (Whipple, "Life and Death"), published in the *Boston Globe*, was a twelve-part serialized biography produced hastily in the wake of the political scandal discussed later in this work. It contained many factual errors and unfounded speculations.
3. NARA-118, 2679.
4. See Craig, *Treasonable Doubt*, 17, 284n1. The other documents mentioned here are in the SMLP-2 archive.
5. See Balkelis, "Opening Gates."
6. Harry White to "Abc" (probably Abraham Wolfson), December 16, 1935, SMLP-2.
7. U.S. Census forms for 1900 and 1910 list his name as Harry White, as does his birth certificate. Bruce Craig found a story in the *Boston Globe* (June 25, 1909) discussing his high school graduating class, which referred to him as Harry Dexter White; Craig, *Treasonable Doubt*, 285n11. In later references, the middle name is almost always included. In another prominent example of this type of assimilation, William S. Paley, the longtime chairman of CBS, was born William Paley in Chicago to Ukrainian Jewish parents in 1901. He added the middle initial when he was twelve.
8. Harry White to Anne Terry White, April 27, 1935, SMLP-2.

9. Some of these details are unverified. The moving date of 1904 is from Nathan White, *Harry Dexter White: Loyal American*, 270. The street address (20 Dyer Avenue) is from Craig, *Treasonable Doubt*, 18.

10. Also see Nathan White, *Harry Dexter White: Loyal American*, 270–71.

11. On October 31, 1926, Harry's Harvard classmate Lauchlin Currie wrote in his diary, after spending a day with Harry visiting Harry's sister Fanny, that Harry had had a sister who committed suicide at the age of twenty-one. The only sister who could fit that description was Ida, who died in May 1903. (Currie provided his diaries and other personal papers to his biographer, Professor Roger Sandilands, who kindly made the relevant excerpts available to me.)

12. Harry's record at Massachusetts Agricultural College is summarized in a recommendation letter from Kenyon L. Butterfield, the college president, April 16, 1917, SMLP-2.

13. Recollections of Barney Kaplan's daughter, provided to me in 2001 and 2015.

14. Nathan White, *Harry Dexter White: Loyal American*, 270, and Anne Terry White, "Autobiography," 110. The award establishing the essay prize is in SMLP-2.

15. This account is based on Anne Terry White, "Autobiography."

16. For example, see Anne Terry to Harry White, May 22 and June 15, 1917, SMLP-2.

17. Harry White to Nathan White, telegram, August 10, 1917, SMLP-2; Anne Terry White, "Autobiography," 139. The official proclamation of the appointment, issued by the president of the United States, was dated August 15, 2017, and is in SMLP-2.

18. The marriage certificate is in SMLP-2. For the history of Temple Israel, see https://www.tisrael.org/our-history/.

19. Alice Couvert to Anne Terry White, August 13, 1918, SMLP-2.

20. These letters are now in SMLP-2.

21. The transfer order is in a scrapbook in SMLP-2. Other details are from Harry's letters to Anne, also in SMLP-2.

22. Bernstein, "All Still," 213.

23. Rees, *Harry Dexter White: A Study in Paradox*, 26.

Chapter 2. The Education of Harry White

1. Rees, *Harry Dexter White: A Study in Paradox*, 27, gives the date of White's enrolment as "February 1922," but White's Stanford transcript (now in SMLP-2) records a full year of coursework at Columbia for the academic year 1921–22.

2. The book list is in SMLP-2.

3. Bernstein, "All Still," 229–30. Also Maurice Bernstein to Anne Terry White, March 4, 1975, family collection.

4. Rees, *Harry Dexter White: A Study in Paradox*, 27, errs by placing the Whites' home in Los Gatos, some twenty miles from Palo Alto. Several letters in the family collection give Los Altos as White's address, and Bernstein, "All Still," 237, confirms it. Bernstein also recalled that he moved with the Whites into Palo Alto after their first year there. Stanford awarded White advanced placement by transferring his credits from the agricultural college and Columbia, in addition to extra credits for "wartime service."

5. These accounts of the careers of the three men are based primarily on letters by and interviews with participants and family members.

6. Dave Everall to Ruth Levitan, July 9, 1980, SMLP-2.

7. Ray Lyman Wilber, president of Stanford University, to White, June 16, 1924, Anne's scrapbooks, family collection.

8. White, "European Loans," 2.

9. Newspaper clipping, in family scrapbook.

10. White to Robert M. La Follette Sr., February 29, 1924, SMLP-2.

11. Notices referring to the lecture, on November 22, 1927, are in one of Anne's scrapbooks, family collection.

12. The appointment letter, dated March 29, 1926, gave the starting date of the appointment as September 1, 1926. The salary was set out in an undated letter to White from the university bursar. That letter noted that the salary was "for the year ending August 31, 1927." Both letters are in Anne's scrapbooks, family collection.

13. The book and article were published as Taussig, *Some Aspects*, and Taussig and White, "Rayon and the Tariff."

14. Harry's Harvard transcript is in SMLP-2. For his dissertation committee, see the record from the Harvard University archives, accessed at http://www .irwincollier.com/harvard-economics-general-examination-lauchlin-currie -and-harry-d-white-1927/.

15. Haberler, *Theory of International Trade*, 3. Haberler placed the second half of the quoted sentence in a footnote.

16. Taussig, *Some Aspects*, 18, recalled that Mill argued in his 1848 classic, *Principles of Political Economy*, that it might be appropriate to impose tariffs "temporarily (especially in a young and rising nation) in hopes of naturalizing a foreign industry." The argument is often traced back further to Alexander Hamilton in 1790, and Irwin, *Against the Tide*, chap. 8, cites an intellectual tradition dating back to the seventeenth century.

17. See Taussig to White, February 11, 1928, SMLP-2. Dates for the trip are from visa stamps in Harry's passport, SMLP-2. Address is from Anne's scrapbooks, family collection.

18. Anne clipped a newspaper story describing the match in detail and kept it in a scrapbook.

19. White, *French International Accounts*, 269.

20. Ibid., 312.

21. See Flanders, *International Monetary Economics*, 236–41. By *late classicals*, Flanders meant a group that was essentially what the Swedish economist Bertil Ohlin called the "Harvard School": Frank Taussig, Jacob Viner (who studied under Taussig at Harvard and taught mainly at Chicago), James W. Angell (who studied under Allyn Young at Harvard and taught mainly at Columbia), John H. Williams (another Taussig student who then taught at Harvard), and White. For more on Taussig's influence and White's anticipation of Keynesian economics, see Alacevich, Asso, and Nerozzi, "Harvard Meets the Crisis."

22. White, *French International Accounts*, frontispiece.

23. White to Mr. J. T. Day, editor at Harvard University Press, May 16, 1933; and Harold Murphy, director of Harvard University Press, to White, May 24, 1933, both in SMLP-2.

24. Taussig to White, May 19, 1933, SMLP-2.

25. For more on Currie's life and work, see Sandilands, *Life and Political Economy of Lauchlin Currie*.

26. Entry for September 26, 1926, Currie's diary, courtesy of Roger Sandilands.

27. Laidler and Sandilands, "Early Harvard Memorandum," reproduced the full text of the 1932 memorandum, the original of which is in SMLP-1, box 12.

28. Ibid., 546–52; emphasis in original.

29. Keynes, *Economic Consequences of the Peace*, and "German Transfer Problem"; Republican Party Platform, June 14, 1932, https://www.presidency.ucsb.edu/documents/republican-party-platform-1932.

Chapter 3. A Brief Academic Career

1. The title and salary are from White's application for a research fellowship from the Social Science Research Council in September 1933, SMLP-2.

2. Craig, *Treasonable Doubt*, 30.

3. See White's fellowship application to the Social Science Research Council, SMLP-2.

4. Taussig to White, September 4, 1933, SMLP-2. Curiously, Taussig's invitation to White initially included reviewing a book by Jacob Viner, but in the event that book (*Studies in the Theory of International Trade*) was not published until 1937.

5. Taussig to White, May 7, 1934, SMLP-2.

6. Harry's manuscript is in SMLP-2, as is a draft of his letter to the *JPE* withdrawing it from consideration. Also see Viner, "Mihail Manoilescu," and Ohlin, "Protectionism."

7. Lecture notes, January 1948, reprinted in Schumpeter, *History*, 1145; emphasis in original.

8. These notes are in SMLP-2. They comprise around 130 pages of handwritten notes, including outlines of potential chapters, a few pages of rough first drafts, notes on books and papers that he was reading, and the occasional

doodle. One page from the middle of a grant application is in the midst of this jumble of papers. That page is the source of the quotation in the preceding paragraph.

9. This quotation is from a handwritten draft of the letter that Harry kept in his own papers and is now in SMLP-2. I have cleaned up the transcription slightly, for example by expanding "int. econ. relations" into "international economic relations," and by breaking the passage into two paragraphs.

10. Viner to White, June 7, 1934, SMLP-2.

Chapter 4. What Next?

1. Gold Reserve Act of 1934, Public Law 73-87, 73rd Congress, H.R. 6976, January 30, 1934, https://fraser.stlouisfed.org/title/?id=1085.

2. For a review of the origins of the Brains Trust in 1932 and 1933, see Edwards, "Academics as Economic Advisers."

3. Specifically, Viner's offer for three months' work was one-third of Harry's academic-year salary and pension benefits plus $200, which works out to about $1,200, or $4,800 at an annual rate. Viner's letters are in SMLP-2.

4. Currie and White were part of a team of economists with temporary appointments to form the Currency and Banking Study Group. The others were Albert G. Hart and Benjamin Caplan, both from the University of Chicago; and Virginius Frank Coe and Edward C. Simmons, both from the Brookings Institution. See U.S. Treasury Press Release of June 24, 1934, box 62, Tax Reform Programs and Studies, Records of the Office of Tax Analysis/Division of Tax Research, General Records of the Department of the Treasury, Record Group 56, National Archives, College Park, Md., http://www.taxhistory.org/Civilization/Documents/Surveys/hst8677-1.html.

5. Unidentified, undated clipping, SMLP-2.

6. Harry White to Anne Terry White, June 26, July 12, and July 26, 1934, SMLP-2.

7. Harry White to Joan White, July 4, 1934, SMLP-2.

8. William Jennings Bryan, speech to the Democratic Party convention, July 9, 1896, http://historymatters.gmu.edu/d/5354/.

9. See especially Fisher, *Stabilizing the Dollar*. For a recent exposition placing Fisher's ideas in historical context, see Edwards, "Academics as Economic Advisers."

10. Keynes, *Treatise on Money*, 299. The "barbarous relic" characterization is in Keynes, *A Tract on Monetary Reform*, 172.

11. Keynes, *Essays in Persuasion*, 183.

12. Laidler, "Rules," nicely summarizes the history of the economic debate over rules vs. discretion in monetary and exchange rate policies. See Rauchway, *Money Makers*, for a detailed account of the warfare within the administration over gold policy.

13. The theory underlying the trilemma was developed in the 1950s by the economists Marcus Fleming and Robert Mundell. For the history of that development, see Boughton, "On the Origins."

14. "Selection of a Monetary Standard for the United States," chap. 15, SMLP-1, box 1.

15. Flood and Isard, "Monetary Policy Strategies." For a history of the use of the gold standard as a contingent rule, see Bordo and Kydland, "Gold Standard as a Rule."

16. Harry White to Anne Terry White, June 29 and July 13, 1934, SMLP-2.

Chapter 5. Settling into Morgenthau's Treasury, 1934–36

1. Harry White to Anne Terry White, July 13 and 16, 1934, SMLP-2.

2. As noted in chapter 3, Harry had applied for a job at the Tariff Commission in 1930 but had withdrawn that application in order to stay at Harvard and pursue an academic career. The commission appears to have been prepared to hire him at that time. See Sidney Morgan, commission secretary, to White, January 16, 1931, SMLP-2. On Haas's background, see Fiorito and Nerozzi, "Viner's Reminiscences," 122n32; and "Treasury Hold Strengthened by Morgenthau," *Chicago Tribune*, September 6, 1934, 23.

3. Treasury appointment letter, November 1, 1934, SMLP-2.

4. Wriston to White, March 1, 1935, and White to Wriston, March 9, 1935, both in SMLP-2.

5. Rees, *Harry Dexter White: A Study in Paradox*, 63, states that the Whites initially lived on Kalmia Road, farther north, toward the Maryland suburbs. He does not give a source for that assertion. Harry's correspondence states clearly that the family moved to the Madison St. address when Anne arrived in September 1934. In March 1935 Henry Wriston sent his letters to White at the Madison St. address.

6. Haas to Morgenthau, memorandum drafted by White, "Managed Currency and the Gold Standard," January 22, 1935, NARA-RG56, box 1. The warning against competitive devaluation is on p. 8. Also see Robinson, "Beggar-My-Neighbour." (Oddly, most modern references to her use of the term render the phrase as "beggar thy [not 'my'] neighbour.")

7. The document, in NARA-RG56, box 1, is headed "Subject: Monetary Policy." It is unaddressed and undated, but this copy (in White's chronological file) is marked in White's handwriting, "Draft submitted to Mr. Haas 11/13/35." The quoted phrase is in the introduction, on p. 1.

8. Ibid., 19. The quotations in the next three paragraphs are from pp. 21–25.

9. Morgenthau to White, April 5, 1935, SMLP-2.

10. Harry White (aboard the *Europa*) to Anne Terry White, April 7, 1935, SMLP-2.

11. Harry White to Anne Terry White on stationery of the Hôtel de Crillon, April 14, 1935, SMLP-2.

12. See White to his division chief, George C. Haas, memoranda, "Personal Report on London Trip" and "Summary of Conversations," both June 13, 1935, SMLP-1, box 1, item 4a. For the British reactions, see Drummond, *Floating Pound*, 192, and his citations of documents in the British Treasury archives. On the State Department reaction, see a secondhand report given in a 1974 oral history interview by John P. Young (a State Department official during World War II), in HSTL, https://www.trumanlibrary.gov/library/oral-histories/youngjp. Harry's personal reaction is in a letter he sent to Anne from the Hague on April 27, 1935, SMLP-2.

13. See Blum, *From the Morgenthau Diaries: Years of Crisis*, 138–49.

14. Minutes of the meeting (unsigned), January 28, 1936, MD 16:70–71.

15. Haas to Morgenthau, memorandum drafted by White, "Restrictions on gold exports," January 29, 1936, NARA-RG56, box 1.

16. Transcript of a meeting, June 4, 1936, MD 26:1–4.

17. For an overview of French policy in this period, see Mouré, *Managing the Franc*, chaps. 6 and 7.

18. The photograph is reproduced in Sandilands, *Life and Political Economy of Lauchlin Currie*, 81.

19. For the exchange on Eccles between Viner and Morgenthau, see transcript of a meeting, September 18, 1936, MD 33:30–32.

20. For Currie's interventions with Eccles, see Sandilands, *Life and Political Economy of Lauchlin Currie*, 97, and Currie, "Recent Developments."

21. Morgenthau to Henrietta Klotz, September 18, 1936, MD 33:78.

22. Haas to Morgenthau, memorandum drafted by White, "Notes on the Foreign Situation," December 28, 1934, 3, NARA-RG56, box 1. For White's analysis of the desperate state of China's finances, see White to Haas, memorandum, "China's Monetary and Banking Systems," August 8, 1935, NARA-RG56, box 1. For more recent analyses of the effects on the Chinese economy, see Friedman, "Franklin D. Roosevelt," and Burdekin, "U.S. Pressure on China." Burdekin disputes Friedman's conclusion that U.S. silver purchases greatly weakened the real economy in China, but both agree that the financial effects were large.

23. It is not clear whether, when, or to whom he sent the note. It was undated but filed chronologically between memoranda dated November 5 and 15, 1934; NARA-RG56, box 1.

24. For Hull's response, see FRUS, 1935, 3:539–40. For background, see Horesh, *Shanghai's Bund*, 140–41.

25. Entry for October 29, 1935, note by Morgenthau, MD 10:247–51.

26. Ibid., 247. Leith-Ross recounted his mission to China in *Money Talks*, 195–226. For further discussion, see Horesh, *Shanghai's Bund*, 139–50.

27. Haas to Morgenthau, memorandum drafted by White, "Supplement to Report on China Submitted September 3, 1935," November 1, 1935, NARA-RG56, box 1.

28. White to Morgenthau, memorandum, "China—Her exchange situation (preliminary draft)," April 17, 1936, MD 21:197–202. Also see Haas

to Morgenthau, memorandum drafted by White, "China," April 9, 1936, NARA-RG56, box 1. Blum, *From the Morgenthau Diaries: Years of Crisis*, 223, discusses the latter memorandum.

29. Bordo, Humpage, and Schwartz, *Strained Relations*, 109.

Chapter 6. Rising into a Position of Influence, 1936–38

1. Treasury appointment letter, October 1, 1936, and Morgenthau to White, July 1, 1937, both in SMLP-2.

2. For the 1936 effort to own a farm, see White to Emil Hakkinen, October 9, 1936, SMLP-2. Hakkinen was an orderly assigned to White when they were in the U.S. Army in France during World War I. They remained friends, but Hakkinen was not available to manage the farm. The background on "Marginal Acres" is from a personal communication from the Currie family to Roger Sandilands in 2013. The timing of the 1937 summer vacation in New Hampshire is from Anne's personal scrapbooks, in the family collection.

3. See White to Mr. and Mrs. William E. Preston (owners of the property), September 17, 1937, SMLP-2.

4. White to George C. Haas, memoranda: "Outline Analysis of Current Situation," February 26, 1935, SMLP-1, box 2 (cited in Rauchway, *Money Makers*, 272n38); "Silver Program Proposed by Senator Thomas," March 14, 1935, NARA-RG56, box 1; and "Recovery Program: The International Monetary Aspect," March 15, 1935, SMLP-1, box 2.

5. On the relationship between Federal Reserve and Treasury policies in contributing to the recession and its resolution, see Meltzer, *History*, chap. 6.

6. Stein, *Fiscal Revolution*, 102.

7. Viner to Morgenthau, April 14, 1938, MD 121:289.

8. Transcript of meeting on "Aid to China," February 2, 1942, MD 491.1:79.

9. White, "Effects of increase in the gold price of the dollar," marked, "[Original] to Mr. Haas," and dated "3/27/37" under White's initials on the last page; NARA-RG56, box 1.

10. Transcript of a meeting with Morgenthau and other Treasury officials on March 29, 1937, pp. 17–18, MD 61:215–53.

11. Transcript of a meeting on May 9, 1938, MD 124.1:8–18.

12. Transcripts of meetings on December 9, 10, and 12, 1938, MD 155.1:162–200 and MD 155.2:50–100, 117–51.

13. Report marked "Prepared by Currie and White, read at Meeting 12-12-38," MD 155.2:152–53.

14. Morgenthau's summary of the meeting with White is in MD 194.1:8. For a summary exposition of the context and the outcome, see Blum, *From the Morgenthau Diaries: Years of Urgency*, 36–42.

15. See especially "The Gold Problem: Summary of Analysis," September 15, 1937, SMLP-1, box 3, item 8e.

16. Eichengreen, *Golden Fetters*, 384. For a recent empirical assessment of the French supply shock and references to other sources, see Cohen-Setton,

Hausman, and Wieland, "Supply-Side Policies." Also see Meltzer, *History*, chap. 6. Meltzer attributes the limited success of the agreement primarily to a failure to understand real (price-level-adjusted) exchange rates.

17. White to Morgenthau, memorandum, "What should our answer be to the British Treasury as to our attitude toward further depreciation of the franc?" April 30, 1938, NARA-RG56, box 2.

18. The 1934 quotation is from White, "Selection of a Monetary Standard for the United States," chap. 17. For the 1936 proposal, see Haas to Morgenthau, memorandum drafted by White, January 11, 1936, "Increase in reserves against deposits in this country owned by residents of foreign countries," NARA-RG56, box 1.

19. Fisher, *100% Money*. For a historical review of the 100 percent reserve proposal, see Lainà, "Proposals."

20. For the 1942 quotation, see the White Plan in Horsefield, *International Monetary Fund*, 3:13. Also see Currie, "Domestic Stability."

21. The phrase appears in paragraph 45 of the February 11, 1942, version of Keynes's "Proposals for an International Currency (or Clearing) Union," in Horsefield, *International Monetary Fund*, 3:13. Keynes used it again in paragraph 31 of the version that Frederick Phillips sent to White on August 28, 1942, in Keynes, *Collected Writings of John Maynard Keynes*, vol. 25 (hereafter cited as KCW-25), 185.

22. For brief reviews of the practice in Latin America, see Díaz Alejandro, "Stories of the 1930s," sec. 1.2, and Bulmer-Thomas, *Economic History*, 219–20.

23. This equivalence was part of economic orthodoxy by the early postwar period. For examples, see Bernstein, "Some Economic Aspects," and Schlesinger, *Multiple Exchange Rates*. The debate is summarized in Blum, *From the Morgenthau Diaries: Years of Crisis*, 149–55.

24. Cordell Hull to Morgenthau, April 2, 1936, MD 20:35–37.

25. Summary of discussion, April 10, 1936, MD 20:341.

26. Viner's report is in MD 21:7–20.

27. White to Haas, "Applicability of Section 303 of the Tariff Act to certain German exports," May 16, 1936, NARA-RG56, box 1.

28. Blum, *From the Morgenthau Diaries: Years of Crisis*, 153–55.

29. Morgenthau (first draft by White) to Roosevelt, October 10, 1938, MD 146:140–41.

30. Transcript of meeting, October 11, 1938, MD 145.2:80.

31. Letter to the editor, *Times* (London), October 5, 1936, in Keynes, *Collected Writings of John Maynard Keynes*, vol. 21, 483.

32. Morgenthau (second draft by White) to Roosevelt, October 15, 1938, MD 146:126.

33. Gold Reserve Act of 1934, section 10(b), https://fraser.stlouisfed.org/title/gold-reserve-act-1934-1085; emphasis added. The first detailed history and analysis of the ESF was by Arthur I. Bloomfield in 1944 ("Operations of the American Exchange Stabilization Fund"). Bloomfield acknowledged that he

was hampered by the secrecy of ESF operations up to that time. For a more recent and informed description of the origin and early activities of the ESF, see Bordo, Humpage, and Schwartz, *Strained Relations*, chap. 3.

34. The ESF's silver purchases are detailed in Bordo, Humpage, and Schwartz, *Strained Relations*, 110–15.

35. White to Haas, memorandum, "Use of the Stabilization Fund," June 15, 1935. White repeated the argument with much the same wording in section V of his November 13, 1935, memorandum, "Monetary Policy." Both memoranda are in NARA-RG56, box 1.

36. The 1999 scheme is discussed in Boughton, *Tearing Down Walls*, 665–72.

37. Morgenthau, aide-mémoire, December 8, 1935, MD 13:120–22.

38. Minutes of meeting, December 31, 1935, MD 14:336–40.

39. Minutes of meeting, January 2, 1936, MD 15:11. The formal agreement, in the form of a letter from the Treasury secretary to the New York Fed, is reproduced in Bordo and Schwartz, "From the Exchange Stabilization Fund."

40. White to Morgenthau, memorandum, May 18, 1938, reporting on a meeting with a State Department official, Herbert Feis, MD 125.2:19–20.

41. For a list of credit arrangements and a brief history of the ESF, see the U.S. Treasury website at https://www.treasury.gov/resource-center/international/ESF/Pages/history-index.aspx. For further discussion, see Henning, *Exchange Stabilization Fund*.

42. Boughton, *Tearing Down Walls*, chap. 10. For a criticism of the roles of the IMF and the ESF in the Mexican crisis, see Schwartz, "From Obscurity to Notoriety."

43. Eichengreen and Irwin, "Trade Blocs," 8.

44. This conclusion has been supported for the postwar era by recent research at the Federal Reserve Bank of New York. See Goldberg, "International Role," and Goldberg and Tille, "Internationalization." For a more skeptical view of developments in the 1930s, see Eichengreen and Irwin, "Trade Blocs." For a critical analysis of the argument that the dollar's international status confers large benefits on the United States, see Eichengreen, *Exorbitant Privilege*.

45. White to Morgenthau, memorandum, "Liberian proposal to purchase U.S. currency," October 9, 1939, MD 216.2:150–51. More background is in a series of cables and memoranda in the same file: 152–73.

46. Transcript of a telephone call between White and Luthringer, October 9, 1939, MD 216.2:148–49.

47. White to Daniel W. Bell, memoranda, "The need for more coins in Liberia," March 16, 1942, and "Letter from Mr. Berle on Liberian Coinage," April 23, 1942, both in NARA-RG56, box 7. The first memorandum was drafted primarily by Frank Southard, the second by J. S. deBeers.

48. Southard and J. S. deBeers to White, memorandum, "Meeting on Liberian coinage in the State Department, May 8, 1942," May 9, 1942, and White to Morgenthau, memorandum drafted by Southard, May 27, 1942, both in NARA-RG56, box 7.

Chapter 7. Preparing for War, 1937–41

1. Transcript of a meeting, April 25, 1938, MD 120:265. Also see appointment letter and Treasury Department Order no. 18, both dated March 25, 1938, SMLP-2. The order describing the new division and its responsibilities is also in U.S. Treasury, *Annual Report for 1938*, 329–30.

2. White to Messersmith, November 7, 1941, SMLP-2. For a summary of Anne's writing career, see her biography on Encyclopedia.com, https://www .encyclopedia.com/arts/news-wires-white-papers-and-books/white-anne -terry.

3. White to Morgenthau, memorandum, "Preliminary report on the possibilities of depriving the aggressor countries of needed strategic war materials," MD 176:279–94. (Other copies are in NARA-RG56, box 2, and SMLP-1, box 6.) The memorandum is dated April 8, 1939, at the top of p. 1 and is marked 4/8/39 at the top of each page; but it is marked 4/10/39 at the bottom of pp. 6 and 8, probably indicating that those pages were revised before White took the memorandum to Morgenthau on April 10. The bottom of p. 1 has a notation that the secretary handed the memorandum to Roosevelt on the 10th. Blum's 1964 account states that Morgenthau persuaded Roosevelt to take appropriate action on April 11.

4. Blum, *From the Morgenthau Diaries: Years of Urgency*, 90, wrote that Harry had opposed these actions, but he seems to have misinterpreted Harry's message. Although much of the memorandum dealt with the limitations and potential costs (a typical "two-handed economist" tactic), the conclusion clearly favored going ahead.

5. White, first draft (October 10, 1938), of Morgenthau to Roosevelt, October 17, 1938, MD 146:145–46.

6. Quoted in Nathan White, *Harry Dexter White: Loyal American*, 41.

7. The full text of White's first draft is in MD 146:135–54. Comments on it by Morgenthau and others are in MD 145.2:77–95. Subsequent drafts and the final text are in MD 146:107–134; Morgenthau's letter to the president, as delivered, is on pp. 107–9.

8. See transcript of a meeting between Morgenthau and a State Department official, Herbert Feis, September 7, 1937, MD 87.2:46–54. Also see minutes of a meeting on June 6, 1938, at which Morgenthau debated the case with Under Secretary of State Sumner Welles, who was presenting Hull's views, and a note of the same date from White (who had attended the meeting) to Morgenthau, MD 127:304–15.

9. Transcript of a meeting, July 8, 1937, MD 78:28. Blum, *From the Morgenthau Diaries: Years of Crisis*, 482–85.

10. White to Morgenthau, memorandum, "Proposal to extend through the Export-Import Bank a long-term loan to China of $50,000,000 to be used to purchase surplus food crops from the United States and possibly some cotton," May 18, 1938, and White and Harold Glasser to Morgenthau, "re: this

morning's conference on Chinese and Haitian loans," June 6, 1938, both in NARA-RG56, box 2. That copy of the June 6 note is marked "HDW:HG:ls 6/6/38" at the bottom of the last page, indicating that Glasser prepared an initial draft at White's direction. Morgenthau's own copy, in MD 127:304–7, lacks that notation but is marked "HDW" in White's handwriting at the bottom of the final page.

11.   For the negotiation and terms of this loan, see Blum, *From the Morgenthau Diaries: Years of Urgency*, 58–63. Blum cites a figure of $26 million for the amount of the loan, but the internal records of the Exim Bank (provided to me pursuant to a request under the Freedom of Information Act) give the amount as $25 million.

12.   White to Morgenthau, memorandum, March 31, 1939, reflecting a first draft by Glasser, NARA-RG56, box 2.

13.   Minutes of meeting between K. P. Chen and Morgenthau, November 8, 1939, MD 221.2:172.

14.   White to Morgenthau, memorandum, "Utilization of our gold holdings," November 20, 1939, NARA-RG56, box 3; White to Morgenthau, memorandum, "'Tin Loan' to China" (November 22, 1939, MD 223:219–21. Also see Blum, *From the Morgenthau Diaries: Years of Urgency*: 123–25.

15.   White to Morgenthau, unsigned note, "The Chinese Ambassador's informal request for advice apropos Chiang Kai-shek's telegram to the President for financial aid," dated in pencil "5-22-40," NARA-RG56, box 3.

16.   "Message for the President," submitted by White to Morgenthau on July 1, 1940, and taken by Morgenthau to Roosevelt, MD 278:87–90.

17.   Blum, *From the Morgenthau Diaries: Years of Urgency*, 347, attributed this scheme to Harry, but the record shows that Morgenthau raised the idea with Soong on July 9. Harry then drafted a formal proposal, which he circulated on July 15. White, draft memorandum for the president, "Preliminary Report on the Feasibility of Financial Assistance to China," July 15, 1940, MD 282.2:90–91.

18.   "Statement by the President," November 30, 1940, MD 334:34. The internal records of the Exim Bank show that the $50 million loan was approved on that date for exports of "strategic materials," guaranteed by the Central Bank of China.

19.   Currie's mission is discussed in Sandilands, *Life and Political Economy of Lauchlin Currie*, 107–12.

20.   See White to Morgenthau, memorandum, "Conversation with Miss Strong about China," February 27, 1941, MD 376:227. White's copy of the memorandum is in NARA-RG56, box 4.

21.   The telephone conversation is summarized in a letter from White to Hemingway, January 27, 1941, MD 351.1:60. The quotation from Hemingway is from Hemingway to Morgenthau, July 30, 1941, MD 433:288.

22.   Hemingway to Morgenthau, July 30, 1941, 5, MD 433:293. For the meeting between Hemingway and Currie, see Moreira, *Hemingway*, 39–40. Moreira

describes the circumstances behind Hemingway's letter on pp. 65–66, on the basis of a letter that Bond sent to Carlos Baker (Hemingway's biographer) in 1966. The letter apparently contained little of substance, as Hemingway was relying on Bond to report orally to White.

23. White to Morgenthau, memorandum, "Hemingway's and Bond's Comments on Chinese Transportation," May 29, 1941, MD 402:215–16.

24. Hemingway's letter, White's reports on it, Morgenthau's cover note to Roosevelt, and Morgenthau's thank-you letter to Hemingway are in MD 433:279–94.

25. White to Morgenthau, memorandum, "Suggested Approach for Elimination of United States–Japan Tension," November 17, 1941, MD 462.2:159–72. The quotations are from pp. 159 and 161.

26. The proposal to expel Germans was not in White's November 17 memorandum to Morgenthau. It was inserted into the final version that Morgenthau sent to Roosevelt on November 18. The rest of the proposal was unchanged.

27. "Memorandum for the President," draft of July 19, 1940, MD 284:131. Morgenthau and White discussed the proposal at two meetings on that date; see MD 284:210–34. Follow-up memoranda are in MD 288:282–92.

28. See FRUS, *Japan: 1931–1941*, 2:264–65; and Blum, *From the Morgenthau Diaries: Years of Urgency*, 377–80.

29. Morgenthau's November 18, 1941, letter to the president (copied to Hull), with attached memorandum, "An Approach to the Problem of Eliminating Tension with Japan and Helping Defeat of Germany," is in MD 463.1:149–65. Morgenthau recounted his interaction with Roosevelt on this topic at a staff meeting on November 24, 1941; MD 464:139–40. Also see Blum, *From the Morgenthau Diaries: Years of Urgency*, 384–86.

30. White's draft, November 27, 1941, along with a second draft with the same date and an insertion by Bernard Bernstein, are in NARA-RG56, box 6. The bulk of Morgenthau's draft is reproduced in Blum, *From the Morgenthau Diaries: Years of Urgency*, 389–91. Blum found the letter among Morgenthau's personal papers at the FDR Library. He seems to have been unaware it was based on a draft by White.

31. White Plan (April 1942); Horsefield, *Twenty Years: Documents*, 63.

32. Morgenthau (marked as drafted, in turn, by Harry White, Bernard Bernstein, and Herman Oliphant) to Roosevelt, November 5, 1938, NARA-RG56, box 2.

33. For Morgenthau's indifference to Brazil's arrears to the private sector, see Blum, *From the Morgenthau Diaries: Years of Urgency*, 52. The rationale for asking for congressional action and the draft resolution are set out in a draft memorandum for the president, February 14, 1939, MD 207.2:170–73. Herbert Feis stated the State Department's objections to the use of the ESF at a meeting on February 15, 1939, MD 207.2:181–82.

34. For Roosevelt's negative reaction to the Treasury proposal, see transcript of Morgenthau's meeting with White and others at 5:20 P.M. on February 15, 1939, MD 207.2:183–86.
35. See paraphrase of White to Morgenthau, telegram, July 23,1940, and Morgenthau's reply, MD 286:150–54.
36. Sumner Welles to Ellis O. Briggs (chargé at the U.S. embassy in Havana), telegram, September 25, 1941, *FRUS*, 1941, vol. 7, document 164. Morgenthau's agreement for White to be made available and to be the chief of mission was made in Morgenthau to Cordell Hull that same day, MD 444:217.
37. Messersmith to White, November 3, 1941, SMLP-2; and Messersmith to Philip S. Bonsal, November 17, 1941, GSM.
38. The final report, "The Central Bank and Stabilization Fund," April 22, 1942, is in SMLP-1, box 6. A preliminary version, prepared in advance of a meeting with the Cuban finance minister in Washington and sent by White to Morgenthau on March 20, 1942, is in MD 509:307–28.
39. On prewar currency boards, see Greaves, *Colonial Monetary Conditions*, and Newlyn, "Colonial Empire." On postwar usage, see Ghosh, Gulde, and Wolf, "Currency Boards," and Hanke, "Currency Boards."
40. "Inter-American Bank," *Federal Reserve Bulletin* (June 1940): 517–25. Also see Helleiner, *Forgotten Origins*, chap. 2.
41. White, "Loans to Latin America for the Industrial Development of Latin America," June 6, 1939, in Morgenthau's "Program to Increase National Income in 1940," MD 196:68–73.
42. Berle to Morgenthau, February 27, 1940, MD 243:196.
43. Blum, *From the Morgenthau Diaries: Years of Urgency*: 57; Collado interview, July 11, 1974, HSTL, https://www.trumanlibrary.gov/library/oral-histories/collado2.
44. White to Morgenthau, memorandum, March 31, 1939, NARA-RG56, box 2. White to Morgenthau, memorandum, "Argentina," May 12, 1939, MD 189.2:76–83. The May 12 memorandum is annotated as having been drafted "chiefly" by Simon Hanson, an expert on Latin America in White's division.
45. Archie Lochhead, memorandum, May 10, 1939, MD 189.1:224. The author of the memorandum is not identified on the document, but the table of contents for the volume attributes it to Lochhead.
46. In the indexes to John Morton Blum's biography of Morgenthau and James McGregor Burns's biography of Roosevelt, the entry for the Soviet Union redirects to Russia.
47. Gaddis, *United States and the Origins of the Cold War*, 37.
48. White first circulated this proposal to Morgenthau in an untitled memorandum on March 31, 1939, NARA-RG56, box 2. A revised version dated June 5, 1939, was included in a briefing book for Morgenthau on the program for economic recovery, MD 196:75–77.
49. White to Morgenthau, June 5, 1939, MD 196:75.

50. White, untitled, five-page, double-spaced manuscript dated June 15, 1940, SMLP-1, box 6.

51. Blum, *From the Morgenthau Diaries: Years of Crisis*, 57.

52. See the transcript and summary of a meeting, October 17, 1940, between Morgenthau and Ambassador Constantin Oumansky, MD 323:59–69.

53. Transcript of a meeting, July 3, 1941, MD 418.1:25–32.

54. White, file memorandum, September 30, 1941, and White to Morgenthau, memorandum, October 29, 1941, both in NARA-RG56, box 5. Also see the report on the meeting that White drafted to send to Averill Harriman in Moscow, MD 445:35.

55. Transcript of a meeting, July 15, 1940, MD 282.2:170.

56. Gass to White, memorandum, "The Value to the United States of Sovereignty over the British Dependencies in the Americas (excluding Newfoundland and Canada)," November 27, 1940, NARA RG-56, box 4. Also see the report by Keynes to a meeting of British ministers, August 23, 1945, in *Collected Writings of John Maynard Keynes*, vol. 24 (hereafter cited as KCW-24), 423.

57. Churchill to Roosevelt, December 7, 1940, MD 337.1:24–43.

58. "Notes on Meeting at the White House with the President at 2:30 P.M., Sunday, December 1, 1940, Concerning Orders Which the British Wish to Place for Airplanes, Munitions, and Ships," MD 334:6–8.

59. For a summary of Lend-Lease activity, see https://history.state.gov/milestones/1937-1945/lend-lease.

60. Including postwar shipments, Lend-Lease assistance totaled $50.2 billion. Net of repayments and reverse shipments, aid totaled around $40 billion. U.S. Congress, Senate Committee on Finance, 93rd Congress, *Foreign Indebtedness to the United States: Briefing Material for the Subcommittee on International Finance and Resources* (October 29, 1973), 5.

61. White's draft, subsequent redrafts, including the tables, and the final text of Morgenthau's testimony are in MD 351.2:15–63. Also see quotation from Morgenthau's testimony in White's draft, "Memorandum for the President: Policy on Lend-Lease and British Dollar Balances," November 17, 1943, MD 678.1:167–71.

62. Transcript of a meeting, February 28, 1941, MD 377:88.

63. See a series of memoranda, White to Morgenthau, August 14, 1941, conveying reports from Coe on Lend-Lease to Great Britain, MD 433:87–96. Additional information on Coe's mission is in NARA-RG56, box 5.

64. Transcript of a meeting, August 15, 1941, in MD 433:169–200.

Chapter 8. The Treasury Goes to War, 1941–43

1. Treasury Department Order no. 43, December 15, 1943. This order was a public announcement of decisions made by Morgenthau a week earlier, on December 8.

2. The decision to ask White to take on the additional responsibility was made at a meeting on February 22, 1943; see MD 611:55–60. For the directive, dated February 25, see MD 612:73. An earlier draft of the directive (dated February 23) described the assignment in slightly more general terms, asking White to "assume full responsibility for the Treasury's participation in all matters affecting foreign fiscal relations arising in connection with the operations of the Army and Navy"; document in SMLP-2.

3. "People of the Week," *United States News*, April 16, 1943, 58.

4. The questions and answers are in SMLP-2.

5. For Morgenthau's directive, see MD 352:67. A scrapbook in SMLP-2 includes a brief newspaper account of the trip, including a photograph of White and two companions on a fishing boat. Anne Terry White to Ruth White, August 6, 1943, ATWP.

6. Letters and scrapbooks of Anne Terry White, family collection.

7. Anne Terry White, tribute to Morgenthau, November 1942, MD 628:82–92.

8. From 1938 to 1945, the committee was formally known as the Special Committee to Investigate Un-American Activities. From 1945 to 1969, its formal name was the House Committee on Un-American Activities. Dies was its chairman from its inception to 1944. The committee was dissolved in 1975.

9. Storrs, *Second Red Scare*, 54–55.

10. For the "Underclerk" confusion, see FBI report of January 5, 1942, file 101-4053, FBI-FOIA, "White," sec. 1:3.

11. The investigation is detailed in FBI file 101-4053, FBI-FOIA, "White," sec. 1. The quoted passages are on pp. 8 and 16.

12. Silvermaster's record of employment in the federal government is in his official "Statement of Federal Service," which the U.S. Civil Service Commission provided to me upon request.

13. Robert P. Patterson to Milo Perkins, head of the Board of Economic Warfare, July 3, 1942, SMLP-2.

14. Transcript of a meeting on "Lend-Lease in Reverse, Russia," December 17, 1943, MD 685:6–11. Another Treasury official, Robert E. McConnell, was also present as an expert on industry requirements.

15. White, "Ten Billion Dollar Reconstruction Arrangement with Russia," January 5, 1944, MD 691:129–31.

16. White to Morgenthau, memorandum, "Proposed U.S. Loan to the U.S.S.R.," March 7, 1944, MD 707:63–74. Also see White, file memorandum, March 18, 1944, MD 711:225–26. For a summary history of the negotiations, see draft memorandum for the president, January 16, 1945, NARA-RG56, box 12.

17. White, "Ten Billion Dollar Reconstruction Arrangement with Russia," January 5, 1944, MD 691:131.

18. "A $10 Billion Reconstruction Credit for the U.S.S.R.," January 10, 1945, MD 808:312–14. See Blum, *From the Morgenthau Diaries: Years of War*, 304–6, for a discussion of the endgame of these negotiations.

19. "Memorandum for the Secretary's files," January 9, 1942, MD 483.2:96–97. The report does not attribute the quoted conclusion on risk to White, but he is the only likely source of it.

20. "Chronology of China Loan Proposal Beginning December 31, 1941," prepared by Frank Coe, Irving Friedman, and Frank Southard in installments from January 30 to March 26, 1942, NARA-RG56, box 6.

21. In addition to the chronology cited in the preceding note, see memorandum for files on a meeting between Soong and White on February 16, 1942, MD 497:221; memorandum for files on a meeting between Soong and U.S. officials on February 19, 1942, MD 498.1:202–5; memorandum for files on a meeting of U.S. officials at the Treasury on February 20, 1942, , to which is attached the first draft of the loan agreement, MD 499.1:208–11; Soong to Daniel W. Bell, March 3, 1942, MD 503.3:67–68; and memorandum for files on a meeting of Treasury officials on March 6, 1942, MD 505:97.

22. See the chronology cited in n. 20; a memorandum for files on a meeting of Treasury officials in White's office on March 20, 1942, MD 509.2:184; transcript of a telephone conversation between Morgenthau and Sumner Welles on March 21, MD 510:6–7; and Soong to Morgenthau, March 21, 1942, promising to keep him informed of the intended uses of the loan proceeds, MD 510:8.

23. Memorandum for files on a meeting in the secretary's office, April 11, 1942, MD 515:276–77.

24. White, memorandum for files on a meeting with Morgenthau on September 29, 1943, MD 668:73–74. Also see Kung to T. V. Soong, telegram, November 17, 1943, agreeing to the termination of the 1941 agreement, NARA-RG56, box 10.

25. White, memorandum for files, September 29, 1943, MD 668:73–74. For a broader discussion of the debate and its outcome, see Blum, *From the Morgenthau Diaries: Years of War*, 87–122, and Rees, *Harry Dexter White: A Study in Paradox*, 154–72.

26. Planning at this stage was preliminary. The venue and date for the summit were firmed up only on November 2, when Chiang accepted Roosevelt's invitation. For background, see Heiferman, *Cairo Conference*.

27. Morgenthau summarized his own itinerary in a joint radio address with Eisenhower, broadcast from Allied Headquarters in Algiers on October 23, 1943. The prepared remarks for the broadcast are in MD 671:89–99. For the instructions to Adler, see MD 670:200–201.

28. MD 685 includes a transcript of the December 17 meeting on pp. 29–36; the December 18 draft prepared by Edward Bernstein and others is on pp. 185–87; and a transcript of a December 20 meeting of Morgenthau, White, and Bernstein is on pp. 182–84.

29. Transcript of a meeting on "China loans," January 18, 1944, MD 695:56–61. Also see transcripts of earlier meetings and related documents in MD 693:59–65 and 108–21.

30. Transcript of a meeting on "China Loans," January 18, 1944, MD 695:56–
      61. Morgenthau had recently read *Shark's Fins and Millet*, a book by the Pol-
      ish journalist Ilona Ralf Sues, based on her years in China, including a stint
      working for Madame Chiang Kai-shek. In this meeting Morgenthau told
      Harry that the book confirmed "what we have always known."

31. Morgenthau to Hu Shih, December 30, 1944, MD 805:306.

32. Transcripts of meetings on "Gold to China," May 15 and 16, 1945, MD
      847:24–38, 50–60. The "rat hole" mention is on pp. 29 and 56; "distasteful"
      follows it on the latter page.

33. Transcripts of meetings on May 16, 1945, MD 847. Clayton's expression of
      reluctance is on p. 57, and his draft letter to Truman is on p. 59. Morgen-
      thau's meeting with Soong is on pp. 62–66.

34. See "Preliminary Agreement between the United States and the United
      Kingdom, February 23, 1942," signed by Sumner Welles (as acting secretary
      of state) and Lord Halifax (British ambassador), http://avalon.law.yale.edu/
      20th_century/decade04.asp. For a discussion, see Blum, *From the Morgen-
      thau Diaries: Years of War*, 122–27.

35. Memorandum for files on a meeting of Phillips, Morgenthau, and White,
      December 22, 1941, MD 476.1:132–33. Exchange of letters between Phil-
      lips and Daniel Bell, January 8, 14, and 22, 1942, MD 487.1:241–45. White
      to Morgenthau, memorandum, March 12, 1942, with an attached report,
      "British Dollar Position in 1942," MD 508.2:103–51.

36. For the origin of the $600 million floor, see transcript of a meeting at the
      U.S. Treasury, June 12, 1941, MD 407:210. On March 17, 1942, during an
      interagency meeting, Morgenthau recalled that Halifax and Phillips had
      told him that they needed $600 million in dollar balances; MD 508.2:67–91.
      On December 22 Thelma Kistler (an economist on Harry's staff), during a
      meeting with Morgenthau, recalled hearing Keynes cite the $600 million
      target during a meeting at the Treasury in July 1941; MD 598.1:187–88. On
      December 23 Stettinius recalled Keynes and Catto citing that figure during
      his (Stettinius's) visit to London in 1942; MD 598.1:246 (where "Catto" is
      rendered as "Catoe" in White's report).

37. Morgenthau initiated the discussions in a telephone call to Acheson on De-
      cember 22, 1942; see transcript, MD 598.1:194–99. Wallace held a seminal
      meeting with Morgenthau, White, Hull, Acheson, and Stettinius on Decem-
      ber 23, MD 598.1:245–49. Wallace's report, dated January 1, 1943, with the
      president's signature of approval, is in MD 603:23–27.

38. White, memorandum for files, "Lunch at the Secretary's invitation, Novem-
      ber 17, 1943," MD 678.1:50–52.

39. "Memorandum for the President: Policy on Lend-Lease and British Dol-
      lar Balances," November 17, 1943, MD 678.1:167–71. A second copy (MD
      678.2:1–5) is marked as drafted by Frank Coe. For the discussion of Cox's
      alternative, see White, file memorandum on a luncheon meeting that Mor-
      genthau and White held with Crowley, Cox, and Currie from the FEA on

November 23, 1943, MD 679:97–98. For the consequences, see Blum, *From the Morgenthau Diaries: Years of War*, 134–39.

40. Transcript of a meeting of the Foreign Financial Policy Committee, October 6, 1944, MD 780:6–18.

41. Robbins, *Wartime Diaries*, 244, 245.

42. Blum, *From the Morgenthau Diaries: Years of War*, 320–26.

Chapter 9. Planning for a Stable Postwar Recovery, 1941–42

1. Address by Wilson to a joint session of Congress, January 8, 1918, http://avalon.law.yale.edu/20th_century/wilson14.asp.

2. For the text of the agreement and a discussion of the context, see Burns, *Roosevelt*, 125–31.

3. White to Morgenthau, memorandum, "British Empire—American cooperation on problems of post-war reconstruction," August 14, 1941, NARA-RG56, box 5.

4. White, "Note for the Secretary's Record," December 15, 1941, MD 473.1:23.

5. White to Sumner Welles, January 6, 1942, attachment, delivered that day by special messenger, with copies to Jacob Viner at the Treasury and to the office of Laurence Duggan at the State Department, NARA-RG56, box 6.

6. Helleiner, *Forgotten Origins*.

7. Editor's commentary, KCW-25:338.

8. The British report was mentioned by Keynes in his August 1942 analysis of the April 1942 White Plan, KCW-25:161.

9. This first draft was published in 1955 as Appendix I of part 30 of an investigation by a subcommittee of the U.S. Senate Judiciary Committee. SMLP-1 holds two drafts, in boxes 3 and 4; an earlier draft is in SMLP-2. I have a copy of the preliminary draft, given to me by Harry's family. It is in a pressboard report cover, which is marked in pencil, "H. Gaston copy." Herbert E. Gaston was assistant secretary of the Treasury, 1939–45.

10. White, "The Future of Gold," 1940 draft, sec. 2:11.

11. White, "The Future of Gold," 1944 draft, sect. 4:6.

12. White, "The Future of Gold," 1940 draft, sec. 3:3.

13. White, file memorandum on a meeting at the State Department held at 11:00 P.M. on January 7, 1942, IMFA-BWC, document BWC1537-01:4–5.

14. A detailed chronology can be found in Frank Southard to Daniel Bell, memorandum, "Resolution on Stabilization Fund of United and Associated Nations to be presented at the Rio Conference," January 15, 1942, NARA-RG56, box 6.

15. The text of the draft resolution was conveyed by Welles to Morgenthau in a January 18, 1942, cable; FRUS, 1942, 5:28–30. The text quoted here is from Frank Southard to Charles Schwarz, internal Treasury Department memorandum, January 20, 1942, NARA-RG56, box 6. The final text, approved as Resolution XV at the Rio conference, was published in the Department of State *Bulletin* (February 7, 1942): 127.

16. Minutes of a discussion between Phillips and Morgenthau, January 22, 1942, MD 487.1:239.
17. White, "Proposal for United Nations Stabilization Fund," April 1942. The portions of the document pertaining to the IMF were published in Horsefield, *International Monetary Fund*, 3:37–82.
18. Morgenthau to Roosevelt, memorandum, May 15, 1942, FRUS, 1942, vol. 1, document 148.
19. A copy of the president's May 16, 1942, memorandum to Morgenthau approving the continuation of "the studies now in progress" is in SMLP-2. For the transcript of the May 25 meeting, see MD 531.2:59–67.
20. Transcript of a telephone call between Hull and Morgenthau, December 8, 1941, MD 470:99.
21. For a profile of Pasvolsky and his role in creating the UN, see Schlesinger, *Act of Creation*, chap. 3. On Pasvolsky's scheme for postwar economic planning, see Penrose, *Economic Planning for the Peace*, 41n4; and Schild, *Bretton Woods and Dumbarton Oaks*, chap. 3.
22. See Dulles, *Chances of a Lifetime*, 170–73; and Srodes, *On Dupont Circle*, 275.
23. Transcript of a meeting in Morgenthau's office, July 2, 1942, and a three-page note that summarized, among other points, the reluctance expressed by State Department officials at an earlier meeting, MD 545:134–61. White's file copy of that note indicates that it was drafted by Frank Southard and that White took it to the July 2 meeting; NARA-RG56, box 8.
24. Transcript of meeting, July 2, 1942, MD 545:134–58. Also see Van Dormael, *Bretton Woods*, 54–55. That work cites the Morgenthau Diaries and a July 11, 1942, State Department memorandum in NARA-RG59, 800.515/555.

Chapter 10. Negotiating with Keynes, 1942–43

1. Keynes to Wilfried Eady, October 3, 1943, KCW-25:356; Harrod, *Life of Keynes*, 537–38. Eady was second secretary in the U.K. Treasury, overseeing the wartime Anglo-American financial negotiations.
2. Skidelsky, *John Maynard Keynes: Fighting for Britain*, 203–9.
3. KCW-25:21–33.
4. Ibid., 28; emphasis in original.
5. Keynes used the terms *clearing union* and *currency union* interchangeably, and he sometimes referred to the proposed institution as a clearing bank.
6. KCW-25, 33. The desire to preserve the system of imperial preferences was a major issue in the debate that ensued in the British Parliament; see Bailey, Bannerman, and Schonhardt-Bailey, "Parliamentary Debates."
7. These terms are from the February 1942 draft of the Keynes Plan; Horsefield, *International Monetary Fund*, 3:7–8.
8. Keynes, "Proposals for an International Currency Union," second draft, November 18, 1941, KCW-25:43.
9. Keynes, "Proposals for an International Currency Union," third draft, December 15, 1941, KCW-25:79.

10. This version of the Keynes Plan was published later in Horsefield, *International Monetary Fund*, 3:3–18. That version omits the first eight paragraphs, which constituted a general introduction. The full version, including the introduction, was published in 1980 in KCW-25:108–39. The two publications numbered the paragraphs differently: KCW-25 used the numbering from the longer document circulated to the British War Cabinet in February 1942, paragraphs 61 through 134. Horsefield's version numbers the paragraphs 1 through 66, corresponding to the original numbers 69 through 134.

11. Keynes to Richard Kahn, May 11, 1942, KCW-25:144.

12. Keynes, "Proposals for an International Currency Union," third draft, December 15, 1941, KCW-25:92.

13. Minutes of these meetings are in IMFA-BWC; see document BWC1537-01.

14. George H. Willis to White, memorandum, "Meeting on the Procedure for Initiating International Consultations on a Stabilization Fund and a Bank for the United Nations, 2:30 P.M., Friday, July 10, 1942," IMFA-BWC, document BWC1359-01:13–14. The "political reasons" point was made by Herbert Feis, representing the State Department.

15. Editor's commentary, KCW-25:157. Leith-Ross claimed that White gave the document to him because White and Phillips "were not on close terms" and that Phillips "had vainly been trying to obtain" a copy; Leith-Ross, *Money Talks*, 298. Keynes, however, noted that his copy came from Phillips; Keynes, "Notes on the Memorandum for Post-War Currency Arrangements transmitted by Sir F. Phillips," KCW-25:160. Also see Van Dormael, *Bretton Woods*, 53–58; and Skidelsky, *John Maynard Keynes: Fighting for Britain*, 246.

16. Keynes to Richard Hopkins, August 3, 1942, KCW-25:158.

17. Ibid., 160.

18. Horsefield, *International Monetary Fund*, 3:52.

19. For this version of the Keynes Plan, see KCW-25:168–95. The transmission of the paper on August 28 was preceded by informal discussions between State Department officials (Pasvolsky and Acheson) and Frederick Phillips of the U.K. Treasury; Berle to Redvers Opie, August 31, 1942, FRUS 1942, vol. 1, document 161.

20. White to Morgenthau, memorandum, "Lord Keynes' Plan for Post-War Monetary Control," September 11, 1942, NARA-RG56, box 8; emphasis in original. Also see Berle, file memorandum, September 10, 1942, FRUS 1942, vol. 1, document 162.

21. For the lists of questions and a summary of the discussion of them, see William H. Taylor, file memorandum, October 7, 1942, IMFA-BWC, document BWC1537-01:23–30. On the subsequent discussion and transmission of the questions, see Taylor to White, memorandum, October 7, 1942, NARA-RG56, box 6. Also see Taylor, minutes of a meeting of the interdepartmental group on October 8, 1942, IMFA-BWC, document BWC1537-01:31–32.

22. The July 21 memorandum, with later notes on the follow-up, is in NARA-RG56, box 8. The September 10 meeting is described in Berle, file memo-

randum, September 10, 1942, FRUS, 1942, vol. 1, document 162. For a discussion, see Van Dormael, *Bretton Woods*, 59–60.

23. Notes on the trip, prepared by White for Morgenthau, November 16, 1942, and White to Morgenthau, memorandum, "Some of the Persons You Talked With," November 3, 1942, both in NARA-RG56, box 6. A detailed report on Morgenthau's movements was prepared jointly by U.S. and British military aides who accompanied him; see "Diary of Trip to Great Britain," memorandum to Morgenthau, November 2, 1942, SMLP-2.

24. The most detailed record of this meeting is in Penrose, *Economic Planning for the Peace*, 48–49. The bulk of Penrose's account was reprinted in Van Dormael, *Bretton Woods*, 62–63. Editor's commentary, KCW-25:196, states that the meeting took place on October 23, and some later works (e.g., Skidelsky, *John Maynard Keynes: Fighting for Britain*, 247) have cited that date as well. Penrose's memoir—written a decade after he sat in on the 1943 meeting—does not give a date, but it mentions that the Americans were to leave for "the Mediterranean" that evening, which would place the meeting on October 27.

25. Editor's commentary, KCW-25:196; appendix 2 of that book, 453–58, lists the changes introduced in the November 9 draft. Also see S. Donald Southworth, minutes of a meeting on December 1, 1942, IMFA-BWC, document BWC1537-01:33–34.

26. Keynes to Roy Harrod, March 4, 1943, and attachment to Keynes to Phillips, April 16, 1943, KCW-25:230, 248.

27. Harrod, *Life of Keynes*, 544–45.

28. Keynes, "Notes on C.U. and S.F.," attachment to a letter to Phillips, April 16, 1943, KCW-25:249.

29. For an early draft of the scarce currency clause, see Horsefield, *International Monetary Fund*, 3:90–91. For the final version, Article VII of the IMF Articles of Agreement, see ibid., 194–95.

30. Keynes to Phillips, December 16, 1942; on January 8, 1943, Phillips replied, "Harry White is showing few signs of life"; KCW-25:200, 205, respectively.

31. Van Dormael, *Bretton Woods*, 63.

32. White, memorandum for files, May 31, 1943, NARA-RG56, box 9. For the minutes of the January 26 meeting and a draft of the invitation letter to governments, see MD 605.2:18–20 or IMFA-BWC, document BWC1537-01:48–50. Also see White to Morgenthau, memorandum, "Response to Your Letter to Finance Ministers," May 3, 1943, MD 630:368–69.

33. Keynes, speech in the House of Lords, May 18, 1943, KCW-25:278.

34. Morgenthau conveyed Roosevelt's instructions at a meeting on April 1, 1943; see MD 622:16.

35. Entry for June 15, 1943, in Robbins, *Wartime Diaries*, 71.

36. The documentation for these meetings is in IMFA-BWC; ten documents in BWC1522, "Meetings, Group on Monetary Plans," 1943.

37. The minutes are in IMFA-BWC, document BWC1522-04. The bilateral meeting with Gromyko and Tepliakov is in a list of White's meetings, in SMLP-2.

38. Muirhead, *Against the Odds*, 91–92. For a detailed discussion of Canada's role, see Rasmussen, "Canada and Bretton Woods." The Canadian Plan is reproduced in Horsefield, *International Monetary Fund*, 3:103–18, and is summarized in Horsefield, *International Monetary Fund*, 1:37–39.

39. Muirhead, *Against the Odds*, 92–94. That account is based both on Rasminsky's papers at the Bank of Canada and on an internal U.S. Treasury memorandum summarizing the meetings. (In an endnote on p. 320, Muirhead cites a file in NARA-RG56 as containing that memorandum, but that file covers a different period and does not include the document in question.)

40. Robertson to Eady, June 3, 1943, with attached notes "written some weeks ago," KCW-25:289–92.

41. The minutes of the meetings are in IMFA-BWC, document BWC1537-03.

42. Keynes to Harrod, April 27, 1943, KCW-25:268. Also see Meltzer, *Keynes's Monetary Theory*, 245.

43. Keynes, "The Synthesis of C.U. and S.F.," June 29, 1943, KCW-25:308.

44. Robertson, "Post-War Monetary Plans."

Chapter 11. The Path to Bretton Woods, 1943–44

1.   "Boston Economist Is Treasury's Quiz Kid," *Boston Globe*, April 8, 1944.

2.   "Taker-Over," *Newsweek*, July 31, 1944, 35. The writer described the California incident as having taken place "just after" the end of World War I, but there is no evidence that the Whites ever visited California until they went there to study at Stanford University in 1923. The incident probably occurred at that time.

3.   Anne's scrapbooks, family collection.

4.   Minutes of the formal meetings are in IMFA-BWC, document BWC1537-04.

5.   Harrod, *Life of Keynes*, 557–58, 635–36.

6.   Harry White to Anne Terry White, n.d., written on the stationery of the office of the U.S. Treasury attaché in London, SMLP-2.

7.   Anne Terry White to Joan and Ruth White, August 12, 1943, SMLP-2. For Craig's interpretation of Harry's opinion of Laski, see Craig, *Treasonable Doubt*, 273–75. For Einstein's proposal for Laski to be named president of Brandeis University, see Sachar, *Brandeis University*, 22–24.

8.   White, "Memorandum of a Conference at the White House," May 18, 1944, IMFA-BWC, document BWC1537-08:19. For summary accounts of Roosevelt's earlier meetings with Keynes, see Rauchway, *Money Makers*, 98–101, 144, 147.

9.   Keynes to Eady, October 3, 1943, KCW-25:356.

10. Ibid., 364. For assessments of Keynes's anti-Semitism, see Chandavarkar, "Was Keynes Anti-Semitic?" and Reder, "Anti-Semitism."

11. Keynes to David Whaley, May 30, 1944, and to Richard Hopkins, June 30, 1944, in *Collected Writings of John Maynard Keynes*, vol. 26 (hereafter cited as KCW-26), 41, 67.

12. Harry White to Keynes, July 24, 1943, KCW-25:337–38; emphasis added.

13. Minutes of a meeting on October 6, 1943, IMFA-BWC, document BWC1537-04:30.

14. Keynes to Eady, October 3, 1943, KCW-25:359.

15. Keynes to Viner, June 9, 1943, and Robertson to Keynes, June 28, 1943, KCW-25:321 and 302, respectively; "The Canadian Plan," Horsefield, *International Monetary Fund*, 3:110.

16. Minutes of a meeting on October 6, 1943, IMFA-BWC, document BWC1537-04:30.

17. James Meade, diary entry for September 28, 1943, in Robbins, *Wartime Diaries*, 119.

18. Diary entry for January 27, 1944, in Wallace, *Price of Vision*, 297.

19. Irving S. Friedman, minutes of a meeting with Hsi Te-mou, March 13, 1944, IMFA-BWC, document BWC1537-05:3. The October 1943 draft of the joint statement is in KCW-25:379–92. The version published in April 1944 is in Horsefield, *International Monetary Fund*, 3:128–35.

20. Many of these developments are discussed in Scott-Smith and Rofe, *Global Perspectives*, especially chaps. 4 through 10.

21. Records of these meetings are in IMFA, "Meetings with the Russian Delegation, Jan.–May 1944," in "Pre–Bretton Woods Meetings—Master file." Acsay, "Planning for Postwar," provides a detailed analysis of the role of the Soviet Union in the negotiations. For a firsthand account, see Mikesell, "Negotiating."

22. Winthrop W. Aldrich, chairman of the Board of Directors of Chase National Bank, speech to the International Chamber of Commerce, April 29, 1943, http://www.ibiblio.org/pha/policy/1943/1943-04-29a.html.

23. For a complete list, see U.S. Department of State, *Proceedings and Documents*, 303–6, and Schuler and Bernkopf, "Who Was at Bretton Woods?" The latter includes additional identifying information but also contains several errors, including incorrect identification of certain people as Soviet spies.

24. Transcript of press conference, excerpted in Bratter, "Steps That Led to Bretton Woods," 1355.

25. U.S. Treasury press release, August 20, 1943, IMFA-BWC, document BWC1361-01.

26. White to Morgenthau, memorandum, "Delay in progress on International Monetary Conference," March 21, 1944, NARA-RG56, box 11.

27. Edward M. Bernstein, minutes of a meeting held April 1, 1944, IMFA-BWC, document BWC1359-01:40–41.

28. For an overview of the congressional resolutions, see Eckes, *Search for Solvency*, 107–9.

29.   Keynes to Harry White, May 24, 1944, KCW-26:27–28. For Keynes's state of health at that time, see Skidelsky, *John Maynard Keynes: Fighting for Britain*, 333–34.

30.   White, minutes of a meeting with Roosevelt, May 18, 1944, IMFA-BWC, document BWC1537-08:19–20.

31.   Edward Bernstein made this point in an interview for the *Washington Post* on the occasion of the fortieth anniversary of the conference; cited in Wachtel, *Money Mandarins*, 27.

32.   Roosevelt approved the plan at a White House meeting on May 25, 1944, attended by Morgenthau, Acheson, and White. See White's minutes, IMFA-BWC, document BWC1537-08:21–23.

33.   Keynes to David Whaley, May 30, 1944, KCW-26:42.

34.   Entry for June 15, 1943, in Robbins, *Wartime Diaries*, 71.

35.   Transcript of a meeting, June 20, 1944, MD 745:132–35.

36.   For a general account of the trip, see Skidelsky, *John Maynard Keynes: Fighting for Britain*, 343. Skidelsky's list of delegations on the trip omits the U.S. representative. For a complete list and the text of the draft that the group produced during the voyage, see MD 747:78–107.

37.   Harry White to Anne Terry White, June 26, 1944, SMLP-2. For the identification of people mentioned in the letter, see Schuler and Bernkopf, "Who Was at Bretton Woods?"

38.   White to Morgenthau, memorandum drafted by Eddie Bernstein, June 22, 1944, IMFA-BWC, document BWC1280-02. The final version is also in MD 746:147–48.

Chapter 12. The Bretton Woods Conference, 1944

1.   For an unofficial but "nearly complete" list of attendees and their affiliations, see Schuler and Bernkopf, "Who Was at Bretton Woods?" The official but less complete list is in U.S. Department of State, *Proceedings and Documents*, 294–306.

2.   Skidelsky, *John Maynard Keynes: Fighting for Britain*, 347.

3.   Blum, *From the Morgenthau Diaries: Years of War*, 258.

4.   Lahey, "Reporter at Bretton Woods," 69.

5.   For a firsthand account, see Mikesell, *Foreign Adventures*, 53.

6.   Transcript of a meeting at Bretton Woods, July 17, 1944, MD 755.1:71–96.

7.   Harry White to Joan and Ruth White, postcard, July 22, 1944, family collection.

8.   For early authoritative histories, see Horsefield, *International Monetary Fund*, vol. 1, and Mason and Asher, *World Bank*. Van Dormael, *Bretton Woods*, is also based heavily on original source material. Most recent studies have been more specialized. Conway, *Summit*, focused more on the human interest stories; Rauchway, *Money Makers*, covered the larger political issues; and Helleiner, *Forgotten Origins*, dealt with the implications for economic development.

9. The phrase is from the April 1942 version of the White Plan; Horsefield, *International Monetary Fund*, 3:65.

10. The British "boat draft" consisted of several documents submitted on June 24, 1944, MD 747:78–107. The "necessary and advisable" proposal is on p. 98. Harry's "not budge" reaction is in a memorandum to Morgenthau, June 25, 1944, MD 747:74.

11. Transcript of a meeting at Bretton Woods, "Instruction of American Delegates—Fund," July 1, 1944, MD 749:7–59. The quotation is from p. 22.

12. E. A. Goldenweiser, "Issues at Bretton Woods," July 29, 1944, 2, EAG, "Bretton Woods" folder.

13. For more on Australia's delay in joining, see Cornish and Schuler, "Australia's Full-Employment Proposals."

14. For the Joint Statement, see Horsefield, *International Monetary Fund*, 3:128–35. The roles of gold and GCE are described on p. 133.

15. U.S. Department of State, *Proceedings and Documents*, 26n.

16. "Informal Minutes, Commission I, United Nations Monetary and Financial Conference at Bretton Woods," 42 (p. 45 of the PDF available online), IMFA-BWC, https://archivescatalog.imf.org/Details/archive/110013587; also reproduced in Schuler and Rosenberg, *Bretton Woods Transcripts*, Kindle location 2252–2397.

17. Entries for July 7 and July 14, 1944, in Robbins, *Wartime Diaries*, 175, 184.

18. U.S. Department of State, *Proceedings and Documents*, 599.

19. "Informal Minutes," 54, IMFA-BWC.

20. Mikesell, *Bretton Woods Debates*, 22–23.

21. Raymond Mikesell to Edward M. Bernstein, memorandum, May 25, 1943, IMFA-BWC, document BWC1529-01.

22. For the transcript of Vinson's report and the commission's consideration of it, see Schuler and Rosenberg, *Bretton Woods Transcripts*, Kindle location 4233–4497. For the full list of recommended quotas, see Horsefield, *International Monetary Fund*, 1:96 (column 6 of table 2).

23. Schuler and Rosenberg, *Bretton Woods Transcripts*, Kindle location 4269–72.

24. "A Suggested Formula for the Determination of Member Country Quotas," June 9, 1943, 2, IMFA-BWC, document BWC1522-07.

25. "Articles of Agreement for the Establishment of an International Monetary Fund, Draft, June 23, 1944," IMFA-BWC, document BWC1265-01:17.

26. U.S. Department of State, *Proceedings and Documents*, 51.

27. Entry for July 14, 1944, and citation to a cable from the U.K. Foreign Office of the same date, Robbins, *Wartime Diaries*, 185, 217n50.

28. Schuler and Rosenberg, *Bretton Woods Transcripts*, Kindle location 4917–4950.

29. McCullough, *Truman*, 404.

30. Keynes, report on the Savannah conference, March 27, 1946, KCW-26:222.

31. Ibid., 216, 221.

Chapter 13. Finishing the Job, 1944–45

1. See transcripts of phone calls, Morgenthau to Hannegan, November 17, 1944, MD 796:35–38; Morgenthau to James Barnes (administrative assistant to the president), November 28, 1944, MD 799:127–30 (Morgenthau recalled Roosevelt's response to his idea of promoting Harry in this phone call); and Morgenthau to Roosevelt, telegram, December 6, 1944, MD 801:169–71.

2. Morgenthau to Roosevelt, memorandum, December 28, 1944, and Roosevelt to Morgenthau, memorandum, same date, MD 805:192–193.

3. Eleanor Roosevelt praised Harry in her My Day newspaper column. See Eleanor Roosevelt, "My Day, December 2, 1941," *Eleanor Roosevelt Papers Digital Edition* (2017), https://www2.gwu.edu/~erpapers/myday/displaydoc.cfm?_y=1941&_f=md056050. In March 1943 she invited Harry and Anne to tea at the White House; the invitation card is in SMLP2.

4. Milo Perkins to White, June 8, 1944, SMLP-2.

5. On the strained relationship, see Fiorito and Nerozzi, "Viner's Reminiscences." A secondhand report of Viner's praise for White's character and ability is in Harold Glasser to Anne Terry White, January 24, 1951, SMLP-2.

6. John P. Young, oral history in HSTL, February 21, 1974, https://www.trumanlibrary.gov/library/oral-histories/youngjp.

7. Entry for June 15, 1943, Robbins, *Wartime Diaries*, 72.

8. McKittrick's comment was recorded by Per Jacobsson (economic adviser at the Bank for International Settlements) in his diary, May 10, 1943, deposited in the Basel (Switzerland) University Library; quoted in Piet Clement (head of the BIS Library) to the author, August 28, 2004. Blum to me, June 16, 2004.

9. Solomon Adler to Bessie White Bloom, November 24, 1956, SMLP-2.

10. Mikesell, *Foreign Adventures*, 54.

11. "Former Aide to White Didn't Suspect Boss," *Holyoke [Mass.] Transcript-Telegram*, November 24, 1953, 1, 10.

12. See Barnes, *Flaubert's Parrot*, 41, and Craig, *Treasonable Doubt*, 379n81. This paragraph was also informed by correspondence between Craig and Joan White Pinkham in 2004–5, copies of which are in the White family collection.

13. Harry White to Ruth and Joan White, July 21, 1944, SMLP-2.

14. White, memorandum for files, August 20, 1944, MD 764:94–95.

15. Morgenthau's record of remarks by Roosevelt at a dinner on July 5, 1944, MPD 6.1:4.

16. White to Morgenthau, memorandum, "Program on the Fund and Bank Projects," September 1, 1944, MD 768:48–50; White to Morgenthau, December 23, 1944, MD 805:69.

17. Morgenthau's record of remarks by Roosevelt at a dinner on July 5, 1944, MPD 6.1:4.

18. See, for example, Edward M. Bernstein, memorandum for files, January 8, 1945, MD 808:69–70.

19. Quoted in the *Washington Post*, September 22, 1944. Harry's address to the People's Lobby was published as White, "International Monetary and Financial Cooperation." For the history of the group, a broad public-interest advocacy organization, see Lee, *Philosopher-Lobbyist*.

20. U.S. Congress, House Committee on Banking and Currency, *Hearings on H.R. 2211*, 66–158, 543–96. Keynes to Edward Bernstein, telegram, May 29, 1945, IMFA-BWC, document BWC1336-02; reprinted in KCW-26:193–94.

21. Eckes, *Search for Solvency*, 167.

22. John H. Crider, "Favor Fund Plan of Bretton Woods," *New York Times*, March 4, 1945, 26.

23. U.S. Congress, Senate Committee on Banking and Currency, *Hearings on H.R. 3314*, 78–80.

24. Ibid., 80–85.

25. See Bloomfield, "Tripartite Agreement," and related research by Henry C. Wallich and others in NYFRB. I am indebted to Max Harris for this reference.

26. See the 1947 third edition of Williams, *Postwar Monetary Plans*. That edition incorporates the original essays from the first (1944) edition, as well as additional material, including the transcript of Williams's 1945 testimony on the Bretton Woods Agreements Act. The key passages from Williams's first paper (published in 1936) and his initial response to the publication of the Keynes and White plans in 1943 are reproduced in Horsefield, *International Monetary Fund*, 3:119–27.

27. U.S. Congress, Senate Committee on Banking and Currency, *Hearings on H.R. 3314*, 134–35.

28. Ibid., 125–32.

29. Ibid., 126.

30. Ibid., 128–29.

31. Ibid., 159–78. The quoted sentence is on p. 163.

32. Ibid., 182–84.

33. Ibid., 233–36.

34. Minutes of a meeting of British officials, August 23, 1945, KCW-24:420–25; Keynes, "Some Highly Preliminary Notes on the Forthcoming Conversations: 9 September 1945," attachment to Keynes to Eady, September 10, 1945, KCW-24:457; and Skidelsky, *John Maynard Keynes: Fighting for Britain*, 404–5.

35. White to Vinson, memoranda, August 31 and September 4, 1945, NARA-RG56, box 13.

36. Keynes, "Some Highly Preliminary Notes on the Forthcoming Conversations: 9 September 1945," attachment to Keynes to Eady, September 10, 1945, KCW-24:457.

37. Ibid., 456–57. Minutes of meetings from September 13 to 20, 1945, are re-produced in KCW-24:466–98. White attended only one of those five meet-ings, on September 14.

38. Keynes to Eady, October 5, 1945, KCW-24:531.

39. Ibid., attachment, "Dr Harry White's Plan," KCW-24:532–35.

40. Entry for November 5, 1945, in Wallace, *Price of Vision*, 506.

41. White, "The Monetary Fund," 207.

42. The original quotation is from a speech by Churchill at the Mansion House on November 10, 1941, https://www.ibiblio.org/pha/timeline/411110awp .html.

43. White, untitled draft manuscript dated November 30, 1945, SMLP-1, box 7.

44. White to Claude Pepper, March 21, 1946, SMLP-2.

45. Quoted by Morgenthau during a staff meeting on January 10, 1945, MD 808:329.

Chapter 14. Dangerous Diversions, 1944–46

1. Gaddis, *United States and the Origins of the Cold War*, 121; Beschloss, *Conquer-ors*, 52; and Craig, *Treasonable Doubt*, 160.

2. Transcript of the hearing, reproduced in Nathan White, *Harry Dexter White: Loyal American*, 63–64.

3. Keynes to John Anderson, October 6, 1944, KCW-26:381.

4. See U.S. Congress, *Morgenthau Diary (Germany)*. For recent repetitions, see Conway, *Summit*, 302–3, and Steil, *Battle of Bretton Woods*, 283. More subtly, Beschloss, *Conquerors*, 156, raises the possibility that promoting Soviet in-terests might have been White's motive, but he stops short of endorsing that view.

5. Morgenthau's record of a meeting with Roosevelt, July 6, 1944, MPD 6.1:3.

6. See Whipple, "Life and Death," part 9, November 24, 1953; Craig, *Treason-able Doubt*, 157–59; and Morgenthau III, *Mostly Morgenthaus*, 353.

7. Morgenthau, "Our Policy toward Germany," part 1. Also see Morgenthau III, *Mostly Morgenthaus*, 352, based on an interview of Josiah DuBois on Feb-ruary 26, 1981.

8. Quoted in Morgenthau III, *Mostly Morgenthaus*, 353–54. The oral history is in HSTL.

9. Penrose, *Economic Planning for the Peace*, 245–46.

10. Josiah DuBois, oral history interview, June 29, 1973, HSTL, https://www .trumanlibrary.gov/library/oral-histories/duboisje.

11. Skidelsky, *John Maynard Keynes: The Economist as Saviour*, 32.

12. Smith, "Rise and Fall."

13. Ibid., and Morgenthau, "Our Policy toward Germany," part 1.

14. Transcript of a meeting, August 17, 1944, MD 763:105.

15. White's copy of the itinerary for the trip is in SMLP-2. Penrose's ac-count mistakenly placed the estate in Wiltshire, the next county to the west. Some accounts relying on Penrose have repeated the error; see, e.g.,

Morgenthau III, *Mostly Morgenthaus*, 362, and Beschloss, *Conquerors*, 75. For a personal account of Morgenthau's visit with his son, see Morgenthau III, *Mostly Morgenthaus*, 359–61.

16. Transcript of a meeting, August 17, 1944, MD 763:117.

17. Penrose, *Economic Planning for the Peace*, 245–47.

18. Ibid., 248.

19. Transcript of a meeting, August 28, 1944, MD 767:6. Also see Pehle to Morgenthau, memorandum, August 21, 1944, MD 764:125.

20. Taylor, memorandum for files, NARA-RG56, box 11.

21. Chief of the Division of Central European Affairs in the State Department [James W. Riddleberger], memorandum, "Suggested Recommendations on Treatment of Germany from the Cabinet Committee for the President," September 4, 1944, http://teachingamericanhistory.org/library/document/documents-regarding-the/. Riddleberger's later report on the September 2 meeting (dated October 28, 1944) is at the same site.

22. Transcript of a meeting, September 4, 1944, MD 768:119.

23. "Suggested Post-Surrender Program for Germany," September 4, 1944, MD 768:164–68. The final version of the plan, which Roosevelt took to Quebec, is reproduced in the front matter of Morgenthau, *Germany Is Our Problem*.

24. "Quebec Directive on Germany," September 15, 1944, MD 772:7–8.

25. White, minutes of a meeting, October 17, 1944, NARA-RG56, box 12.

26. The post-Quebec process is discussed in detail from Morgenthau's perspective in Blum, *From the Morgenthau Diaries: Years of War*, chap. 8. The quotation from the Yalta communiqué is on p. 399.

27. Harry's inscribed copy of *Germany Is Our Problem* is in the White family collection. Morgenthau's 1948 comment is from a condolence letter, now in SMLP2, that he wrote to Anne Terry White. DuBois's recollection is from an interview conducted June 29, 1973, in HSTL, https://www.trumanlibrary.gov/library/oral-histories/duboisje.

28. For histories of the issuance of occupation currencies during World War II, see Southard, *Finances of European Liberation*; and Petrov, *Money and Conquest*.

29. White to Morgenthau, memorandum, "Views of the Belgian Government with Regard to Occupation Currency," December 17, 1942, MD 597:166. Also see Taylor's testimony on October 19, 1953, U.S. Congress, Senate, Executive Sessions of the Senate Permanent Subcommittee on Investigations, 4:3404.

30. Transcript of a meeting in the secretary's office, April 22, 1943, MD 628:36–42.

31. White, "Memorandum Regarding Invasion and Occupation Currencies," March 30, 1943, MD 621:33–34.

32. Transcript of a meeting, April 22, 1943, MD 628:38.

33. Roosevelt's directive is in MD 639:235–42. For a recap of how policy was implemented, see Treasury press release 38-10, August 17, 1943, MD 656:236–40.

34. White, memorandum for files, "re: Occupation Currency," November 26, 1943, MD 680.2:4–6. My tentative identification of Fedotov is from an annotation to an intercepted Soviet cable, "New York KGB Station—Moscow Cables," 96, in WCDA-Venona.

35. Harriman (in Moscow) to Secretary of State Hull, telegram, January 29, 1944, FRUS 1944, British Commonwealth and Europe, vol. 3, https://history.state.gov/historicaldocuments/frus1944v03/d758.

36. Testimony of Alvin W. Hall, October 19, 1953, U.S. Congress, Senate, Executive Sessions of the Senate Permanent Subcommittee on Investigations, 4:3418–19. For an overview of the issue, see Blum, *From the Morgenthau Diaries: Years of War*, 177–88.

37. Blum, *From the Morgenthau Diaries: Years of War*, 188. Also see Harriman to Hull, telegram, February 15, 1944, FRUS 1944, British Commonwealth and Europe, vol. 3, https://history.state.gov/historicaldocuments/frus1944v03/d761.

38. Taylor, file memorandum, "Meeting in Mr. Bell's Office, March 7, 1944," NARA-RG56, box 11. Also see Blum, *From the Morgenthau Diaries: Years of War*, 181–83. Original file memoranda by White are reprinted in U.S. Congress, Senate Committee on Appropriations, 179–84.

39. Testimony of Elizabeth Bentley, October 21, 1953, U.S. Congress, Senate, Executive Sessions of the Senate Permanent Subcommittee on Investigations, 4:3425–29.

40. Schecter and Schecter, *Sacred Secrets*, 122.

41. James Clement Dunn, director of the Office of European Affairs in the U.S. State Department, memorandum of telephone conversation, April 14, 1944, FRUS 1944, British Commonwealth and Europe, vol. 3, https://history.state.gov/historicaldocuments/frus1944v03/d765. Also see Craig, *Treasonable Doubt*, 133.

42. For example, see Petrov, *Money and Conquest*, chap. 5. Petrov's account was based largely on the Senate investigations, and it reflected their biases. For detailed examinations of Harry's alleged complicity, see Rees, *Harry Dexter White: A Study in Paradox*, chap. 12; and Craig, *Treasonable Doubt*, chap. 5.

43. The reasons for this impossibility are set out in Morgenthau to Admiral William D. Leahy, chief of staff to the commander in chief of the army and navy, telegram, March 22, 1944, FRUS 1944, British Commonwealth and Europe, vol. 3, https://history.state.gov/historicaldocuments/frus1944v03/d763.

44. Petrov, *Money and Conquest*, 122, quoting from Harriman to Hull, telegram, April 8, 1944.

45. Kindleberger, *Life of an Economist*, 115. Also see Craig, *Treasonable Doubt*, 114–15, and references therein.

46. "Proposals for the Establishment of a General International Organization," document for "Washington Conversations on International Peace and Security Organization," Dumbarton Oaks, October 7, 1944, http://www.ibiblio.org/pha/policy/1944/441007a.html.

47. For a detailed account, see Russell, *History of the United Nations Charter*.
48. Morgenthau to Joseph Grew, State Department official, March 24, 1945, SMLP-2.
49. Stettinius to White, April 11, 1945, SMLP-2.
50. Harry White to Anne Terry White, April 22, 1945, SMLP-2.
51. White Plan, April 1942, Horsefield, *International Monetary Fund*, 3:72–73.
52. White, undated, handwritten manuscript, titled (as best I can tell) "Political & Economic Int. of Future," SMLP-1, box 9, folder 18. The discussion in the next six paragraphs refers to this manuscript.
53. Untitled typewritten four-page manuscript, marked "H. D. White" and dated November 30, 1945, SMLP-2.
54. Ibid.
55. Harry White to Anne Terry White, April 22, 1945, SMLP-2.
56. Ibid.
57. Harry White to Joan White, April 25, 1945, SMLP-2.
58. Stettinius to Morgenthau, May 21, 1945, Morgenthau to Stettinius, May 29, 1945, and Stettinius to Morgenthau, June 4, 1945, MD 850:52–53, MD 851:112.
59. The negotiations are covered in Russell, *History of the United Nations Charter*, chap. 28.

Chapter 15. The Attack Begins behind the Curtain, 1945

1. Chambers published an autobiography in 1952; Sam Tanenhaus wrote a detailed and broadly sympathetic biography that focused mainly on the Alger Hiss case, in which Chambers played a central role; and Weinstein, *Perjury*, also covered Chambers's role in the Hiss case. For a recounting of Chambers's aliases, see http://whittakerchambers.org/about/aliases/.
2. For an analysis, see G. Edward White, "Alger Hiss's Campaign," 10–11. Also see Weinstein, *Perjury*, 302–3.
3. For accounts of this meeting, see Chambers, *Witness*, 463–71; Tanenhaus, *Whittaker Chambers*, 161–63; and Weinstein, *Perjury*, 291–93. Weinstein notes that the man who helped set up the meeting and who accompanied Chambers to it, an anti-Communist journalist named Isaac Don Levine, later included "Mr. White" in a list of names that "he remembered having been mentioned." Chambers himself, though, acknowledged that he had not mentioned White to Berle; see the story at the end of this section. Craig's attempt to explain the discrepancy (*Treasonable Doubt*, 297n57) is purely speculative. Andrew and Mitrokhin, in *The Sword and the Shield*, 107, 142, stated incorrectly that Chambers included White in the list of names that he gave Berle in 1939.
4. For the full text of Murphy's memorandum, August 28, 1946, see "The Alger Hiss Story," http://algerhiss.com/history/the-flight-to-clear-hisss-name -1950s-1980s/hisss-1978-coram-nobis-petition/chamberss-august-1946 -conversation-with-raymond-murphy/. Weinstein, *Perjury*, 569n25, notes

that the text was also published in the transcript of Alger Hiss's second trial for perjury.

5. Craig, *Treasonable Doubt*, 86–90, 96–99, recounts the employment histories of Adler, Glasser, and the Coe brothers.

6. Chambers, *Witness*, 470.

7. Bentley, *Out of Bondage*, especially chaps. 5 and 11, and Olmsted, *Red Spy Queen*, 18–28, 74–79. Documentation of the activities and identification of Gregory Silvermaster is in the Venona decryptions and Vassiliev Notebooks, both of which are in WCDA.

8. Olmsted, *Red Spy Queen*, 192. Throughout her book, Olmsted carefully explained the many inconsistencies and proven lies in Bentley's shifting stories, but much of Olmsted's own account, including the story of Bentley's interactions with the Silvermaster group, was based directly or indirectly on *Out of Bondage*.

9. NARA-118:2795.

10. Ibid., 2948–50.

11. For details and primary sources, see Craig, *Treasonable Doubt*, 101–2. According to an account in Weinstein and Vassiliev, *Haunted Wood*, 164, a Soviet operative in Washington reported to his superiors in Moscow that Ullmann and Helen Silvermaster were lovers. Olmsted, *Red Spy Queen*, 46, repeats that story as if it were an established fact, but there is no way to know whether the report was based on direct observation or subjective inference from the unusual living arrangement.

12. Draft by White for Morgenthau, "Memorandum for the President," January 5, 1944, NARA-RG56, box 10, and MD 691:129–35. The version in the diary is more limited, as I discuss below. For another brief discussion of this document, see Craig, *Treasonable Doubt*, 151–52.

13. Weinstein and Vassiliev, *Haunted Wood*, 163–64. Although Vassiliev had access to the Soviet archives, the original documents are not available to other researchers. Translations of the notes that Vassiliev made in the archives are available on the website of the Wilson Center: http://digitalarchive.wilsoncenter.org/collection/86/vassiliev-notebooks. The documents the authors refer to must be viewed as unverifiable secondary sources.

14. As was typical of such Treasury documents at that time, the version that was intended for delivery to the president omitted this drafting history. That version is in the Morgenthau Diaries. The notations cited here are on the internal version, in NARA-RG56, box 10.

15. For an extensive biographical summary and other background information on Glasser, see WCDA-Vassiliev, white notebook no. 3, 44–52. It includes what purports to be a biography submitted by Glasser to the NKVD.

16. Notations on some cables indicate that the FBI analyst concluded that Rouble was "probably" Glasser. Other cables omit the qualifier.

17. Summary report on interview, November 10, 1941, FBI-FOIA, "Glasser," part 1:153.

18. Hoover to Vaughan, November 8, 1945, FBI-FOIA, "Silvermaster," part 16:98–100. This document also is in HSTL, https://www.trumanlibrary .gov/library/research-files/j-edgar-hoover-harry-h-vaughan.

19. The FBI surveillance is detailed in several places in FBI-FOIA, "Silvermaster." See, for example, part 45:163–78, which summarizes mail sent to the Whites' home, telephone calls to and from the White family, a telegram sent by the White family, and physical surveillance of Harry White's movements and meetings for the period March 16–31, 1946. For an acknowledgement of the wiretap and its active dates, see D. M. Ladd to H. B. Fletcher, memorandum, February 2, 1950, FBI-FOIA, "White," sec. 1.

20. Internal report, November 16, 1953, FBI-FOIA, "Silvermaster," part 156:111. For a thorough examination of the failures of the FBI's efforts to investigate Soviet espionage in this way, see Theoharis, *Chasing Spies*.

21. "Soviet Espionage in the United States," November 27, 1945, FBI-FOIA.

22. See Hoover, memorandum, November 15, 1945, FBI-FOIA, "Silvermaster," part 16:102.

23. Hoover to Vaughan, February 1, 1946; attachment to letter from Truman to Vinson, February 6, 1946; HSTL, https://www.trumanlibrary.gov/ library/research-files/memo-harry-s-truman-fred-m-vinson-attachment ?documentid=NA&pagenumber=1. The chronology of transmission of this document is in FBI-FOIA, "Silvermaster," part 156:54–56, 65.

24. Truman's cover memorandum to Vinson on February 6 referred to the FBI report's having been forwarded to him by the State Department.

25. Hoover to Vaughan, February 1, 1946, 9.

26. For the legal history of the attorney general's list, see King, "Legal History."

27. For background on Commonwealth College, see Cobb, *Radical Education*.

28. FBI-FOIA, "Silvermaster," part 25:23–32.

29. Harry to Joan, undated; SMLP-2.

30. This identification is based on inferences drawn by the two daughters, as reported to other members of the family.

31. Truman to Vinson, February 6, 1946. The meeting on February 7, 1946, is listed on the calendar at HSTL as taking place at 12:30 P.M., before a lunch scheduled for the president at 1:00 P.M.; https://www.trumanlibrary.gov/ calendar?month=2&day=7&year=2.

Chapter 16. At the International Monetary Fund, 1946–47

1. Entry for November 28, 1945, in Wallace, *Price of Vision*, 524. Also see Walton, *Henry Wallace*, 68.

2. I. F. Stone to Anne Terry White, August 29, 1948, SMLP-2. A few years later, in *Truman Era*, xiv, Stone again assessed Harry as having been "one of the ablest and brightest men in Washington."

3. Stone, *Truman Era*, xiv.

4. Fred Vinson to Truman, "Report to the President on Activities of the National Advisory Council on International Monetary and Financial Prob-

lems," March 4, 1946, https://fraser.stlouisfed.org/files/docs/historical/
martin/17_01_19460308.pdf. For Harry's assessment of the work of the
NAC, see White, "Our Foreign Investment Policy."

5. Coe to Vinson, memorandum, "Problems of Savannah Conference," February 20, 1946, IMF-BWC, document BWC1573-01.

6. William M. Tomlinson, memorandum for files, "Conversation with Lord
Keynes in regard to scheduling first meeting of Governors under the Bret-
ton Woods Agreements," January 19, 1946, SMLP-1, box 9. Tomlinson and
William H. Taylor were the two Treasury officials who met with Keynes in
London on January 18.

7. A transcript exists for a meeting at the U.S. Treasury on June 12, 1941, in
which Keynes and White participated, along with several other American
and British parties, but that meeting did not develop into a debate; MD
407:182–255.

8. "Board of Governors Inaugural Meeting: Functions and Remuneration
Committee," IMFA. This transcript is the source for the following discussion of this meeting. (As of this writing, this file is not available to external
researchers.) For a summary of the proceedings, see Horsefield, *International
Monetary Fund*, 1:130–35.

9. Transcript of a meeting of the IMF Board of Governors at Savannah, Ga.,
March 16, 1946, 11, IMFA. This transcript is the source of the quotes in the
following paragraphs.

10. William H. Taylor, memorandum for files, January 24, 1946, SMLP-1,
box 11.

11. Coe to Vinson, memorandum, "Problems of Savannah Conference," February 20, 1946, IMF-BWC, document BWC1573-01.

12. Harry White to Anne Terry White, March 10, 1946, SMLP-2.

13. See Boughton, "Boxing with Elephants" and "Canada in the Global Financial
System." References to the original sources are in "Boxing with Elephants."

14. Minutes of Executive Board Meeting 1, May 6, 1946, 1–2, IMFA.

15. White, "A Step toward 'One World.'"

16. "Statement Concerning Initial Par Values," Press Release no. 4, December
18, 1946, IMFA. Drafts of the statement were circulated internally as Executive Board Document 138 (EBD/46/138), and revisions 1 through 5.

17. Harry White to Joan White, December 7, 1946, SMLP-2. For his public
assessments, see White, "International Monetary Fund: The First Year" and
"A Step toward 'One World.'"

18. The work of the IMF in 1946–47 is covered comprehensively in Horsefield,
International Monetary Fund, 1: chap. 8.

19. White, unfinished manuscript, "Notes on the Articles of Agreement of the
International Monetary Fund," SMLP-1, box 10. For a summary, see Horsefield, *International Monetary Fund*, 1:138–39.

20. One can only surmise what Harry said during meetings of the Executive
Board. The minutes for that first year recorded only summaries of decisions
that were made, not the arguments advanced by individual directors.

21. An undated partial draft of the speech, including the passage quoted here, is in SMLP-2. The trip to Florida is described in a letter from Harry to Joan White, January 15, 1947, also in SMLP-2.

22. Triffin's work on Latin America while he was an economist at the U.S. Federal Reserve Board is examined in Helleiner, *Forgotten Origins*.

23. IMF Staff Memo 11, "Proposed Mission to Ecuador," January 14, 1947, and minutes of Executive Board Meeting 122, January 17, 1947, both IMFA.

24. Horsefield, *International Monetary Fund*, 1:186. The "feeling its way" phrase is on p. 187. The decision to assign mission to staff instead of directors is covered on p. 198.

25. Personal details are from letters he wrote to Joan, at various stops along the way; SMLP-2.

26. Staff memorandum 84, "Fund Mission to Ecuador," May 1, 1947, IMFA.

27. File, "S812 Mission to Latin America Dr. Harry D. White and Staff," IMFA, box 281, file 8, reference 89337.

28. NARA-118, 2689.

29. Camille Gutt, "Managing Director's Statement Concerning Resignation of Mr. White," Executive Board Circular 174, April 14, 1947, IMFA.

30. Truman to White, April 7, 1947, SMLP-2.

Chapter 17. Freelance Consultant, 1947–48

1. White to William O'Dwyer, April 7, 1947, SMLP-2.

2. These photographs are in a family collection.

3. Henri Bonnet, French ambassador to the United States, to White, September 26, 1947, SMLP-2. The embassy presented the medal to him on March 4, 1948.

4. Paul H. Douglas, professor of economics at the University of Chicago and president of the American Economic Association, to White, November 26, 1947, and undated handwritten draft of White's reply, both SMLP-2.

5. Speculation about a possible appointment was reported by Malcolm R. Hobbs, a journalist for the Overseas News Agency in New York, in an article for the agency's *Washington Letter*, April 22, 1948. The article was reprinted in U.S. Congress, Senate, *Interlocking Subversion: Hearing*, part 30: 2529–30. The full text of Wallace's speech was printed in the *New York Times*, August 22, 1948, 47.

6. Sol Adler to Mrs. Bessie Bloom, November 24, 1956, SMLP-2.

7. Mario Rodriguez, chargé d'affaires at the Chilean embassy in Washington, to White, May 2, 1947, SMLP-2. Also see William L. Clayton, under secretary of state for economic affairs, to Claude G. Bowers, U.S. ambassador to Chile, May 20, 1947, SMLP-2, informing him that "my friend Mr. Harry White" was going to Chile at the invitation of the Chilean government and asking him to extend diplomatic assistance and courtesies to him. As recorded in a 1974 oral history for HSTL, John P. Young (chief of the State Department's Division of International Finance, 1943–65) recalled that the

central bank of Chile asked the U.S. embassy for advice on whether to hire Harry as a consultant. The request got passed up to Dean Acheson (then under secretary of state), who advised the embassy to make a noncommittal reply. Young speculated that Acheson may have heard rumors about White's being suspected of Communist ties. Years later, an embassy official told Young that this reply dissuaded them from proceeding.

8. See Cox to White, October 31, 1947, Professor Isaiah L. Sharfman to White, April 19, 1948, and Anne Terry White to Joan White, April 22, 1948, all SMLP-2.

9. Exchange of letters between White and Antonio Espinosa de los Monteros, the Mexican ambassador to the United States, January 13 and February 19, 1948, SMLP-2.

10. Anne Terry White to Joan White, November 26, 1947, SMLP-2.

11. White, "Proposal for Amendment," 1.

12. Harry introduced the term *trade dollars* in his 1942 plan for the IMF, but only to dismiss the suggestion that the scheme required a new international currency; Horsefield, *International Monetary Fund*, 3:78–82.

13. A copy of the draft, in SMLP-1, box 11, is marked "HDW:atw 4/20/48" at the bottom of the last page, indicating that it was written by Harry White and was typed by Anne Terry White on April 20, 1948. At the top of the first page, in Harry's own hand, it is marked "H D White May 19, 1948." The fact that he signed that copy a month after it was typed and shortly before his trip to Mexico City suggests that he planned to give it to the authorities in Mexico for their use.

14. Ibid.

15. White, "Proposal for Amendment," cover page. Also see minutes of Executive Board Meeting 369, October 7, 1948. Harry's widow, Anne, helped prepare the original manuscript, including typing it, and she was involved in preparing it for the Executive Board. The final version, as circulated in the IMF, included several annotations inserted with her initials (ATW).

16. "Proposal for Amendment to Fund Agreement to Increase Level of World Trade," IMF Executive Board Document 347, Supplement 1, August 23, 1949, IMFA.

17. The lead author of the staff analysis was Jacques J. Polak, then the deputy director of the Research Department. More than a half century later, Polak told me that he and others had found the proposal to be poorly designed. They viewed the official internal circulation and staff analysis of it to have been just a tribute to Harry and a courtesy to his widow.

18. Triffin first presented the theory in a pair of papers published in 1959 in the Italian journal *Banca Nazionale del Lavoro Quarterly Review*. The fullest formulation is in his 1960 book, *Gold and the Dollar Crisis*.

19. For the background to the creation of the SDR and the text of the amendment, see de Vries, *International Monetary Fund: The System under Stress*. For the history of the SDR through the end of the century, see Mussa, Boughton,

and Isard, *Future of the SDR*; Boughton, *Silent Revolution*, chap. 18; and Boughton, *Tearing Down Walls*, chap. 15.

20. For analyses of that growth and its effect on the system, see Fischer, "Globalization and Its Challenges," and Boughton, *Stabilizing International Finance*. The more conventional wisdom about the Bretton Woods system is that it collapsed primarily because of unsustainable macroeconomic policies, especially in the United States, rather than because of the inconsistency between its structure and the successful and widening international sphere of economic growth; see Bordo and Eichengreen, *Retrospective*.

21. Transcript of meeting on "Jewish Evacuation," January 13, 1944, MD 693:192-216. White's copy of the letter to Morgenthau (February 2, 1944), signed along with Herbert E. Gaston, Randolph Paul, John W. Pehle, Ansel F. Luxford, Josiah E. DuBois Jr., and Henrietta Klotz, is in SMLP-2. For a personal account of Morgenthau's involvement, see chap. 29 of his son's memoir, *Mostly Morgenthaus*. Also see Beschloss, *Conquerors*, chaps. 6–9.

22. Harry Magdoff (who served as the intermediary) to Joan White Pinkham, November 17, 1990, White family collection.

23. Ibid.

24. S. Ralph Lazrus to White, February 7, 1947, and June 17, 1947, SMLP-2. For the background to Einstein's withdrawal from the project, see Sachar, *Brandeis University*, 18–22.

25. The original sources for much of this paragraph are the state archives of Israel and the archives of the successor to the Anglo-Palestine Bank. My sources also include an unpublished 2017 manuscript by Professor (Emeritus) Ephraim Kleiman of the Hebrew University of Jerusalem. For a tribute and review of Raisman's career, see Chandavarkar, "Sir (Abraham) Jeremy Raisman." Also see the obituary for Gass in the *New York Times*, January 4, 1990.

26. White to Gass, November 13, 1947, SMLP-2.

27. A caveat is in order regarding this account. White's contributions primarily took the form of letters to Gass that responded to information and suggestions that Gass provided either on his own or on behalf of Hoofien. White's letters are in SMLP-2, but Gass's are not. Some of the basis for Gass's input is in ISA, but for part of what follows I have had to draw inferences from just one side of the correspondence. The plan was set out in a memorandum prepared by Gass for Kaplan: "Some Aspects of the Economic Union proposed by the Majority Report of the UNSCOP," October 7, 1947, and in a technical annex, "Outline of a Monetary System for Palestine under Partition and Economic Union," October 29, 1947. The technical annex was unsigned. Gass's copy and his earlier memorandum are in ISA, file "Oscar Gass, 1947."

28. White to Gass, January 10, 1948, SMLP-2.

29. Kleiman, "Israeli Currency," 10. Also see Hoofien to White, March 15, 1948, SMLP-2.

30. White to Gass, March 18, 1948), draft in SMLP-2; the version received by Gass is in ISA.

31. Ibid.
32. Gass to Hoofien, May 14, 1948, copied to White, SMLP-2.
33. White to Kaplan, memorandum, "Anglo-Palestine Bank and Central Banking Powers," May 28, 1948, ISA, file "Anglo-Palestine Bank [1948 to 1950]," 608–17. Quotes in the following paragraphs are from this memorandum. Also see Kleiman, "Israeli Currency."

Chapter 18. Dealing with the Red Scare, 1947–48

1. Testimony of White, March 24–25, 1948, NARA-118, 2689, 2712. The quote from Sophocles, "Oedipus the King" (translated by David Grene), *The Complete Greek Tragedies: Sophocles I*, at the beginning of the chapter is used by permission of the University of Chicago Press.
2. Testimony of White, March 24, 1948, NARA-118, 2689–91.
3. Testimony of Francis D. O'Brien, March 23, 1948, ibid., 2670–76.
4. Testimony of White, March 25, 1948, ibid., 2713, 2721. For the public speculation about the grand jury, see Robert S. Allen, "Mystery Investigation Flusters Inner Circles," *Washington Post*, August 19, 1947, 13.
5. This grand jury, which was first convened on June 16, 1947, was the same one that had subpoenaed Coe. Unfortunately, the transcripts that were declassified in 1999 contain a long gap between July 31 and November 24, 1947. Coe's testimony would probably have been given very early in August. See index at https://www.trumanlibrary.gov/library/federal-record/records-us-attorneys-and-marshals-transcripts-grand-jury-testimony-alger #series1.
6. Testimony of White, March 24, 1948, NARA-118, 2681–82.
7. See Theoharis, *Chasing Spies*, 96–97, and Craig, *Treasonable Doubt*, 208.
8. Testimony of White, March 25, 1948, NARA-118, 2724. The quotations in the next four paragraphs are from pp. 2733–42.
9. *Washington Times-Herald*, December 28, 1944; clipping from the White family collection in SMLP-2. Also see thank-you letters from White to Bystrov and to Larry Morris (both dated March 26, 1945), in the same collection.
10. Testimony of White, March 25, 1948, NARA-118, 2744.
11. Ibid., 2745–55.
12. White to Oscar Cox, draft letter (marked "very approximate copy"), March 27, 1948, SMLP-2.
13. Testimony of Elizabeth Bentley, March 30, 1948, NARA-118, 2795. A week later, on April 6, 1948, Bentley provided additional details about Harry's alleged involvement, based on what the Silvermasters had told her at various times, but she repeated that she had no firsthand knowledge (2946–53). She testified again in February 1949, after Harry died.
14. *New York Times*, August 1, 1948, 1.
15. Testimony of Whittaker Chambers, August 3, 1948; U.S. Congress, House of Representatives Committee on Un-American Activities, *Hearings*, 563–84. The text also may be accessed at https://famous-trials.com/algerhiss.

16. Feltus to White, August 3, 1948; White to Patterson, draft, August 7, 1948; White to "Dave" (no surname, no date), draft; all in SMLP-2.

17. Liebling, "Whole Story," 139, and editorial, "Due Process for Harry White," *New York Times*, August 18, 1948, 24.

18. For the full text of the hearings, see U.S. Congress, House of Representatives Committee on Un-American Activities, *Hearings*, 877–906. Harry's testimony was also published in Nathan White, *Harry Dexter White: Loyal American*, 20–68.

19. U.S. Congress, House of Representatives Committee on Un-American Activities, *Interim Report*.

20. U.S. Congress, House of Representatives Committee on Un-American Activities, *Hearings*, 881.

21. Ibid.

22. Anne Terry White to Joan White, April 8, 1968, SMLP-2. Also see Whipple, "Life and Death," November 15, 1953, 76; and Craig, *Treasonable Doubt*, 213–14. Whipple's account and others derived from it asserted that Harry got off the train at Fitzwilliam, N.H., but Anne's letter recalls that she met him at Greenfield, some twenty-four miles to the northeast.

Chapter 19. Afterlife

1. The circumstances of White's death and the subsequent unfounded rumors are discussed in Rees, *Harry Dexter White: A Study in Paradox*, 416–18, and Craig, *Treasonable Doubt*, 214–16. For a recent example of the careless repetition of the false suicide story, see Greenfield, "When Enemies Infiltrated."

2. The condolences from Morgenthau and Currie are in SMLP-2.

3. Photostats of the eight pages were published in the *Congressional Record* of House hearings on November 17, 1953. They also were published, alongside a transcription of the text, in Nathan White, *Harry Dexter White: Loyal American*, 82–97. Rees, *Harry Dexter White: A Study in Paradox*, 432–36, reproduced a photocopy of the fourth page of the notes, a transcription of all eight pages, and the text of the report of the handwriting analysis.

4. Examples abound. Rees, *Harry Dexter White: A Study in Paradox*, repeatedly described the set of notes as the "White Memorandum." Tanenhaus, *Whittaker Chambers*, 439, blithely referred to it as "the eight-page memorandum . . . that Harry Dexter White had given Chambers in 1938 for transmittal to Boris Bykov," Chambers's Soviet contact. Craig, *Treasonable Doubt*, 210, referred to it as "the incriminating 'White Memorandum.'" Weinstein, *Perjury*, 211, acknowledged that the notes were written over an extended period, but he still called it "a four-page [*sic*] handwritten memorandum."

5. Morgenthau, meeting notes, January 8, 1938, MD 105:229–30; Haas memorandum, January 10, 1938, MD 105:260–61; notes on Morgenthau's phone call to Taylor, January 10, 1938, MD 105:336–38.

6. "Exchange Control Hit; Morgenthau Says U.S. Will Not Be a Party to Any Plan," *New York Times*, December 24, 1937, 25.

7. Cochran's report, sent by cable from Ambassador Bullitt to Morgenthau on February 15, 1938, is in MD 110:163–74.

8. See Tanenhaus, *Whittaker Chambers*, 312, and Weinstein, *Perjury*, 194–95. For a more skeptical account, see Craig, *Treasonable Doubt*, 54–58. Tanenhaus avers (304) that Chambers gave a copy of Harry's supposed report to the FBI in 1948, but Tanenhaus was confusing the report with the handwritten notes on other topics discussed above.

9. NARA-118, 4513–41.

10. Weinstein, *Perjury*, 553n40, noted that he had seen a statement made by Anne Terry White to her lawyer to the effect that she had received a rug, presumably in this manner, around the reported time. In a personal letter to me in July 2000, Joan Pinkham (the Whites' daughter, who was eight years old and living at home when Silverman gave them the rug) confirmed the account and recalled that the family displayed the rug prominently in the living room for some years, and later in the dining room.

11. See WCDA-Vassiliev, white notebook no. 1, 5, 42.

12. NARA-118, 5419.

13. Ibid., 5637.

14. Ibid., 5544, 5628, and 5630.

15. Joseph McCarthy, speech of February 4, 1954; quoted in Cook, *Nightmare Decade*, 462.

16. "White Scored on Gold," *New York Times*, July 14, 1956, 22.

17. White to Vinson, August 14, 1945, NARA-RG56, box 13.

18. Snow, *Pattern of Soviet Power*, 127.

19. For a detailed analysis, see Craig, *Treasonable Doubt*, 178–95.

20. "Monetary Official Denies He Is Red," *New York Times*, November 10, 1953, 16.

21. U.S. Congress, Senate, Executive Sessions of the Senate Permanent Subcommittee, 4:3403–43.

22. "Taylor's Loyalty Doubted by Panel," *New York Times*, July 22, 1955, 10; and "Taylor Absolved of Red Spying; Loyalty Board Reverses Itself," *New York Times*, January 7, 1956, 1, 7.

23. For Bentley's initial claim to the FBI, see FBI-FOIA, "White," 60. For her grand jury testimony, see NARA-118, 6305.

24. Statements by Chief Counsel Roy M. Cohn and introduction to Coe, testimony, June 3, 1953, U.S. Congress, Senate, Executive Sessions of the Senate Permanent Subcommittee on Investigations, 2:1349, 1351, and 1362–63.

25. Ibid., 1349–66. Other parts of this account are based on interviews with Frank Coe's colleagues and family.

26. WCDA-Venona, "New York KGB 1944" and "New York KGB 1945." Two 1945 cables intercepted in the Venona project refer to "Peak" with the same "possibly" link to Coe, but they provide no further clues about the nature of "Peak's" activities.

27. See, for example, the minutes of a meeting in Morgenthau's office on November 3, 1944, of the "U.S. Committee on Mutual Lend-Lease Aid between the United States and the United Kingdom," MD 791:50–51.
28. WCDA-Vassiliev, black notebook, 78.
29. The case was *Kent v. Dulles*. The full text is at https://supreme.justia.com/cases/federal/us/357/116/case.html. For the background, see Farber, "National Security."
30. FBI-FOIA, "Virginius Frank Coe," 28 (PDF), https://archive.org/details/VirginiusFrankCoe/page/n5. For other anecdotes about Coe's life and work in China, see Rittenberg and Bennett, *Man Who Stayed Behind*.
31. Sweezy led a delegation of economists to China in 1972. See Weber and Semieniuk, "American Radical Economists." The itinerary, which includes the evenings with the Coes, is on the website of Tom Weisskopf, a member of the delegation, at https://sites.lsa.umich.edu/tomweisskopf/. Additional information can be found in the papers of another member, Howard Wachtel, at American University (box 6, "China Trip Notes and Souvenirs"). Fairbank described his visits in letters to Lauchlin Currie, which Roger Sandilands made available to me. On Galbraith and Robinson, see Galbraith, *China Passage*, 48–49, and Turner, *Joan Robinson*, 86–89, 249. Galbraith maintained contact with Coe through the 1970s; see Galbraith to Coe, December 10, 1976, in Galbraith, *Selected Letters*, 467. Morath and Miller describe their visit in their book *Chinese Encounters*.
32. For a more detailed examination of that evidence, see Boughton and Sandilands, "Politics and the Attack." For a full biography, see Sandilands, *Life and Political Economy of Currie*.
33. WCDA-Venona, "New York KGB 1945," 11–13.
34. Craig, *Treasonable Doubt*, 86–87, 313n16. Craig cites an additional cable from the Vassiliev Notebooks that is described in Weinstein and Vassiliev, *Haunted Wood*, 78. That cable, which supposedly described a meeting between Adler and an alleged American Communist named Michael Straight in 1938, is not in the notebooks in WCDA.
35. Horsefield, "Annals," 292–93. Also see U.S. Executive Order no. 10422, January 9, 1953, https://www.archives.gov/federal-register/codification/executive-order/10422.html, and John D. Hickerson, assistant secretary of state, to Ivor Rooth, February 21, 1953, Attachment IV in "United States Executive Order of January 9, 1953," EBAP/53/13, February 24, 1953, IMFA.
36. For the commissioning and early disposition of the busts, see Barbara R. Hughes, memorandum to files, "Busts of Lord Keynes and Harry Dexter White," January 24, 1995, IMFA. Other information in this account is based on recollections by several long-serving IMF staff and my own firsthand observations.
37. The text of the relevant portion of Brownell's speech in this and the next two paragraphs was published in "Text of Brownell's Remarks on Reds," *New York Times*, November 7, 1953, 11.

38. "Close-up of a Ghost," *Life*, November 23, 1953, 31; "One Man's Greed," *Time*, November 23, 1953, 22; Chambers, "Herring and the Thing," 14.

39. Anne Terry White to Joan White, July 30, 1943, SMLP-2. The movie list is in SMLP-2.

40. "Close-up of a Ghost," *Life*, November 23, 1953, 29.

41. In November 1953 Byrnes claimed that when he saw the FBI report in January 1946, he recommended to Truman that he "ask a Senator to move to reconsider the confirmation of White," but Truman "did not think well of that suggestion"; quoted in *Time*, November 16, 1953, 20. Truman's meeting with Vinson and Byrnes took place at 12:30 P.M. on February 7, 1946, the day after the Senate confirmed White, not on February 6, as was widely reported in 1953.

42. Nichols, *Ike and McCarthy*, 86, based on his interview with Brownell's daughter. On Eisenhower's claim, see ibid., 88. On the 1943 meeting, see Morgenthau to Admiral William D. Leahy, memorandum, September 28, 1943, MD 668:53. The 1944 meeting between Eisenhower and White was confirmed by another participant, Fred Smith (like White, assistant to the Treasury secretary); see Smith, "Rise and Fall," which was based on notes that Smith "made directly after the meeting."

Chapter 20. Second Afterlife

1. Anne retained the papers in her possession, as did her daughter Joan, who acquired them upon Anne's death in 1980. After Joan died in 2012, her daughter, Claire A. Pinkham, donated those papers and other personal items to the manuscript library at Princeton University, where they supplement the papers donated by Anne in the 1950s (cited here as SMLP-1 and SMLP-2).

2. U.S. Congress, Senate, *Interlocking Subversion: Hearing*, 84th Cong., part 29, 2368 and 2389.

3. U.S. Congress, Senate, *Interlocking Subversion: Hearing*, 84th Cong., part 30, VI.

4. Ibid., LX.

5. For an overview of the Venona project, see Benson, *The Venona Story*. The cables are posted at https://www.nsa.gov/news-features/declassified-documents/venona/. The texts and a concordance are published at WCDA-Venona.

6. WCDA-Venona, "New York KGB 1944," 34.

7. Blum, *From the Morgenthau Diaries: Years of War*, 304–6.

8. In my article "The Case against Harry Dexter White: Still Not Proven," I questioned whether Harry would have been privy to a conversation between Hull and Wallace. Michael Beschloss, in *Conquerors*, 155n, criticized me for that argument, noting correctly that Harry knew Wallace well. Fair enough, but the main point remains that for Harry to mention to his Soviet counterparts that Wallace favored the loan proposal would not have been a cause for suspicion.

9. "Maj" (Pavel Ivanovich Fedosimov, in New York) to "Viktor" (Pavel Mikhailovich Fitin, in Moscow), telegrams, August 4 and 5, 1944, WCDA-Venona, "New York KGB 1944," 374–79.

10. Andrew and Mitrokhin, in *The Sword and the Shield*, 130, blithely call this incident a meeting between Harry and his "handler."

11. The bracketed text is in the decrypt. "[c]" after "new course" indicates a note to the text, reading, "NOVYJ KURS" in the Russian. If correct, it might be a way of translating 'New Deal.'"

12. Recollections of White's daughters, as reported to me in 2001.

13. Knight, "Selling," 23.

14. Fedosimov to Fitin, telegram, November 20, 1944, WCDA-Venona, "New York KGB 1944," 661–63.

15. Akhmerov, report to Moscow, December 11, 1945, WCDA-Vassiliev, white notebook no. 3, 37.

16. Moscow to New York office, telegram, April 6, 1945, WCDA-Venona, "New York KGB 1945," 151.

17. "Maj" (Stepan Apresyan, in San Francisco) to Fitin, in Moscow, telegrams, May 4 and 5, 1945; and San Francisco to Moscow, May 13, 1945, WCDA-Venona, "San Francisco KGB," 226–29, 234–35.

18. For a detailed history, see Russell, *History of the United Nations Charter*, chap. 28.

19. Venona cable no. 236, May 5, 1945. The cable does not show a closing mark for the purported quotation from "Richard."

20. Harry White to Anne Terry White, April 23, 1945, SMLP-2. WCDA-Venona, "San Francisco KGB," 228.

21. For example, see Weinstein and Vassiliev, *Haunted Wood*, 169.

22. The surname Greinke does not appear in the translated written account that I used. Craig cites the full name in *Treasonable Doubt*, 247.

23. Morgenthau to Roosevelt, October 17, 1938, MD 146:109.

24. Koster, *Operation Snow*, and Schecter and Schecter, *Sacred Secrets*, 33. The quotation in the epigraph is from Pavlov, *Operation Snow*, 49, in a translation from Russian provided to me by Bruce Craig. Also see Craig, *Treasonable Doubt*, 246–51. Craig notes (389n80) that when he interviewed Pavlov, the Russian confirmed that when he wrote that White was never "an agent, it means that we had no relations with him. No relations with him. No relations at all." Kobyakov's confirmation was in an email of December 22, 2003, to Roger Sandilands; author's files.

25. For a review of the transition, see Knight, "Fate of the KGB Archives." The official name of the Soviet intelligence service evolved over time. During the period covered here, the nonmilitary arm was known as the NKVD. The KGB archives include that period as well.

26. Andrew and Mitrokhin, *The Sword and the Shield*, 106.

27. For a discussion of the limitations of the source material, see Knight, "Selling" and "Leonard?" and Chervonnaya, "Vassiliev's Notes."

28. "Statement of Federal Service: Nathan G. Silvermaster," April 15, 1953, U.S. Civil Service Commission.

29. WCDA-Vassiliev, white notebook no. 1, 154. The statement is from an undated report on the activities of Jacob Golos.

30. WCDA-Vassiliev, white notebook no. 1, 21–22; Weinstein and Vassiliev, *Haunted Wood*, 159.

30. Transcript of a telephone conversation between Morgenthau and Frank Knox, July 31, 1941, MD 426:110–11.

32. Transcript of a meeting, August 1, 1941, MD 427.1:31–35. The transcript is slightly garbled. Morgenthau's remark about the bet follows a comment by Foley on another topic, and the transcript fails to note that the speaker has shifted from Foley to Morgenthau. The context makes it clear that Morgenthau made the remark.

33. WCDA-Vassiliev, white notebook no. 1, 34.

34. WCDA-Vassiliev, white notebook no. 3, 2.

35. Weinstein and Vassiliev, *Haunted Wood*, 161.

36. WCDA-Vassiliev, white notebook no. 3, 1.

37. WCDA-Vassiliev, white notebook no. 1, 48.

38. Ibid., 38.

39. Ibid., 48.

40. WCDA-Vassiliev, white notebook no. 3, 25.

41. WCDA-Vassiliev, white notebook no. 1, 71.

42. Ibid., 69.

43. See, for example, Rauchway, *Money Makers*, 176, and West, *Venona*, 307.

44. WCDA-Venona, "New York KGB 1945," 45.

45. WCDA-Vassiliev, white notebook no. 1, 69.

46. WCDA-Vassiliev, white notebook no. 3, 51.

Epilogue: The Legacy Redux

1. Mission statements from the IMF, http://www.imf.org/external/about.htm, and the World Bank, http://www.worldbank.org/en/news/feature/2013/04/17/ending_extreme_poverty_and_promoting_shared_prosperity.

2. Horsefield, *International Monetary Fund*, 3:47. For a full discussion of the British negotiating strategy, see Pressnell, *External Economic Policy*.

3. Keynes Plan of February 1942, Horsefield, *International Monetary Fund*, 3:13. White to Morgenthau, memorandum, "What should our answer be to the British Treasury as to our attitude toward further depreciation of the franc?" April 30, 1938, NARA-RG56, box 2.

4. I have argued this point more fully in Boughton, "The Universally Keynesian Vision."

5. Nathan White, *Harry Dexter White: Loyal American*, 54.

6. Information provided to me by David Eddy. Used by permission.

7. Douglas, *Go East, Young Man*, 382.

8. Examples abound. Skidelsky, *John Maynard Keynes: Fighting for Britain*, 263: "There can be no doubt that . . . White knew that he was betraying his trust." Craig, *Treasonable Doubt*, 263: "He certainly had to have known that he had betrayed the public trust his country had placed in him." Conway, *Summit*, 161: "He undoubtedly knew that he was secretly providing confidential information to the Soviets that was regarded by Moscow as extremely useful."

9. Craig, *Treasonable Doubt*, 101, 320n88, notes that Harry "played a role" in the Treasury's hiring of Perlo. That role consisted of his suggesting to Coe that he consider hiring Perlo after Harry met Perlo "on a social basis."

10. Ezekiel was investigated mainly because his wife, Lucille, was president of the local chapter of the League of Women Shoppers, the same organization that brought Anne Terry White under suspicion in 1942. In addition, Lucille's sister was living with a member of the Communist Party; Storrs, *Second Red Scare*, 103. Similarly, Anne had a sister whose ex-husband (Abe Wolfson) was suspected of being a Communist. For a more general analysis of the attack on members of the League of Women Shoppers and similar groups, see Storrs, "Left-Feminism."

11. For a further discussion of these cases and their context, see Boughton and Sandilands, "Politics and the Attack." For a more general analysis of the effects of loyalty board investigations on individuals and on national policies, see Storrs, *Second Red Scare*.

12. Galbraith to James M. Boughton and Roger J. Sandilands, February 7, 2001, reprinted in Galbraith, *Selected Letters*, 620–21. The journalist I. F. Stone, in *Truman Era*, 48, made a similar observation, writing that White was "too independent in his thinking to tread anybody's line."

Bibliography

Archival Records

ATWP. Anne Terry White Papers, Ax 468, Special Collections and University Archives, University of Oregon Libraries, Eugene.

EAG. E. A. Goldenweiser papers, box 4, Library of Congress.

FBI-FOIA. FBI files declassified and made available in response to requests under the terms of the Freedom of Information Act; https://www.fbi.gov/services/information-management/foipa. The files cited here have been declassified but at the time of this writing are not on the FBI website. PDFs may be available on third-party websites and have been accessed as follows: file 65-56402 ("Silvermaster"), at https://archive.org/details/FBISilvermasterFile/FBI%20File%20Silvermaster%20Part%201%20November%201945; file 101-4053 ("White"), at https://commons.wikimedia.org/wiki/File%3AWhite_01_FBI_File.PDF; file 101-3599 ("Glasser"), at https://archive.org/details/HaroldGlasser/Glasser%2C%20Harold%20001/page/n7/mode/2up; and file 100-96788 ("Virginius Frank Coe"), at https://archive.org/details/VirginiusFrankCoe/page/n5/mode/2up. Page numbers refer to the PDF pagination, not that of the original file.

FRUS. U.S. Department of State, various dates. *Foreign Relations of the United States: Diplomatic Papers*; https://history.state.gov/historicaldocuments/.

GSM. George S. Messersmith Papers, University of Delaware; http://udspace.udel.edu/handle/19716/5973.

HSTL. Harry S. Truman Library; https://www.trumanlibrary.gov/.

IMFA. International Monetary Fund Archives; http://www.imf.org/external/np/arc/eng/archive.htm.

IMFA-BWC. International Monetary Fund Archives, Bretton Woods Collection.

ISA. Israeli State Archives; https://www.archives.gov.il/en/.

MD. Diaries of Henry Morgenthau Jr., April 27, 1933–July 27, 1945. Franklin D. Roosevelt Presidential Library and Museum, digital collection; https://

catalog.archives.gov/search?q=*:*&f.parentNaId=589213&f.level=fileUnit
&sort=naIdSort%20asc&rows=50. These 864 volumes are stored as PDFs,
some volumes being divided into two or three separate files. They are cited
here in the form "MD nnn:ppp" or "MD nnn.x:ppp," where nnn is the volume
number, x is the part number if needed, and ppp is the page number or numbers. Page numbers cited herein refer to the pagination of the PDFs, which is
different from the original pagination of the diaries.

MPD. Presidential Diaries of Henry Morgenthau Jr., January 1, 1938–July 13,
1945. Seven vols. Franklin D. Roosevelt Presidential Library and Museum,
digital collection. Cited in the same manner as the diaries in MD, above.

NARA-118. National Archives and Records Administration, "Records of U.S. Attorneys and Marshalls: Transcripts of Grand Jury Testimony in the Alger Hiss
Case," Record Group 118.

NARA-RG56. National Archives and Records Administration, Records Group
56.12.3, entry 360P, "Records of the Assistant Secretary of the Treasury re:
Monetary and International Affairs. Chronological file of Harry Dexter
White, Nov. 1934–Apr. 1946." College Park, Md., 13 boxes.

NYFRB. Federal Reserve Bank of New York Archives.

SMLP-1. Harry Dexter White Papers, series 1–3; items donated by Anne Terry
White, 1950–55. Seeley G. Mudd Manuscript Library, Princeton University,
Princeton, N.J.

SMLP-2. Harry Dexter White Papers, series 4; items donated by Claire A.
Pinkham beginning in 2013. Seeley G. Mudd Manuscript Library, Princeton
University, Princeton, N.J.

WCDA-Vassiliev. Wilson Center Digital Archive, Vassiliev Notebooks; http://
digitalarchive.wilsoncenter.org/collection/86/vassiliev-notebooks. The collection includes eight notebooks, designated by color and usually a number:
black, white 1–3, and yellow 1–4. It also includes a file guide and an index
with concordance. Page numbers cited here are those of the PDFs, not of the
original notebooks.

WCDA-Venona. Wilson Center Digital Archive, "Venona Project and Vassiliev Index and Concordance," https://www.wilsoncenter.org/article/venona-project
-and-vassiliev-notebooks-index-and-concordance. The collection includes
twelve files of transcriptions of the translations of partially decoded cables between Moscow and Soviet offices in the United States. The index and concordance for the Vassiliev Notebooks covers these files as well. The files cited here
are for 1944 and 1945. The original decryptions are also on the NSA website
at https://www.nsa.gov/news-features/declassified-documents/venona/.

Manuscripts and Publications by Harry Dexter White

Taussig, Frank W. *Some Aspects of the Tariff Question: An Examination of the Development of American Industries under Protection*. 3rd ed., *Continued to 1930, with the
Coöperation of H. D. White*. Cambridge: Harvard University Press, 1931.

Taussig, Frank W., and Harry Dexter White. "Rayon and the Tariff: The Nurture of an Industrial Prodigy." *Quarterly Journal of Economics* 45, no. 4 (August 1931): 588–621.

White, Harry Dexter. "European Loans Floated in the United States from 1919 to 1925." Master's thesis, Stanford University, 1925.

———. *The French International Accounts, 1880–1913*. Cambridge: Harvard University Press, 1933.

———. "Haberler's Der Internationale Handel and Ohlin's Interregional and International Trade." *Quarterly Journal of Economics* 48 (August 1934): 727–41.

———. "International Monetary and Financial Cooperation." In *Some American Problems in 1945 and Suggested Solutions*, 10–13. Washington, D.C.: People's Lobby, 1945.

———. "The International Monetary Fund: The First Year." *Annals of the American Academy of Political and Social Science* 252 (July 1947): 21–29.

———. "The Monetary Fund: Some Criticisms Examined." *Foreign Affairs* 23 (January 1945): 195–210.

———. "Our Foreign Investment Policy." *Young Democrat* (May 1946): 21, 29.

———. "Postwar Currency Stabilization." *American Economic Review (Papers and Proceedings)* 33 (March 1943): 382–87.

———. "Proposal for Amendment to Fund Agreement to Increase Level of World Trade." IMF Executive Board Document no. 347. October 14, 1948. IMF Archives.

———. "Proposal for United Nations Stabilization Fund and a Bank for Reconstruction and Development of the United and Associated Nations: Preliminary Draft." April 1942. IMF Archives.

———. "A Step toward 'One World': The IMF Sets Exchange Rates." *Dun's Review* 55 (September 1947): 14–16.

Other Sources

Acsay, Peter Josef. "Planning for Postwar Economic Cooperation: U.S. Treasury, the Soviet Union, and Bretton Woods, 1933–1946." Ph.D. dissertation, Saint Louis University, 2000. http://centerforfinancialstability.com/brettonwoods_docs.php.

Adler, Solomon. *The Chinese Economy*. London: Routledge & Kegan Paul, 1957.

Alacevich, Michele, Pier Francesco Asso, and Sebastiano Nerozzi. "Harvard Meets the Crisis: The Monetary Theory and Policy of Lauchlin B. Currie, Jacob Viner, John H. Williams, and Harry D. White." *Journal of the History of Economic Thought* 37, no. 3 (September 2015): 387–410.

Andrew, Christopher, and Vasili Mitrokhin. *The Sword and the Shield: The Mitrokhin Archive and the Secret History of the KGB*. New York: Basic Books, 1999.

Bailey, Andrew, Gordon Bannerman, and Cheryl Schonhardt-Bailey. "The Parliamentary Debates in the United Kingdom." In *The Bretton Woods Agreement: Together with Scholarly Commentaries and Essential Historical Documents*, edited by Naomi Lamoreaux and Ian Shapiro, chap. 5. New Haven: Yale University Press, 2019.

Baker, Carlos. *Ernest Hemingway: A Life Story*. New York: Charles Scribner's Sons, 1969.

Balkelis, Tomas. "Opening Gates to the West: Lithuanian and Jewish Migrations from the Lithuanian Provinces, 1867–1914." *Ethnicity Studies* (2010): 41–66.

Barnes, Julian. *Flaubert's Parrot*. London: Jonathan Cape, 1984.

Benson, Robert L. *The Venona Story*. CreateSpace Independent Publishing Platform, 2012. Also published online by the U.S. National Security Agency; https://www.nsa.gov/Portals/70/documents/about/cryptologic-heritage/historical-figures-publications/publications/coldwar/venona_story.pdf.

Bentley, Elizabeth. *Out of Bondage*. New York: Devin-Adair, 1951.

Bernstein, Edward M. "Some Economic Aspects of Multiple Exchange Rates." *International Monetary Fund Staff Papers* 1 (September 1950): 224–37.

Bernstein, Maurice. "All Still: Life among a Thousand Siblings." Undated manuscript, in author's files.

Beschloss, Michael. *The Conquerors: Roosevelt, Truman, and the Destruction of Hitler's Germany, 1941–1945*. New York: Simon & Schuster, 2002.

Bloomfield, Arthur I. "Operations of the American Exchange Stabilization Fund." *Review of Economics and Statistics* 26, no. 2 (May 1944): 69–87.

———. "The Tripartite Agreement of 1936 as an Alternative to the Keynes and White Plans." NYFRB folder "Postwar International Monetary Organization, 1943."

Blum, John Morton. *From the Morgenthau Diaries: Years of Crisis, 1928–1938*. Boston: Houghton Mifflin, 1959.

———. *From the Morgenthau Diaries: Years of Urgency, 1938–1941*. Boston: Houghton Mifflin, 1965.

———. *From the Morgenthau Diaries: Years of War, 1941–1945*. Boston: Houghton Mifflin, 1967.

Bordo, Michael D., and Barry Eichengreen, eds. *A Retrospective on the Bretton Woods System: Lessons for International Monetary Reform*. Chicago: University of Chicago Press, 1993.

Bordo, Michael D., Owen F. Humpage, and Anna J. Schwartz. *Strained Relations: U.S. Foreign Exchange Operations and Monetary Policy in the Twentieth Century*. Chicago: University of Chicago Press, 2015.

Bordo, Michael D., and Finn E. Kydland. "The Gold Standard as a Rule: An Essay in Exploration." *Explorations in Economic History* 32 (1995): 423–64.

Bordo, Michael D., and Anna J. Schwartz. "From the Exchange Stabilization Fund to the International Monetary Fund." NBER Working Paper 8100. Cambridge, Mass.: National Bureau of Economic Research, 2001.

Boughton, James M. "Boxing with Elephants: Can Canada Punch above Its Weight in Global Financial Governance?" CIGI Research Paper 28. Waterloo, Ont.: Centre for International Governance Innovation, 2014.

———. "Canada in the Global Financial System." In *Crisis and Reform: Canada and the International Financial System*, edited by Rohinton P. Medhora and Dane Rowlands. Waterloo, Ont.: Centre for International Governance Innovation, 2014.

———. "The Case against Harry Dexter White: Still Not Proven." *History of Political Economy* 33, no. 2 (Summer 2001): 219–39.

———. "On the Origins of the Fleming-Mundell Model." *IMF Staff Papers* 50, no. 1 (2003): 1–9.

———. *Silent Revolution: The International Monetary Fund, 1979–1989*. Washington, D.C.: International Monetary Fund, 2001.

———. *Stabilizing International Finance: Can the System Be Saved?* Essays in International Finance, no. 2. Waterloo, Ont.: Centre for International Governance Innovation, 2014.

———. *Tearing Down Walls: The International Monetary Fund, 1990–1999*. Washington, D.C.: International Monetary Fund, 2012.

———. "The Universally Keynesian Vision of Bretton Woods." In *The Bretton Woods Agreement: Together with Scholarly Commentaries and Essential Historical Documents*, edited by Naomi Lamoreaux and Ian Shapiro, chap. 4. New Haven: Yale University Press, 2019.

Boughton, James M., and Roger J. Sandilands. "Politics and the Attack on FDR's Economists: From the Grand Alliance to the Cold War." *Intelligence and National Security* 18, no. 3 (Autumn 2003): 73–99.

Bratter, Harbert M. "Steps That Led to Bretton Woods." *Commercial and Financial Chronicle* 160, no. 4320 (1944): 1347, 1355–56.

Bulmer-Thomas, Victor. *The Economic History of Latin America since Independence*. 3rd ed. Cambridge: Cambridge University Press, 2014.

Burdekin, Richard C. K. "U.S. Pressure on China: Silver Flows, Deflation, and the 1934 Shanghai Credit Crunch." *China Economic Review* 19 (June 2008): 170–82.

Burns, James MacGregor. *Roosevelt: The Soldier of Freedom, 1940–1945*. New York: Harcourt Brace Jovanovich, 1970.

Chambers, Whittaker. "The Herring and the Thing." *Look*, December 29, 1953, 14–18.

———. *Witness*. Washington, D.C.: Regnery, 1952.

Chandavarkar, Anand. "Sir (Abraham) Jeremy Raisman, Finance Member, Government of India (1939–1945): Portrait of an Unsung Statesman Extraordinaire." *Economic and Political Weekly* 36, no. 28 (July 14–20, 2001): 2641–55.

———. "Was Keynes Anti-Semitic?" *Economic and Political Weekly* 35, no. 19 (May 6, 2000): 1619–24.

Chervonnaya, Svetlana. "Alexander Vassiliev's Notes and Harry Dexter White." Documents Talk, http://documentstalk.com/wp/harry-dexter-white-in-alexander-vassilievs-notes-on-kgb-foreign-intelligence-files/.

Cobb, William H. *Radical Education in the Rural South: Commonwealth College, 1922–1940*. Detroit: Wayne State University Press, 2000.

Cohen-Setton, Jérémie, Joshua K. Hausman, and Johannes F. Wieland. "Supply-Side Policies in the Depression: Evidence from France." NBER Working Paper 22140 (March 2016). http://www.nber.org/papers/w22140.

Conway, Edmund. *The Summit: The Biggest Battle of the Second World War—Fought behind Closed Doors.* London: Little, Brown, 2014. (The title of the U.S. edition is *The Summit: Bretton Woods, 1944: J. M. Keynes and the Reshaping of the Global Economy.* New York: Pegasus, 2015.)

Cook, Fred J. *The Nightmare Decade: The Life and Times of Senator Joe McCarthy.* New York: Random House, 1971.

Cornish, Selwyn, and Kurt Schuler. "Australia's Full-Employment Proposals at Bretton Woods: A Road Only Partially Taken." In *The Bretton Woods Agreement: Together with Scholarly Commentaries and Essential Historical Documents,* edited by Naomi Lamoreaux and Ian Shapiro, chap. 8. New Haven: Yale University Press, 2019.

Craig, R. Bruce. *Treasonable Doubt: The Harry Dexter White Spy Case.* Lawrence: University Press of Kansas, 2004.

Currie, Lauchlin. "Domestic Stability and the Mechanism of Trade Adjustment to International Capital Movements." In *Explorations in Economics: Notes and Essays Contributed in Honor of F. W. Taussig,* 46–56. New York: McGraw-Hill, 1936.

———. "Recent Developments in International Monetary Relations, October 1936." Reprinted in *Journal of Economic Studies* 31, no. 3–4 (2004): 310–12.

———. "Some Theoretical and Practical Implications of J. M. Keynes' General Theory." In *The Economic Doctrines of John Maynard Keynes,* 15–27. New York: National Industrial Conference Board, 1938.

de Vries, Margaret Garritsen. *The International Monetary Fund, 1966–1971: The System under Stress.* Washington, D.C.: International Monetary Fund, 1976.

Díaz Alejandro, Carlos F. "Stories of the 1930s for the 1980s." In *Financial Policies and the World Capital Market: The Problem of Latin American Countries,* edited by Pedro Aspe Armella, Rudiger Dornbusch, and Maurice Obstfeld, 5–40. Chicago: University of Chicago Press, 1983.

Douglas, William O. *Go East, Young Man: The Early Years.* New York: Random House, 1974.

Drummond, Ian M. *The Floating Pound and the Sterling Area, 1931–1939.* Cambridge: Cambridge University Press, 1981.

Dulles, Eleanor Lansing. *Chances of a Lifetime: A Memoir.* Upper Saddle River, N.J.: Prentice-Hall, 1980.

Eckes, Alfred E., Jr. *A Search for Solvency: Bretton Woods and the International Monetary System.* Austin: University of Texas Press, 1975.

Edwards, Sebastian. "Academics as Economic Advisers: Gold, the 'Brains Trust,' and FDR." NBER Working Paper 21380 (July 2015).

Eichengreen, Barry. *Exorbitant Privilege: The Rise and Fall of the Dollar and the Future of the International Monetary System.* Oxford: Oxford University Press, 2011.

————. *Golden Fetters: The Gold Standard and the Great Depression, 1919–1939.* Oxford: Oxford University Press, 1992.

Eichengreen, Barry, and Douglas A. Irwin. "Trade Blocs, Currency Blocs and the Reorientation of World Trade in the 1930s." *Journal of International Economics* 38 (1995): 1–24.

Farber, Daniel A. "National Security, the Right to Travel, and the Court." *Supreme Court Review* 289 (1981): 263–290. https://lawcat.berkeley.edu/record/1111673?ln=en.

Fiorito, Luca, and Sebastiano Nerozzi. "Viner's Reminiscences from the New Deal (February 11, 1953)." In *Research in the History of Economic Thought and Methodology*, edited by Warren J. Samuels, Jeff E. Biddle, and Ross B. Emmett, 75–136. (Bingley, U.K.: Emerald, 2009).

Fischer, Stanley. "Globalization and Its Challenges." *American Economic Review* 93 (May 2003): 1–30.

Fisher, Irving. *100% Money: Designed to Keep Checking Banks 100% Liquid; to Prevent Inflation and Deflation; Largely to Cure or Prevent Depressions; and to Wipe Out Much of the National Debt.* New York: Adelphi, 1935.

————. *Stabilizing the Dollar: A Plan to Stabilize the General Price Level without Fixing Individual Prices.* New York: Macmillan, 1920.

Flanders, M. June. *International Monetary Economics, 1870–1960.* Cambridge: Cambridge University Press, 1990.

Flood, Robert P., and Peter Isard. "Monetary Policy Strategies." *IMF Staff Papers* 36, no. 3 (September 1989): 612–32.

Friedman, Milton. "Franklin D. Roosevelt, Silver, and China." *Journal of Political Economy* 100 (February 1992): 62–83.

Gaddis, John Lewis. *The United States and the Origins of the Cold War, 1941–1947.* New York: Columbia University Press, 1972.

Galbraith, John Kenneth. *A China Passage.* Boston: Houghton Mifflin, 1973.

————. *The Selected Letters of John Kenneth Galbraith.* Edited by Richard P. F. Holt. New York: Cambridge University Press, 2017.

Gardner, Richard N. *Sterling-Dollar Diplomacy in Current Perspective: The Origins and the Prospects of Our International Economic Order.* New York: Columbia University Press, 1980.

Ghosh, Atish R., Anne-Marie Gulde, and Holger C. Wolf. "Currency Boards: The Ultimate Fix?" IMF Working Paper WP/98/8 (January 1998).

Goldberg, Linda. "The International Role of the Dollar: Does It Matter If This Changes?" Federal Reserve Bank of New York Staff Report no. 522 (October 2011).

Goldberg, Linda, and Cédric Tille. "The Internationalization of the Dollar and Trade Balance Adjustment." Federal Reserve Bank of New York Staff Report no. 255 (August 2006).

Goode, James M. *Best Addresses: A Century of Washington's Distinguished Apartment Houses.* Washington, D.C.: Smithsonian Institution Press, 1988.

Greaves, Ida. *Colonial Monetary Conditions*. Colonial Research Studies no. 10. London: Her Majesty's Stationery Office, 1953.

Greenfield, Daniel. "When Enemies Infiltrated the White House," *Frontpage Mag*, March 10, 2013. http://www.frontpagemag.com/fpm/180831/when-enemies-infiltrated-white-house-daniel-greenfield.

Grene, David, and Richmond Lattimore, eds. *The Complete Greek Tragedies: Sophocles I*. Chicago: University of Chicago Press, 1954.

Haberler, Gottfried. *The Theory of International Trade with Its Applications to Commercial Policy*. New York: Macmillan, 1936.

Hanke, Steve. "Currency Boards." In *Exchange-Rate Regimes and Capital Flows: The Annals of the American Academy of Political and Social Science*, edited by George S. Tavlas and Michael K. Ulan, 87–105. Thousand Oaks, Calif.: Sage, 2002.

Harrod, Roy F. *The Life of John Maynard Keynes*. London: Macmillan, 1951.

Heiferman, Ronald Ian. *The Cairo Conference of 1943: Roosevelt, Churchill, Chiang Kai-shek and Madame Chiang*. Jefferson, N.C.: McFarland, 2011.

Helleiner, Eric. *The Forgotten Origins of Bretton Woods: International Development and the Making of the Postwar Order*. Ithaca: Cornell University Press, 2014.

Henning, C. Randall. *The Exchange Stabilization Fund: Slush Money or War Chest?* Washington, D.C.: [Peterson] Institute for International Economics, 1999.

Horesh, Niv. *Shanghai's Bund and Beyond: British Banks, Banknote Issuance, and Monetary Policy in China, 1842–1937*. New Haven: Yale University Press, 2009.

Horsefield, J. Keith. "Annals of the Fund." Internal document; draft of Horsefield, *The International Monetary Fund, 1945–1965: Twenty Years of International Monetary Cooperation*, Vol. 1, *Chronicle*. Washington, D.C.: International Monetary Fund, 1969.

———. *The International Monetary Fund, 1945–1965: Twenty Years of International Monetary Cooperation*. Vol. 1, *Chronicle*. Washington, D.C.: International Monetary Fund, 1969.

———, ed. *The International Monetary Fund, 1945–1965: Twenty Years of International Monetary Cooperation*. Vol. 3, *Documents*. Washington, D.C.: International Monetary Fund, 1969.

Irwin, Douglas A. *Against the Tide: An Intellectual History of Free Trade*. Princeton: Princeton University Press, 1996.

Keynes, John Maynard. *The Collected Writings of John Maynard Keynes*. Vol. 21, *Activities, 1931–1939: World Crises and Policies in Britain and America*. Edited by Elizabeth Johnson and Donald Moggridge. London: Macmillan, 1978.

———. *The Collected Writings of John Maynard Keynes*. Vol. 24, *Activities, 1944–1946, The Transition to Peace*. Edited by Donald Moggridge. London: Macmillan, 1979.

———. *The Collected Writings of John Maynard Keynes*. Vol. 25, *Activities, 1940–1944, Shaping the Post-War World: The Clearing Union*. Edited by Donald Moggridge. London: Macmillan, 1980.

———. *The Collected Writings of John Maynard Keynes*. Vol. 26, *Activities, 1941–1946, Shaping the Post-War World: Bretton Woods and Reparations*. Edited by Donald Moggridge. London: Macmillan, 1982.

———. *The Economic Consequences of the Peace*. London: Macmillan, 1919.

———. *Essays in Persuasion*. New York: Harcourt, Brace, 1932.

———. *The General Theory of Employment, Interest and Money*. London: Macmillan, 1936.

———. "The German Transfer Problem." *Economic Journal* 39 (1929): 1–7.

———. *A Tract on Monetary Reform*. London: Macmillan, 1923.

———. *Treatise on Money*. Vol. 2, *The Applied Theory of Money*. London: Macmillan, 1930.

Kindleberger, Charles P. *The Life of an Economist: An Autobiography*. Oxford: Blackwell, 1991.

King, Donald L. "The Legal Status of the Attorney General's 'List.'" *California Law Review* 44, no. 4 (1956): 747–61. https://lawcat.berkeley.edu/record/1109515.

Kleiman, Ephraim. "Harry Dexter White and the Establishment of Israeli Currency." Unpublished manuscript, 2017.

Knight, Amy. "The Fate of the KGB Archives." *Slavic Review* 52, no. 3 (Autumn 1993): 582–86.

———. "Leonard?" *Times Literary Supplement*, June 26, 2009, 8–9.

———. "The Selling of the KGB." *Wilson Quarterly* 24 (Winter 2000): 16–23.

Koster, John. *Operation Snow: How a Soviet Mole in FDR's White House Triggered Pearl Harbor*. Washington, D.C.: Regnery, 2012.

Lahey, Edwin A., "A Reporter at Bretton Woods." *New Republic*, July 17, 1944, 67–69.

Laidler, David E. W. "Rules, Discretion and Financial Policies in Classical and Neoclassical Monetary Economics." *Economic Issues* 7, pt. 2 (2002): 11–23.

Laidler, David E. W., and Roger J. Sandilands. "An Early Harvard Memorandum on Anti-Depression Policies: Introductory Note." *History of Political Economy* 34, no. 3 (2002): 515–52.

Lainà, Patrizio. "Proposals for Full-Reserve Banking: A Historical Survey from David Ricardo to Martin Wolf." *Economic Thought* 4, no. 2 (2015). http://et.worldeconomicsassociation.org/papers/proposals-for-full-reserve-banking-a-historical-survey-from-david-ricardo-to-martin-wolf/.

Lee, Mordecai. *The Philosopher-Lobbyist John Dewey and the People's Lobby, 1928–1940*. Albany: State University of New York Press, 2015.

Leith-Ross, Frederick. *Money Talks: Fifty Years of International Finance. The Autobiography of Sir Frederick Leith-Ross*. London: Hutchinson, 1968.

Liebling, A. J. "The Whole Story." *New Yorker*, November 13, 1948, 134–45.

Lippmann, Walter. *U.S. Foreign Policy: Shield of the Republic*. Boston: Little, Brown, 1943.

Manoilescu, Mihail. *The Theory of Protection and International Trade*. London: P. S. King & Son, 1931.

Mason, Edward S., and Robert E. Asher. *The World Bank since Bretton Woods*. Washington, D.C.: Brookings Institution, 1973.

McCullough, David. *Truman*. New York: Simon and Schuster, 1992.

Meltzer, Allan H. *A History of the Federal Reserve*. Vol. 1, *1913–1951*. Chicago: University of Chicago Press, 2003.

———. *Keynes's Monetary Theory: A Different Interpretation*. Cambridge: Cambridge University Press, 1988.

Mikesell, Raymond F. *The Bretton Woods Debates: A Memoir*. Princeton: Princeton University Department of Economics, 1994.

———. *Foreign Adventures of an Economist*. Eugene: University of Oregon Press, 2000.

———. "Negotiating at Bretton Woods, 1944." In *Negotiating with the Russians*, edited by Raymond Dennett and Joseph E. Johnson. Boston: World Peace Foundation, 1951.

Morath, Inge, and Arthur Miller. *Chinese Encounters*. New York: Farrar, Straus & Giroux, 1979.

Moreira, Peter. *Hemingway on the China Front: His WWII Spy Mission with Martha Gellhorn*. Washington, D.C.: Potomac Books, 2006.

Morgenthau, Henry, Jr. *Germany Is Our Problem: A Plan for Germany*. New York: Harper & Brothers, 1945.

———. "Our Policy toward Germany." Serialized in the *New York Post*, November 24–29, 1947.

Morgenthau, Henry, III. *Mostly Morgenthaus: A Family History*. New York: Ticknor & Fields, 1991.

Mouré, Kenneth. *Managing the Franc Poincaré: Economic Understanding and Political Constraint in French Monetary Policy, 1928–1936*. Cambridge: Cambridge University Press, 1991.

Muirhead, Bruce. *Against the Odds: The Public Life and Times of Louis Rasminsky*. Toronto: University of Toronto Press, 1999.

Mussa, Michael, James M. Boughton, and Peter Isard, eds. *The Future of the SDR in Light of Changes in the International Financial System*. Washington, D.C.: International Monetary Fund, 1996.

Newlyn, W. T. "The Colonial Empire." In *Banking in the British Commonwealth*, edited by R. S. Sayers. Oxford: Oxford University Press, 1952.

Nichols, David A. *Ike and McCarthy: Dwight Eisenhower's Secret Campaign against Joseph McCarthy*. New York: Simon & Schuster, 2017.

Ohlin, Bertil. "Protectionism and Non-Competing Groups." *Weltwirtschaftliches Archiv* 33 (1931): 30–35.

Olmsted, Kathryn S. *Red Spy Queen: A Biography of Elizabeth Bentley*. Chapel Hill: University of North Carolina Press, 2002.

Parton, James. *The Life of Horace Greeley, Editor of "The New York Tribune": From His Birth to the Present Time*. 1855. Reprint, Boston: Houghton Mifflin, 1889.

Pavlov, Vitaly. *Operation Snow: Half a Century in KGB Foreign Intelligence*. Moscow: Geya Publishers, 1996.

Penrose, E. F. *Economic Planning for the Peace*. Princeton: Princeton University Press, 1953.

Petrov, Vladimir. *Money and Conquest: Allied Occupation Currencies in World War II*. Baltimore: Johns Hopkins Press, 1967.

Pressnell, L. S. *External Economic Policy since the War*. Vol. 1, *The Post-War Financial Settlement*. London: Her Majesty's Stationery Office, 1986.

Rasmussen, Kathleen Britt. "Canada and Bretton Woods." In *Global Perspectives on the Bretton Woods Conference and the Post-War World Order*, edited by Giles Scott-Smith and J. Simon Rofe, 167–86. London: Palgrave Macmillan, 2017.

Rauchway, Eric. *The Money Makers: How Roosevelt and Keynes Ended the Depression, Defeated Fascism, and Secured a Prosperous Peace*. New York: Basic Books, 2015.

Reder, Melvin W. "The Anti-Semitism of Some Eminent Economists." *History of Political Economy* 32, no. 4 (2000): 833–56.

Rees, David. *Harry Dexter White: A Study in Paradox*. New York: Coward, McCann, & Geoghagan, 1973.

Rittenberg, Sidney, and Amanda Bennett. *The Man Who Stayed Behind*. New York: Simon and Schuster, 1993.

Robbins, Lionel. *The Wartime Diaries of Lionel Robbins and James Meade, 1943–1945*. Edited by Susan Howson and Donald Moggridge. London: Macmillan, 1990.

Robertson, Dennis H. "The Post-War Monetary Plans." *Economic Journal* 53 (December 1943): 352–60.

Robinson, Joan. "Beggar-My-Neighbour Remedies for Unemployment." In *Essays in the Theory of Employment*, by Joan Robinson. Oxford: Basil Blackwell, 1937.

Russell, Ruth B., assisted by Jeannette E. Muther. *A History of the United Nations Charter: The Role of the United States, 1940–1945*. Washington, D.C.: Brookings Institution, 1958.

Sachar, Abram L. *Brandeis University: A Host at Last*. Waltham, Mass.: Brandeis University Press, 1995.

Sandilands, Roger. J., *The Life and Political Economy of Lauchlin Currie*. Durham, N.C.: Duke University Press, 1990.

Schecter, Jerrold, and Leona Schecter. *Sacred Secrets: How Soviet Intelligence Operations Changed American History*. Dulles, Va.: Brassey's, 2002.

Schild, Georg. *Bretton Woods and Dumbarton Oaks: American Economic and Political Postwar Planning in the Summer of 1944*. New York: St. Martin's, 1995.

Schlesinger, Eugene Richard. *Multiple Exchange Rates and Economic Development*. Princeton: Princeton University Press, 1952.

Schlesinger, Stephen C. *Act of Creation: The Founding of the United Nations*. Boulder, Colo.: Westview, 2003.

Schuler, Kurt, and Mark Bernkopf. "Who Was at Bretton Woods?" New York: Center for Financial Stability. 2014.www.centerforfinancialstability.org/bw/Who_Was_at_Bretton_Woods.pdf.

Schuler, Kurt, and Andrew Rosenberg. *The Bretton Woods Transcripts* (e-book). New York: Center for Financial Stability, 2012.

Schumpeter, Joseph A. *History of Economic Analysis*. New York: Oxford University Press, 1954.

Schwartz, Anna J. "From Obscurity to Notoriety: A Biography of the Exchange Stabilization Fund." NBER Working Paper 5699. Cambridge, Mass.: National Bureau of Economic Research, 1996.

Scott-Smith, Giles, and J. Simon Rofe. *Global Perspectives on the Bretton Woods Conference and the Post-War World Order*. London: Palgrave Macmillan, 2017.

Skidelsky, Robert. *John Maynard Keynes: The Economist as Saviour, 1920–1937*. London: Macmillan, 1992.

———. *John Maynard Keynes: Fighting for Britain, 1937–1946*. London: Macmillan, 2000. (The title of the U.S. edition is *John Maynard Keynes: Fighting for Freedom, 1937–1946*. New York: Viking, 2001.)

Smith, Fred. "The Rise and Fall of the Morgenthau Plan." *United Nations World*, March 1947, clipping, SMLP-2.

Snow, Edgar. *The Pattern of Soviet Power*. New York: Random House, 1945.

———. *Red Star over China*. New York: Random House, 1938.

Southard, Frank A., Jr. *The Finances of European Liberation, with Special Reference to Italy*. New York: King's Crown Press, 1946.

Srodes, James. *On Dupont Circle: Franklin and Eleanor Roosevelt and the Progressives Who Shaped Our World*. Berkeley, Calif.: Counterpoint, 2012.

Steil, Benn. *The Battle of Bretton Woods: John Maynard Keynes, Harry Dexter White, and the Making of a New World Order*. Princeton: Princeton University Press, 2013.

Stein, Herbert. *The Fiscal Revolution in America: Policy in Pursuit of Reality*. 2nd ed. Washington, D.C.: AEI Press, 1996.

Stone, I. F. *The Truman Era*. New York: Monthly Review Press, 1953.

Storrs, Landon R. Y. "Left-Feminism, the Consumer Movement, and Red Scare Politics in the United States, 1935–1960." *Journal of Women's History* 18, no. 3 (2006): 40–67.

———. *The Second Red Scare and the Unmaking of the New Deal Left*. Princeton: Princeton University Press, 2012.

Tanenhaus, Sam. *Whittaker Chambers: A Biography*. New York: Random House, 1997.

Theoharis, Athan. *Chasing Spies: How the FBI Failed in Counterintelligence and Promoted the Politics of McCarthyism in the Cold War Years*. Chicago: Ivan R. Dee, 2002.

Triffin, Robert. *Gold and the Dollar Crisis*. New Haven: Yale University Press, 1960.

———. "The Return to Convertibility: 1926–1931 and 1958–? or Convertibility and the Morning After." *Banca Nazionale del Lavoro Quarterly Review* 48 (March 1959): 3–57.

———. "Tomorrow's Convertibility: Aims and Means of National Monetary Policy." *Banca Nazionale del Lavoro Quarterly Review* 48 (June 1959): 131–200.

Turner, Marjorie Shepherd. *Joan Robinson and the Americans*. Armonk, N.Y.: M. E. Sharpe, 1989.

U.S. Congress. House of Representatives Committee on Banking and Currency. *Hearings on H.R. 2211, a Bill to Provide for the Participation of the United States in the International Monetary Fund and the International Bank for Reconstruction and Development.* 79th Cong., 1st sess., 1945.

———. House of Representatives Committee on Un-American Activities. *Hearings Regarding Communist Espionage in the United States Government.* 80th Cong., 2nd sess., 1948.

———. House of Representatives Committee on Un-American Activities. *Interim Report on Hearings Regarding Communist Espionage in the United States Government.* 80th Cong., 2nd sess., 1948.

———. Senate. Executive Sessions of the Senate Permanent Subcommittee on Investigations of the Committee on Government Operations. 83rd Congress, 1st session, 1953.

———. Senate. *Interlocking Subversion in Government Departments. Hearing before the Subcommittee to Investigate the Administration of the Internal Security Act and Other Internal Security Laws of the Committee on the Judiciary, United States Senate.* 83rd Cong., 2nd sess., 1953.

———. Senate. *Interlocking Subversion in Government Departments. Report of the Subcommittee to Investigate the Administration of the Internal Security Act and Other Internal Security Laws to the Committee on the Judiciary, United States Senate.* 83rd Cong., 1st sess., July 30, 1953.

———. Senate. *Interlocking Subversion in Government Departments. Hearing before the Subcommittee to Investigate the Administration of the Internal Security Act and Other Internal Security Laws of the Committee on the Judiciary, United States Senate.* 84th Cong., 1st sess., part 29, June 15, 1955.

———. Senate. *Interlocking Subversion in Government Departments. Hearing before the Subcommittee to Investigate the Administration of the Internal Security Act and Other Internal Security Laws of the Committee on the Judiciary, United States Senate.* 84th Cong., 1st sess., part 30, August 30, 1955.

———. Senate Committee on Appropriations, Armed Services and Banking and Currency. *Occupation Currency Transactions: Hearings.* 80th Cong., 1st sess., 1947.

———. Senate Committee on Banking and Currency. *Bretton Woods Agreements Act: Hearings on H.R. 3314.* 79th Cong., 1st sess., 1945.

———. Senate Committee on the Judiciary. Subcommittee to Investigate the Administration of the Internal Security Act and Other Internal Security Laws. *Morgenthau Diary (Germany).* 90th Cong., 1st sess., 1967.

U.S. Department of State. *Proceedings and Documents of the United Nations Monetary and Financial Conference, Bretton Woods, New Hampshire, July 1–22, 1944.* Washington, D.C.: U.S. Government Printing Office, 1948.

U.S. Treasury. *Annual Report of the Secretary of the Treasury on the State of the Finances for the Fiscal Year Ended June 30 1938.* Washington, D.C.: U.S. Government Printing Office, 1939.

Van Dormael, Armand. *Bretton Woods: Birth of a Monetary System.* London: Macmillan, 1978.

Viner, Jacob. "Mihail Manoilescu on the Theory of Protection." *Quarterly Journal of Economics* 40, no. 1 (February 1932): 121–25.

Wachtel, Howard M. *The Money Mandarins: The Making of a Supranational Economic Order*. Rev. ed. Armonk, N.Y.: M. E. Sharpe, 1990.

Wallace, Henry A. *The Price of Vision: The Diary of Henry A. Wallace, 1942–1946*. Edited by John Morton Blum. Boston: Houghton Mifflin, 1973.

Walton, Richard J. *Henry Wallace, Harry Truman, and the Cold War*. New York: Viking, 1976.

Weber, Isabella Maria, and Gregor Semieniuk. "American Radical Economists in Mao's China: From Hopes to Disillusionment." *Research in the History of Economic Thought and Methodology* 37A (2019): 31–63.

Weinstein, Allen. *Perjury: The Hiss-Chambers Case*. New York: Random House, 1997.

Weinstein, Allen, and Alexander Vassiliev. *The Haunted Wood: Soviet Espionage in America—The Stalin Era*. New York: Random House, 1998.

West, Nigel. *Venona: The Greatest Secret of the Cold War*. London: HarperCollins, 1999.

Whipple, Charles L. "Life and Death of Harry Dexter White." Serialized in the *Boston Globe*, November 15–27, 1953.

White, Anne Terry. "An Autobiography." Undated typewritten manuscript, in ATWP.

———. *Men before Adam*. New York: Random House, 1942.

White, G. Edward. "Alger Hiss's Campaign for Vindication." *Boston University Law Review* 83, no. 1 (2003): 1–14.

White, Nathan I. *Harry Dexter White: Loyal American*. Boston: Independent Press [for Bessie (White) Bloom, Waban, Mass.], 1956.

Williams, John H. *Postwar Monetary Plans and Other Essays*. 3rd ed. New York: Alfred A. Knopf, 1947.

Index